Virtual Technologies for Business and Industrial Applications:
Innovative and Synergistic Approaches

N. Raghavendra Rao
VIT University, India

BUSINESS SCIENCE REFERENCE

Hershey · New York

Director of Editorial Content:	Kristin Klinger
Director of Book Publications:	Julia Mosemann
Acquisitions Editor:	Lindsay Johnston
Development Editor:	Christine Bufton
Publishing Assistant:	Casey Conapitski
Typesetter:	Keith Glazewski
Production Editor:	Jamie Snavely
Cover Design:	Lisa Tosheff
Printed at:	Yurchak Printing Inc.

Published in the United States of America by
Business Science Reference (an imprint of IGI Global)
701 E. Chocolate Avenue
Hershey PA 17033
Tel: 717-533-8845
Fax: 717-533-8661
E-mail: cust@igi-global.com
Web site: http://www.igi-global.com

Library of Congress Cataloging-in-Publication Data

Virtual technologies for business and industrial applications : innovative and synergistic approaches / N. Raghavendra Rao, editor.
    p. cm.
  Includes bibliographical references and index.
  Summary: "This book provides research related to the concept of virtual reality and developing business models using this concept"--Provided by publisher.
  ISBN 978-1-61520-631-5 (hbk.) -- ISBN 978-1-61520-632-2 (ebook) 1. Virtual reality--Industrial applications. 2. Manufacturing processes--Computer simulation. I. Rao, N. Raghavendra, 1939- II. Title.

  QA76.9.C65V573 2010
  670.42'7--dc22

                                2009049085

British Cataloguing in Publication Data
A Cataloguing in Publication record for this book is available from the British Library.

Table of Contents

Section 1
Business Models in Virtual Environment

Section 2
Virtual Technologies in Manufacturing Sector

Section 3
Virtual Reality Concepts in Service Sector

Section 4
Virtual Modeling in Virtual Communities and Static Images

Detailed Table of Contents

Section 1
Business Models in Virtual Environment

The author states a new era has set in the business environment. Globalization, market consolidation, vertical market strategies and mergers are presenting new trends in business enterprises to adapt themselves in this phenomenon. Now it has become a necessity for many enterprises to look for a new approach which can help them to face the new realities in business. Business enterprises must combine facts and ideas to create new knowledge that will drive their organization in the right direction through innovation. Integration of the elements such as virtual organizations, virtual teams, virtual reality, human centered assets and sophisticated concepts of information and communication technology can be considered as innovation driver. In present globalization scenario many business processes are needed to be completed in a less turnaround time. A business model for a business process can be invented through virtual reality.

Virtual Reality applications strive to simulate real or imaginary scenes with which users can interact and perceive the effects of their actions in real time. Adding haptic information such as vibration, tactile array, and force feedback enhances the sense of presence in virtual environments. Haptics interfaces present new challenges in the situation where it is crucial for the operators to touch, grasp and manipulate rigid/soft objects in the immersive virtual worlds. Soft-touch haptics modeling is the core component in feeling and manipulating dynamic objects within the virtual environments. For adding the haptic sensations with interactive soft objects, the authors first present multiple force-reflecting dynamics in Loop subdivision surfaces, and further the haptic freeform deformation of soft objects through mass-spring Bezier volume lattice. The haptic constraint modeling based on metaballs is experimented to intuitively control the interactive force distribution within the dynamically constructed constraint, making the soft-touch simulation of objects simple to manipulate with enhanced realism.

Collision detection is one of the enabling technologies in many areas, such as virtual assembly simulation, physically-based simulation, serious games, and virtual-reality based medical training. The author provides a number of techniques and algorithms that provide efficient, real-time collision detection for virtual objects. Further the author indicates that they are applicable to various kinds of objects and are easy to implement.

Business Process Modeling is a fast growing field in business and information technology, which uses visual grammars to model and execute processes within an organization. However, many analysts present such models in a 2D static and iconic manner that is difficult to understand by many stakeholders. Difficulties in understanding such grammars can impede the improvement of processes within an enterprise due to communication problems. They present in their chapter a novel framework for intuitively visualizing animated business process models in 3D Virtual Environments. They also explain that virtual environment visualizations can be performed with present 2D business process modeling technology, thus providing a low barrier to entry for business process practitioners. Two case studies have been discussed from film production and healthcare domains. These cases illustrate the ease with which these visualizations can be created. They suggest that this approach can be generalized to other executable workflow systems and for any application domain being modeled.

Section 2
Virtual Technologies in Manufacturing Sector

The authors explain in their chapter a virtual reality machine shop environment has been developed capable of simulating the operation of a three axis milling machine and it has been integrated with a graphical model for the calculation of quantitative data affecting the machined surface roughness. This model determines the machined surface topomorphy as a cloud of points, retrieved from the visualization system Z buffer. Their study describes the developed model for milling processes simulation in a virtual environment and the determination of the surface roughness of the processed surfaces. The methodology for the verification of the quantitative data acquired by the system is also presented. The results obtained in their study have been verified with the data determined in cutting experiments and by another numerical model that has been integrated to the system.

They indicate the current issues existing in current assembly work in their chapter. They explain the established theoretical basis with the reasons that Augmented Reality systems could provide cognitive support and augmentation. They analyze the foundations for assembly feasibility evaluation and discuss possible innovative ways which would provide an efficient and robust solution for these problems of realism and efficiency in design and assembly processes. Their   proposed platform considers the multiple dependencies in different manufacturing sectors that allow the work to be conducted in a simultaneous way rather than sequential order.

Section 3
Virtual Reality Concepts in Service Sector

Marketers have long been fascinated by the possibility of understanding how consumers think and what factors stimulate favorable reactions to marketing stimuli. Marketers are now beginning to utilize neuromarketing techniques to map patterns of brain activities to ascertain how consumers evaluate products, objects, or marketing messages. Neuromarketing is relatively a new field of marketing that utilizes computer-simulated environments, such as Virtual Reality (VR) or Immersive Virtual Reality (IVR) technologies combined with neuroimaging technologies, such as Functional Magnetic Resonance Imaging (fMRI), Quantitative Electroencephalography (QEEG), Magnetoencephalography (MEG), and other means of studying human neurological responses. Marketers need this information to help gain favorable reactions to their marketing stimuli and to predict which product designs and marketing messages will appeal most and be on consumer's minds when the prospects are ready to buy.

Chapter 8

Rui Wang, The University of Sydney, Australia
Xiangyu Wang, The University of Sydney, Australia

They explain in their chapter the use of Second Life as a virtual environment to help the commercial sector in marketing process. They present the use of Immersive Virtual Reality concept to design a distributed marketing system for commercial sector based on the Benford's Mixed Reality boundaries theory and Motivated Learning Agents model. They propose a system framework in their chapter. Further they discuss boundaries as well as agents' factors in their framework.

Chapter 9

Sofia Bayona, Universidad Rey Juan Carlos, Spain
José Miguel Espadero, Universidad Rey Juan Carlos, Spain
José Manuel Fernández-Arroyo, Hospital Severo Ochoa, Spain
Luis Pastor, Universidad Rey Juan Carlos, Spain
Ángel Rodríguez, Universidad Politécnica de Madrid, Spain

This chapter concentrates on the advantages that virtual reality can offer to the Healthcare Sector. After a brief introduction, the authors explain the areas where VR techniques can be successfully applied. They describe some existing VR applications in healthcare sector. The developments of a VR surgery simulator, with all the aspects that make this process challenging, are presented in their chapter. They analyze the difficulties specific to healthcare environments while designing and development of VR applications. They conclude with future prospects of VR in the Healthcare Sector.

Section 4
Virtual Modeling in Virtual Communities and Static Images

Chapter 10

Rafael Capilla, Universidad Rey Juan Carlos, Spain

The phenomenon of virtual reality has crossed geographical and social barriers since virtual reality applications started to be used massively by non expert users. The development of highly cost and complex virtual reality applications for concrete domains and highly skilled users have widen its scope to the general public, which exploits Internet to create, share, and configure virtual communities of users and avatars that transcend organizational, political, cultural and social barriers. The author analyses the social impact of different software platforms and environments that can be used to create virtual communities. Further the author indicates how these platforms provide different collaborative capabilities among their members. The author also analyzes the impact of virtual reality technology in the creation and use of virtual communities and outlines the benefits and drawbacks in a globalization context.

Chapter 11

Mercedes Farjas Abadía, Universidad Politécnica de Madrid, Spain
Manuel Sillero Quintana, Universidad Politécnica de Madrid, Spain
Pedro Ángel Merino Calvo, Universidad Politécnica de Madrid, Spain

The authors indicate in their chapter that it has been practice to present a human figure by using simple drawings and techniques that help to reflect the movement of human body segments. Further they mention cartographic techniques have advanced features to capture and present in 3D representation systems. In recent years cartographic technique is being used in many sciences. This technique is yet to be applied in the area of virtual technology. The advent of the laser acquisition system enables to acquire data without discrimination on points and to get quick 3D models. The authors state that this system help them to work directly on the concept of surface and to analyze it from the uniqueness of the detail, compared to traditional systems which capture points for, later, imaging surfaces from them. A research group has been formed consisting of graduates in Physical Activity and Sport and in Cartography. The aim of this research group is to bring together both sciences and to improve techniques of capturing and representing of the human body. This group is working on this project. They have some results from their work .Initial results are presented in their chapter to readers. They are continuing with their research work.

Chapter 12

Mercedes Farjas, Universidad Politécnica de Madrid, Spain
Francisco J. García-Lázaro, Universidad Politécnica de Madrid, Spain
Julio Zancajo, Universidad de Salamanca, Spain
Teresa Mostaza, Universidad de Salamanca, Spain
Nieves Quesada, Universidad Politécnica de Valencia, Spain

The authors present laser scanner systems as a new method of automatic data acquisition for use in archaeological research. The operation of the equipment is briefly described. The results are presented from its application in two Spanish archaeological sites: Abrigo de Buendía (Cuenca), Atapuerca (Burgos). Point cloud measuring photogrammetric methods are revised with these systems. Photogrammetry has been widely used in heritage documentation and in no way is to be relegated by the new scanning techniques. Instead, Photogrammetry upgrades its methods by applying digital approaches so that it becomes competitive in both, operational costs and results. Nevertheless, Photogrammetry and laser scanner systems should be regarded as complementary rather than competing techniques. To illustrate photogrammetric methods their application to generate the Digital Surface Model of an epigraph is described. The authors' research group endeavours to combine teaching and research in its different fields of activity. Initial data are acquired in project-based teaching situations and international seminars or other activities. Students thus have the opportunity to become familiar with new methodologies while collecting material for analytical studies.

Preface

In the present globalization scenario enterprises have started realizing that the only place where they could grow is outside the Country. For this to happen, they have to become internationally not just competitive but internationally acceptable as suppliers or service providers. Managing business knowledge as well as innovative process of conducting business is required in the present globalization scenario. The important factor for the success on the business landscape is innovation. Innovation is no longer confined to research and development of an enterprise. Whatever way the innovation is generally defined, business leaders and management thinkers are convinced of its value to business. It would to be apt to recall Peter Drucker's observation on "Innovation": he says that innovation is not science or technology but value. There are two types of innovation. They are incremental and radical innovation. Incremental innovation talks about improving, expanding or extending the existing business models, processes, products and services. In the case of radical innovation it refers to creation of something new. Critical business needs decide the type of innovation to be adopted. Growth of a business depends on the ability of business to innovate. Integration of the knowledge management concepts, business process reengineering, human centered assets and sophisticated concepts of information and communication technologies can be considered as foundation for innovation. Virtual reality concept makes innovation a reality.

Virtual reality essentially refers to the presentation of system generated data made available in such a way that those who use it perceive the information at their disposal as having similar or enhanced characteristics in business models. The line dividing simulated tasks and their real world counter parts is very thin. The ability to get real world perceptions interactively through systems explains the interest associated with three dimensional graphics in virtual reality. The synergy between real and simulated facts yields a real effectiveness. It will be more effective if the system and its artifacts are to be active rather than a passive display. The essential element of virtual reality is that interactive simulation with navigation among widely scattered heterogeneous data bases. This results in logical, numerical processing and wide range of visualization functions. Virtual reality concept helps to unlock the innovative thinking in enterprises for carrying out incremental and radical innovation in their organization. Virtual reality concepts help enterprises to accomplish their ambitious goals with new innovation improvement incentives. The new initiatives help generating alternative ideas by taking inputs from different sources and structuring through virtual reality applications. Virtual reality concepts will increase the chances of successfully diffusing knowledge, technology and process. It will definitely provide scope for innovation to emerge. The contributors of this book are from academics who are doing research related to the concept of virtual reality and developing business models using this concept.

In the introductory chapter Rao states that rapid changes are taking place in global economy. Therefore it has become a necessity for enterprises to respond to these changes. Innovation in the business is the solution to face these changes. The importance of Collaborative technology and Knowledge Management Systems is explained for developing a business innovation models. Hanqiu Sun and Hui Chen explain in their chapter that Virtual Reality applications strive to simulate real or imaginary scenes with which users can interact and perceive the effects of their actions in real time. Adding hap tic information such as vibration, tactile array and force feed back enhances the sense of presence in virtual environments. The chapter written by Bilalis Nicolaos and Petousis Markos talks about their virtual reality environment model. This model stimulates the operation of a three axis milling machine and it is integrated with a graphical model for the calculation of quantitative data affecting the machined surface roughness. Gabriel Zachmann describes that collision detection is one of the enabling technologies in many areas such as virtual assembly simulation, physically-based simulation, serious games, and virtual reality based medical training. Rui (Irene) Chen, Xiangyu Wang, and Lei Hou talk about augmented reality systems that could provide cognitive support and augmentation. Further they discuss the possible innovative ways for efficient and robust solutions in design assembly processes. Ross Brown and Rune Rasmussen observe that business process modeling is a fast growing field in business and information technology. Harrison R. Burris and Shahid A. Sheikh suggest that neuromarketing techniques help marketers to ascertain how consumers evaluate products, objects or marketing messages. Further they explain neuromarketing is relatively a new field of marketing that utilizes computer simulated environments. Two cases studies pertaining to film production and health care sector are discussed in support of virtual environment visualizations. Rui Wang and Xiangyu Wang talk about the use of immersive virtual reality concept to design a distributed marketing system for commercial sector based on Ben ford's mixed reality boundaries theory and motivated learning agents model. Sofia Bayona, Jose Miguel, Jose Manuel, Luis Pastor and Angel Rodriguez indicate the advantages of virtual reality in the health care sector. They explain about the development of a VR surgery simulator. Rafael Capilla analyzes the impacts of virtual reality technology in the creation and use of virtual communities and outlines the benefits and drawbacks in a globalized context. Mercedes Farjas Abadia, Manuel Sillero Quintana and Pedro Angel Merino Calvo present the research work of a group who are working on the techniques of Capturing and representing the image of human body. The results obtained by the research group are presented in their chapter. The chapter written by Mercedes Farjas, Francisco J. Garcia Lazaro, Julio Zancajo, Teresa Mostaza and Nieves Quesada discuss about laser scanned systems as a new method of automatic data acquisition for use in archaeological research.

This book provides comprehensive view of virtual reality concepts being used with collaborative technologies across multiple sectors such as manufacturing, healthcare, marketing and business organizations. This book would be useful in libraries for reference of research scholars, in research and development departments, as a course supplement to the students pursuing computer science related subjects and as a resource for software professionals.

N. Raghavendra Rao
VIT University, India

Acknowledgment

At the outset, I would like to thank all the chapter authors for their excellent contributions. I would like to offer my special thanks to IGI Global for the opportunity to edit the publication. The editorial guidance provided by Christine Bufton was excellent.

I would like to acknowledge the role of the reviewers and editorial team (Dr. L. Jeganathan, Dr. Hariharanath, Dr. E. V. Prasad and Mr. Ramesh Gopalaswamy) for their continuous support. Finally, I would like to thank my wife Meera for her continuous encouragement and support in my scholastic pursuits.

N. Raghavendra Rao
Editor

Section 1
Business Models in Virtual Environment

Chapter 1
Innovation through Virtual Technologies

N. Raghavendra Rao
VIT University, India

ABSTRACT

Rapid changes are taking place in global economy. It has become a necessity for enterprises to respond to these changes. Innovation in the business is the solution to face these changes. Identifying the right type of technology, knowledge and process are the main elements in designing an innovative method. Two business models are discussed for creating innovation models. Some of the concepts in information and communication technology and management are applied in these business models. Further, this chapter talks about the contribution of global virtual teams in designing and developing ideas for innovation.

INTRODUCTION

It is apt to recall the observation of Peter Drucker on Innovation: "A business enterprise has two and only two basic functions; Marketing and Innovation. Marketing and Innovation produce results; all the rest are cost". The dividing factors in the market are niche markets and unique products or services. Innovation is needed to achieve the above factors in the present competitive market. Innovation is no longer related to the activities confined to research and development in an enterprise on the new products or adding new features to their existing products. Innovation may be classified under two categories. They are technical innovation and business process innovation. Convergence of information and communication technologies continues to provide many new concepts under technological innovation. This convergence is also enabling many business process innovations to take place in business enterprises. All these innovations present some exciting opportunities for business enterprises to compete in the global market. This chapter provides an overview of some of the concepts in information and communication technology. Further it suggests how these concepts can be made use of developing a business model by using new ideas and methods.

DOI: 10.4018/978-1-61520-631-5.ch001

NEED FOR A BUSINESS MODEL

Globalization which was initially viewed with fear and distrust has opened up huge new markets for many countries. This has been focusing on the need for innovative approach in conducting business by enterprises. The world is poised to take a huge leap at the rate innovation is gaining popularity as a result of the enhanced sharing of information and collaborative possibilities opened by the convergence of information and communication technology. Dimitris N.Chorafas and Heinrich Steinhann (1995) rightly say: "Innovation always provides the opportunity to be first in the market with new products and services as well as to help shape the methodology and the tools while locking out the competition."

INVENTION AND INNOVATION

The terms "Invention" and "Innovation" are used interchangeably. Actually these are separate and distinct concepts. Invention means designing and creating something which has never been made before. The classic examples are invention of the light bulb by Thomas Edison, and invention of telephone by Alexander Graham Bell. Louis Pasteur came up with vaccines. Innovation deals with bringing in new methods and ideas resulting in the required changes in an enterprise. The American heritage Dictionary defines innovation as "that which is newly introduced". The term "INNOVATE" derives from a Latin word which means to "Renew". In the present business context, innovation is taking interesting ideas and transforming them into usable solutions for business problems. Invoking of human minds leads to Innovation. It is interesting to note the observations of Narayanan V.K and Liam Fashefy (2004) on Mind Invoking: "The capacity to invoke visions about an organization's alternative futures or aspirations about the customer value generating possibilities of the firm's next generation of prod-

ucts depend singularly upon the mind's ability to invoke (conceptually) views of the future, views that could not exist except through the thought processes of mind-endowed creatures."

COLLABORATIVE TECHNOLOGY

Information and Communication technology provides infrastructure for Virtual Collaboration. Due to technological advancements many concepts are emerging in this technology. Virtual reality, Data Warehouse, Data Mining, Text mining, Intelligent Systems, Web Based Intelligent Systems and Grid Computing are among the number of concepts provided by this technology.

History of Virtual Reality

Digital simulation has emerged after the advent of computers. Contribution to the concept of simulation was a video presentation combined with the mechanical flight simulator in 1952. It was considered as birth of virtual reality in that year. The US Airforce, US Navy and NASA have provided the funds to the university laboratories for the activities related to Virtual Reality. The US Airforce had an idea about immersing pilots into training simulators at Wright Patterson Airforce base in Dyton, Ohio. The pilots got the simulated experience of being inside an aircraft by being able to test specific flight situations at any point in time. This and projects similar to this, have indicated that computer simulation and the associated visualization could be applied to create valuable scenario for training.

Another application related to virtual reality has taken place by the development of fuel-flow simulators for the space shuttle. This helped the technicians to monitor fuel storage and usage. This was known as the virtual environment work station project. The main focus of this project was to combine sources as process monitoring, live video, and work station input. As the technology

Figure 1. Element in virtual reality

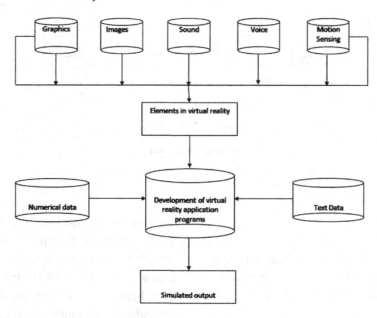

got integrated, it has provided a single environment in which the user world have control over various information sources through the use of dynamic interactive windows. Consequent to this the new uses of virtual reality have started gaining importance, funding for the project related to virtual reality have also increased.

Concept of Virtual Reality

Before any major change has to be effected in a business enterprise in the area of product development or adding new features in the existing product or changing a business process, the enterprise would like to visualize before it is implemented. Visualization of the above activities are possible through simulation. This kind of simulation can be termed as virtual reality. The concept of virtual reality facilitates in visualizing the new ideas for business purposes. The elements constituting virtual reality are audio, voice, graphics, images, sound and motion sensing. These elements along with numerical and textual data facilitate the creation of real time simulation. Business enterprises

have choices to evaluate their new ideas by making use of the concept of virtual reality. (Figure 1) elements in virtual reality gives an overview of the integration of the various elements. Simulated outputs resulted from virtual reality application programs help to visualize and visibilize the proposed ideas of business enterprises. They also facilitate to visualize hypothetical cases in business and interact with the applications developed under virtual reality concepts. It may be noted that the concept of multimedia is required in virtual reality applications. The following terms are associated in virtual reality environment. The concept of virtual reality is the seed of innovation for developing a business model.

Visualization

Information and communication technology has made visualization process as important component in the development of advanced business applications. Presentation of output through simulated data facilitates to analyze and take decisions.

Figure 2. Grid computing in virtual organizations

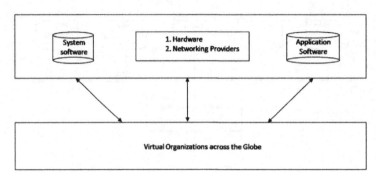

Visibilization

Visibilization makes mapping of physical reality with virtual reality for end users to understand the output generated through simulated data.

Visitraction

Visitraction is the process of visualization of concepts, characteristics or phenomena lacking a direct physical interpretation. This results in establishing link between the concepts and ideas.

Grid Computing

Grid computing helps to co-ordinate sharing of resources distributed in global virtual organizations. The enormous competitive pressure in the business and industry sectors designing a product or services are expected to take place in far less turnaround time. They need a system that supports capturing of data, analyzing of data and results in a business model. The concept of grid computing is very useful in the present globalization scenario.

It would be apt to quote Johy Joseph and Craig Fellenstein (2004) on Grid Computing: "Grid computing solutions are constructed using a variety of technologies and open standards. Grid computing, in turn provides highly stable, highly secure and extremely high performance mechanisms for discovering and negotiating access to remote computing resources in a seamless manner.

This makes it possible for the sharing of computing resources, on an unprecedented scale, among an infinite number of geographically distributed groups." It may be noted from their explanation that sharing of resources by dynamic grouping individuals and multi groups is the push factor in global virtual teams for the goal set to them. (Figure 2). Grid Computing in Virtual Organization explains how the resources can be shared by Virtual Organization.

It is interesting to note the views on network economy by Mahendhiran Nair, Tengu Mohd. Assman and Shariffa Adeen (2009): "The rise of the network economy, smaller nations such as Finland, Hongkong, Ireland, Singapore and Taiwan have shown their ability to rapidly enhance their competitiveness, and in some sectors of the economy, these smaller economies have surpassed the traditional economic super power. Much of their success is attributed to 'Creative Capital' and the development of a resilient National Innovation Ecosystem that continuously adapts to global technological change."

Data Warehouse

Humphries, Hawkins, and Dy (1999) explained that data warehouse is a concept in Information Technology. It may be noted that a Data Warehouse is central store of data that is extracted from operational data. The information in Data Warehouse is subject oriented, non-volatile and of a historic nature. Data Warehouse tends to contain extremely large data sets. There are different definitions of Data Warehouse. The essence of these definitions is extraction of the data from the legacy systems in enterprises integrating with data from the various sources for analyzing purposes. It can be said that the purpose of Data Warehousing is (1) to slice and dice through data, (2) to operate analytical process and (3) to support the decision process.

Data Mining

Knowledge in 'know discovery in data warehouse' means relationships and patterns between data and elements. The term 'Data Mining' is used exclusively for identifying knowledge in Data Warehouse. Pieter Adrains and Dolf Zantinge (1996) have classified four types of knowledge in Data Mining. They are (1) Shallow Knowledge – Information can be easily retrieved from databases using a query tool such Structured Query Language (SQL). (2) Multi Dimensional Knowledge – Information can be analyzed by using online analytical processing tools (OLAP). (3) Hidden Knowledge – Data can be found relatively, easily by using pattern recognition or machine learning. (4) Deep Knowledge – Information that is stored in the Data Warehouse can only be located if one has a clue that indicates where to look for.

Text Mining

The analysis in respect of textual data stored in text database is carried out through text mining. Like data mining it identifies relationships in the vast amount of text data.

Intelligent Systems

There are certain concepts in Information Technology which can be made use in developing a knowledge management system. They are (1) Case based Systems – this contains cases that maintain unique expert experiences. (2) Artificial Neural Networks – this uses artificial neurons executable on systems to imitate the human brain. (3) Genetic Algorithms – this helps to find useful knowledge by modifying the natural selection process. (4) Fuzzy Logic – this helps to improve decision process by making use of symbolic reasoning and mathematical calculations.

Web Based Intelligent Systems

Wide usage of internet services has led to web based intelligent systems being developed. Semantic web is an emerging concept in web services. This concept talks about the representation of data on World Wide Web. Resource Description Frame Work (RDF) is used to integrate a variety of applications using XML. Ontology is used as a tool for the collection of RDF statements and making logical inferences among them.

KNOWLEDGE MANAGEMENT

Knowledge Management is a process. This process helps to create a business innovation model. Some of the concepts related to Knowledge Management are explained below.

Historical Back Ground of Knowledge Management

The concept of knowledge management is not new. The focus and approach has been changing over a period of time. One may observe from the literature on the history of information and knowledge that the basic pattern of behavior remained consistent over a period of centuries concerning the role of information and knowledge. History provides many examples. Emperors in china in the olden days always surrounded themselves with advisors who were scholars first, politicians second. Roman emperors like the ancient Greeks consulted educated priests to gain an insight into the possible future. Indian kings seemed to be concerned with creation of knowledge among people by allocating places for schools and libraries. Practices in management of knowledge and information have changed significantly in space and time. The people who manage information and whose knowledge is being managed are undergoing changes. In the present era group dynamics dominate.

Evolution of Knowledge Management

In the pre-industrial era agriculture was the basis of nation's economy, then the concentration was to learn more about farming. In the post industrial era manufacturing became the basis of nation's economy, then the concentration was more about learning manufacturing techniques Nick Bontis (2002) rightly observes that the first evidence of codification of knowledge may have its roots in scientific management. Fredic Taylor attempted to formalize worker's experience and tacit skills into objective rules and formulas.

Organizational Knowledge Base

Knowledge representation in documents, manuals, e-mails and databases can be considered as "Explicit Knowledge". Knowledge found in business processes, product and services can be termed as "Embedded Knowledge". Undocumented Knowledge that is captured during discussions, meetings and interaction with persons inside and outside one's own organization can be termed as 'Tacit Knowledge'.

Knowledge Harvesting

The word "Harvesting" generally applies to agriculture and refers to the practice of increasing the yield of cultivable land. In the same way organizational databases can be considered as equivalent to cultivable land, where the employee's wisdom is the "Manure" with the help of which data is converted into useful information. "Knowledge Harvesting" is an integrated set of processes that capture the often hidden insight of human expertise in business.

Business Intelligence

The word "Intelligence" means the application of information, skills, experiences and reasoning to solve business problems. It is apt to recall Efraian Turban, Jay E. Aronson and Ting-Peng Liang's (2005) on business intelligence. They say it involves acquiring data and information from wide variety of sources and utilizing them in decision making. Further they indicate the business analysts add an additional dimension to business intelligence: Models and solution methods.

Intellectual Capital or Assets

Intellectual Capital or Intellectual assets are two terms mentioned frequently in the present knowledge economy. The word 'Capital' or 'Asset' as suffix to "Intellectual" is not used in strict accounting terminology. It is only a term referred for "intangible Assets". It may be noted that the meaning of both the terms is the same. The components of intangible assets are generally classified under four heads. (1) Market Assets represent business enterprise's brand image, distribution network and collaboration. (2) Intellectual Property assets are patents, copyrights, design rights, trademarks and trade secrets. (3) Human Centered Assets indicate knowledge and entrepreneurial ability of employees in business enterprise. (4) Infrastructure assets consists of business processes, methods and information systems. These will enable business enterprises to conduct their business smoothly. In this context it is interesting to note the observation of Michael J. English and William H. Baker, Jr (2006): "Internationally, by joining a knowledge-sharing network, an organization can learn rapidly via best practices and

Figure 3.Components in a global virtual team

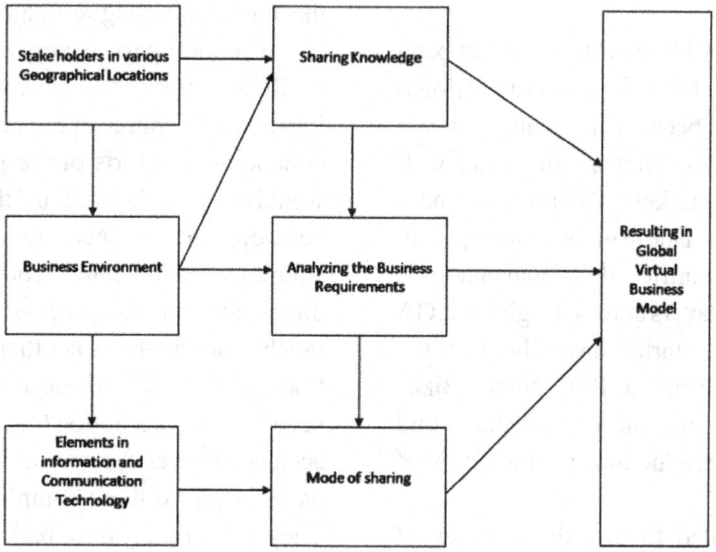

lessons learned and developed its own path to growing and leveraging its intellectual capital."

VIRTUAL ORGANIZATIONS

Globalization has created Virtual Organizations. The role of global virtual teams in developing a business innovation model is described in the ensuing paragraphs.

Global Virtual Teams

The members of global virtual teams who work at different locations in the globe need to share their knowledge. The constant interaction among the members of the global team is to accomplish the task assigned to them. Information and communication technology facilitates them to achieve their goal. (Figure 3). Components in a Global Virtual Team illustrate the relationship between the different components for effective interaction among the members of the team. Virtual teams because of the global distance, supporting members rely more heavily on communications and information technologies to facilitate interaction

and coordinate work than members who share a common physical environment. The process in global virtual team development is composed of a series of actions and interactions that bring about a result.

Shared understanding among the members of the global virtual team is a collective way of organizing and communicating relevant knowledge as a way of collaborating results in a global virtual business model. It is interesting to note the observation of Rohit Agarwal and Patricia Brown (2007) on business environment: "The environment plays an important role in the innovation process. A successful innovator taps into the environment to come up with an idea that would drive change – Change that can be adopted by markets and customers and monetized. An innovator must be in constant touch with the environment to understand the changing landscape, spot pain points, recognize parallel trends, and tune into competitive faces that shape the innovation cycle." In other words the global virtual team can successfully integrate ideas and business environments towards the achievement of developing a business model.

Case Illustration 1

An Indian base ROA Motor Bikes Ltd has been manufacturing motor bikes for Indian and Global markets. They have been in the market over a period of two decades. Their products are well received in both the markets. Their market share has been encouraging. Due to globalization policy followed by many countries, the global market is now open to many players across the globe. ROA motor Bikes Ltd has started losing hold on the market due to globalization. ROA Motor Bikes Ltd has decided to innovate new methods and business process in production and marketing of their motor bikes.

They have decided to hire the services of the domain experts who have rich experience in innovating methods and business processes in the motor bikes sector. They have identified the domain experts located in France and Korea. It has been agreed among them that domain experts and their team members will operate from their respective countries. Further it has been agreed to use the concepts of virtual reality and Grid Computing in developing business models for ROA Motor Bikes Ltd.

The domain experts have developed a business model that considers real world requirements for which parameters are created on the basis of their requirements. Simulated version of a motorbike has been designed and experiments have been carried out in computer systems. The domain experts team members have immersed themselves in every aspect of design and testing. Working in front of a large screen of a computer has given a sense of being actually testing a motorbike in a real world situation. The concept of virtual reality has helped them to look from the real world situation. The domain experts have created a three dimensional image of a motorbike. They made it possible for the user to move through and around the image. They have proved that virtual reality imitates the way the real motorbike looks and moves. They have made the information in databases to simulate. The users have understood that the line dividing simulated tasks and their real world counter parts is very thin.

ROA motorbikes Ltd has proved that by tapping into multiple source of expertise, knowledge and collaborative efforts of the global virtual teams would integrate the ideas and the process of product development. Engineering activities and design solutions are inherently complex across several dimensions and the processing requirements are much more intense than that of traditional solutions of the past. These complexities fall into several areas of solution that span across industry sectors all over the world. The domain experts have described these complexities in four areas. They are (1) analysis of real time data for finding out specific pattern (2) Creating parameters for studying and verifying the different aspects of the systems (3) Modeling experiments to create new designs and (4) simulating the activities to verify the accuracy in the business models. The domain experts have made use of the concepts in grid computing for analysis and modeling activities. They have used grid computing discipline which provides mechanisms for resources sharing by forming one or more virtual teams providing specific sharing capabilities. (Figure 4) business model created by domain experts gives an overview of the steps in creating a business model for designing and testing a motorbike.

Case Illustration 2

OAR Ltd. is a management and information technology consultants based in India. Their team consists of Professionals who have rich experience in the areas of knowledge management and information and communication technology. OAR Ltd. has been in consultancy business over a period of two decades. Their consultancy and information technology based business solution has helped many of their clients in Western and Middle and Eastern countries to increase their turnover and expanded their markets. The consultants of OAR

Figure 4. Business model created by domain experts

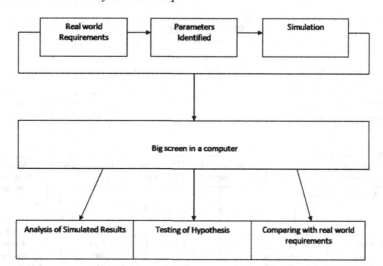

Ltd. are located in different parts of the globe. In recent times their valuable clients have started feeling the impact of competition due to globalization policy followed by many countries. One of the clients of OAR Ltd. has felt that managing technical knowledge as well as innovative process in conducting business is the way to remain competitive in the global market and requested them to design a knowledge repository system for their organization. They wanted to make use of the knowledge repository system for the purpose of business innovative process in their organization. In response to their request OAR Ltd., has decided to develop a business model for knowledge repository system. They have decided to make use of unique knowledge of their team members and resources located across the globe to develop a business model for knowledge repository system. They have applied the concepts of knowledge management in management and information technology disciplines.

Methodology

OAR Ltd. has developed a business model for knowledge repository system by relating the concepts in intellectual assets, data ware, data mining

and text mining. The important element in this model is the resource for knowledge. How broad or narrow, its knowledge base depends upon the requirements of a business enterprise. A business enterprise has to access the industrial scenario for their products. This will help the enterprise to know its competitive advantages and disadvantages in the market. Further it will help them to identify the gaps in their system. Innovative processes can be used for bridging the existing gaps by making use of knowledge repository system. OAR Ltd has suggested categorizing and increasing the information within the repository system. This system represents a valuable means to manage the explicit sharing, combination of application and renewal of organizational knowledge. The knowledge repository system helps knowledge innovators and knowledge workers to create intelligent systems for their analysis and business strategy. (Figure 5) resource for knowledge base helps the core team in a business enterprise to identify the core areas where they need to concentrate from their business perspective. Resource for knowledge base is the main element to develop a business model for knowledge repository system. (Figure 6) knowledge Repository system gives an over view for using it for innovation.

Figure 5. Resource for knowledge base

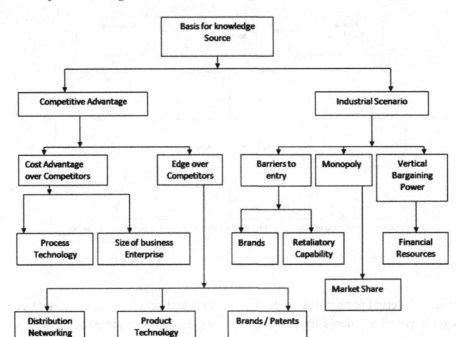

Figure 6. Knowledge for repository system

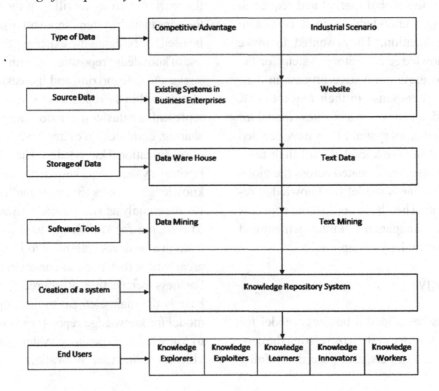

Figure 7. Relationship in knowledge management

CONCEPTS IN IT DISCIPLINE (DATA MINING)	CONCEPTS IN MANAGEMENT DISCIPLINE
Sallow Knowledge	Knowledge Learners
Multi-Dimensional Knowledge	Knowledge Exploiters
Hidden Knowledge	Knowledge Explorers
Deep Knowledge	Knowledge Innovators

Summary of Above Illustrations

A global enterprise takes advantage of unique knowledge and resources where ever they are located. It may be information communication technology expert or domain expert. Till recently the standard model of innovation has been a linear process from research through to design, development and then manufacturing. Now many of these processes are carried out concurrently and collaborating through information communication technology. Case illustration: 1 demonstrates how wide range of technologies can stimulate innovation. Case illustration: 2 explains that the need for business enterprises needs to evaluate the core competence in relation with their products and services. The elements in external competency are patents, brands, monopoly and trade secrets.

The element in internal competency consists of process technology, distribution channels, advantages in costing and size of plants. While talking of core competence of the corporation, Prahalad and Hamel (2001) observe that core competencies are the collective learning in the organization, especially how to coordinate diverse production skills and integrate multiple streams of technologies. Knowledge repository system helps an enterprise to evaluate their core competence. Further it establishes the relationship between two disciplines in knowledge management. (Figure 7) relationship in knowledge management shows the relationship in two disciplines.

(Figure 8) concepts in the management discipline helps to identify the competence and intellectual assets.

Figure 8. Concepts in the management discipline

CORE COMPETENCE	INTELLECTUAL ASSETS
Elements in External Competence	Market Assets and Intellectual Property
Elements in Internal Competence	Human Centered Assets and Infrastructural Assets

Knowledge networking is needed in the present business scenario. It is a process of Management discipline and Information technology discipline where people share information, knowledge and experiences to develop new knowledge for handling new situations. Knowledge Repository System stimulates innovation through knowledge transfer.

FUTURE TRENDS

While stressing the need for funding on innovation Judy Estrin (2009) says "Competition for funding can bring out the best in innovators, but it can have the opposite impact if the resources are too scarce." The two thrusts of knowledge – innovation and sharing are fundamental foundations for generating business opportunities. Innovation converts knowledge into new products, services and processes. Collaborative business networks are another source of innovation and economic development. Ted Fuller, Paul Argyle and Paul Moran (2004) rightly say that we make links between foresight as an interpretative process i.e.; personal competence in an entrepreneurial context and the sustainability of the enterprise i.e.; the organizational ability to maintain or improve fitness in a changing landscape, and hence survive or grow.

CONCLUSION

Information and communication technology has increased virtualization in business activities and ways of working. Virtualization overcomes time and distance. The term 'virtual' is now appearing in many forms. The two cases of illustrations have indicated how business models can be developed by applying the concepts in two disciplines. The business models explain how to adopt innovative approach in invoking vision for business enterprises by applying the concept of "Mind Invoking."

REFERENCES

Adrians, P., & Zantige, D. (1996). *Data Mining*. London: Addison-Wesley.

Agarwal, R., & Brown, P. (2007). *How Innovators connect*. Mumbai, India: Himalaya Publishing House.

Bontis, N. (2002). Managing organizational Knowledge by diagnosing Intellectual Capital. In Weicho, C., & Bontis, N. (Eds.), *The Strategic Management of Intellectual Capital and organizational knowledge*. Oxford, UK: Oxford University Press.

Chorafas, D. N., & Steinhann, H. (1995). *An Introduction to Visualizaton, Virtual Reality*. Upper Saddle River, NJ: Prentice Hall.

English, M. J., & Baker, W. H. Jr. (2006). *Winning the knowledge transfer race*. New Delhi: Tata McGraw Hill.

Estrin, J. (2009). *Closing the innovation gap*. New Delhi: Tata McGraw Hill.

Fuller, T., Argyle, P., & Moran, P. (2004). Meta-rules for Entrepreneurial Foresight. In Soukas, H. T., & Shepherd, J. (Eds.), *Managing the Future*. Oxford, UK: Blackwell Publishing.

Humphries, M., Hawkins, M. W., & Dy, M. C. (1999). *Data Warehousing: Architecture and Implementation. Englewood Cliffs, NJ: Prentice Hall.Joseph, J., & Fellenstein, C. (2004). Grid Computing*. New Delhi: Pearson Education.

Nair, M., Assman, T. M., & Shariffadeen. (2009). Managing Innovation in the Network Economy: Lessons for Countries in the Asia Pacific Region. In S. Akhtar & P. Arinto (Eds.), *Digital Review of Asia Pacific 2009 – 2010 Managing Innovation in the Network Economy*. New Delhi: Sage Publications.

Narayanan, V. K., & Fashey, L. (2004). Invention and Navigation as contrasting metaphors of the pathways to the future. In Tsoukas, H., & Shepherd, J. (Eds.), *Managing the Future*. Oxford, UK: Blackwell Publishing.

Prahalad, C. K., & Hamel, G. (2001). The Core Competence of the Corporation. In Zack, M. H. (Ed.), *Knowledge and Strategy*. New Delhi: Butterworth Heinemann.

Turburn, E., Aronson, J. E., & Liang, T.-P. (2005). *Decision Support Systems and Intelligent Systems*. New Delhi: Prentice Hall of India Private Ltd.

Chapter 2
Soft–Touch Haptics Modeling of Dynamic Surfaces

Hanqiu Sun
The Chinese University of Hong Kong, Hong Kong

Hui Chen
Chinese Academy of Sciences and The Chinese University of Hong Kong, China

ABSTRACT

Virtual Reality applications strive to simulate real or imaginary scenes with which users can interact and perceive the effects of their actions in real time. Adding haptic information such as vibration, tactile array, and force feedback enhances the sense of presence in virtual environments. Haptics interfaces present new challenges in the situation where it is crucial for the operators to touch, grasp and manipulate rigid/soft objects in the immersive virtual worlds. Soft-touch haptics modeling is the core component in feeling and manipulating dynamic objects within the virtual environments. For adding the haptic sensations with interactive soft objects, the authors first present multiple force-reflecting dynamics in Loop subdivision surfaces, and further the haptic freeform deformation of soft objects through mass-spring Bezier volume lattice. The haptic constraint modeling based on metaballs is experimented to intuitively control the interactive force distribution within the dynamically constructed constraint, making the soft-touch simulation of objects simple to manipulate with enhanced realism.

INTRODUCTION

Haptics studies the modality of touch and associated sensory feedback. In contrast to the other sensory channels such as visual and auditory, haptic interaction is the only technique that can provide touch-enabled dynamic & interactive 3D display to users. It is an active research field to improve the immersive reality of virtual environments (Chen & Sun, 2006), especially in simulations where it is crucial for the operators to touch, grasp and manipulate the virtual soft objects realistically as in the physical world. Soft-touch haptics modeling is the core component in feeling and manipulating dynamic objects within the virtual environments. Augmenting soft-touch realism in deformable objects provides new touch characteristic in addition with graphical display, and covers a wide range

DOI: 10.4018/978-1-61520-631-5.ch002

of applications (Aamisepp & Nilsson, 2003) such as geometric modeling, computer animation, and on-line game development.

We present soft-touch haptics modeling and rendering mainly in three themes: multiple force-reflecting dynamics in Loop subdivision surfaces; soft-touch physical freeform deformations; force constraints in interactive design. Loop subdivision is designed to generalize the recurrence relations for the three-directional quartic box splines to triangular meshes of arbitrary topology (Loop, 1987). Because triangular meshes arise in many applications, Loop subdivision becomes one of the most popular subdivision schemes. Subdivision surfaces are motivated to uniformly model any complex surfaces of arbitrary topology. Dynamic subdivision surfaces allow the shape editing of limit surfaces by applying forces interactively on the control meshes, and thus enable the creation of intuitive interface for geometric modeling such as modeling with clay dough. We incorporate the 6-DOF haptic interface in the dynamic modeling of Loop surfaces, where the dynamic parameters are computed easily without subdividing the control mesh recursively. During the haptic interactions, the contact point is traced and reflected to the rendering of updated graphics and haptics. Based on the multi-resolution surfacing representation, our approach permits the users to touch the virtual objects at the varying detailed surfacing levels, and manipulate the dynamics by applying the intuitive forces through the real-time haptic interface.

With the development of haptics techniques, implementing a realistic physics engine within games is possible. Lander simulated bouncy and trouncy response of particles under Newton's dynamics (Lander, 1999) and also mimicked crush effect of large massive objects via matrix deformation (Lander, 2000) in game development. However, the system didn't reflect the realistic force feedback to the players besides deformation in game engine. The demand for realistic haptic feedbacks at high refresh rate leads to additional computation complexity. Integrating non-physical

methods with haptic feedbacks is not natural, and cannot provide realistic physical simulation of deformable objects. In our study, we propose the dynamic simulation of mass-spring systems and flexible control of free-form deformation technique in interactive haptics modeling. Through distributing physical properties including mass, spring and damping coefficients of the object to the bounded Bezier volume lattice, the deformations of the object in response to the haptic avatar follow the physical laws and acquire high working rate. Our haptic-freeform model provides touch-enabled simple interface and efficient performance in the flexible deforming controls, then letting the objects move in a dynamic, cartoon-like touching style.

How to add force constraints in interactive design is a challenge task that needs further investigation. Constrained deformation based on metaballs is a flexible technique for designing closed surfaces, and provides simple solutions for creating blends, ramifications and advanced human character design, but short of dynamic interaction of touch sensation. Our work is to apply soft-touch interaction during the process of such constrained deformations. The deformation based on metaball constraint yields a local result which satisfies the desired displacement precisely on the constraint skeleton C, and does not affect the points outside the effective radius R of the metaball M. We study how to apply soft-touch sensation in such deformation using metaball constraints, thus users can feel and control the deforming process during the interactions. Haptic-constraint tools, such as disk and sphere-volume constraints, are experimented during the haptic deformable modeling, in which the soft-touch manipulation is instantly reflected to users intuitively via the interacting interface.

The overall objective of this chapter is to facilitate the interactive haptics modeling of dynamic surfaces, soft-touch freeform objects and constrained deforming manipulation in real time. We first study multiple force-reflecting dynamics in Loop subdivision surfaces, and further the haptic freeform deformation of soft objects through physical Bezier volume lattice. The constrained haptic deformations based on the metaballs are experimented to effectively control the interactive force distribution within the influence range, making the deformable simulation of soft-touch objects easy to control and manipulate.

BACKGROUND

Haptic rendering refers to the computational methods used to determine the forces resulted when we interact with virtual objects. During point-based haptic interaction model, only the end point of the haptic device, also known as the haptic interface point (HIP), interacts with virtual objects. Traditional methods of producing convincing haptic rendering through manipulating point avatar with models can be classified into two groups: *penalty-based methods* and *constraint-based methods*. In *penalty-based methods* (Massie & Salisbury, 1994), force proportional to the amount of penetration into a virtual object is applied to the haptic device. This approach however has some drawbacks, including force discontinuity when across a sub-volume boundary and breaking down for objects with complex polygonal meshes. On the other hand, *constraint-based methods* (Zilles & Salisbury, 1995; Ruspini et al., 1997) are well designed for generating convincing interaction forces for objects modeled as rigid polyhedral.

Haptic simulation of deformable objects needs to estimate not only the deformation of the object nodes in space, but also the interaction forces with the object and resulted evaluations that are reflected to users via haptic device. Usually a force model generating interaction forces is loosely coupled in *geometry-based methods*. Colgate et al. (1995) proposed a virtual coupling scheme to bring between the haptic interface and the virtual environment successfully. The extension of geometry-based techniques to haptic display

of deformable objects has applications in haptic sculpting (Chen & Sun, 2002) and CAD system (Higashi et al., 2002; Chen et al., 2007). In *physics-based methods*, the computation of interaction forces is part of physics-based models, so we don't need a separate model for forces generation. McDonnell et al. (2001) developed a haptic sculpting system based on a subdivision solid and mass-spring modeling. Dachille et al. (2001) established a similar system through dynamic NURBS (D-NURBS) to combine NURBS and mass-spring modeling. James & Pai (1999) and Basdogan (2001) had made modeling simplifications due to the limited computational power to implement real-time FEM with haptic displays. Haptics and physically-based interactions have got especially focus in surgery simulation (Puangmali et al., 2008), fabrics (Volino et al., 2007) and hair simulations (Magnenat-Thalmann et al., 2007). In general, physically-based deformation methods require intensive computation, and the demand for realistic haptic feedbacks at high refresh rate leads to the additional computation complexity. On the other hand, integrating non-physical methods with haptic feedback is not natural and cannot provide realistic physical simulation of soft object deformation.

The main requirements with these algorithms, including our work, are the following:

- The reflection forces should be stable and smooth at a high force refreshing rate around 1kHz;
- The exhibition of object deformations should be smooth and carry out the physical-realistic behaviors;
- Force constraints have to be designed to control the deformations and to make the simulation more intuitive and simple to manipulate.

These requirements in interactive haptics modeling are realized in the recent researches presented here. In the following, we present the advances in force-reflecting dynamics in multi-resolution Loop subdivision surfaces, the fast haptics freeform deformation of soft objects through mass-spring Bezier volume lattice, and how to establish the haptic constraint deformation based on the interactive metaballs, to control and manipulate the deformable simulation more easily and intuitively.

DYNAMIC LOOP SUBDIVISION SURFACES

The sense of touch, while allowing for active exploration in haptic simulation of deformable objects, is spatially focused and has a far lower bandwidth than the visual sense (Fritz & Barner, 1999; Kokjer, 1987). Thus, the rate at which information is exchanged through touch is far less than that achieved through visual perception. In addition, most haptic devices utilize point interactions, during which only the end point of the haptic device interacts with virtual objects, resulting in a low bandwidth and further complicating data exploration.

Multi-resolution techniques can provide a solution to address the issues of low information bandwidth and data complexity. Asghar & Barner (2001) developed wavelet based nonlinear multi-resolution techniques for scientific visualization utilizing haptic implementation method to interact with 2D surface. Subdivision surfaces have advantages to uniformly model any complex surfaces of arbitrary topology. Physics-based dynamic subdivision surfaces (Mandal et al., 2000; Qin et al., 1998, 2001) allow the shape editing of limit surfaces by applying forces interactively on the control meshes, and thus enable the creation of intuitive interface for geometric modeling such as modeling with clay dough.

Qin et al. (1998) first introduced the "physical quantity" into dynamic Catmull–Clark surfaces to the visualization of medical datasets. Their method subdivided the faces around extraordinary points recursively in order to compute dynamic parameters, including mass matrix, damping matrix, and stiffness matrix, and obtained only approximate results from linear equations with quickly increasing orders. Mandal et al. (2000) gave approximate solutions of dynamic parameters for the modified butterfly subdivision scheme, and Du & Qin (2000) proposed a method for interactive sculpting of dynamic PDE surfaces, which are usually defined on a regular domain. It is difficult to use PDE surfaces to model complex surfaces of arbitrary topology by patching and trimming. Using parameterizations for subdivision surfaces of arbitrary topologies, including Catmull–Clark surfaces and Loop surfaces (Stam, 1998a, b), it is potential indeed to evaluate the dynamic parameters exactly without actually subdividing the control meshes (Qin et al., 2002).

Haptic Modeling of Dynamic Surfaces

The computation of haptic control loop is strongly influenced by the complexity of the object. Due to the multi-resolution surfaces, the intermediate representation of constraint-based method (Adachi et al., 1995; Chen et al., 2000) is applied.

Haptic Interaction

(Figure 1a) shows the general model used for feeling an object with a point-based contact interaction. Based on the position, velocity and displacement information of a moving haptic sensing point P, force is generated as follows:

$$F = F_a + F_r + F_s$$

where F_a is the vector sum of ambient forces independent of the object, such as gravitational or buoyant forces; F_r is a motion retarding force proportional to velocity; F_s is a stiffness force normal to the object; and F describes the resultant

Figure 1. Force generation profile: (a) Force components; (b) Intermediate representation

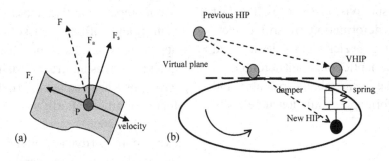

force applied to the user location at position P, it is then the sum of the above three components.

The haptic interface renders the force feedback of a contact point with 6-DOF input is incorporated. The translation controlled by 3-DOF is treated in a classical manner. When activating the stylus switch, each displacement of the stylus along the 3 axes is directly applied to the virtual object in the VEs. As for the virtual plane used as intermediate representation, $D_N \bullet (x - p) = 0$ make the constraint of virtual haptic interface point moving along the virtual plane, here D_N is the normal of the virtual plane, p is the base point of the virtual plane, and x describes the position of the VHIP as shown in (Figure 1b). The other 3-DOF input, roll, pitch, and yaw, describes the rotation mode of the object. When rotating the avatar of the haptic device, each value specifies the rotate angle along the corresponding axis. The constraint along the virtual plane is made accordingly, $D_N \times D_T >= 0$, here D_N is the normal of the virtual plane, D_T is the orientation of the stylus switch.

(Figure 1b) shows the intermediate representation of a virtual object. If the collision is detected between the haptic interaction point (HIP) and the rendered object, the virtual plane of the object is generated using the normal evaluated, giving the direction of the interaction force. The magnitude of the force is a function of the HIP velocity and surface penetration depth. Virtual haptic interac-

tion point (VHIP) describes the point constrained on this virtual plane and corresponds to the shortest distance between the HIP and the object. Thus, the interaction force based on a spring-damper model is obtained as follows:

$$F = K_{spring}d + K_{damping}v$$

Where d is the displacement between HIP and VHIP, v is the velocity of the HIP, K_{spring} is the spring constant, and $K_{damping}$ is the damping ratio. The stiffness of the rendered surface can be controlled by $K_{damping}$.

Loop Subdivision Surfaces

A Loop surface is defined as the limit of a sequence of finer and finer meshes generated by subdividing an initial control mesh recursively. Dynamic Loop subdivision surfaces allow the shape editing of limit surfaces by applying forces interactively on the control meshes, and thus enable the creation of intuitive interface for dynamic geometrical modeling.

Loop subdivision surfaces are designed to generalize the box splines to triangular meshes of arbitrary topology. In each refinement step, a triangle is divided into four pieces by updating each old vertex and introducing a new vertex for each edge of the old control mesh, as shown in (Figure 2a). We show the connectivity structures of the local vertices for updating an old vertex and

Figure 2. Loop Subdivision: (a) triangle subdivision; (b) updating an old vertex; (c) evaluating the new vertex for an edge

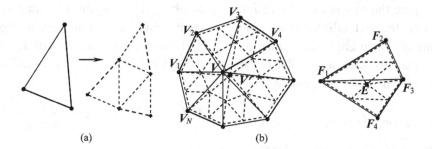

(a)   (b)

evaluating the new vertex for an edge in (Figure 2b) and (Figure 2c), respectively, and list the corresponding formulae as follows:

$$\mathbf{V}' = (1 - \alpha_N)\mathbf{V} + \frac{\alpha_N}{N}\sum_{i=1}^{N}\mathbf{V}_i, \text{ and}$$

$$\mathbf{E} = \frac{3}{8}(\mathbf{F}_1 + \mathbf{F}_3) + \frac{1}{8}(\mathbf{F}_2 + \mathbf{F}_4),$$

where $N \geq 3$ is the valence of V, i.e. the number of the edges sharing V, and

$$\alpha_N = \frac{5}{8} - \frac{\left(3 + 2\cos(2\pi / N)\right)^2}{64}.$$

After one time of subdivision, there are obviously two types of vertices in the resulting mesh: one is directly obtained from an old vertex and called vertex point, e.g. V'; and the other is generated corresponding to an edge and accordingly called edge point, just like E. Note that each vertex point has the same valence as the corresponding old vertex, but all edge points are newcomers and have valence 6.

A vertex with valence other than 6 is regarded as an extraordinary point. After one subdivision step, all extraordinary points are isolated in the control mesh. Without loss of generality, we assume that all extraordinary points are isolated in the initial triangular mesh so that each triangular face contains one extraordinary point at most. In the mesh away from extraordinary points, Loop subdivision is equivalent to the subdivision manner of the three-directional quartic box spline, so the surface can be parameterized using triangular Bezier patches derived from the box splines (Lai, 1992).

If there are m vertices and d faces in the initial control mesh, then the i-th limit surface patch can be rewritten as

$$\mathbf{s}_i^{\mathrm{T}} = \mathbf{J}_i \mathbf{C}_{s_i} = \mathbf{J}^* \mathbf{R}_i \mathbf{C}_0,$$

where $\mathbf{C}_0 = (\mathbf{c}_1, \cdots, \mathbf{c}_m)^{\mathrm{T}}$ contains all m control vertices, and $\mathbf{R}_i$ is an $(N+6) \times m$ picking matrix (each row is filled with zeros except for a one in a certain column). Then, a whole Loop surface can be expressed formally as follows:

$$\mathbf{s}^{\mathrm{T}} = \sum_{i=1}^{d}\mathbf{J}_i\mathbf{C}_{s_i} = \sum_{i=1}^{d}\mathbf{J}^*\mathbf{R}_i\mathbf{C}_0 = \mathbf{J}\mathbf{C}_0,$$

where $\mathbf{J} = \sum_{i=1}^{d}\mathbf{J}^*\mathbf{R}_i$, hence the Loop surface can also be regarded as the sum of all control vertices multiplied by the corresponding basis functions. Here, $\mathbf{J}$ and $\mathbf{J}^*$ can be called the global generalized basis functions and the local generalized basis functions, respectively, accordingly to their defined surface regions.

Dynamic Model of Loop Surfaces

In order to compute the dynamics deformation of Loop surfaces, the methods for evaluating dynamic parameters in the Lagrangian equation are derived, and then two schemes to solve linear equations derived from the Lagrangian equation are presented.

If we regard the control vertices $\mathbf{C}_0$ as a function related to the time t in a pure physical system, the Lagrangian dynamics equation is satisfied:

$$\mathbf{M}\ddot{\mathbf{C}}_0 + \mathbf{D}\dot{\mathbf{C}}_0 + \mathbf{K}\mathbf{C}_0 = \mathbf{F}_p, \qquad (1)$$

where $\mathbf{M}$, $\mathbf{D}$ and $\mathbf{K}$ are the mass, damping and stiffness matrices, respectively, and $\mathbf{F}_p$ is the generalized force vector. Let μ be the density of mass, γ be the coefficient of damping, then the mass matrix and the damping matrix are evaluated as follows:

$$\mathbf{M} = \iint \mu \mathbf{J}^T \mathbf{J} dv dw, \quad \mathbf{D} = \iint \gamma \mathbf{J}^T \mathbf{J} dv dw.$$

The stiffness matrix can be obtained by computing the "thin-plate-energy" for each face (Halstead et al., 1993; Qin et al., 1998):

$$K = \iint (\alpha_{11} J_v^T J_v + \alpha_{22} J_w^T J_w + \beta_{11} J_{vv}^T J_{vv} + \beta_{12} J_{vw}^T J_{vw} + \beta_{22} J w_{ww}^T J_{ww}) dv dw,$$

where α_{ii} and β_{ij} are the characteristic springiness coefficients. Let f be the entire external force applied on the surface, then the force vector $\mathbf{F}_p$ is given as follows:

$$\mathbf{F}_p = \iint \mathbf{J}^T \mathbf{f}^T dv dw.$$

Solving the Dynamics Equations

For the Lagrangian dynamics equation, a two-order differential equation, we replace all derivatives with their discretized approximations first and then use the iteration method to solve the resulting time-varying algebraic system. As the central difference is the best approximation to a derivative, we use central differences to discrete the dynamics equation, in the following,

$$\ddot{\mathbf{C}}_0(t) = \frac{\mathbf{C}_0(t + \Delta t) - 2\mathbf{C}_0(t) + \mathbf{C}_0(t - \Delta t)}{\Delta t^2},$$

$$\dot{\mathbf{C}}_0(t) = \frac{\mathbf{C}_0(t + \Delta t) - \mathbf{C}_0(t - \Delta t)}{2\Delta t},$$

then the dynamics equation $\mathbf{M}\ddot{\mathbf{C}}_0(t) + \mathbf{D}\dot{\mathbf{C}}_0(t) + \mathbf{K}\mathbf{C}_0(t) = \mathbf{F}_p(t)$ can be rewritten as follows:

$$(2\mathbf{M} + \mathbf{D}\Delta t)\mathbf{C}_0(t + \Delta t) = (4\mathbf{M} - 2\Delta t^2 \mathbf{K})\mathbf{C}_0(t) + (\mathbf{D}\Delta t - 2\mathbf{M})\mathbf{C}_0(t - \Delta t) + 2\Delta t^2 \mathbf{F}_p(t)$$

$$(2)$$

Initially we assume that $\mathbf{C}_0(-\Delta t) = \mathbf{C}_0(0)$, and then we can solve the time-varying algebraic system (2) by recursively computing $\mathbf{C}_0((n + 1)\Delta t)$ from the linear equation:

$$(2\mathbf{M} + \mathbf{D}\Delta t)\mathbf{C}_0((n + 1)\Delta t) = (4\mathbf{M} - 2\Delta t^2 \mathbf{K})\mathbf{C}_0(n\Delta t) + (\mathbf{D}\Delta t - 2\mathbf{M})\mathbf{C}_0((n - 1)\Delta t) + 2\Delta t^2 \mathbf{F}_p(n\Delta t)$$

$$(3)$$

according to the known values $\mathbf{C}_0(n\Delta t)$ and $\mathbf{C}_0((n - 1)\Delta t)$ till $\mathbf{C}_0((n + 1)\Delta t) = \mathbf{C}_0(n\Delta t)$ approximately or the iterative time has reached the maximum number set in advance. Note that the coefficient matrix of the linear equation (3), i.e. $(2\mathbf{M} + \mathbf{D}\Delta t)$, is constant, so we can solve the linear equation (3) efficiently during the iteration process only with one time of LU-decomposition of the coefficient matrix.

Figure 3.

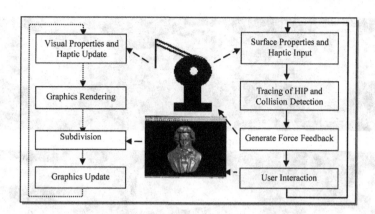

For the local solution of linear system, we regard all vertices in the ρ rings around the vertex v as the influence region of a force applied to v, denoted by Reg(v), where ρ is some integer. Let Dis($\cdot,\cdot$) denote the distance of two vertices in graph theory. If the sequence of edges $\{v_0 v_1, v_1 v_2,...,v_{k-1} v_k\}$ gives the shortest path connecting v_0 with v_k, then Dis(v_0, v_k) = k. Accordingly, we can define Reg(v) more precisely, i.e., Reg(v) = $\{w \mid \text{Dis}(v, w) \leq \rho\}$. If all n forces are applied to the vertices $v_1, v_2,...,$ and v_n in the control mesh, respectively, then the total influence region is $\bigcup_{j=1}^{n} \text{Reg}(\mathbf{v}_j)$, which is supposed as $\{V_1, V_2,..., V_{m_0}\}$. We solve these m_0 vertices only, while fixing all other vertices in the control mesh. Thus, the linear equation (3) has been simplified from m-order to m_0-order.

Interactive Haptics Modeling

In order to integrate the visual and haptic feedbacks seamlessly in interactive haptic modeling, four major components are designated, including virtual-world representation of Loop subdivision surfaces, reacting force computation, the communication links, and interactive modeling interface. The following diagram shows the parallel control architecture for interactive haptic modeling, which supports the dynamic multi-resolution surfaces in touch-enabled VR simulation. (See Figure 3)

Visual properties of objects are derived from Loop subdivision surfaces and sent to the pipeline for graphics update/rendering in the left processing loop. During the processing, the surfacing objects are generated from a simple mesh to more fine details of the surface by applying Loop subdivision schemes. The virtual haptic environment has been developed to provide the realistic force feedback to the users, while touching and deforming the objects of multi-resolution surfaces in the right processing loop. During the interactive modeling, the dynamic multi-resolution surface subsystem and haptics subsystem read the new status of the object and refresh them in the next iteration. A decouple method is applied between the graphics and haptics because of different refresh rates. The sense of touch is much more sensitive than vision, so a realistic haptic interaction must run at a high frequency, about 1000Hz. The graphics sub-system is running as a servo loop at rate of 30Hz. Based on the multi-resolution surfacing representation, kinesthetic-based properties of the object, such as shape and object stiffness, can be conveyed to users through the sense of touch.

Loop subdivisions construct the multi-resolution surfaces in the virtual scene, which are interacted through the 6-DOF haptic interface for dynamic modeling of Loop subdivision surfaces, shown in (Figure 4). (Figure 4a) shows kettle data after 1 time subdivision, and (Figure 4b) the

Figure 4. (a)-(c) Subdivision and deformation of kettle data; (d)-(f) hole & hill data

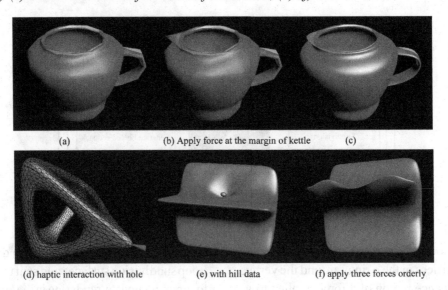

(a) (b) Apply force at the margin of kettle (c)

(d) haptic interaction with hole (e) with hill data (f) apply three forces orderly

resulted model when force is applied to simulate the pulling at the margin of kettle. As for the high frequency of haptics feedback (> 1000Hz), the interactive force is applied only at the coarse triangle mesh (low-resolution surface) to acquire the real-time performance. Once the force is transmitted to the object, the coarse deformation first quickly appears as shown in (Figure 4b), and then further subdivision for finer & smooth visual effect of the deformed object is progressively generated, see (Figure 4c). (Figure 4d) and (Figure 4e) show the examples of interactive haptics modeling on hole and hill data, and (Figure 4f) shows the dynamic simulation resulted by applying the three interactive forces on the surface wall of hill data orderly.

SOFT-TOUCH FREEFORM DEFORMATION

Haptic interface enables the users to directly perform physical interaction with the computer-generated objects that other modalities cannot supply, such as stiffness, vibration, pressure, and temperature. One important use of haptics applies in the entertainment business, where haptics has been used to give the players force feedback during the events occurring in interactive computer games. Physics simulation (Hecker, 1996) with force feedback enabled the players immersive themselves in high-end games is the next frontier in the game development. In 1990s, the desktop force-feedback joysticks and wheels were introduced for interactive games and digital entertainment. These devices work well in simulating the recoil of a gun in shooting games, or the vibration of a steering wheel in racing vehicles. These are however limited in the degrees of freedom and sensitivity, making them hard to be applied for the more advanced game applications.

Haptic simulation of deformable objects needs to estimate not only the deformation of the object nodes in space, but also the magnitude and direction of interaction forces that are reflected to the user via a haptic device. Similar with deformable modeling methods in graphical display, techniques to render force-reflecting deformable objects can be basically grouped into *geometry-based* and *physics-based*. A force model generating interaction forces is loosely coupled in *geometry-based methods*. The extension of geometry-based techniques to haptic display of deformable objects

Figure 5. Mass-spring Bezier volume lattice: hidden masses and springs are removed for the clarity of illustration

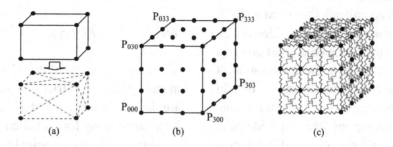

(a)   (b)   (c)

has applications in haptic sculpting (Dachille et al., 1999), and CAD system (Edwards & Luecke, 1996; Higashi et al., 2002). In *physics-based methods*, the computation of interaction forces is part of physics-based models, so we don't need a separate model for forces generation. McDonnell et al. (2001) developed a haptic sculpting system based on a subdivision solid and mass-spring modeling, where mass-spring modeling is used to reduce complexity of manipulating geometric elements and force is given to the subdivision solid. Adding force feedback in deformable modeling has advantages to increase intuition, to control deformations, and to support the development of physical constraints.

Haptic Modeling of Freeform Deformations

Rather than the precise physical simulations in the virtual surgical environment, haptics feedback in interactive gaming is mainly a method to mimic the exaggerated fanciful animations to the players, enhancing attraction and impression of the system. Motivated by the efficient simulation of dynamic models and the free-form deformation in interactive modeling, we propose the soft-touch dynamic freeform deformations that incorporate the dynamic simulation of mass-spring systems and the flexible control of free-form deformation, which can easily simulate force feedback of the avatars in dragging, hitting and crashing motions,

letting the objects move in a dynamic, cartoon-like soft touch style.

Physically-Based Bezier Volume Lattice

We construct the intermediate physically-based Bezier volume space of the object in the following: a tensor product trivariate Bernstein polynomial, a Bezier volume, is chosen as the underlying intermediate parametric space for the object representation and the further haptics-based interactive modeling. The interactive haptic manipulation with the control points of the lattice updates the shape of the intermediate space and the embedded object deformed accordingly.

The initial Bezier volume structure for object utilized is formed into a cubic shape, and the control points are set to form a 4×4×4 regular coordinate grid, shown in Figure 5(b). To attach a Bezier volume to an object, the resting state of Bezier volume block would match the bounding box of the object, and each vertex from its current (x,y,z) object coordinate must be converted to the (u,v,w) lattice position. Physical properties of the object are assigned to the bounding Bezier volume of the object to construct the intermediate physical Bezier volume space for further haptic interactions. Instead of utilizing the mass-spring model which commonly connects the mass points and springs on the object, a mass-spring system is attached to the bounding Bezier volume of the object to simulate dynamic free-form deformations.

The mass of each control point is assigned according to the mass distribution on the object. The springs connected control points aligned with the lattice are then connected, shown as side-springs in (Figure 5c). As the lattice connected only via side-springs may collapse in the deformation, it is necessary to put crossbeam supports shown in cross springs on the lattice. (Figure 5a) is a simple example of 3D mass-spring lattice for one cube unit, above is the original cube, and in lower it comprises eight point masses connected by 28 damped linear springs: 12 run along the edges of the cube, 12 traverse face diagonals, and the remaining 4 lie along the body diagonals. Totally 27 cubes are involved and 504 springs are set for constructing mass-spring Bezier volume lattice of each object (See Figure 4c): 180 parallel to the edges of the cube, 216 traverse face diagonals, and 108 lie along the body diagonals within the object.

Dynamic Freeform Deformation

The physical Bezier volume lattice is constructed through masses and connected springs, the dynamics of control points is governed by the Newton's Second Law of motion. The displacement of the *i*th control point $u_i \in \mathrm{R}^3$ due to an external force F_i is given as follows,

$$m_i \ddot{u}_i + d_i \dot{u}_i + \sum_j \frac{k_{ij}(|r_{ij}| - l_{ij})}{|r_{ij}|} r_{ij} = F_i$$

where m_i is the mass of the point i, d_i is the damping constant of the same point, r_{ij} is the vector distance between point i and point j, l_{ij} and k_{ij} are the rest length and stiffness of the spring connecting two mass points respectively. The right-hand term F_i is the sum of other external forces (e.g. gravity or other user applied forces). The motion equations for the entire system are assembled from the motions of the mass points in the Bezier volume lattice. Concatenating the position vectors of the N individual masses into a single 3N-dimensional

position vector U, then the Lagrange's dynamics equation is satisfied,

$$M\ddot{U} + D\dot{U} + KU = F \qquad (4)$$

where M, D and K are the $3N \times 3N$ mass, damping and stiffness matrices respectively. M and D are diagonal matrices and K is banded because it encodes spring forces which are the functions of distances between neighboring mass points only. The vector F is a $3N$-dimensonal vector representing the total external forces on the mass control points. To solve the Lagrange's dynamics equation (4), we first replace all derivatives with their discretized approximations, central difference, and then use the iteration method to solve the resulting time-varying algebraic system.

Interactive Haptic Deformation

During the deformation or movement of the soft object, real-time haptic interaction needs to be modeled in response to the object accordingly. To simplify the process, the simulation of point-to-plane model is applied here in interactive haptic response. If a collision occurs, the haptic response needs to be computed, with two vectors representing the motion parallel and tangential to the normal of the collision.

$$\vec{V}_n = (\vec{N} \bullet \vec{V})\vec{N} \qquad \vec{V}_t = \vec{V} - \vec{V}_n \qquad \vec{V}' = \vec{V}_t - K_r \vec{V}_n$$

where $\vec{V}_n$ is the amount of the normal force applied to the resulting force; $\vec{V}_t$ is the parallel one; $\vec{V}'$ is the velocity of the particle after collision; K_r is the coefficient of restitution. If K_r is 1, an elastic response is acquired; if it is 0, the particle sticks to the plane. Multi-collisions are treated similarly through the mechanical coupling of an implicit integration progress.

In order to accordingly deform the object within the intermediate mass-spring Bezier volume lattice, each vertex in the object must be

Figure 6. (a) Original homogeneous star object. (b) Haptic deformation & rotation around four anchor nodes. (c) Stretch around one anchor node

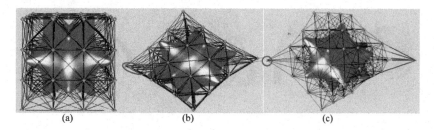

(a)   (b)   (c)

passed through trivariate Bernstein polynomial function, to evaluate its deformed position. The Bernstein basis functions serve as the role of relating the control points in the mass-spring Bezier volume lattice to the vertices in the object. The scale value between 0 and 1 of (*u,v,w*) of each vertex in the object is calculated in advance, and plugged into the basis functions for each control point. The out pops a point weight that relates the vertex in the object to that control point. The sum of all the 64 point weights on any vertex is equal to 1 due to the nature of the Bezier basis functions, and the sum of the influences at any point along the curve is always equal to 1. Once the weight values are calculated for each vertex in the object, the object is deformed accordingly to the movement of the mass-spring Bezier volume lattice, through physically based deformation of the control points.

External forces must be applied from the haptic avatar to directly manipulate the object in the virtual scene. Besides gravity forces applied to particles putting down the object, drag forces are used for making the object floating around. The drag force is simulated with Hook's law via a spring tied to the particle and haptic avatar, having the form $F = K_s d + K_d v$. The second part of the formula is viscous drag through multiplying a damping constant with the velocity to prevent too much bounce and add stability to the system. Two drag forces can be applied at the same time to simulate the two hands' motion of the player. The soft objects are interacted with homogeneous

and isotropic materials. The homogeneous lattice is composed of nodes with mass and springs of same stiffness, and anisotropy of the model by setting different stiffness for springs in the vertical and horizontal directions. A transversely isotropic lattice with springs along y-axis ten times smaller than that along x- and z-axis is composed, which experiences smaller deformation and is stretched less outwards under the same pulling force. Effects on different materials have been studied by varying spring stiffness.

Anchor nodes are set to infinite mass in the model to create special-effect simulation in interactive haptic deformation, shown in (Figure 5). The mass of anchor nodes are 1000 times larger than the other nodes. In (Figure 5b), four anchor nodes are set on the left corner of the object in ellipse to simulate a rotational axis during the haptic deformation. (Figure 5c) sets one anchor node, and more stretched deformation of the whole star is acquired in comparison with (Figure 5b). Special effects of the soft object deformation can be simulated easily with the specified anchor node(s). (Figure 6) shows the surface model of a clown head, in which two anchor nodes are set on the lower left ear circled in ellipse. The haptic drag forces are applied on the right ear to simulate the shaking head from left to right with laughing. The larger force has been perceived while dragging the head through the haptic input. Real-time force feedbacks are replied to the user during the haptic input, in relation to the interacting process. The dynamic-freeform model can be easily coupled in

Figure 7. Interactive haptic deformation of cartoon clown, by pulling at right corner with two anchor nodes circled in red, showing the shaking head with laughing

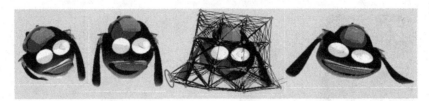

game development to augment force feedbacks of the avatar, while dragging, clashing or exploring in the virtual worlds.

CONSTRAINED HAPTICS MODELING

Haptic simulation of deformable objects needs to estimate not only the object deformation but also the interacting forces that are reflected to users via the haptic device. Adding soft-touch realism in deformable objects provides new touch characteristic in addition with graphical display and covers a wide range of applications, such as geometric modeling (Foskey et al., 2005), computer animation (Chen et al., 2007), and on-line game development (Seo et al., 2007). Haptic manipulation involves direct interaction with soft objects being explored, during which interactive haptic constraints need to be developed to control the deformations flexibly and to make the soft-touch simulation more realistically.

Constraint deformation is efficient in producing controlled spatial deformations. Constraints are usually set on vertices with user-specified displacements to drive the deformation of the object, namely Simple Constrained Deformation (SCODEF), first introduced by Borrel & Rappoport (1994). The displacement of any point to be deformed is the blend of the local B-spline basis functions determined by the constraint points. Further the generalized SCODEF deformation method has been extended on subdivision surface (Lanquetin et al., 2006) and NURBS surfaces

(Clapes et al., 2008) to permit the satisfaction of geometrical constraints. Another typical constraint deformation method is Radial Basis Functions (RBFs) (Botsch & Kobbelt, 2005). RBFs assumed surface smoothness as a minimal constraint, and animations were produced by controlling an arbitrary sparse set of control points on or near the surface of the model. The general idea of constraint deformation (Witkin, 2001) in physically-based modeling is to include not only particles and forces, but restrictions on the way the particles are permitted to move. The key issue in constraint dynamics is to model the particles obey Newton's laws, and at the same time the geometric constraints.

Metaball Constraints

Currently, the modeling process of metaball-constraint deformations is lack of dynamic interaction via touch sensation. Our objective is to incorporate intuitive haptic interaction with constrained metaballs during deformation process. In our proposed haptic-constraint modeling, first the constraint skeleton C_i attached with haptic input is attracted to the target location on the object to be deformed. When haptic avatar moves nearby, guiding force F_a and torque T_a take into effect to guide the users place the constraint skeleton to the target position and direction. Then, manipulating force F_d and torque T_d are generated with the operation of haptic-constraint tool to govern the deformation of the object. Metaball M is constructed dynamically in relation with the movement of constraint skeleton and the distance of force transfer area. Finally, local influenced area on the object is deformed accordingly.

A generalized metaball $M = \langle S, F(d(P,C),R) \rangle$ centered on the skeleton C is defined by a boundary surface S and a potential function $F(d(P,C),R)$ as follows,

$$S = \{P(x, y, z) \in S \mid d(P,C) = R\}$$

$$F(d(P,C),R) = f(d, R) \circ d(P,C)$$

where $d(P,C)$ is a distance function which defines the minimal distance from point $P(x, y, z)$ in 3D space to the individual points $Q(u, v, w)$ on the skeleton C; and $f(d, R)$ is a weight function drops from 1 on the skeleton C to 0 beyond the effective radius R of the skeleton, here Wyvill's degree six polynomial (Nishita & Nakamae, 1994) is adopted as the weight function, because this function blends well and can avoid the calculation of square root.

The deformations of the object based on metaball constraints are generated in the following: Suppose $P(x, y, z)$ is a point on the object in $\mathbf{R}^3$, then $Deform(P): \mathbf{R}^3 \rightarrow \mathbf{R}^3$ is a deformation function which maps P to $Deform(P)$. Let C be a constraint skeleton as above, ΔD be its displacement, and $M = \langle S, F(d(P,C), R) \rangle$ be the metaball centered on the same skeleton. The deformation function is defined as:

$$Deform(P) = P + \Delta D \cdot F(d(P,C),R)$$

Study the potential function of metaball, we have:

$$Deform(P) = \begin{cases} P + \Delta D & d(P,C) = 0 \\ P + \Delta D \cdot f(d,R) & 0 < d(P,C) \leq R \\ P & d(P,C) > R \end{cases}$$

Therefore, the deformation based on metaball constraint yields a local result which satisfies the desired displacement precisely on the constraint skeleton C, and does not affect the points outside the effective radius R of the metaball M. Accordingly, deformation function with n constraints has

$$Deform(P) = P + \sum_{i=1}^{n} \Delta D_i F(d(P, C_i), R_i)$$

The displacement of point P is the blend of the displacements of constraint skeletons weighted by the potential functions of their corresponding metaballs.

Haptic-Constraint Modeling

Given constraint skeleton embedded in the haptic tool, first comes the guiding mode of haptic manipulation. Often the targets are located within the narrow valley or places that are difficult to catch, thus guiding force and torque are taken into effect to help the users place a constraint skeleton to target position and direction on the object. Haptic input is attached to the center O_c of constraint skeleton C_p and pulled towards the target location O_t. Local coordinate of haptic avatar $o''x''y''z''$ is defined with the origin at the end of stylus in haptic device, which is at the center O_c of constraint skeleton, and the y-axis is consistent with the direction of stylus, which is perpendicular to the constraint skeleton. The local coordinate $o'x'y'z'$ is defined at the target location O_t. When haptic avatar is moving into the adjacent area within the distance r of target location, guiding force F_a and torque T_a are taking into effect to guide the user placing the haptic constraint tool to the target location.

$$F_a = k_a(|\vec{h}| - r)\frac{\vec{h}}{|\vec{h}|} + k_v |(\vec{v} \cdot \vec{h})| \frac{\vec{v}}{|\vec{v}|} \quad |\vec{h}| - r < 0$$

$$T_a = k_\theta \frac{1}{\theta} + k_\omega(\vec{\omega} \cdot \theta)$$

where $\vec{h} = \overrightarrow{HIP - O_c}$, HIP is the position of haptic input point, k_a and k_θ are the coefficients

Figure 8. Haptic feedback model during the soft-touch manipulation

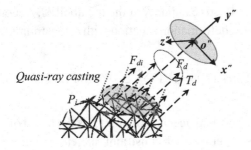

of guiding force and torque respectively, and k_v and k_ω are the coefficients to resist the moving velocity $\vec{v}$ and angular velocity $\vec{\omega}$ of haptic input.

Once the constraint skeleton is attached to the target location on the object, users start to deform the object in the manipulating mode. Interactive manipulating force and resulted haptic-constraint deformation based on metaballs are generated during the soft-touch modeling. (Figure 8) outlines the haptic feedback model during interactive soft-touch manipulation. After constraint skeleton is attached to the target location, quasi-ray-casting method along target direction is applied on the sampled discrete points on the skeleton shown in dotted line. Discrete points P_i of the metaball skeleton on the object are acquired and dynamic manipulating forces are generated via tracing the movement of these points. Finally the composed manipulating force replied to haptic device and the accompanied torque are given as follows:

$$F_{di} = k_{si}(|\,\vec{h}_i\,| - l_{d_i}) + k_{di}\vec{v}_i \quad F_d = \sum_{i=1}^{n} F_{di}$$

$$T_{di} = (|\,\vec{h}_i\,| - l_{di}) \times F_{di} \quad T_d = \sum_{i=1}^{n} T_{di}$$

where k_{si} and l_{di} are the spring coefficient and the rest length of spring tied to the point P_i, k_{di} is the damping coefficient in relation to velocity $\vec{v}_i$ of the same point. F_d and T_d are the final composed

force feedback and torque replied to the user via haptic device.

Haptic Deformation of Interactive Metaballs

The deformation of the object during interactive haptic manipulation is governed by the physics-based deformation of constraint skeleton and dynamically constructed metaball. The movement of constraint skeleton C_i on the object is governed by the Newton's second law of motion. The displacement of the ith vertex u_i within target area on the object to an external force F_i is given as follows,

$$m_i\ddot{u}_i + d_i\dot{u}_i + \sum_j \frac{k_{ij}(|\,\overrightarrow{u_iu_j}\,| - l_{ij})}{|\,\overrightarrow{u_iu_j}\,|}\overrightarrow{u_iu_j} = F_i$$

(5)

where m_i is the mass of the vertex i, d_i is the damping constant of the same point, l_{ij} and k_{ij} are the rest length and stiffness of the spring connecting two mass points respectively. The right-hand term F_i is the sum of external forces (e.g. gravity or other user applied dragging forces). This equation is solved numerically with the central difference method along time steps. Dynamic metaball of constraint skeleton C_i with effective radius R_i is then constructed,

$$R_i = \Delta D_i + \Delta T_i$$

where ΔD_i is the skeleton displacement of constraint C_i computed by equation (5) and ΔT_i is the distance of force transfer area, here average distance of four layers is selected as the optimum force transfer depth.

With the construction of dynamic constraint metaball, an intuitive interface of the haptic manipulation is set up through attaching a local coordinate system to each constraint C_i attached to the haptic input. Let the local coordinate system at haptic constraint C_i be $o'x'y'z'$, and the destination coordinate system be $o''x''y''z''$ after

Figure 9.

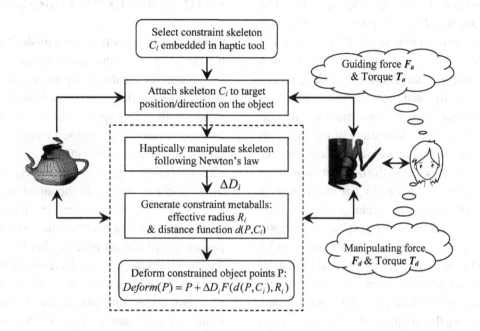

movement and rotation. M is the transformation matrix made up of translation matrix $T(d_x,d_y,d_z)$ in relation with displacement of skeleton computed dynamically in equation (5) and rotation matrix $R(\theta_x,\theta_y,\theta_z)$, having $M = T(d_x,d_y,d_z) R(\theta_x,\theta_y,\theta_z)$. For any point P to be deformed within dynamic constraint metaballs, we first transform it into the local coordinate system and obtain P', then multiply P' with transformation matrix M', having

$$M' = T(d_x',d_y',d_z')R(\theta_x',\theta_y',\theta_z'),$$

$$(d_x',d_y',d_z') = F(d(P,C_i),R_i)(d_x,d_y,d_z) \text{ and}$$

$$(\theta_x',\theta_y',\theta_z') = F(d(P,C_i),R_i)(\theta_x,\theta_y,\theta_z).$$

The following diagram shows the framework of interactive haptic-constraint modeling based on metaballs. The constraint skeleton C_i attached with haptic input is attracted to the target location on the object to be deformed. When haptic avatar moves nearby, guiding force F_a and torque T_a take into effect to guide the users place the constraint skeleton to the target position and direction.

Then, manipulating force F_d and torque T_d are generated with the interactive haptic-constraint tool to govern the deformation of the object. Metaball is constructed dynamically in relation with constraint skeleton and human interactive behavior. The effective radius R_i of metaball is determined with the movement ΔD_i of constraint skeleton, and the distance of force transfer area. Here distance of four surrounding layers is selected as the optimum force transfer depth (Choi et al., 2003). The appropriate distance function $d(P,C_i)$ is selected according to the shape of skeleton. Finally, local influenced area on the object is deformed accordingly. (See Figure 9)

Force Evaluations

(Figure 10) records the guiding force of point-picking constraint tool when interacting with star object of 8640 triangles. The force in evaluation is the force computed before reflecting to the haptic device at the sampling rate of 1KHz. (Figure 10a) records the relationship between guiding force and the displacement of $h = HIP$

$- C_i$, where the stiffness coefficient k_a is 0.3N/ mm and the threshold of attractive radius r is 5mm. Discrete cyan plus signs show the original sample data of the force and the blue dash line is a cubic polynomial fitting of the data, where the coefficient to resist the moving velocity k_v is 0.001mm²/s. Similarly, discrete green circles and the red line record the sample and fitting data with k_v is 0.004mm²/s. Higher velocity guides the user moving into or away from the target at the boundary of attractive field with higher coefficient of k_v. (Figure 10b) records the relationship between guiding force and the moving velocity of haptic interaction point, where k_v is 0.001mm²/s and r is 5mm. Discrete cyan plus signs and blue dash line are the sample and cubic polynomial fitting data with k_a is 0.3N/mm, discrete green circles and red line are the sample and cubic polynomial fitting data with k_a is 0.5N/mm. Higher k_a results in larger force to guide the user reach the target. In (Figure 10c), the mesh grid and discrete red circles are the expected and sampled force under the control of displacement and velocity, where k_a is 0.3N/mm and k_v is 0.004mm²/s. We observe that the guiding force is the compound of attracting force in reverse direction to displacement h and the moving force under the direction to velocity.

FUTURE RESEARCH DIRECTIONS

Our studies in interactive haptic modeling simulate the tangible and immersive experiences during the object deformations, by adding the physical realism interacting with subdivision surfaces, dynamic freeform space, and interactive meta-ball constraints. The proposed work is extensible to support users perceptually experience the virtual objects with different materials through the tangible interfaces in the augmented virtual worlds. It is important to perform the subject experiments from the user groups, to test how the perception of virtual objects simulated through the haptic interactions replicate or differ from the touch with the real objects. To distinguish from different materials through touch perception, groups of users can be organized for the tests of the same experimental configuration involving both virtual and real objects. Establishing more accurate method to overcome the limitations of current haptic interaction model will improve the immersive simulation of force experience in virtual environments. We will further investigate how on realize more realistic physical properties in soft-touch haptic modeling, and extend the dynamic deforming Loop surfaces, incorporating the 6-DOF haptic interaction, to the dynamic modeling of other subdivision surfaces similarly.

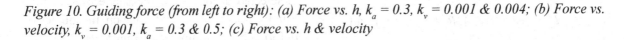

Figure 10. Guiding force (from left to right): (a) Force vs. h, k_a = 0.3, k_v = 0.001 & 0.004; (b) Force vs. velocity, k_v = 0.001, k_a = 0.3 & 0.5; (c) Force vs. h & velocity

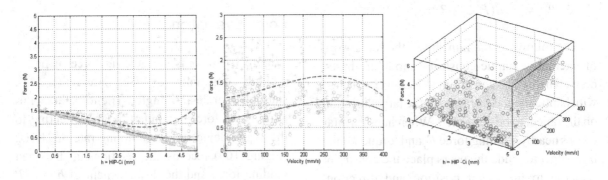

In general, haptic perception and manipulation can be further constructed uniformly in the multi-resolution rendering framework. For the object with different data resolutions, multiple physical properties can be revealed in relation to larger force applied, such as texture properties. Interactive force rendering methods can be integrated and selected dynamically to enhance the diversity of force perceptions in virtual environments. In haptic constraint modeling, if we generalize the potential function to a Bezier function in haptic constraint tools, more control freedoms can be obtained. With the embedded free-form deformations, our approach is somehow limited to the coarse representation of the interested object to be deformed through manipulating the bounded volume. Like the anchor nodes used in the system, void nodes may be simulated to represent the hole or air region within the object or more closely approximated object space. The future work includes investigating force evaluation methods and haptic contact models, and in addition integrating them into the unified haptic-scene framework, for the rich and dexterous experiences in large, touch-enable virtual environments.

CONCLUSION

Haptics is an active research topic to enhance the realism of immersive virtual environments, which provides the important, bidirectional sensorial channel in touch-enabled interactive applications. This chapter presents the related work on adding soft-touch haptics interaction in feeling and manipulating dynamic objects within the virtual environments. First, haptic modeling of Loop subdivision surfaces is efficiently established. It supports the shape editing of limit surfaces by applying forces interactively on the subdivision surfaces, and the dynamic parameters are computed easily without subdividing the control mesh recursively. Following, haptic simulation of dynamic free-from deformations through

mass-spring Bezier volume lattice is flexibly set up. The approach integrates the merits of Bezier volume and free-form deformation technique, so that it is simple to determine parametric space, has intuitive and effective controls, and apply the physical properties for real-time simulation in the soft-touch virtual environment. Moreover, interactive metaball constraints are incorporated with haptics interface to control the deforming process, making the simulation of deformable objects simple to manipulate via the touch. Interactive haptics modeling based on metaballs effectively control the force propagation through the potential function distribution, within the influence range of constrained deformations.

REFERENCES

Aamisepp, H., & Nilsson, D. (2003). *Haptic Hardware Support in 3D Game Engine*. Master of Science thesis, Department of Computer Science, Lund Institute of Technology.

Adachi, Y., Kumano, T., & Ogino, K. (1995). Intermediate Representation for Stiff Virtual Objects. In *Proc. IEEE Virtual Reality Annual Intl. Symp* (pp. 203-210).

Asghar, M. W., & Barner, K. E. (2001). Nonlinear Multiresolution Techniques with Applications to Scientific Visualization in a Haptic Environment. *IEEE Transactions on Visualization and Computer Graphics*, 7(1), 76–93. doi:10.1109/2945.910825

Basdogan, C. (2001). Real-time Simulation of Dynamically Deformable Finite Element Models Using Modal Analysis and Spectral Lanczos Decomposition Methods. In Medicine Meets Virtual Reality (pp. 46-52).

Borrel, P., & Rappoport, A. (1994). Simple Constrained Deformation for Geometric Modeling and Interactive Design. *ACM Transactions on Graphics*, 13(2), 137–155. doi:10.1145/176579.176581

Botsch, M., & Kobbelt, L. (2005). Real-time Shape Editing Using Radial Basis Functions. [Proceedings of Eurographics]. *Computer Graphics Forum, 24*(3), 611–621. doi:10.1111/j.1467-8659.2005.00886.x

Chen, H., & Sun, H. (2002). Real-time Haptic Sculpting in Virtual Volume Space. In *International Conference Proceedings of ACM VRST 2002* (pp. 81-88).

Chen, H., & Sun, H. (2006). Body-based Haptic Interaction Model for Touch-enabled Environments. *MIT Journal of PRESENCE: Teleoperators and Virtual Environments, 15*(2), 186–203. doi:10.1162/pres.2006.15.2.186

Chen, H., Sun, H., & Jin, X. (2007). Interactive Soft-touch Dynamic Deformation. *Journal of Computer Animation and Virtual Worlds, 18*, 153–163. doi:10.1002/cav.171

Chen, K. W., Heng, P. A., & Sun, H. (2000). Direct Haptic Rendering of Isosurface by Intermediate Representation. In *International Conference Proceedings of ACM VRST 2000 (*pp. 188-194).

Choi, K. S., Sun, H., & Heng, P. A. (2003). Interactive Deformation of Soft Tissues with Haptic Feedback for Medical Learning. *IEEE Transactions on Information Technology in Biomedicine, 7*(4), 358–363. doi:10.1109/TITB.2003.821311

Clapes, M., Gonzalez-hidalgo, M., Mir-Torrres, A., & Palmer-Rodriguez, P. A. (2008). Interactive Constrained Deformations of NURBS Surfaces: N-SCODEF. In Articulated Motion and Deformable Objects 2008 (LNCS5098, pp. 359-369). Berlin: Springer-Verlag.

Colgate, J. E., Stanley, M. C., & Brown, J. M. (1995). Issues in the Haptic Display of Tool Use. In *Proc. Of IEEE/RSJ International Conference on Intelligent Robots and Systems* (pp. 140-145).

Dachille, F., Qin, H., & Kaufman, A. (2001). A Novel Haptics-based Interface and Sculpting System for Physics-based Geometric Design. *Journal of Computer Aided Design, 33*(5), 403–420. doi:10.1016/S0010-4485(00)00131-7

Dachille, F., Qin, H., Kaufman, A., & El-sana, J. (1999). Haptic Sculpting of Dynamic Surfaces. In *ACM Symposium on Interactive 3D Graphics 1999* (pp. 103-110).

Du, H., & Qin, H. (2000). Direct Manipulation and Interactive Sculpting of PDE Surfaces. *Journal of Comput Graph Forum (Eurographics 2000), 19*(3), 261–270.

Edwards, J., & Luecke, G. (1996). Physically based Models for Use in a Force Feedback Virtual Environment. In *Japan/USA Symposium on Flexible Automation, ASME 1996* (pp. 221-228).

Foskey, M., Otaduy, M. A., & Lin, M. C. (2005). ArtNova: Touch-enabled 3D Model Design. In *International Conference on Computer Graphics and Interactive Techniques* (pp.188-195).

Fritz, J. P., & Barner, K. E. (1999). Design of a Haptic Data Visualization System for People with Visual Impairments. *IEEE Transactions on Neural Systems and Rehabilitation Engineering, 7*(3), 372–384.

Halstead, M., Kass, M., & DeRose, T. (1993). Efficient, Fair Interpolation Using Catmull-Clark Surfaces. In *Computer Graphics (Proceedings of SIGGRAPH '93)* (pp. 35-44).

Hecker, C. (1996). *Physics, the Next Frontier* (pp. 12–20). Game Developers Magazine.

Higashi, M., Aoki, N., & Kaneko, T. (2002). Application of Haptic Navigation to Modify Free-form Surfaces Through Specified Points and Curves. *Journal of Computing and Information Science in Engineering, 2*, 265–276. doi:10.1115/1.1559581

James, D., & Pai, D. (1999). ARTDEFO: Accurate Real Time Deformable Objects. In *SIGGRAPH Conference Proceedings* (pp.65-72).

Lai, M. J. (1992). Fortran Subroutines for B-nets of Box Splines on Three- and Four-directional Meshes. *Numerical Algorithms*, *2*, 33–38. doi:10.1007/BF02142204

Lander, J. (1999). *Graphic Content - collision response: bouncy, trouncy, fun* (pp. 15–19). Game Developers Magazine.

Lander, J. (2000). Graphic Content - in This Corner: the Crusher. *Game Developer Magazine*, 17-22.

Lanquetin, S., Raffin, R., & Neveu, M. (2006). Generalized SCODEF Deformations on Subdivision Surfaces. In Articulated Motion and Deformable Objects (LNCS 4069, pp.132-142). Berlin: Springer-Verlag.

Loop, C. (1987). *Smooth Subdivision Surfaces based on Triangles*. MS thesis, Department of Mathematics, University of Utah.

Magnenat-Thalmann, N., Montagnol, M., Bonanni, U., & Gupta, R. (2007). Visuo-Haptic Interface for Hair. In *2007 International Conference on Cyberworlds* (pp. 3-12).

Mandal, C., Qin, H., & Vemuri, B. C. (2000). A Novel FEM-based Dynamic Framework for Subdivision Surfaces. *Computer Aided Design*, *32*, 479–497. doi:10.1016/S0010-4485(00)00037-3

Massie, T. H., & Salisbury, J. K. (1994). The PHANToM Haptic Interface: A Device for Probing Virtual Object. In *Proceedings of the ASME Winter Annual Meeting, Symposium on Haptic Interfaces for Virtual Environment and Teleoperator Systems*.

McDonnell, K., Qin, H., & Wlodarczyk, R. (2001). Virtual Clay: a Real-time Sculpting System with Haptic Toolkits. In *Proc. of 2001 ACM Symp. on Interactive 3D Graphics* (pp. 179-190).

Nishita, T., & Nakamae, E. (1994). A Method for Displaying Metaballs by Using Bezier Clipping. *Computer Graphics Forum*, *13*(3), 271–280. doi:10.1111/1467-8659.1330271

Puangmali, P., Althoefer, K., Seneviratne, L. D., Murphy, D., & Dasgupta, P. (2008). State-of-the-Art in Force and Tactile Sensing for Minimally Invasive Surgery. *IEEE Sensors Journal*, *8*(4), 371–381. doi:10.1109/JSEN.2008.917481

Qin, H., Mandal, C., & Vemuri, B. C. (1998). Dynamic Catmull-Clark Subdivision Surfaces. *IEEE Transactions on Visualization and Computer Graphics*, *4*(3), 215–229. doi:10.1109/2945.722296

Qin, K., Chang, Z., Wang, H., & Li, D. (2002). Physics-based Loop Surface Modeling. *Journal of Computer Science and Technology*, *17*(6), 851–858. doi:10.1007/BF02960776

Qin, K., Wang, H., Li, D., Kikinis, R., & Halle, M. (2001). Physics-based Subdivision Surface Modeling for Medical Imaging and Simulation. In *Proceedings of MIAR'2001*, Hong Kong (pp. 117-124).

Ruspini, D. C., Kolarov, K., & Khatib, O. (1997). The Haptic Display of Complex Graphical Environments. In *SIGGRAPH 97 Conference Proceedings* (pp. 345 – 352).

Seo, Y., Lee, B. C., Kim, Y., Kim, J. P., & Ryu, J. (2007). K-HapticModeler: A Haptic Modeling Scope and Basic Framework. In *IEEE International Workshop on Haptic, Audio and Visual Environments and Games HAVE 2007* (pp. 136 – 141).

Stam, J. (1998a). Evaluation of Loop Subdivision Surfaces. In SIGGRAPH'98.

Stam, J. (1998b). Exact Evaluation of Catmull-Clark Subdivision Surfaces at Arbitrary Parameter Values. In *Computer Graphics (Proceedings of SIGGRAPH '98)* (pp. 395-404).

Volino, P., Davy, P., Bonanni, U., Luible, C., Magnenat-Thalmann, N., Mäkinen, M., & Meinander, H. (2007). From Measured Physical Parameters to the Haptic Feeling of Fabric. *The Visual Computer*, 23(2), 133–142. doi:10.1007/s00371-006-0034-2

Witkin, A. (2001). *Constrained Dynamics*. SIGGRAPH.

Zilles, C. B., & Salisbury, J. K. (1995). A Constraint-based God-Object Method for Haptic Display. In *Proceedings of the 1995 IEEE/RSJ International Conference on Intelligent Robots and Systems* (pp. 146-151).

ADDITIONAL READING

Avila, R. S. (1998). The Nuts and Bolts of Using Touch Interfaces With Computer Graphics Applications. In *SIGGRAPH 1998 Course Notes #1*. Physical Interaction.

Avila, R. S. (1999). From Basic Principles to Advanced Applications. In *SIGGRAPH 1999 Course Notes #38*. Haptics.

Benchmann, D. (1998). Multimensional Free-Form Deformation Tools. In. *Proceedings of Eurographics*, *1998*, 102–110.

Blinn, J. F. (1982). A Generalization of Algebraic Surface Drawing. *ACM Transactions on Graphics*, 1(3), 235–256. doi:10.1145/357306.357310

Bloomenthal, J., Bajaj, C., Blinn, J., Cani-Gasuel, M., Rockwood, A., Wyvill, B., & Wyvill, G. (1997). *An Introduction to Implicit Surfaces*. Los Altos, CA: Morgan Kaufmann Publishers.

Bloomenthal, J., & Shoemake, K. (1991). Convolution Surfaces. *Computer Graphics*, 25(4), 251–256. doi:10.1145/127719.122757

Bloomenthal, J., & Wyvill, B. (1990). Interactive Techniques for Implicit Modeling. *Computer Graphics*, 24(2), 109–116. doi:10.1145/91394.91427

El-Sana J., & Varshney A. (2000). Continuously-adaptive Haptic Rendering. *Virtual Environments*, 135–144.

Faloutsos, P., Panne, M., & Terzopoulos, D. (1997). Dynamic Free-Form Deformations for Animation Synthesis. *IEEE Transactions on Visualization and Computer Graphics*, 3(3), 201–214. doi:10.1109/2945.620488

Glencross, M., Vhalmers, A. G., Lin, M. C., Otaduy, M. A., & Gutierrez, D. (2006). Exploiting Perception in High-fidelity Virtual Environments. In SIGGRAPH 2006 course note 24.

Gregory, A., Mascarenhas, A., Ehmann, S., Lin, M. C., & Manocha, D. (2000). Six Degree-of-Freedom Haptic Display of Polygonal Models. In *Proceedings of IEEE Visualization* (pp. 139-146, 549).

Jin, X., Li, Y., & Peng, Q. (2000). General Constrained Deformations Based on Generalized Metaballs. *Computers & Graphics*, 24, 219–231. doi:10.1016/S0097-8493(99)00156-9

Kim, Y. J., Otaduy, M. A., Lin, M. C., & Manocha, D. (2003). Six-Degree-of-Freedom Haptic Display Using Incremental and Localized Computations. *MIT Journal of Presence: Teleoperators and Virtual Environments*, 12(3), 277–295. doi:10.1162/105474603765879530

Kojekine, N., Savchenko, V., Senin, M., & Hagiwara, I. (2002). Real-time 3D Deformations by Means of Compactly Supported Radial Basis Functions. In Proceedings of Eurographics (pp. 35-42).

Kokjer, K. J. (1987). The Information Capacity of the Human Fingertip. *IEEE Transactions on Systems, Man, and Cybernetics, 17*(1). doi:10.1109/TSMC.1987.289337

Lamousin, H., & Waggenspack, W. (1994). NURBS-based Free-Form Deformation. *IEEE Computer Graphics and Applications, 14*(9), 59–65. doi:10.1109/38.329096

Mark, W., Randolph, S., Finch, M., Van Verth, J., & Taylor, R. M., II. (1996). Adding Force Feedback to Graphics Systems: Issues and Solutions. In *SIGGRAPH 96 conference proceedings* (pp. 447–452).

McLaughlin, M. L., Hespanha, J. P., & Sukhatme, G. S. (2002). *Touch in Virtual Environments: Haptics and the Design of Interactive Systems.* New York: Prentice Hall PTR.

McNeely, W. A., Puterbaugh, K. D., & Troy, J. J. (1999). Six Degree of-Freedom Haptic Rendering Using Voxel Sampling. In *Proc. ACM SIGGRAPH Int. Conf. on Computer Graphics and Interactive Techniques* (pp. 401-408).

Nishimura, H., Hirai, M., & Kawai, T. (1985). Object Modeling by Distribution Function and a Method of Image Generation. *Transactions on IECE, 68*(4), 718–725.

Noh, J. Y., Fidaleo, D., & Neumann, U. (2000). Animated Deformations with Radial Basis Functions. In *Proceedings of the 2000 ACM Symposium on Virtual Reality Software and Technology* (pp. 166-74).

Otaduy, M. A., & Lin, M. C. (2003). Sensation Preserving Simplification for Haptic Rendering. In *Proc. of ACM SIGGRAPH* (pp. 543-553).

Otaduy, M. A., & Lin, M. C. (2006). A Modular Haptic Rendering Algorithm for Stable and Transparent 6-DoF Manipulation. *IEEE Transactions on Robotics, 22*(4), 751–762. doi:10.1109/TRO.2006.876897

Srinivasan, M. A., & Basdogan, C. (1997). Haptics in Virtual Environments: Taxonomy, Research Status, and Challenges. *Computer Graphics, 21*(4), 393–404. doi:10.1016/S0097-8493(97)00030-7

Sun, H., Wang, H., Chen, H., & Qin, K. H. (2007). Touch-enabled Haptic Modeling of Deformable Multi-resolution Surfaces. *Journal of Virtual Reality: Research. Development and Applications, 11*, 45–60.

Yoshihiro, K., Megumi, N., Tomohiro, K., Hiroshi, O., & Masaru, K. (2005). Interaction Model Between Elastic Objects for Haptic Feedback Considering Collisions of Soft Tissue. *Computer Methods and Programs in Biomedicine, 80*(3), 216–224. doi:10.1016/j.cmpb.2005.09.001

Zhang, J., Payandeh, S., & Dill, J. (2002). Haptic Subdivision: An Approach to Defining Level-of-detail in Haptic Rendering. In *Proceedings of 10th Symposium on Haptic Interfaces for Virtual Environment and Teleoperator Systems* (pp. 201–208).

Chapter 3
Collision Detection:
A Fundamental Technology for Virtual Prototyping

Gabriel Zachmann
Clausthal University, Germany

ABSTRACT

Collision detection is one of the enabling technologies in many areas, such as virtual assembly simulation, physically-based simulation, serious games, and virtual-reality based medical training. This chapter will provide a number of techniques and algorithms that provide efficient, real-time collision detection for virtual objects. They are applicable to various kinds of objects and are easy to implement.

INTRODUCTION

In the product development process of manufacturing industries, prototyping is an essential step. Prototypes represent important features of a product that are to be investigated, evaluated, and improved. They are used to analyse design alternatives, to plan assembly lines, to support managment decisions, or to market studies by showing a new model to potential customers.

The vision of virtual prototyping is to utilize virtual reality techniques for design evaluations and presentations based on a digital model instead of physical prototypes.

One of the most challenging classes of virtual prototyping in manufacturing industries are *functional simulations virtual assembly simulations,* and *ergonomic studies*. These are VR applications that usually comprise a lot of interaction among objects and interaction between the user and virtual objects.

In order to make the virtual objects behave exactly like real objects, fast and exact collision detection of polygonal objects undergoing rigid motions or deformations is an enabling technology in many virtual prototyping applications (and many other applications of computer graphics). It is a fundamental problem of the dynamic simulation of rigid bodies, simulation of natural interaction with objects, and haptic rendering.

DOI: 10.4018/978-1-61520-631-5.ch003

For example, in virtual assembly simulations, parts should be rigid and slide along each other.

It is very important for a VR system to be able to do all simulations and renderings at interactive frame rates. Otherwise, the feeling of immersion and even the usability of the VR system will be impaired. For instance, haptic rendering is very demanding because it requires the collision detection algorithms to handle at least 1000 collision queries per second for each pair of objects.

Virtually all approaches to this problem utilize some kind of acceleration data structure. One particular requirement in the context of product engineering and virtual prototyping is that this auxiliary data structure is to be built fairly fast and efficiently. This is important because manufacturing industries do not want to store any auxiliary data in their product data management systems.

In this chapter, we will first describe some of the approaches to collision detection that we have developed in recent years, targeted at differing scenarios and conditions. Then, we will highlight some scenarios in virtual prototyping where collision detection is an enabling technology.

BACKGROUND

BVH Based Methods

Bounding volume hierarchies have proven to be a very efficient data structure for rigid collision detection, and, to some extent, even for deformable objects.

One of the design choices with BV trees is the type of BV. In the past, a wealth of BV types has been explored, such as spheres (Hubbard, 1996; Palmer & Grimsdale, 1995), OBBs (Gottschalk, Lin & Manocha, 1996), DOPs (Klosowski, Held, Mitchell, Sowrizal & Zikan, 1998; Zachmann, 2009), Boxtrees (Bala, Walter & Greenberg, 2003; Zachmann, 2002), AABBs (van den Bergen, 1997; Larsen, Gottschalk, Lin & Monocha, 1999), and convex hulls (Ehmann & Lin, 2001).

Space Subdivision Methods

Another alternative are space-subdivision approaches, for instance by an octree (Kitamura, Smith, Takemura & Kishino, 1998) or a voxel grid (Mcneely, Puterbaugh & Troy, 1999). In general, non-hierarchical data structures seem to be more promising for collision detection of deformable objects (Agarwal, Basch, Guibas, Hershberger & Zhang, 2000; Fisher & Lin, 2001; Huh, Metaxas & Badler, 2001), although some geometric data structures suggest a natural BV hierarchy (Lau, Chan, Luk & Li, 2002). Deformable collision detection is not the focus of our work presented here.

GPU Based Methods

A clever way to utilize graphics hardware was presented by Knott & Pai (2003). Based on the observation that an intersection can occur if and only if an edge of one object intersects the other one, they render edges of one object and polygons of the other. This even works for deformable geometry. Unlike many previous approaches, objects do not need to be convex. However, they must still be closed. Furthermore, it seems to work robustly only for moderate polygon counts.

A hybrid approach was proposed by Govindaraju, Redon, Lin & Manocha (1996). Here, the graphics hardware is used only to detect potentially colliding objects, while triangle-triangle intersections are performed in the CPU. While this approach alleviates previous restrictions on object topology, its effectiveness seems to degrade dramatically when the density of the environment increases.

The approach presented by Argawal, Krishnan, Mustafa & Venkatasubramanian (2003) can compute the penetration depth using graphics hardware, but only for convex objects.

Earlier image-based methods include (Baciu & Wong, 2002; Baciu & Wong, 2003; Lombardo, Cani & Neyret, 1999; Myszkowski, Okunev & Kunii, 1995; Shinya & Forgue, 1991).

Penetration Depth and Proximity

A classical approach for proximity queries is the GJK algorithm (Gilbert, Johnson & Keerthi, 1988; van den Bergen, Fast & Robust, 1999). It derives the distance between a pair of convex objects, by utilizing the Minkowski sum. It is also possible to extend GJK in order to compute the penetration depth (Cameron, 1997).

In (Johnson & Cohen, 1998) a generalized framework for minimum distance computations that depends on geometric reasoning is presented. It also includes time-critical properties.

PQP creates a hierarchy of rectangle swept spheres. Distance computations are performed between these volumes on the hierarchical tree (Larsen, Gottschalk, Lin & Monocha, 1999). Moreover, it uses specialized algorithms to improve the efficiency of distance calculations. We used it in this paper to compute the ground truth for the proximity queries.

Another package, supporting proximity queries between any convex quadrics is SOLID (van den Bergen, 2001). It uses axis aligned bounding boxes and the Minkowski difference between convex polytopes together with several optimization techniques.

SWIFT++ provides a convex surface decomposition scheme and a modified Lin-Canny closest feature algorithm to compute approximate as well as exact distance between general rigid polyhedra (Ehmann & Lin, 2001).

Sphere trees have also been used for distance computation in the past (Hubbard, 1995; Mendoza & Sullivan; 2006; Quinlan, 1994). The algorithms presented there are interruptible and they are able to deliver approximative distances. Moreover, they all compute a lower bound on the distance, because of using outer hierarchies, while our ISTs derive an upper bound. Thus, a combination of these approaches with our ISTs could deliver good error bounds in both directions.

Johnson & Willemsen (2003) compute local minimum distances for a stable force feedback computation and uses spatialized normal cone pruning for the collision detection. However, it is not applicable to penetration depth estimation.

DEEP is a technique based on Dual-space Expansion for Estimating the Penetration depth between convex polytopes in 3D. The algorithm incrementally seeks a "locally optimal solution" by walking on the surface of the Minkowski sums. The surface of the Minkowski sums is computed implicitly by constructing a local Gauss map. In practice, the algorithm works well when there is high motion coherence in the environment and is able to compute the optimal solution in most cases.

Surveys and Books

Some good surveys on collision detection can be found in (Jimenez, Thomas & Torras, 2001; Lin, Manocha, Cohen & Gottschalk, 1996; Teschner, Kimmerle, Zachmann, Heidelberger, Raghupathi, Fuhrmann, Cani, Faure, Magnetat-Thalmann & Strasser, 2004; Teschner, Heidelberger, Manocha, Govindaraju, Zachmann, Kimmerle, Mezger & Fuhrmann; 2005). In addition, there are two books (Ericson, 2004; van den Bergen, 2003).

MINIMAL HIERARCHICAL COLLISION DETECTION

In this section, we present a bounding volume hierarchy (BVH) that allows for extremely small data structure sizes while still performing collision detection as fast as other classical hierarchical algorithms in most cases (Zachmann, 2002). The hierarchical data structure is a variation of axis-aligned bounding box trees. In addition to being very memory efficient, it can be constructed efficiently and very fast. It has been invented independently several times and under different names (Ooi, McDonell & Sacks-Davis, 1987; Wächter & Keller, 2006; Zachmann, 2002).

We also propose a criterion to be used during the construction of the BVHs that is formally

Figure 1.Only one value per axis needs to be recomputed for the overlap test

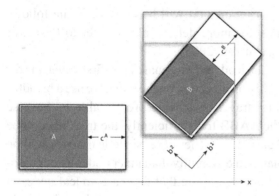

derived. The idea of the argument is general and can be applied to other bounding volume hierarchies as well.

Restricted Boxtrees

In a BV hierarchy, each node has a BV associated that completely contains the BVs of its children. Usually, the parent BV is made as tight as possible. In binary AABB trees, this means that a parent box touches each child box on 3 sides on average, because of the way the set of polygons is partitioned (usually alog one axis). In our experience, for about half of all nodes the volume of empty space between its bounding box and its parent's bounding box is 10% or less.

Consequently, our hierarchy never stores a complete box explicitly. Instead, each node stores only one side of an AABB, in particular that one which cuts off the most empty space from the father box. Overall, a node consists of just one float, representing the distance from one of the sides of the parent box, plus the ID of the axis, plus one pointer to the left child (assuming siblings are stored contiguously).

Because each box in such a hierarchy is restricted on most sides, we call this a *restricted boxtree*.

The overlap test between a pair of BVs is the elementary step in all hierarchical collision detec-

tion algorithms, which accounts for the majority of the runtime.

With the BVs of the restricted boxtree, there are a number of algorithms possible to test a given pair for overlap. We have devised a test that was also dubbed elsewhere the "SAT lite" test (van den Bergen, 1997). We have found this test to yield the most efficient collision detection with restricted boxtrees.

Assume we are given two boxes A and B (See Figure 1). The general idea of our test is to compute an axis-aligned box that tightly encloses B in the coordinate system of A (this is equivalent to projecting B onto the three axes of A). This computation can be sped up very efficiently by utilizing the fact that we already know that the parent boxes of A and B must overlap. For the same reason, the overlap tests of the children can be sped up significantly.

After performing the "SAT lite" test on 3 axes, we reverse the roles of A and B, which completes the test along all 6 axes.

A GENERAL HEURISTIC FOR CONSTRUCTING GOOD BVHS

The performance of any hierarchical collision detection depends not only on the traversal algorithm, but also crucially on the quality of the hierarchy, i.e., the construction algorithm.

The generally adopted aproach is top-down, i.e., we start with the complete set of polygons. In the first step, we enclose this by a BV of the chosen type. Then, we choose a so-called *splitting axis* (this could be one of the coordinate axes). Then, we make one plane sweep along that axis, where each plane position yields a partition of the given set of polygons. Once we have determined the right plane position, we can recursively process the two sets of polygons.

The main question during this process is: which plane position yields the best partition of the set of polygons, in the sense of fastest collision queries on average.

By applying Minkowsky sums, we have found evidence that good BVHs can be obtained if the total volume of the children of a given BV is minimized.

OBJECT-SPACE INTERFERENCE DETECTION ON PROGRAMMABLE GRAPHICS HARDWARE

Currently, the performance of graphics hardware (GPUs) is progressing faster than general-purpose CPUs. The main reason is an architecture that combines *stream processing* (Kapasi, Rixner, Dally, Khailany, Ahn, Mattson & Owens, 2003) and SIMD processing. In addition, the programmability of the GPU has increased drastically over the past few years. Overall, today a programmer can write *kernels* for all stages of the graphics pipeline that are automatically executed in parallel on an indefinite number of processing units. This has led many researchers to investigate exploitation of the GPU for other computations, such as matrix computations, ray tracing, distance field computation, etc.

Many algorithms have been proposed to utilize graphics hardware for the problem of collision detection. They can be classified into techniques that make use of the depth and stencil buffer tests, and those that compute discrete distance fields. In any case, the problem is approached in *image space*, i.e., it is discretized.

To our knowledge, we have presented the first algorithm that performs collision detection completely on the GPU and in *object space* (Gress & Zachmann, 2003). Our method is based on previous hierarchical collision detection algorithms. However, all computations during this traversal, including the final triangle intersection tests, are performed in vertex and fragment programs on the GPU. The algorithm has no requirements on the

shape, topology, or connectivity of the polygonal input models.

This method will be outlined in the following; for more details, please refer to (Gress & Zachmann, 2003).

Instead of traditional depth-first traversals for collision detection on the CPU, we use a breadth-first traversal scheme. To be able to traverse the AABB trees efficiently, the trees have to be balanced. Furthermore, since leaf nodes will be handled differently than inner nodes by our algorithm, we require that there are no leaf nodes in the tree other than at the lowest hierarchy level.

Since we traverse the tree breath-first and since at each hierarchy level only certain node pairs are to be visited, we have to store the indices of these node pairs temporarily during the traversal. For this purpose, we use a 2D buffer, which we will refer to in the following as *node pair index map*.

This buffer contains an array of index sets as follows. Let $L_j = \{i \,|\, AABB(S_i) \text{ overlaps } AABB(T_j)\}$. Putting the contents of set L_j in the 2D buffer at row j, stored successively starting at the first pixel in this row, the complete buffer consists of m horizontal lines of different lengths. The lengths of all these lines (or, more precisely, their start and end points) are stored in a vertex array.

In addition, we require a second temporary 2D buffer, that we call *overlap count map*. This buffer consists of multiple levels, exactly as much as there are hierarchy levels in the AABB trees. As the node pair index map, also each level of the overlap count map consists of m horizontal lines of different lengths. The contents of the overlap count map are constructed during the AABB tree traversal at each hierarchy level L as follows.

At first, all those AABB node pairs that are to be visited at the considered level L are checked for overlap. Each such node pair corresponds to one entry in the overlap count map at level L. If the AABB overlap test of a certain node pair was positive and thus the corresponding child nodes are to be visited when processing the next hierarchy level, the number of these child nodes is written into the corresponding entry of the overlap count map. Otherwise the entry of the overlap count map is set to *0*. How this is done using the GPU is described in (Gress & Zachmann, 2003).

If this step results in a map containing only *0*-entries (what can be determined using an occlusion query), all AABB overlap tests have been negative, and therefore the two objects definitively do not collide.

Otherwise, the AABB tree traversal is continued as follows. Before the iteration proceeds to the next hierarchy level, the node pair index map has to be updated, as well as the vertex array containing the start and end points of the horizontal lines contained in this map. This is done in two steps. First, the vertex array is updated, as well as $0, ..., L-1$ of the overlap count map. Second, the information contained in levels $0, ..., L$ of the overlap count map is used to construct the node pair index map required as input for processing the next hierarchy level.

The whole process is repeated for all hierarchy levels as long as there are positive AABB overlap tests. If the last hierarchy level is reached, instead of testing AABB overlaps, triangle intersection tests are performed on the GPU for all leaf node pairs that have to be visited according to the node pair index map. Using an occlusion query, we obtain the number of intersecting triangle pairs for the considered objects. If required, the actual list of intersecting triangles can be obtained via read-back from graphics memory.

TIME-CRITICAL COLLISION DETECTION USING ADB-TREES

It has often been noted previously, that the *perceived quality* of a virtual environment and, in fact, most interactive 3D applications, crucially depends on the real-time response to collisions (Uno & Slater, 1997). At the same time, humans cannot distinguish between physically correct and *physically plausible* behavior of objects

(at least up to some degree) (Barzel, Hughes & Wood, 1996).[1]

Therefore, we have introduced the novel framework of collision detection using an average-case approach, thus extending the set of techniques for plausible simulation (Klein & Zachmann, 2003; Klein & Zachmann, 2003).To our knowledge, this is the first time that the *quality* of collision detection can be decreased in a controlled way (while increasing the speed), such that a numeric *measure* of the quality of the results is obtained (which can then be related to the perceived quality). The methods presented in this section can be applied to virtually any hierarchical collision detection algorithm.

Conceptually, the main idea of the new algorithm is to consider *sets of polygons*} at inner nodes of the BV hierarchy, and then, during traversal, check pairs of sets of polygons. However, we neither check pairs of polygons derived from such a pair of polygon sets, nor store any polygons with the nodes. Instead, based on a small number of parameters describing the *distribution* within the polygon sets, we will derive an estimation of the probability that there *exists* a pair of intersecting polygons. This has two advantages:

1. The application can control the runtime of the algorithm by specifying the desired "quality" of the collision detection (to be defined later).
2. The probabilities can guide the algorithm to those parts of the BV hierarchies that allow for faster convergence of the estimate.

The idea of our algorithm is to guide and to abort the traversal by the *probability* that a pair of BVs contains intersecting polygons. The design of our algorithm was influenced by the idea to develop an algorithm that works well and efficient for most practical cases - in other words, that works well in the average case. Therefore, we estimate the probability of a collision within a pair of BVs by some characteristics about the

Figure 2. We partition the intersection volume by a grid Then, we determine the probability that there are collision cells where polygons of different objects could intersect (highlighted in grey). For the sake of illustration, only one polygon of each BV is shown

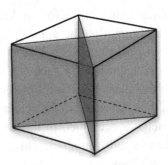

Figure 3. A cubic collision cell c with side length a. $Area_c(A)$ and $Area_c(B)$ must be at least $MaxArea(c) = a^2\sqrt{2}$, which is exactly the area of the two quadrangles

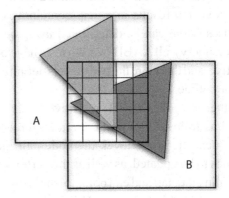

average distribution of the polygons, but we do not use the exact positions of the polygons during the collision detection.

Conceptually, the intersection volume of BVs A and B, $A \cap B$, is partitioned into a regular grid (See Figure 2). If a cell contains *enough* polygons of one BV, we call it a *possible collision cell* and if a cell is a possible collision cell with respect to A and also with respect to B, we call it a *collision cell*. This is motivated by the following observation. Consider a cubic cell containing exactly one polygon from A and one from B, resp., both having maximal size, then we must have exactly the configuration shown in (Figure 3), i.e., an intersection. Obviously, a set of polygons is not planar (usually), so even if their total area is larger than the one of the single polygons depicted in (Figure 3), there might still not be an intersection. But since almost all practical objects have bounded curvature in most vertices, the approximation by a planar polygon fits better and better as the polygon set covers smaller and smaller a surface of the object.

Given the total number of cells in $A \cap B$, the number of possible collision cells from A and B, resp., lying in $A \cap B$, we can compute the probability that there are at least x collision cells in $A \cap B$. This

probability can be used to estimate the probability that the polygons from A and B intersect.

For the computations, we assume that the probability of being a possible collision cell is evenly distributed among all cells of the partitioning because we are looking for an algorithm that works well in the average case where the polygons are uniformly distributed in the BVs.

An outline of our traversal algorithm is shown in (Figure 1). Function computeProb estimates the probability of an intersection between the polygon sets of two BVs. By descending first into those sub-trees that have highest probability, we can quickly increase the confidence in the result and determine the end of the traversal. Basically, we are now dealing with priorities of pairs of nodes, which we maintain in a priority queue. It contains only pairs whose corresponding polygons can intersect. The queue is sorted by the probability of an intersection. Instead of a recursive traversal, our algorithm just extracts the front node pair of the queue and inserts a number of child pairs.

The quality and speed of the collision detection strongly depends on the accuracy of the probability computation. Several factors contribute to that, such as the kind of partitioning and the size of the polygons relative to the size of the cells.

Table 1.

Algorithm 1: Our algorithm traverses two BV hierarchies by maintaining a priority queue of BV pairs sorted by the probability of an intersection.
traverse (A,B)
input: A, B = two nodes of the two hierarchies, resp.
Data: q = a priority queue
k:=0
q.insert (A,B,1)
while q *is not empty* **do**
A,B:= q.pop
forall *children* A [i] *and* B [j] **do**
P:= computeProb(A [i], B [j])
if p$\geq$p$_{min}$**then**
k++
if k$\geq$k$_{min}$ **then**
return *"collision"*
if p>0 **then**
q.insert(A [i], B [j],p)
return *"no collision"*

Further details can be found in [38, 37].

There are two other important parameters in our traversal algorithm, p_{min} and k_{min}, that affect the quality and the speed of the collision detection. Both can be specified by the application every time it performs a collision detection. A *pair of collision nodes* is found if the probability of an intersection between their associated polygons is larger than p_{min}.

A collision is reported if at least k_{min} such pairs have been found. The smaller p_{min} or k_{min}, the shorter is the runtime and, in most cases, the more errors are made.

COLLISION DETECTION OF POINT CLOUDS

Point sets, on the one hand, have become a popular shape representation over the past few years. This is due to two factors: first, 3D scanning devices have become affordable and thus widely available (Rusinkiewicz, Hall-Holt & Levoy, 2002) second, points are an attractive primitive for rendering complex geometry for several reasons (Bala, Walter & Greenberg, 2003; Pfister, Zwicker, van Baar & Gross, 2000; Rusinkiewicz & Levoy, 2000; Zwicker, Pfister, van Baar & Gross, 2002)

Interactive 3D computer graphics, on the other hand, requires object representations that provide fast answers to geometric queries. Virtual reality applications and 3D games, in particular, often need very fast collision detection queries. This is a prerequisite in order to simulate physical behavior and in order to allow a user to interact with the virtual environment.

So far, however, little research has been presented to make point cloud representations suitable for *interactive* computer graphics. In particular, there is virtually no literature on determining collisions between two sets of points.

In this section, we present our algorithm to check whether or not there is a collision between two point clouds. The algorithm treats the point cloud as a representation of an implicit function that approximates the point cloud.

Note that we never explicitly reconstruct the surface. Thus, we avoid the additional storage overhead and an additional error that would be introduced by a polygonal reconstruction.

We also present a novel algorithm for constructing point hierarchies by repeatedly choosing a suitable subset. This incorporates a hierarchical sphere covering, the construction of which is motivated by a geometrical argument.

This hierarchy allows us to formulate two criteria that guide the traversal to those parts of the tree where a collision is more likely. That way, we obtain a *time-critical* collision detection algorithm that returns a "best effort" result should the time budget be exhausted. In addition, the point hierarchy makes it possible that the application can specify a maximum "collision detection resolution", instead of a time budget.

Figure 4.Our approach constructs a point hier-archy, where each node stores a sample of the points underneath, which yields different levels of detail of the surface. In addition, we store a sphere covering of the surface of each node. Note that in our implementation we compose a sphere covering of many more spheres

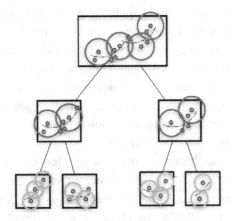

Overview of our Approach

A point cloud P_A can be viewed as a way to define a function $f_A(x)$ such that the implicit $f_A(x) = 0$ approximates P_A.

The idea of our algorithm is to create a hier-archy where the points are stored in its leaves. At each inner node, we store a sample of the point cloud underneath, a simple BV (such as a box), and a sphere covering for the part of the surface corresponding to the node (See Figure 4). The point cloud samples effectively represent a simplified surface, while the sphere coverings define a neighborhood around it that contains the original surface.

The sphere coverings, on the one hand, can be used to quickly eliminate the possibility of an intersection of parts of the surface. The simplified point clouds, on the other hand, together with the sphere coverings, can be used to determine kind of a likelihood of an intersection between parts of the surface.

Table 2.

Algorithm 2: Outline of our hierarchical algorithm for point cloud collision detection.
traverse (A,B)
if *simple BVs of A and B do not overlap* **then**
return
if *sphere coverings do not overlap* **then**
return
if *A and B are leaves* **then**
Return *approx. distance between surfaces inside*
forall *children* A_i *and* B_j **do**
Compute priority of pair (A_i, B_j)
Traverse (A_i, B_j) with largest priority first

Given two such point cloud hierarchies, two objects can be tested for collision by simultaneous traversal (See Figure 2), controlled by a priority queue. For each pair of nodes that still needs to be visited, our algorithm tries to estimate the likelihood of a collision, assigns a priority, and descends first into those pairs with largest prior-ity. A pair of leaves is interrogated by a number of test points.

In order to make our point hierarchy memory efficient, we do not compute an optimal sphere covering, nor do we compute an optimal sample for each inner node. Instead, we combine both of them so that the sphere centers are also the sample.

Surface Definition

We define the surface of a point cloud implicitly based on weighted least squares. For sake of completeness, we will give a quick recap of that surface definition in this section; please refer to (Klein & Zachmann, 2004; Klein & Zachmann, 2004; Klein & Zachmann, 2004) for the details.

Let N points $p_i \in \mathbf{R}^3$ be given. Then, the im-plicit function $f: \mathbf{R}^3 \to \mathbf{R}$ describes the distance of a point x to a plane given by a point $\mathbf{a}(\mathbf{x})$ and the normal $\mathbf{n}(\mathbf{x})$:

$$f(\mathbf{x}) = \mathbf{n}(\mathbf{x}) \cdot (\mathbf{a}(\mathbf{x}) - \mathbf{x}) \tag{1}$$

The point a(x) is the weighted average

$$\mathbf{a}(\mathbf{x}) = \frac{\sum_{i=1}^{N} \theta\left(\left\| \mathbf{x} - \mathbf{p}_i \right\|\right) \mathbf{p}_i}{\sum_{i=1}^{N} \theta\left(\left\| \mathbf{x} - \mathbf{p}_i \right\|\right)} \tag{2}$$

and the normal n(x) is defined by weighted least squares, i.e., n(x) minimizes

$$\sum_{i=1}^{N} (\mathbf{n}(\mathbf{x}) \cdot (\mathbf{a}(\mathbf{x}) - \mathbf{p}_i))^2 \theta\left(\left| \left| \mathbf{x} - \mathbf{p}_i \right| \right|\right) \tag{3}$$

for fixed x and under the constraint $\| \mathbf{n}(\mathbf{x}) \| = 1$.

This is exactly the smallest eigenvector of matrix **B** with

$$b_{ij} = \sum_{i=1}^{N} \theta\left(\left\| \mathbf{x} - \mathbf{p}_k \right\|\right)\left(\mathbf{p}_{k_i} - \mathbf{a}(\mathbf{x})_i\right)\left(\mathbf{p}_{k_j} - \mathbf{a}(\mathbf{x})_j\right) \tag{4}$$

In the following, we will use the kernel

$$\theta(\mathbf{d}) = e^{-\mathbf{d}^2 / \mathbf{h}^2} \tag{5}$$

where the global parameter *h* (called *bandwidth*) allows us to tune the decay of the influence of the points, which is theoretically unbounded. It should be chosen such that no holes appear, yet details are preserved.

In practice, we consider a point $\mathbf{p}_i$ only if, $\theta\left(\left| \left| \mathbf{x} - \mathbf{p}_i \right| \right|\right) > \theta_\mu$, which defines a *horizon of influence* for each $\mathbf{p}_i$. However, now there are regions in $\mathbf{R}^3$ where only a small number of $\mathbf{p}_i$ are taken into account for computing $\mathbf{a}(\mathbf{x})$ and $\mathbf{n}(\mathbf{x})$. We amend this by dismissing points x

for which the number *c* of $\mathbf{p}_i$ taken into account would be too small. Note that *c* and $_{,\mu}$ are independent parameters. (We remark here that [1] proposed an amendment, too, although differently specified and differently motivated.)

Overall, the surface *S* is defined as the constrained zero-set of *f*, i.e.,

$$S = \left\{ \left\{ \mathbf{x} \mid f(\mathbf{x}) = 0, \# \left\{ \mathbf{p} \in P : \left\| \mathbf{p} - \mathbf{x} \right\| < r_\varepsilon \right\} > c \right\} \tag{6}$$

where Equation 5 implies $r_\varepsilon = h \cdot \sqrt{\left| \log \theta_\varepsilon \right|}$.

We approximate the distance of a point *x* to the surface *S* by $f(\mathbf{x})$. Because we limit the region of influence of points, we need to consider only the points inside a BV *A* plus the points within the r_ε-border around *A*, if $\mathbf{x} \in A$.

Point Cloud Hierarchy

In this section, we will describe a method to construct a hierarchy of point sets, organized as a tree, and a hierarchical sphere covering of the surface.

In the first step, we construct a binary tree where each leaf node is associated with a subset of the point cloud. In order to do this efficiently, we recursively split the set of points by a top-down process. We create a leaf when the number of cloud points is below a threshold. We store a suitable BV with each node to be used during the collision detection process. Since we are striving for maximum collision detection performance, we should split the set so as to minimize the volume of the child BVs (Zachmann, 2002).

Note that so far, we have only partitioned the point set and assigned the subsets to leaves.

In the second step, we construct a simplified point cloud and a sphere covering for each level of our hierarchy. Actually, we will do this such that the set of sphere centers are exactly the simplified point cloud. One of the advantages is that we need virtually no extra memory to store the simplified point cloud.

Simultaneous Traversal of Point Cloud Hierarchies

In this section we will explain the details of the algorithm that determines an intersection, given two point hierarchies as constructed above.

Utilizing the sphere coverings of each node, we can quickly eliminate the possibility of an intersection of parts of the surface. Note that we do not need to test all pairs of spheres. Instead, we use the BVs of each node to eliminate spheres that are outside the BV of the other node.

As mentioned above, we strive for a time-critical algorithm. Therefore, we need a way to estimate the likelihood of a collision between two inner nodes A and B, which can guide our algorithm shown in (Figure 2).

Assume for the moment that the sample points in A and B describe closed manifold surfaces $f_A = 0$ and $f_B = 0$, resp. Then, we could be certain that there is an intersection between A and B, if we would find two points on f_A that are on different sides of f_B.

Here, we can achieve only a heuristic. Assuming that the points P'_A are close to the surface, and that f'_B is close to f_B, we look for two points $\mathbf{p}_1, \mathbf{p}_2 \in P'_A$ such that $f'_B(\mathbf{p}_1) < 0 < f'_B(\mathbf{p}_2)$.

In order to improve this heuristic, we consider only test points $\mathbf{p} \in P'_A$ that are outside the $\mathbf{r}_B$-neighborhood around f_B, because this decreases the probability that the sign of $f_B(\mathbf{p}_1)$ and $f_B(\mathbf{p}_2)$ is equal.

Overall, we estimate the likelihood of an intersection proportional to the number of points on both sides.

This argument holds only, of course, if the normal $\mathbf{n}_B(\mathbf{x})$ in Equation 1 does not "change sides" within a BV B.

When the traversal has reached two leaf nodes, A and B, we would like to find a test point $\mathbf{p}$ such that $f_A(\mathbf{p}) = f_B(\mathbf{p}) = 0$ (where f_A and f_B are defined over P_A and P_B, resp.).

In practice, such a point cannot be found in a reasonable amount of time, so we generate randomly and independently a constant number of test points $\mathbf{p}$ lying in the sphere covering of object A. Then we take

$$d_{AB} \approx \min_{\mathbf{p}} \left\{ \left| f_A(\mathbf{p}) \right| + \left| f_B(\mathbf{p}) \right| \right\} \tag{7}$$

as an estimate of the distance of the two surfaces.

More details can be found in (Klein & Zachmann, 2004).

KINETIC CONTINUOUS COLLISION DETECTION OF DEFORMABLE OBJECTS

Virtual environments with dynamically deforming objects play an important role in many applications, including medical training simulations, pre-operative planning, entertainment, and virtual assembly simulations.

Usually, a BVH is constructed in a pre-processing step, but if the object deforms, the hierarchy becomes invalid. In order to still use this well-known method for deforming objects, it is necessary to update the hierarchies after the deformation happened.

We propose an event-based approach for continuous collision detection. The rationale is as follows: We all know that motion in the physical world is normally continuous. So, if an animation is discredited by very fine time intervals, a brute-force approach to the problem of updating BVHs and checking for collisions would need to do this at each of these points in time, possibly utilizing swept BVs between successive times. However, changes in the *combinatorial structure* of a BVH and, analogously, collisions only occur at *discrete* points in time. Therefore, we propose to utilize an event-based approach to remedy this unnecessary frequency of BVH updates and collision checks.

Exploiting this observation, we present the novel *kinetic separation list*, which enables continuous inter- and intra-object collision detection for arbitrary deformations such that checks between bounding volumes (BVs) and polygons are done only when necessary, i.e., when changes in the moving front really happen.

This way, the continuous problem of continuous collision detection is reduced to the discrete problem of determining exactly those points in time, where the combinatorial structure of our kinetic separation list changes.

We use the framework of kinetic data structures (KDS) for the design and the analysis of our algorithms. To use this framework, it is required that a *flightplan* is given for every vertex. This flightplan may change during the motion, maybe by user interaction or by physical events (like collisions). Many deformations caused by simulations satisfy these constraints, like keyframe animations and many other animation schemes.

The kinetic separation list is based on the kinetic AABB tree. In contrast to conventional AABB trees, only the combinatorial structure of the hierarchy is stored instead of real vertex positions of the BVs. An update of the hierarchy is only necessary, if this combinatorial structure changes, which happens much less frequent than changes of vertex positions. However, the kinetic AABB trees utilize the temporal and spatial coherence only for the update of an individual hierarchy.

Our kinetic separation list extends the same principle to collision detection between pairs of objects. We maintain the combinatorial structure of a separation list of a conventional recursion tree.

As a natural consequence of this event-based approach, collisions are detected automatically in the right order, so there is no further ordering required like in many other approaches. Therefore, our kinetic separation list is well suited for collision response.

Kinetic Data Structures

In this section we give a quick recap of the kinetic data structure framework and its terminology. The kinetic data structure framework (KDS) is a framework for designing and analyzing algorithms for objects (e.g. points, lines, polygons) in motion, which was invented by (Bach, Guibas & Hershberger, 1997). The KDS framework leads to event-based algorithms that sample the state of different parts of the system only as often as necessary for a special task. This task can be, for example, the convex hull of a set of moving points and it is called the *attribute* of the KDS.

A KDS consists of a set of elementary conditions, called *certificates*, which prove altogether the correctness of the attribute.

Those certificates can fail as a result of the motion of the objects. These certificate failures, the so-called *events*, are placed in an *event-queue*, ordered according to their earliest failure time. If the attribute changes at the time of an event, the event is called *external*, otherwise the event is called *internal*. Thus, sampling of time is not fixed, but determined by the failures of some conditions.

The quality of a KDS is measured by four criteria: A good KDS is *compact*, if it requires only little space, it is *responsive*, if we can update it quickly in case of a certificate failure. It is called *local*, if one object is involved in not too many events. This guarantees that we can adjust changes in the flighplan of the objects quickly. And finally, a KDS is *efficient*, if the overhead of internal events with respect to external events is reasonable.

In case of the kinetic AABB tree, the objects are a set of m polygons with n vertices; in the case of the kinetic separation list, they are a pair of BVs or a pair of polygons. Every vertex p_i has a flightplan $f_{p_i}(t)$. This might be a chain of line segments in the case of a keyframe animation or algebraic motions in the case of physically-based simulations. The flightplan is assumed to use $O(1)$ space and the intersection between two flightplans can be computed in $O(1)$ time. The flightplan may change during simulation by user interaction or physical phenomena, including collisions. In this case, we have to update all events the vertex is involved in.

The attribute is, in the case of the kinetic AABB tree, a valid BVH for a set of moving polygons. An event will happen, when a vertex moves out of its BV. In the case of the kinetic separation list, the attribute is a valid separation list, i.e., a list of non overlapping BVs in the traversal tree. An event will happen, if two BVs in the traversal tree will overlap, or if their fathers does not overlap anymore.

The Kinetic AABB-Tree

In this section, we give a short recap of the kinetization of the well-known AABB tree (Zachmann & Weller, 2006).

We build the tree by any algorithm that can build a static BVH. However, instead of storing the actual extends of the AABBs with the nodes, we store references to those points, that determine the bounding box. For the theoretical runtime analysis, we assume that the height of the BVH is logarithmic.

After building the hierarchy, we compute the initial set of events. Basically, an event will happen, if a vertex leaves its box, i.e., if it "overtakes" that vertex that currently realizes the respective extent of its box (which is only stored in the form of a reference to that realizing vertex).

During runtime, we just have to process all those events in the event queue with a timestamp smaller than the current query time. When an event happens, we simply have to replace the old maximum or minimum along the axis, with the new one, and compute a new event for this BV. In addition, we have to propagate this change possibly to the upper BVs in the BVH.

In (Zachmann & Weller, 2006) we showed, that our kinetic AABB tree is compact, local, responsive, and efficient. Furthermore, the BVH is valid at every point of time, not only at the query times as is the case with most other update algorithms, like bottom-up or top-down approaches. Moreover, the total number of events is bounded by nearly $O(n \log n)$.

For a detailed description of the kinetic AABB, we would like to refer the interested reader to (Zachmann & Weller, 2006).

The Kinetic Separation

So far, the kinetic AABB tree utilizes the temporal and, thus, combinatorial coherence only for the updates of individual hierarchies. In this section, we will describe a novel KDS specifically for detecting collisions between pairs of objects.

Our so-called *kinetic separation list* builds on the kinetic AABB tree and utilizes an idea described in (Chen & Li, 1999; Ponamgi, Cohen, Lin & Manocha, 1995) for rigid bodies. Given two kinetic AABB trees of two objects O_1 and O_2, we traverse them once for the initialization of the kinetic incremental collision detection. Thereby, we get a list, the so-called *separation list*, of overlapping BVs in the BV test tree (BVTT) (See Figure 5). We call the pairs of BVs in the separation list *nodes*. This list contains three different kinds of nodes: Those which contain BVs that do not overlap (we will call them the *inner nodes*), leaves in the BVTT, where the BV pairs do not overlap (the *non-overlapping leaves*), and

Figure 5. This figure shows the complete traversal tree of two given BVHs. The overlapping nodes are colored red, the non overlapping nodes are colored blue. When we perform a collision check, we get a BVTT. Those BV pairs, where the traversal stops, build a list in this tree. We call it the separation list. This list consists of inner nodes, whose BVs do not overlap (B, 3), leaf nodes, where the BVs are leaves in the BVH that do not overlap (G, 5) and finally non-overlapping leaf nodes which contain leaves of the BVHs which do overlap (F, 6).

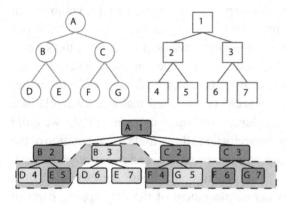

finally, leaf nodes in the BVTT that contain pairs of overlapping BVs, the so called *overlapping leaves*.

During run-time, this list configuration changes at discrete points in time, when one of the following events happens:

- *BV-overlap event*: This event happens, when the pair of BVs of a node in the separation list which did not overlap so far, do overlap now. Thus, this event can happen only at inner nodes and non-overlapping leaves.
- *Fathers-do-not-overlap event*: This event happens, if the BVs of a father of an inner node or a non-overlapping leaf in the BVTT do not overlap anymore his could be inner nodes or non-overlapping leaves.

- *Leaves-do-not-overlap event*: The fathers-do-not-overlap event cannot occur to overlapping leaves, because if their fathers do not overlap, then the leaves cannot overlap in the first place. Therefore, we introduce the leaves-do-not-overlap event.
- *Polygons-collide event*: A collision between two triangles can only happen in overlapping leaves. If a non-overlapping leaf turns into an overlapping leaf, we have to compute the collision time and insert an adequate event into the event queue.

BV-change event: Finally, we need an event that remarks changes of the BV hierarchies. This event is somewhat comparable to flightplan updates of the kinetic AABB tree, but it is not exactly the same: This is, because an object in the separation list is composed of two BVs of different objects O_1 and O_2 and the flightplans are attributes of the vertices of only one single object. Therefore, not every flightplan update of an object affects the separation list.

In addition, a BV-change event happens, if the combinatorial structure of a BV in the separation list changes. Since we use kinetic AABB trees as BVH for the objects, this can happen only if a tree event or a leaf event in the BVH of an object happens. Surely, not all events cause changes at the separation list.

It is fairly straight-forward to show that our data structure and update algorithms are *compact, responsive, efficient*, and *local* (Gress & Zachmann, 2006; Weller & Zachmann, 2006; Zachmann & Weller, 2006).

In addition, we implemented our algorithms in C++ and tested the performance on a PC with a 3 GHz Pentium IV. Timings of our implementation and comparisons can be found in (Gress & Zachmann, 2006; Weller & Zachmann, 2006; Zachmann & Weller, 2006).

PROXIMITY AND PENETRATION QUERIES USING INNER SPHERE TREES

BVHs guarantee very fast responses at query time, so long as no further information than the set of colliding polygons is required for the collision response. However, most applications require much more information in order to resolve or avoid the collisions.

One way to do this is to compute the exact time of contact of the objects. This method is called continuous collision detection. Another approach, called penalty methods, is to compute repelling forces based on the penetration depth. However, there is no universally accepted definition of the penetration depth between a pair of polygonal models (Ong & Gilbert, 1996; Zhang, Kim, Varadhan & Manocha, 2007). Mostly, the minimum translation vector to separate the objects is used, but this may lead to discontinuous forces.

Another approach is to avoid penetrations or contacts before they really happen. In this case, the minimum distance between the objects can be used to compute repelling forces.

Haptic rendering requires update rates of at least 200 Hz, but preferably 1kHz to guarantee a stable force feedback. Consequently, the collision detection time should never exceed 5 msec.

One example of an approach that offers fairly constant query times are voxel-based methods like the Voxmap Pointshell algorithm (VPS), where objects, in general, have to be voxelized (the "voxmap") and covered by a point cloud (the "point shell"). This can be very memory consuming and produce aliasing artifacts due to the discretization errors.

We have developed a novel geometric data structure, the *Inner Sphere Trees* (IST), that provides hierarchical bounding volumes from the *inside* of an object, and a unified algorithm that can compute for a pair of objects, based on their ISTs, both an approximate minimal distance and the approximate penetration volume (Weller &

Zachmann, 2009; Weller & Zachmann, 2009; Weller & Zachmann, 2009). One of the advantages of this approach is that the application does not need to know in advance which situation currently exists between the pair of objects

Our ISTs and, consequently, the collision detection algorithm are independent of the geometry complexity; they only depend on the approximation error.

The main idea is that we do not build an (outer) hierarchy based on the polygons on the boundary of an object. Instead, we fill the interior of the model with a set of non-overlapping simple volumes that approximate the object's volume closely. In our implementation, we used spheres for the sake of simplicity, but the idea of using inner BVs for lower bounds instead of outer BVs for upper bounds can be extended analogously to all kinds of volumes. On top of these inner BVs, we build a hierarchy that allows for fast computation of the approximate proximity and *penetration volume*.

The penetration volume corresponds to the water displacement of the overlapping parts of the objects and, thus, leads to a physically motivated and continuous repulsion force. According to Fisher & Lin (2001) it is "the most complicated yet accurate method" to define the extent of intersection, which was also reported earlier by O'Brien & Hodgins (1999). However, to our knowledge, there are no algorithms to compute it efficiently as yet.

Our data structure can support all kinds of object representations, e.g. polygon meshes or NURBS surfaces. The only precondition is that they be watertight. In order to build the hierarchy on the inner spheres, we utilize a recently proposed clustering algorithm that allows us to work in an adaptive manner.

The results shows that our new data structure can answer both kinds of queries at haptic rates with a negligible loss of accuracy.

Figure 6. These images show the different stages of our sphere packing algorithm. First, we voxelize the object (left) and compute distances from the voxels to the closest triangle (second image; transparency = distance). Then, we pick the voxel with the largest distance and put a sphere at its center. We proceed incrementally and, eventually, we obtain a dense sphere packing of the object (right).

Creation of the Inner Sphere Tree

In this section we describe the construction of our data structure. In a first step, we want a watertight object to be densely filled with a set of non-overlapping spheres. The volume of the object should be approximated well by the spheres, while their number should be small. In a second step, we create a hierarchy over this set of spheres.

For squared objects, spheres seem not to be a good choice as filling volumes. However, they compensate this disadvantage because of the trivial overlap test and their rotationally invariance. Moreover, it is easy, in contrast to AABBs or OBBs, to compute the exact intersection volume.

The Sphere Packing

Filling objects densely with smaller volumes is a highly non-trivial task and still an active field of research, even when restricted to spheres (Birgin & Sobral, 2008; Schuermann, 2006). We present a simple heuristic that offers a good trade-off between accuracy and speed in practice.

This heuristic is currently based on a distance field. We start with a flood filling voxelization, but instead of simply storing whether or not a voxel is filled, we additionally store the distance d from the center of the voxel to the nearest point on the surface, together with the triangle that realizes this distance.

After this initialization, we use a greedy algorithm to generate the inner spheres. All voxels are stored in a priority queue, sorted by their distance to the surface. Until the p-queue is empty, we extract the maximum element, i.e. the voxel V^* with the largest distance d^*. We create an inner sphere with radius d^* and centered on the center of the voxel V^*. Then, all voxels whose centers are contained in this sphere are deleted from the p-queue. Additionally, we have to update all voxels V_i with O_1 and $d_i < d^*$ and distance $\left(V_i, V^*\right) < 2d^*$. This is because they are now closer to the sphere around V^* than to a triangle on the hull. Their d_i must now be set to the new free radius.

After his procedure, the object is filled densely with a set of non-overlapping spheres. The density, and thus the accuracy, can be controlled by the number of voxels.

Building the IST

Our sphere hierarchy is based on the notion of a *wrapped hierarchy* (Agarwal, Guibas, Nguyen, Russel & Zhang, 2004), where inner nodes are tight BVs for all their leaves, but they do not necessarily bound their direct children. Compared to layered hierarchies, the big advantage is that the inner BVs are tighter. We use a top-down approach to create our hierarchy, i.e., we start at the

Figure 7. This figure shows the results of our hierarchy building algorithm based on batch neural gas clustering with magnification control. All of those inner spheres that share the same color are assigned to the same bounding sphere. The left image shows the clustering result of the root sphere, the right images the partitioning of its four children.

root node that covers all inner spheres and divide these into several subsets.

The partitioning of the inner spheres has significant influence on the performance during runtime. Previous algorithms for building ordinary sphere trees, like the medial axis approach (Bradshaw & O'Sullivan, 2004; Hubbard, 1995) work well if the spheres constitute a *covering* of the object and have similar size, but in our scenario we use disjoint inner spheres that exhibit a large variation in size. Other approaches based on the *k-center problem* work only for sets of points and do not support spheres.

So, we decided to use the *batch neural gas* clustering algorithm (BNG) known from artificial intelligence (Cottrell, Hammer, Hasenfuß & Villmann, 2006). BNG is a very robust clustering algorithm, which can be formulated as stochastic gradient descent with a cost function closely connected to quantization error. Like *k-means*, the cost function minimizes the mean squared euclidean distance of each data point to its nearest center. But unlike k-means, BNG exhibits very robust behavior with respect to the initial cluster center positions (the *prototypes*): they can be chosen arbitrarily without affecting the

convergence. Moreover, BNG can be extended to allow the specification of the *importance* of each data point. More details can be found in (Weller & Zachmann, 2009; Weller & Zachmann, 2009; Weller & Zachmann, 2009).

Overall, we first compute a bounding sphere for all inner spheres (at the leaves), which becomes the root node of the hierarchy. To do that, we use the fast and stable smallest enclosing sphere algorithm proposed in (Gärtner, 1999). Then, we divide the set of inner spheres into subsets in order to create the children. To do that, we use the extended version of batch neural gas with magnification control. We repeat this scheme recursively (See Figure 7) for some clustering results.

In the following, we will call the spheres in the hierarchy that are not leaves *hierarchy spheres*. Spheres at the leaves, which were created in the previous section, will be called *inner spheres*. Note that hierarchy spheres are not necessarily contained completely within the object.

BVH Traversal

Our algorithm(s) for answering proximity queries and for computing the penetration volume work similarly to the classic recursive schemes that simultaneously traverse two given hierarchies (Zachmann, 1998). As a by-product, our algorithm can return a witness realizing the separation distance in the case of non-collision, and a partial list of intersecting polygons in the case of a penetration.

In the following, we describe algorithms for these two query types, but it should be obvious how they can be modified in order to provide an approximate yes-no answer. This would further increase the speed.

First, we will discuss the two query types separately, in order to point out their specific requirements and optimizations. Then, we explain how they can be combined into a single algorithm.

Proximity Queries

Our algorithm for proximity queries works like most other classical BVH traversal algorithms. We simply have to maintain, in addition, a lower bound for the distance. If a pair of leaves, which are inner spheres, is reached, we update the lower bound so far (see Algorithm 3).

During traversal, there is no need to visit branches of the bounding volume test tree that are farther apart than the current minimum distance, because of the bounding property. This guarantees a high culling efficiency.

Improving Runtime. In most collision detection scenarios, there is a high spatial and temporal coherence, especially when rendering at haptic rates. Thus, in most cases, those spheres realizing the minimum distance in a frame are also the closest spheres in the next frames, or they are at least in the neighborhood. Therefore, using the distance from the last frame yields a good initial bound for pruning during traversal. Thus, in our implementation we store pointers to the closest spheres as of the last frame and use their current distance to initialize *minDist* in Algorithm 3.

If the application is only interested in the distance between a pair of objects, then, of course,

Table 3.

Algorithm 3: checkDistance(A, B, minDist).
input: A, B. = spheres in the inner sphere tree
in/out: minDist = overall minimum distance seen so far
if   *A and B are leaves* **then**
// end of recursion
minDist $= \min\{distance(A,B)\,minDist\}$
else
// recursion step
forall *children* a[i] *of A* **do**
P:= **forall** c **forall** *children* b[j] *of B* **do**
if $distance(a[i],b[j]) < minDist$ **then**
checkDistance$(a[i],b[j],minDist)$

a further speed-up can be gained by abandoning the traversal once the first pair of intersecting inner spheres is found (in this case the objects must overlap).

Moreover, our traversal algorithm is very well suited for parallelization. During recursion, we compute the distances between 4 pairs of spheres in one single SIMD implementation, which is greatly facilitated by our hierarchy being a 4-ary tree.

As mentioned before, during recursion we test one sphere against four others simultaneously, which can be computed as quickly as a single sphere-sphere test by utilizing the SIMD instructions of modern CPUs.

Improving Accuracy. Obviously, Algorithm 3 returns only an approximate minimum distance, because it utilizes only the distances of the inner spheres for the proximity query. Thus, the accuracy depends on their density.

Fortunately, it is very easy to alleviate these inaccuracies by simply assigning the closest triangle (or a set of triangles) to each inner sphere. After determining the closest spheres with Algorithm 3, we add a subsequent test that calculates the exact distance between the triangles assigned to those spheres. This simple heuristic reduces the error significantly even with relatively sparsely filled objects, and it does not affect the running time.

Penetration Volume Queries

In addition to proximity queries, our data structure also supports a new kind of penetration query, namely the *penetration volume*. This is the volume of the intersection of the two objects, which can be interpreted directly as the amount of the repulsion force, if it is considered as the amount of water being displaced.

Obviously, the algorithm to compute the penetration volume (see Algorithm 4) does not differ very much from the proximity query test: we simply have to replace the distance test by an overlap test and maintain an accumulated overlap volume during the traversal.

Filling the Gaps. The algorithm described earlier results in densely filled objects. However, there still remain small voids between the spheres that cannot be completely compensated by increasing the number of voxels.

As a remedy, we assign an additional, *secondary radius* to each inner sphere, such that the volume of the secondary sphere is equal to the volume of all voxels whose centers are contained within the radius of the primary. This guarantees that the total volume of all secondary spheres equals the volume of the object, within the accuracy of the voxelization, because each voxel volume is accounted for exactly once.

Certainly, these secondary spheres may slightly overlap, but this simple heuristic leads to acceptable estimations of the penetration volume. (Note, however, that the secondary spheres are not necessarily larger than the primary spheres.)

Improvements. Similar to the proximity query implementation, we can utilize SIMD paralleliza-

Table 4.

Algorithm 4: computeVolume(A, B, totalOverlap)
input: A, B. = spheres in the inner sphere tree
in/out: total Overlap = overall volume of intersection
if   *A and B are leaves* **then**
//end of recursion
totalOverlap += overlapVolume(A, B)
else
//recursion step
forall *children* a[i] *of A* **do**
P:= **forall** c **forall** *children* b[j] *of B* **do**
if $overlap(a[i], b[j]) > 0$ **then**
computeVolume$(a[i], b[j], \text{totalOverlap})$

tion to speed up both the simple overlap check and the volume accumulation.

Furthermore, we can exploit the observation that a recursion can be terminated if a hierarchy sphere (i.e., an inner node of the sphere hierarchy) is completely contained inside an inner sphere (leaf) of the other IST. In this case, we can simply add the total volume of all of its leaves to the accumulated penetration volume. In order to do this quickly, we store the total volume

$$Vol_i(S) = \sum_{S_j \in Leaves(S)} Vol(S_j), \qquad (8)$$

where S_j are all inner spheres below S in the BVH.

This can be done in a preprocessing step during hierarchy creation.

Time-Critical Computation of Penetration Volume

In most cases, a penetration volume query has to visit many more nodes than the average proximity query. Consequently, the running time on average is slower, especially in cases with heavy overlaps.

In the following, we will describe a variation of our algorithm for penetration volume queries that guarantees a predefined query time budget. This is essential for time-critical applications such as haptic rendering.

A suitable strategy to realize time-critical traversals is to guide the traversal by a priority queue Q Then, given a pair of hierarchy spheres S and R a simple heuristic is to use $Vol(S \cap R)$ for the priority in Q. In our experience, this would yield acceptable upper bounds.

Unfortunately, this simple heuristic also leads to very bad lower bounds in cases where only a relatively small number of inner spheres can be visited (unless the time budget permits an almost complete traversal of all overlapping pairs).

A simple heuristic to derive an estimate of the lower bound could be to compute

$$\sum_{\substack{(R,S) \in Q}} \sum_{\substack{R_i \in ch(R), \\ S_j \in ch(S)}} Vol\left(R_i \cap S_j\right) \qquad (9)$$

where $ch\ (S)$ is the set of all direct children of node S.

Equation 9 amounts to the sum of the intersection of all direct child pairs of all pairs in the p-queue Q. Unfortunately, the direct children of a node are usually not disjoint and, thus, this estimate of the lower bound could actually be larger than the upper bound.

In order to avoid this problem, we introduce the notion of *expected overlap volume* in order to estimate the overlap volume more accurately.

The only assumption we make is that for any point inside S, the distribution of the probability that it is also inside one of its leaves is uniform.

Let (R,S) be a pair of spheres in the p-queue. We define the *density* of a sphere as

$$p(S) = \frac{Vol_l(S)}{Vol(S)} \qquad (10)$$

with $vol_l(S)$ defined similarly to equation 8 as the accumulated volume of all inner spheres below S.

This is the probability that a point inside S is also inside one of its leaves (which are disjoint). Next, we define the *expected overlap volume* $\overline{Vol}$ (R, S) as the probability that a point is inside $R \cap S$ and also inside the intersection of one of the possible pairs of leaves, i.e.,

$$\overline{Vol}(R,S) = p(S) \cdot p(R) \cdot Vol(R \cap S)$$
$$= \frac{Vol_l(R) \cdot Vol_l(S) \cdot Vol(R \cap S)}{Vol(R) \cdot Vol(S)}$$
$$\qquad (11)$$

In summary, for the whole queue we get the expected overlap volume

$$\sum_{(R,S) \in Q} \overline{Vol}(R,S) \qquad (12)$$

Clearly, this volume can be maintained during traversal quite easily.

More importantly, this method provides a much better heuristic for sorting the priority queue: if the difference between the expected overlap $\overline{Vol}$ (R, S) and the overlap $Vol\left(R \cap S\right)$ is large, then it is most likely that the traversal of this pair will give the most benefit toward improving the bound;

Table 5.

Algorithm 5: compVolumeTimeCritical(A, B)
input: A, B. = root spheres of the two ISTs
estOverlap $= \overline{Vol}$ (A, B)
Q =empty priority queue
Q.push(A, B)
while Q not empty & time not exceeded **do**
(R,S) = Q.pop()
if R and S are not leaves **then**
P:= **forall** eestOverlap $-= \overline{Vol}$ (R, S)
forall $R_i \in children\ of\ R, S_j \in children\ of\ S$ **do**
estOestOverlap $+= \overline{Vol}(R_i, S_j)$
Q.push (R_i, S_j)

consequently, we insert this pair closer to the front of the queue.

Algorithm 5 shows the pseudo code of this approach. (Note that $p(S) = 1$ if S is a leaf, and therefore $\overline{Vol}(R, S)$ the exact intersection volume at the leaves.)

The Unified Algorithm

In the previous sections, we introduced the proximity and the penetration volume computation separately. However, it is of course possible to combine both algorithms. This yields a unified algorithm that can compute both the distance and the penetration volume.

To that end, we start with the distance traversal. As soon as we find the first pair of intersecting inner spheres, we simply switch to the penetration volume computation.

This is correct because all pairs of inner spheres we visited so far did not overlap and thus they could not increase the penetration volume. Thus, we do not have to visit them again and can continue with the traversal of the rest of the hierarchies using the penetration volume algorithm. If we do not meet an intersecting pair of inner spheres, the unified algorithm still reports the minimal separating distance.

Collision Response

In this section, we describe how to use the penetration volume to compute continuous forces in order to enable a stable haptic rendering. Mainly, there exist three different approaches to resolve collisions: the penalty-based method, the constraint-based method and the impulse-based method. The constraint-based approach computes constraint forces that are designed to cancel any external acceleration that would result in interpenetrations. Unfortunately, this method has at least quadratic complexity in the number of contact points. The impulse-based method resolves contacts between objects by a series of impulses in order to prevent interpenetrations. It is applicable to real-time simulations but the forces may not be valid for bodies in resting contact.

So, we decided to use the penalty-based method, that computes penalty forces based on the interpenetration of a pair of objects. The main advantages are its computational simplicity, which makes it applicable for haptic rendering, and its ability to simulate a variety of surface characteristics. Moreover, the use of the penetration volume eliminates inconsistent states that may occur when only a penetration depth (e.g.~a minimum translational vector) is used.

Contact Forces

Algorithm 4, and its time-critical derivative, return a set of overlapping spheres or potentially overlapping spheres, resp. We compute a force for each of these pairs of spheres (R_i, S_j) by:

$$\mathbf{f}\left(R_i\right) = \left(k_c\right) Vol\left(R_i \bigcap S_j\right) \mathbf{n}(R_i) \qquad (13)$$

where k_c is the contact stiffness, $Vol\left(R_i \bigcap S_j\right)$ is the overlap volume, and $\mathbf{n}(R_i)$ is the contact normal.

Accumulating all pairwise forces gives the total penalty force:

$$\mathbf{f}\left(R\right) = \sum_{R_i \bigcap S_j \neq \varnothing} \mathbf{f}\left(R_i\right) \qquad (14)$$

In order to compute normals for each pair of spheres, we augment the construction process of the ISTs: in addition to storing the distance to the object's surface, we store a pointer to the triangle that realizes this minimum distance. While creating the inner spheres by merging several voxels we accumulate a list of triangles for every inner sphere. We use the normals of these triangles to compute normal cones, which are defined by an

axis and an angle. They tightly bound the normals of the triangles that are stored in the list of each inner sphere.

During force computation, the axes of the normal cones c_R and c_S are used as the directions of the force, since they will bring the penetrating spheres outside the other object in the direction of the surface normals. Note that $\mathbf{f}\left(R_i\right) \neq \mathbf{f}\left(S_j\right)$. If the cone angle is too large (i.e., $\alpha \approx \pi$), then we simply use the vector between the two centers of the spheres.

Obviously, this force is continuous in both cases, because the movement of the axes of the normal cones and also the movement of the centers of the spheres are continuous, provided the path of the objects is continuous. (See Figure 8) for results from our benchmark.

Torques

In rigid body simulation, the torque π is usually computed as $\pi = \left(P_c - C_m\right) \times \mathbf{f}$, where P_c is the point of collision, C_m is the center of mass of the

Figure 8. Left: magnitude (solid) and direction (dotted) of the force arising between two copies of the object shown in the middle, one of which is being moved on a pre-recorded path. Right: torque magnitude (solid) and direction (dotted) in the same scene.

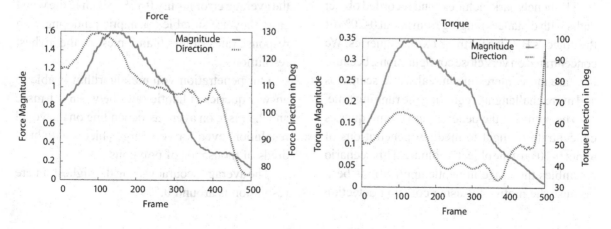

object and $\mathbf{f}$ is the force acting at P_c. Like in the section before, we compute the torque separately for each pair $\left(R_i, S_j \right)$ of intersecting inner spheres:

$$\pi \left(R_i \right) = \left(P_{\left(R_i, S_j \right)} - C_m \right) \times \mathbf{f} \left(R_i \right) \qquad (15)$$

Again, we accumulate all pairwise torques to get the total torque:

$$\pi \left(R \right) = \sum_{R_i \cap S_j \neq \varnothing} \pi \left(R_i \right) \qquad (16)$$

We define the point of collision $P_{\left(R_i, S_j \right)}$ simply as the center of the intersection volume of the two spheres. Obviously, this point moves continuously if the objects move continuously. In combination with the continuous forces $\mathbf{f} \left(R_i \right)$ this results in a continuous torque.

Results

We have implemented our new data structure in C++. The testing environment consists of a PC running Windows XP with an Intel Pentium IV 3GHz dual core CPU and 2GB of memory. The initial distance field was computed using a slightly modified version of Dan Morris' *Voxelizer* (Morris, 2006).

The benchmark includes hand recorded object paths with distances ranging from about 0-20% of the object's BV size for the proximity queries. We concentrated on very close configurations, because they are more interesting in real world scenarios and more challenging regarding the running time.

The paths for the penetration volume queries concentrate on light to medium penetrations of about 0-10% of the object's volume. This scenario resembles the usage in haptic applications best, because the motive for using collision detection

algorithms is to avoid heavy penetrations. However, we also included some heavy penetrations of 50% of the object's volume to stress our algorithm.

We used highly detailed objects with a polygon count ranging up to 370k to test the performance and the quality of our algorithm.[2] The quality of the resulting distances and penetration volumes is closely related to the quality of the underlying voxelization. Consequently, we voxelized each object in different resolutions in order to evaluate the trade-off between the number of spheres and the accuracy.

We computed the ground truth data for the proximity queries with the PQP library. We also included the running time of PQP in our plots, even if the comparison seems to be somewhat unfair, because PQP computes exact distances. However, it shows the impressive speed-up that is achievable when using approximative approaches. Moreover, it is possible to extend ISTs to support exact distance calculations, too.

To our knowledge, there are no implementations available to compute the exact penetration volume efficiently. In order to still evaluate the quality of our penetration volume approximation, we used a tetrahedralization to compute the exact volume. Even though we speed it up by a hierarchy built on the tetrahedra, the running time of this approach is in the order of 0.5 sec/frame.[3]

The results of our benchmarking show that our ISTs with the highest sphere resolution have an average speed-up of 50 compared to PQP, while the average error is only 0.15%. Even in the worst case, they are suitable for haptic rendering with response rates of less than 2 mesc in the highest resolution.

Our penetration volume algorithm is able to answer queries at haptic rates between 0.1 msec and 2.5 msec on average, depending on the voxel resolution, even for very large objects with hundreds of thousands of polygons.

The average accuracy using the highest sphere resolution is around 0.5%.

Figure 9. Tools snap onto screws and are constrained. Also, they are placed automatically at an ergonomic position within the hand by the system (©1999 FhG-IGD/BMW; used with permission.)

Figure 10. The window regulator has to be installed with two hands; the "ghost" paradigm signals collisions system (©1999 FhG-IGD/BMW; used with permission.)

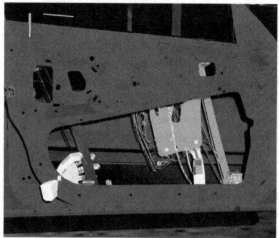

APPLICATIONS

In this section, we will touch upon a few scenarios in virtual prototyping in car industries that require very efficient collision detection (Gomes de Sa & Zachmann, 1998; Gomes de Sa & Zachmann, 1999).

The Tail-Light

The first scenario is the disassembly of the tail-light of a car. First, the covering in the car trunk must be turned down, in order to get access to the fastening of the lights. To reach the screws fixing the tail-light, the fastening needs to be pulled out.

Then the tail-light itself can be unscrewed by a standard tool. After all screws are taken out, the tail-light cap can be disassembled by pulling it out from the outside.

The Door

This scenario is much more complex and more difficult in that both hands and various tools must be utilized.

The first task is to put the lock in its place in the door. This is quite difficult in the real world, because it is very cramped inside the door and the lock cannot be seen very well during assembly. Screws have to be fastened while the lock is held in its place (Figure 9).

Next, the window-regulator is to be installed (Figure 10). This task needs both hands, because the window-regulator consists of two parts connected to each other by flexible wires. After placing the bottom fixtures into slots, they must be turned upright, then the regulator screws can be fixed.

Finally, several wires must be layed out on the inner metal sheet, clipped into place, and connected to various parts. However, this part of the assembly was not performed in VR.

Physically-Based Simulation

Many mechanical components comprise articulated kinematic chains. These could be simple "door-like" mechanisms, i.e., permanent joints with one rotational degree of freedom (DOF), such as hoods, lids, etc.; other very simple ones are sliding mechanisms (one translational DOF), for example the seat of a car. Inverse kinematics of these and other articulated chains can be simulated on-line.

A lot of the parts in a vehicle are flexible: wires, hoses, plastic tanks, etc. It is still a major challenge to simulate all these different types of flexible parts with reasonable precision and at interactive rates. In particular, simulation of the interaction of flexible objects with the surrounding environment and the user's hands by a general framework in virtual environments is, to our knowledge, still unsolved.

We have implemented hoses and wires in our VR system as simple models based on B-splines: the wires or hoses are attached at both ends to other, non-flexible parts, and they can be pushed or pulled by a user's hand.

Verification of Designs without Force-Feedback

Although there is a long history of research in force feedback, VR systems with force feedback are still rarely found in every-day use for a number of reasons (such as working volume, inability to render hard contacts, costs, etc.). Without force feedback, however, assembly tasks are more difficult in VR than in the real in world, because humans can perform even quite complicated tasks without seeing their hands or tools merely based on auditory, haptic and kinaesthetic feedback. Therefore, we have developed a lot of interaction paradigms trying to compensate for any missing haptic feedback.

In order to help the user placing parts, we have developed two kinds of *snapping* paradigms: the first one makes objects snap in place when they are released by the user and when they are sufficiently close to their final position. The second snapping paradigm makes tools snap onto screws when sufficiently close and while they are being utilized (See Figure 9). The second paradigm is implemented by a 1-DOF rotational constraint which can be triggered by events.

The major problems is: how can we verify that a part can be assembled by a human worker? A simple solution is to turn a part being grasped into what we call a *ghost* when it collides with other parts: the solid part itself stays at the last valid, i.e., collision-free, position while the object attached to the user's hand turns wireframe (See Figure 10).

However, invalid positions can be "tunneled". Therefore, we have developed *rubber band* paradigm: the object is no longer attached rigidly to the virtual hand; instead, it "follows" the hand as far as it can go without penetrating any other parts. We have implemented a physically-based simulation, so that the object can glide along other parts; in our earlier implementation, there was no gliding, which caused the moving object to get stuck in tight environments. So, at any time it can assume only valid positions. Of course, exact and fast collision detection is a prerequisite.

This is only a first step. A completely reliable verification will check the virtual hand for collisions as well. Also, the hand and/or part should slide along smooth rigid objects to make assembly easier for the user.

Documentation

If a certain assembly task cannot be done, then the result of the verification session should be a precise as well as intuitive understanding why that is. A number of techniques have been implemented in order to investigate and document a possible failure of assembly.

During assembly/disassembly, the path of any part can be recorded and edited in VR. Saved paths can then be stored in the PDM system.

While parts are being moved, the sweeping envelope can be traced out. It does not matter whether the part is moved interactively by the user or on an assembly path.

During an assembly simulation, a variety of feedbacks can be combined which will be given if the user tries to move an object at an invalid position: acoustic feedback, tactile feedback by a Cybertouch™ glove, and visual feedback. Visual feedback can be provided in several ways: whole parts can be highlighted, or the polygons which would have intersected at the invalid position can be highlighted.

FUTURE WORK

Although the area has been an active field of research over the past two decades in the computer graphics and robotics communities, there are still a number of open questions and opportunities for future research.

With almost all acceleration data structures, an open issue is how they can be adapted when the underlying geometry deforms, short from rebuilding the whole hierarchy. There are some cases, in which this can be efficiently, such as when the deformation of the geometry is restricted or known in advance. But it is largely an open question in the case of general deformations.

The construction of bounding volume hierarchies still poses some open questions as well. One of them is how to better estimate the costs (for the run-time traversal) of a split among the polygons during the top-down construction (or the benefit of a merge of two cells during a bottom-up construction). By approximating the cost equation to a higher order, one could possibly arrive at a kind of "look-ahead" criterion for the construction algorithm, which could result in better hierarchies.

The idea of filling objects from the inside with "bounding" volumes offers a lot of potential for further exploration. First of all, the intermediate distance field should be replaced by a different data structure, for instance a Voronoi diagram. Another interesting task is to explore other uses of "inner bounding volume hierarchies", such as ray tracing or occlusion culling. Furthermore, a GPU implementation of the force computation should result in further speed-ups. This is possible, because the forces and torques depend only

on computations on a set of independent pairs of spheres, which is (almost) trivially parallelizable. Another option could be the investigation of inner volumes other than spheres. This could improve the quality of the volume covering, because spheres do not fit well into square objects.

CONCLUSION

In this chapter, we have reviewed some of the current methods and algrotihms in the area of collision detection.

We have presented a hierarchical BV data structure, the *restricted BoxTree,* that needs arguably the least possible amount of memory among all other BV trees while performing about as fast as DOP trees. The basic idea can be applied to all BV hierarchies.

We have presented a method for interference detection using programmable graphics hardware. Unlike previous GPU-based approaches, it performs all calculations in object-space rather than image-space, and it imposes no requirements on shape, topology, or connectivity of the polygonal input models.

We have also presented a general method to turn a conventional hierarchical collision detection algorithm into one that uses probability estimations to decrease the quality of collision detection in a controlled way. Thus, using this method, any hierarchical collision detection algorithm can be made time-critical, i.e., it computes the best answer possible within a given time budget.

Furthermore, we have presented our approach to collision detection of point clouds, which is, to the best of our knowledge, still the only one. It works even for non-closed surfaces, and it works directly on the point cloud (and the implicit function defined by that), i.e., there is no polygonal reconstruction.

And, finally, we have presented some work for very efficient penetration volume and proximity query computation. This is needed for many applications such as clearance checking and physically-based simulation.

REFERENCES

Adamson, A., & Alexa, M. (2004). Approximating Bounded, Non-orientable Surfaces from Points. *Shape Modeling Internations*. Retrieved from http://www.computer.org/portal/web/csdl/doi/10.1109/SMI.2004.1314511

Agarwal, P., de Berg, M., Gudemundsson, J., Hammar, M., & Haverkort, H. (2002). Box-Trees and R-Trees with Near-Optimal Query Time. *Discrete & Computational Geometry, 28,* 291–312.

Agarwal, P., Guibas, L., Nguyen, A., Russel, D., & Zhang, L. (2004). Collision Detection for Deforming Necklaces. In CGTA: Computational Geometry: Theory and applications, 28(2-3), 137-163.

Agarwal, P., Krishnan, S., Mustafa, N., & Venkatasubramanian, S. (2003). Streaming Geometric Optimization Using Graphics Hardware. In *11th European Symposium on Algorithms*.

Agarwal, P. K., Basch, J., Guibas, L. J., Hershberger, J., & Zhang, L. (2002). Deformable free space tiling for kinetic collision detection. *The International Journal of Robotics Research, 21*(3), 179–197.

Bach, J., Guibas, L., & Hershberger, J. (1997). Data Structures for Mobile Data. In *SODA: ACM-SIAM Symposium on Discrete Algorithms (A Conference on Theoretical and Experimental Analysis of Discrete Algorithms)*. Retrieved from http://citeseer.ist.psu.edu/145907.html

Baciu, G., & Wong, W. S.-K. (2002). Hardware-assisted self-collision for deformable surfaces. In *Proceedings of the ACM Symposium on Virual Reality Software and Technology (VRST)* (pp. 129-136). Retrieved from http://doi.acm.org/10.1145/585740.585762

Baciu, G., & Wong, W. S.-K. (2003). Image-Based Techniques in a Hybrid Collision Detector. *IEEE Transactions on Visualization and Computer Graphics, 9,* 254–271.

Bala, K., Walter, B., & Greenberg, D. P. (2003, July). Combining edges and points for interactive high-quality rendering. In *Proceedings of SIGGRAPH, 22,* 631–640.

Barzel, R., Hughes, J., & Wood, D. N. (1996). Plausible Motion Simulation for Computer Graphics Animation. In R. Boulic & G. Hégron (Eds.), *Proceedings of the Eurographics Workshop Computer Animations and Simulation* (pp. 183-197).

Birgin, E. G., & Sobral, F. N. C. (2008). Minimizing the object dimensions in circle and sphere packing problems. *Computers & OR, 35*(7), 2357-2375. Retrieved from http://dx.doi.org/10.1016/j.cor.2006.11.002

Bradshaw, G., & O'Sullivan, C. (2004). Adaptive medial-axis approximation for sphere-tree construction. *ACM Transactions on Graphics, 23*(1), 1–26. Retrieved from http://visinfo.zib.de/ELlib/Show?EVL-2004-1.

Cameron, S. (1997). Enhancing GJK: Computing Minimum and Penetration Distances between Convex Polyhedra. In *Proceedings of International Conference on Robotics and Automation* (pp. 3112-3117).

Chen, J.-S., & Li, T.-Y. (1998). Incremental 3D Collision Detection with Hierarchical Data Structures. In *Proceedings of the ACM symposium on Virtual reality software and technology table of contents* (Vol. 22, pp. 139-144). Retrieved from http://portal.acm.org/citation.cfm?id=293701.293719

Cottrell, M., Hammer, B., Hasenfuß, A., & Villmann, T. (2006). Batch and Median Neural Gas. *Neural Networks, 19*(6-7), 762–771.

Ehmann, S. A., & Lin, M. C. (2001). Accurate and Fast Proximity Queries Between Polyhedra Using Convex Surface Decomposition. *Computer Graphics Forum, 20*, 500–510.

Ericson, C. (2004). *Real-Time Collision Detection*. San Francisco: Morgan Kaufman.

Fisher, S., & Lin, M. (2001). Fast Penetration Depth Estimation for Elastic Bodies Using Deformed Distance Fields. In *Proceedings of International Conference on Intelligent Robots and Systems (IROS)*. Retrieved from http://gamma.cs.unc.edu/DDF/

Fisher, S. M., & Lin, M. C. (2001). *Fast Penetration Depth Estimation for Elastic Bodies Using Deformed Distance Fields*.

Gärtner, B. (1999). Fast and Robust Smallest Enclosing Balls. In J. Nesetril (Eds.), *Lecture Notes in Computer Science* (Vol. 1643, pp. 325–338). Retrieved from http://link.springer.de/link/service/series/0558/bibs/1643/16430325.htm

Gilbert, E. G., Johnson, D. W., & Keerthi, S. S. (1988). A Fast Procedure for Computing the Distance Between Complex Objects in Three-Dimensional Space. *IEEE Journal on Robotics and Automation, 4*, 193–203.

Gomes de Sa, A., & Zachmann, G. (1998). Integrating Virtual Reality for Virtual Prototyping. In *Proceedings of the 1998 ASME Design Engineering Technical Conferences*. DETC98/CIE-5536.

Gomes de Sa, A., & Zachmann, G. (1999). Virtual Reality as a Tool for Verification of Assembly and Maintenance Processes. *Computers & Graphics, 23*, 389–403.

Gottschalk, S., Lin, M., & Manocha, D. (1996). OBB-Tree: A Hierarchical Structure for Rapid Interference Detection. In H. Rushmeier (Eds.), *SIGGRAPH 96 Conference Proceedings* (pp. 171–180), New Orleans, Louisiana.

Govindaraju, N., Redon, S., Lin, M. C., & Manocha, D. (2003 July). Cullide - Interactive Collision Detection Between Complex Models in Large Environments Using Graphics Hardware. In *Proceedings of Graphics Hardware*, San Diego, California (pp. 41-50). Retrieved from http://graphics.stanford.edu/papers/photongfx/

Gress, A., & Zachmann, G. (2003). Object-Space Interference Detection on Programmable Graphics Hardware. In M. L. Lucian & M. Neamtu (Eds.), *SIAM Conf. on Geometric Design and Computing* (pp. 311–328).

Gress, A., & Zachmann, G. (2006). *GPU-ABiSort: Optimal Parallel Sorting on Stream Architectures* (Technical Report IfI-06-11). Clausthal-Zellerfeld, Germany: TU Clausthal. Retrieved from http://cg.in.tu-clausthal.de/publications.shtml

Hubbard, P. M. (1995). Collision detection for interactive graphics applications. In IEEE Transactions on Visualization and Computer Graphics (Vol. 1, pp. 218–230).

Hubbard, P. M. (1996). Approximating Polyhedra with Spheres for Time-Critical Collision Detection. *ACM Transactions on Graphics, 15*, 179–210.

Huh, S., Metaxas, D. N., & Badler, N. I. (2001 November). Collision Resolutions in Cloth Simulation. In *IEEE Computer Animation Conference*, Seoul, Korea.

Jimenez, P., Thomas, F., & Torras, C. (2001). 3D Collision Detection: a Survey. *Computers & Graphics, 25*(2), 269–285.

Johnson, D. E., & Cohen, E. (1998). A Framework for Efficient Minimum Distance Computations. In *Proceedings of the IEEE International Conference on Robotics and Automation (ICRA-98)* (pp. 3678–3684).

Johnson, D. E., & Willemsen, P. (2003). Six Degree-of-Freedom Haptic Rendering of Complex Polygonal Model. In *HAPTICS* (pp. 229–235). Retrieved from http://csdl.computer.org/comp/proceedings/haptics/2003/1890/00/18900229abs.htm

Kapasi, U. J., Rixner, S., Dally, W. J., Khailany, B., Ahn, J. H., Mattson, P., & Owens, J. D. (2003). Programmable Stream Processors. In IEEE Computer (pp. 54–61).

Kitamura, Y., Smith, A., Takemura, H., & Kishino, F. (1998). A Real-Time Algorithm for Accurate Collision Detection for Deformable Polyhedral Objects. *Presence (Cambridge, Mass.)*, *7*(1).

Klein, J., & Zachmann, G. (2003). ADB-Trees: Controlling the Error of Time-Critical Collision Detection. In 8th International Fall Workshop Vision, Modeling, and Visualization (VMV.). Munich, Germany: University München.

Klein, J., & Zachmann, G. (2003). Time-Critical Collision Detection Using an Average-Case Approach. In *Proceedings of ACM Symposium on Virtual Reality Software and Technology (VRST)* (pp. 22–31). Retrieved from http://www.gabrielzachmann.org/

Klein, J., & Zachmann, G. (2004). Nice and Fast Implicit Surfaces over Noisy Point Clouds. In *SIGGRAPH Proceedings*. Retrieved from http://www.gabrielzachmann.org/

Klein, J., & Zachmann, G. (2004). Point Cloud Collision Detection, Computer Graphics forum. In []. Retrieved from http://www.gabrielzachmann.org/]. *Proceedings of EUROGRAPHICS*, *23*, 567–576.

Klein, J., & Zachmann, G. (2004). Point Cloud Surfaces using Geometric Proximity Graphs. *Computers & Graphics*, *28*, 839–850. Retrieved from http://dx.doi.org/10.1016/j.cag.2004.08.012.

Klein, J., & Zachmann, G. (2004). Proximity Graphs for Defining Surfaces over Point Clouds. In M. Alexa, M. Gross, H.-P. Pfister, & S. Rusinkiewicz (Eds.), *Symposium on Point-Based Graphics* (pp. 131–138). Zürich, Switzerland: ETHZ. Retrieved from http://www.gabrielzachmann.org/

Klosowski, J. T., Held, M., Mitchell, J. S. B., Sowrizal, H., & Zikan, K. (1998). Efficient Collision Detection Using Bounding Volume Hierarchies of k-DOPs. *IEEE Transactions on Visualization and Computer Graphics*, *4*, 21–36.

Knott, D., & Pai, D. K. (2003). CInDeR: Collision and Interference Detection in Real-Time Using Graphics Hardware. In *Proceedings of Graphics Interface*, Halifax, Nova Scotia, Canada, June 11-13. Retrieved from http://www.cs.rutgers.edu/~dpai/papers/KnottPai03.pdf

Larsen, E., Gottschalk, S., Lin, M., & Monocha, D. (1999). *Fast proximity queries with swept sphere volumes*. Technical Report TR99-018.

Larsson, T., & Akenine-Möller, T. (2001). *Collision Detection for Continuously Deforming Bodies* (pp. 325–333). Eurographics.

Lau, R., Chan, O., Luk, M., & Li, F. (2002). A Collision Detection Method for Deformable Objects. In *Proceedings of the ACM Symposium on Virtual Reality Software and Technology (VRST)* (pp. 113–120). Retrieved from http://doi.acm.org/10.1145/585740.585760

Lin, M., Manocha, D., Cohen, J., & Gottschalk, S. (1996). Collision Detection: Algorithms and Applications. In Laumond, J.-P., & Overmars, M. (Eds.), *Proceedings of Algorithms for Robotics Motion and Manipulation* (pp. 129–142).

Lombardo, J.-C., Cani, M.-P., & Neyret, F. (1999). Real-time collision detection for virtual surgery. In *Proceedings of Computer Animation*, Geneva, Switzerland, May 26-28. Retrieved from http://www.evasion.imag.fr/Publications/1999/LCN99

Mcneely, W. A., Puterbaugh, K. D., & Troy, J. J. (1999). Six Degrees-of-Freedom Haptic Rendering Using Voxel Sampling. In. *Proceedings of SIGGRAPH*, *99*, 401–408.

Mendoza, C., & O'Sullivan, C. (2006). Interruptible collision detection for deformable objects. *Computers & Graphics*, *30*, 432–438. Retrieved from http://dx.doi.org/10.1016/j.cag.2006.02.018.

Mezger, J., Kimmerle, S., & Etzmuss, O. (2003). Hierarchical Techniques in Collision Detection for Cloth Animation. *Journal of WSCG*. Retrieved from http://wscg.zcu.cz/wscg2003/Papers_2003/G97.pdf

Morris, D. (2006). *Algorithms and Data Structures for Haptic Rendering: Curve Constraints, Distance Maps, and Data Logging*. Technical Report 2006-06.

Myszkowski, K., Okunev, O. G., & Kunii, T. L. (1995). Fast collision detection between complex-solids using rasterizing graphics hardware. *The Visual Computer*, *11*, 497–512.

O'Brien, J. F., & Hodgins, J. K. (1999). Graphical modeling and animation of brittle fracture. In *SIGGRAPH '99: Proceedings of the 26th annual conference on Computer graphics and interactive techniques*, New York, NY, USA (pp. 137–146).

Ong, C., & Gilbert, E. (1996). Growth Distances: New Measures For Object Separation And Penetration. *IEEE Transactions on Robotics and Automation*, *12*(6), 888–903.

Ooi, B., McDonell, K., & Sacks-Davis, R. (1987). Spatial kd-tree: An indexing mechanism for spatial databases. In IEEE COMPSAC (pp. 433–438).

Palmer, I. J., & Grimsdale, R. L. (1995). Collision Detection for Animation using Sphere-Trees. *In Proceedings of EUROGRAPHICS* (Vol. 14, pp. 105–116).

Pfister, H., Zwicker, M., van Baar, J., & Gross, M. (2000). Surfels: Surface Elements as Rendering Primitives. In *Proceedings of SIGGRAPH* (pp. 335–342). Retrieved from http://visinfo.zib.de/EVlib/Show?EVL-2000-69

Ponamgi, M., Cohen, J., Lin, M., & Manocha, D. (1995). Incremental Algorithms for Collision Detection between General Solid Models. In *Proceedings of the third ACM symposium on Solid modeling and applications* (pp. 293-304). Retrieved from http://portal.acm.org/citation.cfm?id=218076.

Quinlan, S. (1994). Efficient distance computation between non-convex objects. In *Proceedings of International Conference on Robotics and Automation*. (pp. 3324–3329). Retrieved from http://eprints.kfupm.edu.sa/36777/1/36777.pdf

Rusinkiewicz, S., Hall-Holt, O., & Levoy, M. (2002). Real-time 3D model acquisition. *ACM Transactions on Graphics*, *21*, 438–446.

Rusinkiewicz, S., & Levoy, M. (2000). *QSplat: A Multiresolution Point Rendering System for Large Meshes*. In *Proceedings of SIGGRAPH* (pp. 343–352). Retrieved from http://visinfo.zib.de/EVlib/Show?EVL-2000-73

Schuermann, A. (2006). On packing spheres into containers (about Kepler's finite sphere packing problem). *Documenta Mathematica*, *11*, 393–406. Retrieved from http://arxiv.org/abs/math/0506200.

Shinya, M., & Forgue, M.-C. (1991). Interference detection through rasterization. *The Journal of Visualization and Computer Animation*, *2*, 132–134.

Teschner, M., Heidelberger, B., Manocha, D., Govindaraju, N., Zachmann, G., Kimmerle, S., et al. (2005). Collision Handling in Dynamic Simulation Environments. In *Eurographics Tutorial # 2* (pp. 1–4). Retrieved from http://www.gabrielzachmann.org/

Teschner, M., Kimmerle, S., Zachmann, G., Heidelberger, B., Raghupathi, L., Fuhrmann, A., et al. (2004). Collision Detection for Deformable Objects. In *Proceedings of Eurographics State-of-the-Art Report*, Grenoble, France (pp. 119–139). Retrieved from http://www.gabrielzachmann.org/

Uno, S., & Slater, M. (1997 March). The sensitivity of presence to collision response. In *Proceedings of IEEE Virtual Reality Annual International Symposium (VRAIS)*, Albuquerque, New Mexico (pp. 95).

van den Bergen, G. (1997). Efficient Collision Detection of Complex Deformable Models using AABB Trees. *Journal of Graphics Tools, 2*(4), 1–13.

van den Bergen, G. (1999). A Fast and Robust GJK Implementation for Collision Detection of Convex Objects. *Journal of Graphics Tools: JGT, 4*(2), 7–25.

van den Bergen, G. (2001). 3D Game Objects. In *Game developers conference*. Proximity Queries and Penetration Depth Computation on.

van den Bergen, G. (2003). *Collision Detection in Interactive 3D Environments*. San Francisco: Morgan Kaufman.

Wächter, C., & Keller, A. (2006). Instant Ray Tracing: The Bounding Interval Hierarchy. In T. Akenine-Möller & W. Heidrich (Eds.), *Eurographics Workshop/ Symposium on Rendering* (pp. 139–149). Retrieved from http://www.eg.org/EG/DL/WS/EGWR/EGSR06/139-149.pdf

Weller, R., & Zachmann, G. (2006). Kinetic Separation Lists for Continuous Collision Detection of Deformable Objects. In *Third Workshop in Virtual Reality Interactions and Physical Simulation (Vriphys)*, Madrid, Spain, November 6-7. Retrieved from http://cg.in.tu-clausthal.de/papers/vriphys06/vriphys_kinetic_separation_list.pdf

Weller, R., & Zachmann, G. (2009 June). Inner Sphere Trees for Proximity and Penetration Queries. In *Robotics: Science and Systems Conference (RSS)*, Seattle, WA, USA. Retrieved from http://cg.in.tu-clausthal.de/research/ist

Weller, R., & Zachmann, G. (2009). Stable 6-DOF Haptic Rendering with Inner Sphere Trees, in International Design Engineering Technical Conferences & Computers and Information. In *Engineering Conference.* (IDETC/CIE), San Diego, CA, USA. September. Retrieved from http://cg.in.tu-clausthal.de/research/ist

Weller, R., & Zachmann, G. (2009 August). A Unified Approach for Physically-Based Simulations and Haptic Rendering. In *Sandbox 2009: ACM SIGGRAPH Video Game Proceedings*, New Orleans, LA, USA. Retrieved from http://cg.in.tu-clausthal.de/papers/siggraph09/IST-SiggraphGames.pdf

Zachmann, G. (1998 March). Rapid Collision Detection by Dynamically Aligned DOP-Trees. In *Proceedings of IEEE Virtual Reality Annual International Symposium* (VRAIS '98), Atlanta, Georgia (pp. 90–97).

Zachmann, G. (2002). Minimal Hierarchical Collision Detection. *In Proceedings of ACM Symposium on Virtual Reality Software and Technology (VRST)*. Hong Kong, China, (pp. 121– 128). November 11-13. http://www.gabrielzachmann.org/

Zachmann, G., & Weller, R. (2006). Kinetic Bounding Volume Hierarchies for Deformable Objects. In *ACM Int'l Conf. on Virtual Reality Continuum and Its Applications (VRCIA)*. Hong Kong, China, June 14-17. Retrieved from http://www.gabrielzachmann.org/

Zhang, L., Kim, Y. J., Varadhan, G., & Manocha, D. (2007). Generalized penetration depth computation. *Computer Aided Design, 39*, 625–638. Retrieved from http://dx.doi.org/10.1016/j.cad.2007.05.012.

Zwicker, M., Pfister, H., van Baar, J., & Gross, M. (2002). EWA Splatting. *IEEE Transactions on Visualization and Computer Graphics, 8,* 223–238. Retrieved from http://csdl.computer.org/comp/trans/tg/2002/03/v0223abs.htm.

ENDNOTES

[1] Analogously to rendering, a number of human factors determine whether or not the "incorrectness" of a simulation will be noticed, such as the mental load of the viewing person, cluttering of the scene, occlusions, velocity of the objects and the viewpoint, point of attention, etc.

[2] Please visit cg.in.tu-clausthal.de/research/ist to watch some videos of our benchmarks.

[3] This is due to bad BV tightness and the costly tetrahedron-tetrahedron overlap volume calculation.

Chapter 4
Virtual Environment Visualisation of Executable Business Process Models

Ross Brown
Queensland University of Technology, Australia

Rune Rasmussen
Queensland University of Technology, Australia

ABSTRACT

Business Process Modelling is a fast growing field in business and information technology, which uses visual grammars to model and execute processes within an organisation. However, many analysts present such models in a 2D static and iconic manner that is difficult to understand by many stakeholders. Difficulties in understanding such grammars can impede the improvement of processes within an enterprise due to communication problems. In this chapter, we present a novel framework for intuitively visualising animated business process models in 3D Virtual Environments. We also show that virtual environment visualisations can be performed with present 2D business process modelling technology, thus providing a low barrier to entry for business process practitioners. Two case studies are presented from film production and healthcare domains that illustrate the ease with which these visualisations can be created. This approach can be generalised to other executable workflow systems, for any application domain being modelled.

INTRODUCTION

Games and related virtual environments have been a fast growing area of the entertainment industry. The classic reference is that games are now approaching the size of Hollywood box office sales (Boyer, 2008). Books are now appearing on its influence on business (Edery & Mollick, 2008), and it is one of the key drivers of present hardware development, especially with hardware manufactures providing solutions for graphics processing, physics simulation and interaction devices like the Nintendo Wiimote. Some of this game technology is now available as general purpose bundled applications on operating systems, including such examples as Aero on Windows, and Time Machine on the Apple Mac.

DOI: 10.4018/978-1-61520-631-5.ch004

In addition to this continued growth in the area of games, there are a number of factors that are increasing the influence of Games Technology and 3D Virtual Environments on Business IT systems. Firstly, the average age of gamers is approaching the mid thirties (ESA, 2008). Therefore, a number of people who are in management positions in large enterprises are experienced in using 3D entertainment environments. Secondly, due to demand for more computational power in CPU and Graphical Processing Units (GPUs), average desktop machines and recent laptops are capable of supporting a game or virtual environment. It should be noted that the demonstrations at the end of this chapter were developed at the Queensland University of Technology (QUT) on a normal Software Operating Environment, with a standard Intel Dual Core CPU and basic Intel graphics option.

What this means is that business computing is on the verge of being able to ubiquitously utilise Virtual Environment technology due to:

1. A broad range of workers being regularly exposed to 3D Virtual Environment software via games and related technologies.
2. Standard desktop computing power now being strong enough to potentially roll out a Virtual Environment solution across an entire enterprise.

In addition to this technological change emerging into business software spaces, we can also draw upon the communication capabilities of such 3D virtual spaces. 3D visualisation of data is a mainstream concept in many scientific and business fields (Hansen & Johnson, 2005). The inclusion of the third dimension of depth to 2D representations opens up many possibilities with regards to embedding high dimensional data into interactive visualisations. Once animation is included, the possibilities of encoding further information into these extra dimensions creates arrangements that are potentially superior for

spatially organised tasks (Tavanti & Lind, 2001). While this superior efficacy is still an ongoing debate (Cockburn & McKenzie, 2004), the novelty and physical attractiveness of such 3D environments continues to offer the possibility of compelling new environments for business system users.

Virtual Environments take this 3D visualisation concept further to generate a sense of presence within a computerised synthetic world, where the ego centre of the individual using the environment is placed within the representation as what is known as an Avatar (Lessig, 2000). The placement "In World" of the user facilitates the ability to communicate with the avatar of another person who is in the environment, and to interact in a collaborative, networked manner with data and process representations.

We believe such visual simulation environments can have a great impact in the application area of Business Process Modelling. Much research has been carried out into the usage of such environments for business via co-creation of content amongst other approaches (Bonsu & Darmody, 2008), but this has not been supported by the development of facilitating technology to ease the development burden for businesses seeking to use such virtual worlds. We believe that a key problem in the usage of such environments for business purposes, especially in the areas of business process management, is the absence of appropriate tools to facilitate easy modelling of business processes for consumption by stakeholders within an enterprise.

Present 2D tools offered to business process modellers suffice for the iconic and static representations used by process modelling experts, but no similar tools have been developed in the space of business process modelling for 3D Virtual Environments. Therefore, the main aim of this chapter is to describe the possibilities of visualising and interacting with business processes within virtual worlds, and to outline the software tools and approaches required for the average business analyst to be able to observe business process models being executed.

The first section of this chapter (Using Virtual Worlds in Business Process Management) will outline the communication capabilities of such environments, giving possibilities for business process modelling applications, where enterprises need to create, manage and improve their business processes, and then communicate their processes to stakeholders, both process and non-process cognisant. The second section (A Business Process Modelling Virtual Environment Framework) will describe a theoretical framework for developing business process virtual worlds with executable software. From this a software framework will be derived that supports the translation of common modelling tool formats into 3D Virtual Worlds. Section Three (Business Process Animation Case Studies) will cover two case studies of executing business processes using our prototype software. The first case study is a film production process model, and the second, a health case study. The final sections (Future Research Directions and Conclusion) will detail the next phase of research and development for this software framework, in an effort to make this process even easier for non-programmers.

USING VIRTUAL ENVIRONMENTS IN BUSINESS PROCESS MANAGEMENT

Business Process Management (BPM) has been a recent high priority growth sector within the business and IT communities, receiving its own Magic Quadrant report from Gartner (Hill, Cantara, Kerremans, & Plummer, 2009). Businesses have, in many cases, moved over to a form of enterprise modelling that is process centric. The benefits of such an abstraction of processes is the ability to model, measure, and improve those processes, and therefore improve the bottom line of a business in a systematic fashion (Lewis & Slack, 2003). A

key factor in the success of such business process management initiatives is the ability to accurately model (via Business Process Modelling) the enterprise in question. Such a process is difficult, time consuming, often involves external consultants and large amounts of monetary resources.

Precision of modelling is a major issue in this process. Any mistakes in the process of developing a business process model will cause problems later on in the execution and management of such business processes. If the model is inaccurate, then any process of measurement and refinement will cause errors to occur, and will thus be costly to the bottom line of the business. The main thesis of this chapter is, that 3D Virtual Environment representations allow complete simulation and interaction with a model of the business processes, bringing far more accuracy in modelling, and so will save money in the long term.

Inspiration for the use of 3D Virtual Environments comes from a number of application domains that have invested heavily in the area of virtual environment simulation. Military (Smith, 2006), Aerospace (Rolfe & Staples, 1988) and Medical (Gallagher et al., 2005) simulators, have all received heavy investment for visualising domain specific processes in 3D. All of these domains involve scenarios where the cost from limited understand and poor execution of processes is potentially life threatening and economically expensive. It is in these domains that a deep understanding of processes, and the ability to precisely implement these processes is paramount, thus the use of high quality simulation technology.

While the life threatening nature of process training is not typically present in business process models, virtual environment simulations offer a panoply of interactions that bring the educational experience closer to role playing, without the costs and risks involved in defining training scenarios in reality. They also offer the capacity for users to replay the simulation, and learn from mistakes in a less costly fashion. They contribute to independent exploration of scenarios and spaces, and since they are digital environments, such spaces can be annotated to provide insight into their improvement. This is one of the key contributions of such virtual worlds, to be able to experience the simulation as a very close copy, and to then comment on the representation with precision, due to the ability to interact with the process model in a free manner.

A number of training and communication outcomes from this work map well to BPM. Virtual environments facilitate the ability to see the process as a visualisation, to observe its function over time, and then to interact and change the parameters of the representation in a visual fashion. Virtual environments are simulation systems with attractive and intuitive to use visual interfaces that map in most cases directly to the domain application scenario being simulated. In other words, the distance between the reality and the representation is minimised as much as possible. This is a major component of such systems, as they give an ability, via the simulation, to experience a close version of real processes. This precision is vital in any of the process development life cycle stages, as we wish the process to be refined to a high level of fidelity, from "as is" to "to be" processes, in order to support utilisation and future improvement (Jörg Becker, Martin Kugeler, & Rosemann, 2003).

Presently, business process modelling has not taken on the use of virtual environments to model business processes with any sense of structure. Some systems have explored using animations in 3D to illustrate the process model (Interactive-Software, 2008) and some have used 2.5D simulations as commercial solutions (OnMap, 2008), but they do not use readily available tools to give the process modeller the ability to rapidly develop fully interactive visualisations in 3D.

Notwithstanding these other systems, when modelling business processes, usually a set of 2D static diagrams are generated, and a number of systems can be used to indicate the workflow of an organisation over time in a discrete time simulation (Rozinat, Wynn, van der Aalst, ter

Hofstede, & Fidge, 2009). These modelling tools are often noted to be an important factor in the success of process modelling projects (Bandara, Gable, & Rosemann, 2005). A number of process model notations are used, and frequently discussed for their relative capabilities (Recker, 2006). An example is shown below in (Figure 1) of two process models, one in Business Process Modelling Notation (BPMN) (OMG, 2006), an increasingly popular conceptually oriented modelling grammar, and YAWL (W.M.P. van der Aalst & ter Hofstede, 2005) an executable process modelling grammar.

The content of such Business Process Models is, however, very arcane to naive stakeholders. The problem is that such an iconic representation is compact and thus quickly understood by experts, in much the same fashion as a terse mathematical equation, but for naïve viewers, it is hard to understand. In addition, there is evidence of over complicating the notations created (Muehlen & Recker, 2008). For example, concepts of choice, shown as or-splits, are abstracted into iconic representations, that may not be represented in an intuitive manner. Such complicated representations take time to understand, creating a hurdle for process modelling naïve stakeholders.

These process models are typically stored in what are known as process repositories, which are searchable databases of process diagrams (Weber & Reichert, 2008). Further obfuscation occurs, especially with large process models, as the shear size and complexity of such hierarchical models precludes easy understanding of the enterprise. This problem is exacerbated when dealing with enterprises that may have thousands of large models in their repository.

We can conclude that compact 2D notations are exceedingly efficient representations for experts, but very difficult to understand for clients, and other non-process cognisant stakeholders in an organisation being modelled. The confusion in the validation process translates to a number of problems for the business process life cycle:

Figure 1. Illustration of two diagrammatic forms of process models used in BPM. The top diagram is an example of an executable form of a film production process model developed in the YAWL grammar. The bottom diagram is a Health Traumatology process model developed using the BPMN grammar

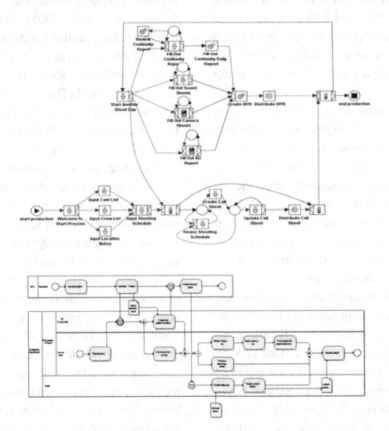

1. Confusion during the validation stages with clients – how can they communicate back to the modeller that they have captured the subtleties of the process in the diagram, without an understanding of the subtleties of the diagrammatic notation used?

2. Inconsistencies in any final implementation, whether executable or not in nature. Any mistakes are embedded in the process models as conceptual and configuration errors, thus misleading people who access the repository to ascertain how an organisation performs its work.

3. Follow on losses from the incorrect modelling of the processes in process improvement stages. Any of the gains from process im-

provement may be affected due to incorrect modelling of the processes in the first place.

We therefore postulate that virtual environment technology is most useful for communication purposes, involving the enhancement of insight by a process stakeholder that will provide flow on benefits to an organisation.

We believe that the value proposition to the BPM community is that any increase in insight and understanding of process models will by default reap savings in the development of any processes, and their optimisation thereafter. 3D Virtual Environment visualisations of business processes offer intuitive simulations that every stakeholder can engage with easily, as they are functionally the closest simulation possible with modern technology. However, this benefit must be weighed up against the effort involved in creating 3D visualisations of said business processes. The benefit must be seen from the perspective of the bottom line of a company. However, we believe there is a strong case from other manufacturing process domains, that the use of such 3D simulations can reap savings, as long as modelling costs are kept low. Companies have for some time now routinely used simulation software in order to test products, to make sure that it meets client specifications (Wolfgang et al., 2002). The thesis of this chapter is that this is the same for developing a complex process model. Clear communication of the structure of a business process, both in space and in time, will lead to fewer misunderstandings, and thus less loss of resources. A corollary of such an argument is the projected need for easy to use 3D process modelling tools to be provided to business analysts.

However, present Virtual Environment modelling tools are hard to use, requiring programming capabilities on the part of the designer. This will need to change in order to allow business analysts to easily use virtual environment technology. By analogy, we may look at the history of desktop publishing and word processing. Early 80s word processors were hard to use; involving arcane text commands and mark up in order to format a document. Professional publishers needed highly skilled operators to generate professionally formatted books. Now, ordinary users can create polished documents using templates that are useful for business communication. Virtual Environments are at the same stage as these word processors were in their infancy. The design tools are powerful, but difficult for naive users to grasp, and as such require much training to use effectively. Environments such as Second Life (Linden, 2008) have gone a long way to providing modelling and animation toolsets, but these tools still exhibit a lack of affordance for the task of modelling business processes. In particular,

they lack an integrated approach to the modelling process that goes beyond the simple scripting of object animations.

Technology being developed by the games industry offers insight into solving this problem. Games often ship with design tools for users to augment and modify game environments. These tools are typically used by game designers in games studios, who do not have a strong programming background, and will have the design tools developed for them by programmers to easily build game levels (Rouse, 2000). Often these editors allow the integration of models and pre-created animations to create lively interactive environments for the carrying out of game missions. These missions can be seen by analogy as a form of game workflow (Brown, Lim, Wong, Heng, & Wallace, 2006), similar to the concept of workflow as used in Process-aware Information Systems. Furthermore, games companies release these game editors to the public, enabling lay people to easily modify their games with these tools – thus the tools are highly developed and easy to use for non-game development experts.

Present modelling tools in the BPM community may come with components that support discrete simulation methods. A number of products have the ability to simulate the execution of business process models, including: ARIS (IDS-Scheer, 2008), Casewise (CaseWise, 2008) and others. Discrete simulation of process models (Rozinat et al., 2009) and related agent-based techniques (Zhao & Cao, 2007) remain an active research topic.

What has to be stated is that the simulation models are still 2D, and often do not incorporate spatial information, or effective representations of the objects in question being used in the process model being developed. While 2D is of course very useful, it is missing a vital third dimension that is now desired for representing complex processes and data (Tavanti & Lind, 2001). This dimension by default allows the encoding of extra information, and provides the extra interaction possibilities that allow deeper insight into the model, by giving the ability to literally manipulate in three and not two dimensions.

Other work has proposed the use of role based visualisations for the representation of process models (Bobrik, Bobrik, Reichert, & Bauer, 2005) and some have developed 3D visualisations for process modelling (Interactive-Software, 2008). None have approached this work in a thorough manner, defining a complete approach to such visualisations or a set of novel visualisation techniques. We believe there are a number of issues that need to be addressed in order to advance the possibilities of business process modelling and execution within such 3D virtual environments. Many of these issues revolve around the functionality of the BPM modelling tools being used.

A BUSINESS PROCESS MODELLING VIRTUAL ENVIRONMENT FRAMEWORK

In the main, the concept of using 3D for visualising business processes has not been exploited. Some reasons for not exploring 3D virtual environments given include: difficulty of use, lack of maturity in business process modelling with regards to 2D models of business processes let alone 3D, extra effort to model the details, and lack of research into how one represents a business process in 3D.

Difficulty of use is a misnomer, as games have shown that 3D environments are being used by people of many ages to entertain themselves, and soon tools will emerge that will be used for work more and more often, especially in product development collaboration scenarios (Tahmincioglu, 2008) (Rozwell, 2008).

Process modelling still has some way to go with regards to formalising its approaches. The use of complex visualisations of business processes requires an appropriate layer of technology and expertise to be in place. While BPM tools are well developed, there is a lack of standardisa-

tion present to fully take up the offerings of 3D Virtual Environments. Research has indicated that the tools presently have an influence on the success of process modelling projects (Bandara et al., 2005), and thus we can state that the tools required to develop such 3D visualisations are not present at the moment to easily create BPM Virtual Environments.

A major issue is the newness of the field. Virtual reality has for many years required high-end technology to be implemented, costing hundreds of thousands of dollars. Games technology that now exceeds previous simulation system capacities is now available in consumer form, and along with high-speed home networking, has brought this technology into home and SME business environments. The research on how to use this technology in the Business Process Management application domain in a broad sense has simply not been performed. Present research, while addressing in some way the issues of 3D virtual environment based process modelling (IBM, 2008; Interactive-Software, 2008), have not looked at developing technology to ease the modelling task in any way, let alone rigorously investigated the techniques and tools required to visualise a business process in 3D Virtual Environments.

VISUAL MODELLING REQUIREMENTS ANALYSIS

Extreme visual fidelity, while emotionally impacting, is not necessarily essential to improving the understanding of a process. Many visualisation systems utilise animation and interaction capabilities that are not photo-realistic in nature, and in fact, usage of non-photo realistic representations are considered superior in certain visualisation applications (Gooch, Gooch, Shirley, & Cohen, 1998). This means that the quality of the virtual environment does not have to be so computationally expensive that it requires vast amounts of power to create the visualisation, thus allowing viable 3D Business Process Visualisations to be made available on laptop and standard desktop systems available today.

It can be stated as a maxim, that Interactive Visualisations are about elegant sufficiency of representation. The use of obfuscating "Chart Junk," as described famously by Tufte (Tufte, 1983), is to be avoided at all costs, as it actually clouds the perception of the information within the representation. Thus, the general approach to business process management visualisation should be around the need to communicate, and less about the need to impress stakeholders. We can therefore see that in general, this places a boundary on requirements for such visualisations, placing them within the reach of the equipment, and potentially the modelling skills, of a typical business analyst.

It must be stated, that in a similar manner to the present 2D diagrammatic representations, business process modelling does not need high fidelity representations in 3D in order to be successful. Three dimensional business process visualisations only require a number of key components to make the visualisation usable:

1. Spatial organisation of objects used in the process model that is, positioning tasks within a floor plan in a building or on a terrain.
2. 3D representations of objects for use in world entire websites are devoted to selling such artefacts, thus it can be easily extended to typical physical business system resources (photocopiers, terminals, mobile phones and people, amongst other things).
3. Object animations that illustrate the actions that resources perform, either on their own, or with another resource.
4. Representations of decision structures involved in the processes. This means the translation of such choice representations from the 2D, to a similarly recognisable construct in the 3D virtual world, via either

an abstract representation as an artefact, or the animation of a human resource involved in the decision process.

5. Representation of the more abstract IT components of a process model. For instance, the representation of the components of an IT transaction system being used in a bank.

Taking these requirements, we now create a framework indicating the major components of any software needed to model processes in 3D virtual environments.

BUSINESS PROCESS VISUALISATION CONCEPTUAL FRAMEWORK

We have endeavoured to analyse and develop a framework that is focussed on the execution and analysis of Workflow. Workflow is a subsection of Business Process Management that deals with the execution of process models to coordinate work within enterprises (W.M.P. van der Aalst & van Hee, 2004). This also makes the domain applicable to animation systems, due to the fact that the technology implicitly executes process models, and thus can be extended to easily illustrate those processes executing in a 3D virtual world. Furthermore, the more abstract aspects of conceptual modelling that are a component of BPM, can still be represented due to a number of technological advances, including the ability to translate conceptual grammars such as BPMN into executable representations (Decker, Dijkman, Dumas, & García-Bañuelos, 2008).

For this framework, we will take a workflow-oriented viewpoint to the representation of Business Processes, and will refine the framework to suit conceptual modelling approaches in the future. From this point on the term Workflow, and its technologies, will be the reference point for framework construction, as an entry point into the field of BPM. Workflow models have three com-

Figure 2. Example of a form, with fields drawn from the Data Perspective in the YAWL4Film workflow model

monly articulated views or perspectives: control, data, and resource.

The Control Perspective is the temporal ordering of tasks, such that they represent the ordering of things to be performed in the process, including the choices made by human resources in the organisation. A business process visualisation in 3D must seek to represent the discrete tasks that resource(s) execute. Thus the requirements for such a representation will be to have a location that the resource performs the action, and an appropriate interaction with the object(s) to be used for the task. Decisions need to be represented, in essence an OR-Split (W.M.P. van der Aalst & ter Hofstede, 2005), whereby a resource makes a choice from a number of tasks available to be executed. A parallel set of items (known as an And-Split), can be serialised and represented as a set of tasks performed by a resource in series (W.M.P. van der Aalst & ter Hofstede, 2005). An example control perspective is shown at the top of (Figure 1).

The Data Perspective represents the supporting data model for the executable workflow model. This includes work data assigned to the task, and supporting information used in automated

decisions. This is the level in which spatial and temporal information about the visualisation is stored. Spatial information pertaining to where the tasks are performed, and what visual representation the task is performed with is stored in this perspective as annotation information. Additional form-based information attached to the work item, can be directed to representations within the virtual world. An example of a form that is generated for filling in by a worker is shown below in (Figure 2).

Such data may be represented as a form, for the worker to fill in as part of their work, or as meta-data to be transmitted for processing by the worklist client. The worklist being a list of work items to be completed by a worker engaged with the workflow system. For example, a work item may require the filling out of an invoice with purchase details: invoice number, client name, date, item description, number to ship and so on. This information is transmitted from the workflow system and will need to be interpreted, transformed, and represented in world as either a live form, or as a supporting item of visual information. It is these annotations that we refer to later in our framework for generating animated visualisations.

Resource perspectives incorporate the roles and tasks of people in the organisation (human resources) and the non-human resources involved in the project (Nick Russell, Wil M.P. van der Aalst, Arthur H.M. ter Hofstede, & Edmond, 2005). The resource view relates directly to the avatar involved in the virtual environment representation, as the representation of the resource involved in the process. A virtual environment system will involve session management, which requires the user of the system to login and then register a session with the business process system. Such executable models have a worklist dissemination approach that requires a login session to allow the worker to receive work items.

In effect, this resource model maps directly to the representation offered in a virtual world. For an avatar to be part of the visualisation of the process model, it should be logged into the process

Figure 3. Process Model Visualisation Framework, showing the major components required to provide a visualisation of workflow in a 3D Virtual World. We have implemented the Animation Agent component of this framework at this stage

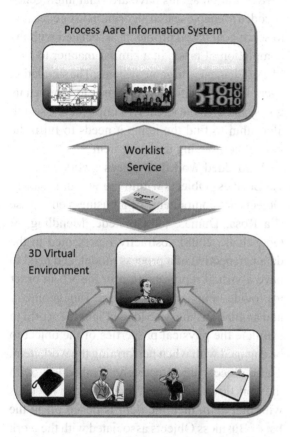

system. The avatar then becomes part of a running workflow case on the process system, and will receive work items according to the resource model of the workflow system with which the avatar is interacting. For example, an office worker will receive work items that pertain to the printing and photocopying of said documents. Whereas, a management avatar will be required to analyse and sign such documents and pass them onto other people in the organisation. Effectively, the session management in a virtual world system will map to the session management system operating with a workflow system, and its resource model used to allocate work (Nick Russell et al., 2005).

In Figure 3 we show the relationship between the various components, and how they are implemented in our Virtual Environment Business Process Visualisation Framework.

From the diagram we see the major constructs of the visualisation framework. A virtual world, in order to illustrate workflow occurring within the enterprise, needs to link to the workflow system via a service. This service extracts the work items for the person logged in via the virtual world, and then hands the worklist to the Worklist Supervisor, which manages the session for the logged in user. Therefore, there is an instance of the supervisor for each person logged into the world. It should also be noted that any simulated agent can be logged in automatically, and so artificial agents in this scheme can be used to simulate many people within a working process. This means that a complete enterprise can be modelled within a Virtual Environment in a scalable manner.

The supervisor controls the logged in workflow session for the user, and checks that particular work items are executed correctly. Each work item is atomic in the modelling of workflow for the enterprise, however, we now have to model the actual actions to be performed in order to complete the work item. Each work item comes annotated with a data structure containing a series of virtual world items that have to be interacted with, in order to complete the task. For example, the processing of a purchase at a store will include such tasks as scanning the bar code of the items, processing the payment from the buyer, removing security devices, and packaging for sale. Each is required to finish the sale, and to provide a convincing simulation of the work.

It should be noted that the supervisor module may be a human monitoring the work in a hidden manner for training purposes, or may be an AI system that checks for the completion of the work item by counting the correct interactions with virtual business objects within the environment. Allowing a human into the loop of being a supervisor opens up other educational possibilities

Figure 4. Illustration of the interactions possible with the in-world workflow system. On the top left the avatar is being controlled for Animation. On the top right is an illustration of the Supervisor Embedding virtual objects with workflow item interactions (embedded objects highlighted with a circle). On the bottom is an example of a Heads Up Display (HUD), which shows an Explicit List of the workflow items to be performed (to the right of the image), allowing direct interaction with the workflow list, as per a normal terminal based workflow system

within the framework, including interdiction by the supervisor during training scenarios in-world.

BUSINESS PROCESS INTERACTIONS

The worklist may be exposed to the user in the virtual world in three modes: animation, embedding and explicit worklists. These modes are an extension of the nature of workflow in normal business process systems. The workflow interaction modes are illustrated in the following (Figure 4).

Animation is the simplest example that animates the avatar to complete the workflow, as a single person interacting with the executing workflow. This is illustrated by the avatar being

lead through the process model, under the control of the Supervisor. As the avatar completes each work item it checks it in to the workflow system, as would a worker in the same scenario.

Simulation agents have artificial intelligence encoded to enable search algorithms to be executed to solve goal based problems associated with the completion of tasks, in a similar manner to Non Player Characters in game systems. The simulation agent interacts with the supervisor to be given its goals, and then the agent will implement a search algorithm to find the items it needs to fulfil the goal of completing the work item.

Embedded Workflow places a work item into the Business Objects within the world. Business Objects are components of a business enterprise (La Rosa, Dumas, ter Hofstede, Mendling, & Gottschalk, 2008) abstractly represented in the data perspective of a process model, and need to have a virtual representation in the VE in order to provide simulation capabilities. Thus geometry and animations must be loaded into the world to simulate the physical properties of the object to be engaged with when performing the work item. These objects are effectively "Embedded" with the workflow task items. When an avatar interacts with that item, then the item is ticked off in the list of Business Objects associated with the work item being executed.

This provides an intuitive method for user interaction with the workflow system, providing a natural interface via objects within the environment. For example, when a phone in the virtual world is picked up and used, this is registered as making a call, which is noted in the list of objects interacted with by the supervisor.

A human user may directly interact with the workflow system by using a Heads Up Display (HUD) as they traverse the environment, with work items displayed as lists of tasks to be performed. This gives a similar experience to that when using a normal workflow system with a terminal, laptop or PDA delivering work items to the worker via a list interface for checkin and checkout.

Figure 5. Snapshot of a screen showing the YAWL process modelling editor, with the task variables for Input Cast List in the YAWL4Film example case study.

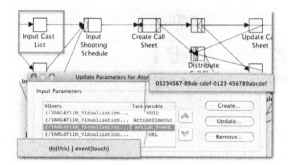

BUSINESS PROCESS ANIMATION CASE STUDIES

We have begun to develop tools to support the visualising business processes in 3D worlds. We have integrated a business process modelling tool YAWL, with the Second Life 3D Virtual Environment. We have chosen this as the first entry point, as the industry uses similar 2D modelling tools, and they represent a repository of verified and validated process representations that can be used to test the efficacy of 3D animation in this domain. The intent of these case studies were to analyse the feasibility of using YAWL to model a process and to see an animation of the process occur in the virtual environment implementation, Second Life.

An open source workflow tool has been developed called Yet Another Workflow Language (YAWL), which enables the detailed modelling of business processes using a sophisticated executable language (W.M.P. van der Aalst & ter Hofstede, 2005). YAWL is amenable to the task of linking to Second Life, due to its service oriented architecture, and encapsulated interfaces to the workflow being executed. In the design of the software, the process of worklist presentation to the worker is abstracted out into a service, from which a custom worklist service can be created.

As a first stage in this description, we will show now how the animation framework is used for the modelling and execution phases. The intention is to illustrate that a typical 2D process modelling tool can be used, via additional annotations, to encode key aspects of the visualisation required, and then be executed by an in-world interaction process.

Animation Modelling

Part of the purpose of this research is to allow a business process modeller to easily develop virtual environment visualisations by utilising typical process modelling tools, such as those used in products by ARIS, Oracle and YAWL. As discussed in the Virtual Modelling Requirements for such a system, the process model needs to have a set of virtual environment objects made available within that world, to enable the physical modelling of the environment within which the process model is embedded.

Assuming such virtual Business Objects are already in the virtual environment, then the process model needs to be able to reference them, to say that a particular task is related to this virtual object item. Two variables need to be added as annotations to the process model in order for this to occur. Firstly, the object must be identified. Second Life offers a unique object identifier called a UUID, which is a string of characters generated by the Second Life server software upon object creation. Thus if the object exists in world, then this UUID will enable the workflow service to find it and relate it to a Work Item for the avatar. See Figure 5.

Note the main two variables required to link the process to an animation in Second Life – *UUID* or Object Identifier and *Action_Event* or what needs to be executed upon interaction with the object. Example values that can be entered are shown in the breakout boxes for the two variables.

Figure 6. Overview diagram of the linking of the YAWL Workflow system with Second Life via a custom service. Note that the approach is inherently distributed, with the YAWL server we used residing at QUT, Australia, and the Visualisation being generated at the Second Life server in the US, and potentially viewable anywhere

Animation Execution

Once the link is made via the annotation of the workflow, the model then needs to be executed within the workflow tool. In order to provide a 3D virtual environment interface to the worklist, we developed a custom service module to link the Second Life environment with the worklist interface in YAWL. In effect, this means that objects to be associated with workflow tasks within Second Life can animate the traversal of a workflow control network, causing an avatar to change locations and act out the tasks contained within the business process model. The overall implementation architecture is illustrated in (Figure 6).

The avatar animation implementation works in a stepwise fashion as follows:

1. User logs into Second Life, and is assigned an avatar, as is normal for such systems.
2. A Supervisor Object is made available within the virtual world location presently occupied by the avatar. The representation is arbitrary (we use a sphere for the example), but this can be a metaphor, such as an employment ID card
3. The avatar attaches the Supervisor Object to their body. The Supervisor Object executes code to login a session with the YAWL workflow tool located on a server, external to the Second Life servers at Linden Labs.

4. The Supervisor takes control of the avatar so that YAWL now has control and can, via worklist commands, direct the avatar to the spatial locations where work is to be carried out.

This Supervisor attachment and control process is illustrated in the following screen images in (Figure 7).

In order to establish the feasibility of using such a system with typical process modelling tools, we have implemented two animation scenarios based on YAWL process models, one a production process model from the film industry, and another from the healthcare sector. The intention of these demonstrations is to illustrate the ability of the animation framework to allow a process modeller to use their 2D tools to model the workflow, and then to have the process model be animated within a full 3D virtual Environment.

THE YAWL4FILM CASE STUDY

The first demonstration uses a substantial process model drawn from a project being run within the QUT BPM research group called YAWL4Film (Ouyang, La Rosa, ter Hofstede, Dumas, & Short-land, 2008). This is a project seeking to introduce process modelling to the film industry, to facilitate efficient management of the film production pro-

Figure 7.Illustration of the process of handing control to the YAWL system via a "Supervisor Object," in this case a red sphere. Once the object is attached, it logs in a workflow session to the YAWL system via the custom worklist handler service, and then extracts the work items from the custom worklist service to animate the avatar executing the process model

cess, to assist with multi-site film shoots, and to help the Australian film industry to be competitive via process modelling efficiency gains.

(Figure 8) illustrates the process model developed by the YAWL4Film team. (Figure 9) shows still images from the animation generated by the YAWL/Second Life service. The illustration shows a sample of snapshots of tasks being performed by an avatar controlled by the YAWL4Film film process model. In order to generate the animation, the process model was annotated as previously mentioned with UUID values for the objects involved with the task, and the Action_Value required for that particular work item. Thus, according to the set of five points mentioned previously in the Business Process Modelling User Requirements Section, we have representations of the spatial locations of tasks, the human and non-human resources used, and animations illustrating the execution of the film production process. We have also shown how to easily annotate a process model with extra information in order to generate the visualisation. This shows the feasibility of offering such tools to business modellers, with a minimum of extra training.

HEALTHCARE CASE STUDY

In this case study the application domain is from the Healthcare Sector, with a patient visitation scenario, used to illustrate the flexibility of the software framework we have developed. Here we have used YAWL to model a parallel set of items to be carried out by a doctor on his rounds. The same software is used, but in this case the process model and the inventory on the Second Life Island are changed. The virtual world example is from a Hospital model created by the Auckland University Medical School, in New Zealand.

What should be noted here is the ability to easily change scenarios, and to thus illustrate the spatial location of the processes for many scenarios. Business Object inventory at Auckland hospital was reused for this example; we simply started the process modelling system on their Second Life Island, with a different process configuration, and the animation was captured. This illustrates the points made earlier in this chapter that the use of the process modelling framework easily allows for such process visualisations, as many of these virtual worlds have abundant content that can be refactored for use in many application domains. This is a key contribution of this work, to abstract out the process modelling from the content within

Figure 8. An illustration of the process model of the film production process for YAWL4Film. The images are snap shots from the executing animation of the process model in Second Life, to illustrate how the process model maps to the tasks being carried out by the avatar that has logged in to the YAWL workflow system

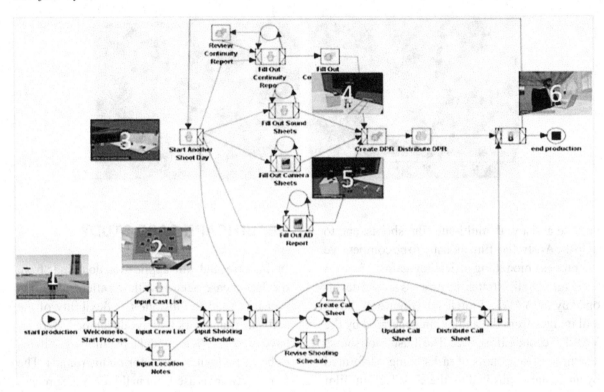

Figure 9. Larger versions of the images in (Figure 8), showing the animated execution of the workflow system

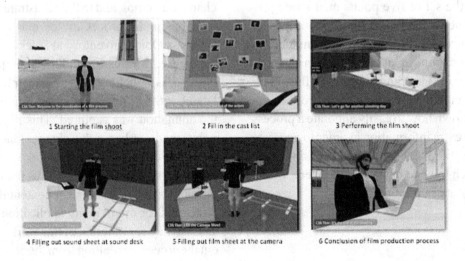

Figure 10. Illustration of a patient visitation process model, showing the daily rounds of a doctor

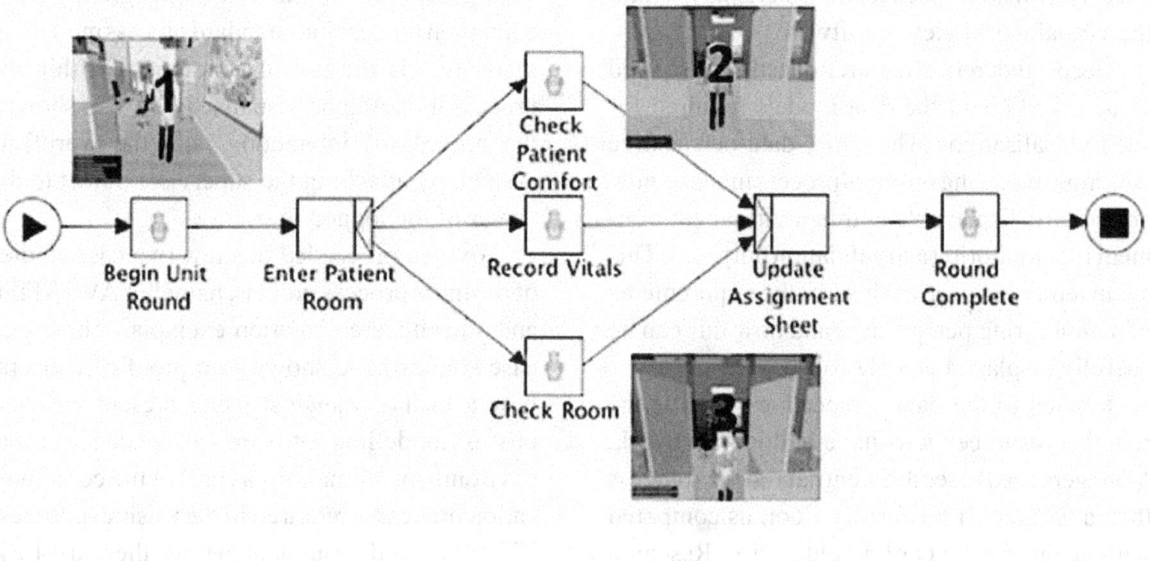

a virtual environment, for ease of modification. See Figures 10 and 11.

FUTURE RESEARCH DIRECTIONS

Future work revolves around the implementation and testing of the rest of the framework, in addition to the animation framework we have developed, including new simulation avatars with AI capabilities, embedded workflow items and explicit worklists for direct interaction by human virtual world users. These components will provide many more possibilities in the area of workflow

simulation and communication, leading to better modelling of systems.

In addition to the general presentation of, and interaction with, workflow items in the virtual world, there are many other visualisation opportunities within this field. Major work needs to be performed into generalising the visual interface to show avatars making choices, avatars interfacing with each other, and to develop representations of the internal IT infrastructure represented in the visualisation (for example, representations of transaction status, workflow monitoring data flows and so on). This will require the augmentation of the 3D world with data perspectives shown

Figure 11. Larger images from the health example, showing the avatar being animated at different stages of the workflow model

1 Beginning a patient round   2 Checking patient comfort   3 Checking the room

as new 3D glyphs in the world itself, or as a 2D overlay of data on the Heads Up Display within the virtual world viewer software.

Deeper theoretical research questions also need to be asked about the data models required for such visualisations. The entire data perspective within an executing business process model is now potentially displayable within a virtual environment for monitoring and validation purposes. This again requires a deep analysis of the requirements of a monitoring perspective, and how this can be usefully displayed in a 3D world.

Related to the data perspective views is the role that resource views have in this framework. Managers need to see different data about a process than a worker on the factory floor, as compared with again to a CEO of an enterprise. Research will be carried out into the visualisations required for different roles within the process development life cycle, and how these 3D visualisations of process models can be used in validation and communication processes for the benefit of all process stakeholders.

Finally, what needs to be assessed most of all is the role of such software within the BPM community. We need to ascertain how this framework can be used in an effective manner that is of most benefit to stakeholders. This framework, and its future implementations, will need to be usable in order to have impact. Further work is required to investigate how such modelling tools will be incorporated into the tools and approaches used by business analysts and modellers as they engage clients.

CONCLUSION

In this chapter we have shown a complete conceptual visualisation framework for Business Process Models in Virtual Environments. We have illustrated the visual and interaction requirements, and have identified the major software constructs required to develop a complete virtual environ-

ment based, business process modelling system.

We have shown the ease of integrating a 3D animation process into standard process modelling software, via the use of annotations within the process model to be visualised. We also showed the process of interacting with the workflow system, by attaching the supervisor object to the avatar of the logged in user.

We then proceeded to show two case studies of business process models, namely YAWL4Film and a healthcare visitation exemplar. These two case studies have shown as a proof of concept, how a business analyst using present business process modelling software, can create 3D virtual environment animations as part of the communication processes required in the Business Process Lifecycle. At this moment in time, the software is at the level of being able to animate a workflow, by controlling an avatar.

We believe this is a successful first entry point into a rich Greenfield research area, linking games technology with Business Process Modelling, that will provide great assistance to practitioners in their modelling and communication tasks.

ACKNOWLEDGMENT

The authors wish to thank Scott Diener (Auckland University, New Zealand) for his assistance in providing a hospital simulation from his Second Life Island, Long White Cloud, and Florian Cliquet for developing early prototype animation code.

REFERENCES

Bandara, W., Gable, G., & Rosemann, M. (2005). Factors and Measures of Business Process Modeling: Model Building Through a Multiple Case Study. *European Journal of Information Systems, 14*(4), 347–360. doi:10.1057/palgrave. ejis.3000546

Bobrik, R., Bobrik, R., Reichert, M., & Bauer, T. (2005). *Requirements for the visualization of system-spanning business processes.* Paper presented at the Sixteenth International Workshop on Database and Expert Systems Applications.

Bonsu, S. K., & Darmody, A. (2008). Co-creating Second Life. *Journal of Macromarketing, 28*(4), 355–368. doi:10.1177/0276146708325396

Boyer, B. (2008). *MGS4 Dominates June NPD, Drives PS3 Sales.* Retrieved October 2008, from http://www.gamasutra.com/php-bin/news_index.php?story=19476

Brown, R. A., Lim, A. E., Wong, Y. L., Heng, S.-M., & Wallace, D. M. (2006). Gameplay workflow: a distributed game control approach. In *2006 International Conference on Game Research and Development*, Fremantle, Australia.

CaseWise. (2008). *CaseWise.* Retrieved October 2008, from http://www.casewise.com

Cockburn, A., & McKenzie, B. (2004). Evaluating Spatial Memory in Two and Three Dimensions. *International Journal of Human-Computer Studies, 61*(30), 359–373. doi:10.1016/j.ijhcs.2004.01.005

Decker, G., Dijkman, R., Dumas, M., & García-Bañuelos, L. (2008). Transforming BPMN Diagrams into YAWL Nets. In *Business Process Management* (pp. 386–389). Berlin: Springer. doi:10.1007/978-3-540-85758-7_30

Edery, D., & Mollick, E. (2008). *Changing the Game: How Video Games Are Transforming the Future of Business.* Upper Saddle River, NJ: FT Press.

ESA. (2008). *Industry Facts.* Retrieved October 2008, from http://www.theesa.com/facts/index.asp

Gallagher, A. G., Ritter, E. M., Champion, H., Higgins, G., Fried, M. P., & Moses, G. (2005). Virtual Reality Simulation for the Operating Room Proficiency-Based Training as a Paradigm Shift in Surgical Skills Training. *Annals of Surgery, 241*(2), 364–372. doi:10.1097/01.sla.0000151982.85062.80

Gooch, A., Gooch, B., Shirley, P. S., & Cohen, E. (1998). A Non-Photorealistic Lighting Model for Automatic Technical Illustration. In SIGGRAPH 98 (pp. 447-452).

Hansen, C. D., & Johnson, C. R. (Eds.). (2005). *The Visualization Handbook.* Amsterdam: Elsevier-Butterworth Heinemann.

Hill, J. B., Cantara, M., Kerremans, M., & Plummer, D. C. (2009). *ID Number: G00164485 Magic Quadrant for Business Process Management Suites.*

IBM. (2008). *Innov8 Web Site.* Retrieved March 2008, from http://www-304.ibm.com/jct03001c/software/solutions/soa/innov8.html

IDS-Scheer. (2008). *ARIS.* Retrieved October 2008, from http://www.ids-scheer.com

Interactive-Software. (2008). *Interactive Software Systems.* Retrieved October 2008, from http://www.interactive-software.de/

Jörg Becker. Martin Kugeler, & Rosemann, M. (Eds.). (2003). Process Management: A Guide for the Design of Business Processes. Berlin: Springer-Verlag.

La Rosa, M., Dumas, M., ter Hofstede, A. H. M., Mendling, J., & Gottschalk, F. (2008). Beyond Control-Flow: Extending Business Process Configuration to Roles and Objects. In *27th Proceeding of International Conference on Conceptual Modeling*, Barcelona, Spain.

Lessig, L. (2000). *Code and Other Laws of Cyberspace.* New York: Basic Books.

Lewis, M., & Slack, N. (Eds.). (2003). *Operations Management: Critical Perspectives on Business and Management*. London: Routledge.

Linden. (2008). *Second Life*. Retrieved October 2008, from http://www.secondlife.com

Muehlen, M. Z., & Recker, J. (2008). How Much Language is Enough? Theoretical and Practical Use of the Business Process Modeling Notation. In *20th International Conference on Advanced Information Systems Engineering (CAiSE 2008)*, Montpellier, France.

OMG. (2006). *Business Process Modeling Notation Specification*. Retrieved March 29, 2008, from www.bpmn.org

OnMap. (2008). *OnMap*. Retrieved April, 2008, from http://www.onmap.fr/

Ouyang, C., La Rosa, M., ter Hofstede, A. H. M., Dumas, M., & Shortland, K. (2008). Toward Web-Scale Workflows for Film Production. *Internet Computing, IEEE, 2008*(October), 53–61. doi:10.1109/MIC.2008.115

Recker, J. (2006). *Process Modeling in the 21st Century*. Retrieved October 2008, from http://www.bptrends.com/publicationfiles/05-06-ART-ProcessModeling21stCent-Recker1.pdf

Rolfe, J. M., & Staples, K. J. (Eds.). (1988). *Flight Simulation*. Cambridge, UK: Cambridge University Press.

Rouse, R. (2000). *Designing Design Tools*. Retrieved October 2008, from http://www.gamasutra.com/features/20000323/rouse_01.htm

Rozinat, A., Wynn, M. T., van der Aalst, W. M. P., ter Hofstede, A. H. M., & Fidge, C. J. (2009). *Workflow Simulation for Operational Decision Support*. Accepted for Data and Knowledge Engineering.

Rozwell, C. (2008). *Michelin Uses Virtual Environment to Teach Complex Material*. Stamford, CT: Gartner.

Russell, N., van der Aalst, W. M. P., ter Hofstede, A. H. M., & Edmond, D. (2005). *Workflow Resource Patterns: Identification, Representation and Tool Support*. Paper presented at the CAiSE 2005.

Smith, R. (2006). Technology Disruption in the Simulation Industry. *The Journal of Defense Modeling and Simulation: Applications, Methodology. Technology (Elmsford, N.Y.), 3*(1).

Tahmincioglu, E. (2008). First Stop: Second Life. *Business Week: Small Biz,* 41-45.

Tavanti, M., & Lind, M. (2001). *2D vs 3D, implications on spatial memory*. Paper presented at the IEEE Symposium on Information Visualization (INFOVIS 2001).

Tufte, E. (1983). *The Visual Display of Quantitative Information*. Cheshire, CT: Graphics Press.

van der Aalst, W. M. P., & ter Hofstede, A. H. M. (2005). YAWL: Yet Another Workflow Language. *Information Systems, 30*(4), 245–275. doi:10.1016/j.is.2004.02.002

van der Aalst, W. M. P., & van Hee, K. (2004). *Workflow Management Models, Methods, and Systems*. Boston: MIT Press.

Weber, B., & Reichert, M. U. (2008). Refactoring Process Models in Large Process Repositories. In *20th Int'l Conf. on Advanced Information Systems Engineering (CAiSE '08)* (pp. 124-139). Montpellier, France: Springer Verlag.

Wolfgang, M.-W., Reginald, J., Meehae, S., Jochen, Q., Haibin, W., & Yongmin, Z. (2002). Best modeling methods: virtual factory: highly interactive visualisation for manufacturing. In *Proceedings of the 34th conference on Winter simulation: exploring new frontiers*. San Diego, CA: Winter Simulation Conference.

Zhao, H., & Cao, J. (2007). A business process simulation environment based on workflow and multi-agent. In Industrial Engineering and Engineering Management (pp. 1777-1781).

Section 2
Virtual Technologies in Manufacturing Sector

Chapter 5
A Virtual Environment for Machining Operations Simulation and Machining Evaluation

Bilalis Nicolaos
Technical University of Crete, Greece

Petousis Markos
Technological Educational Institute of Crete, Greece

ABSTRACT

A virtual reality machine shop environment has been developed capable of simulating the operation of a three axis milling machine and it has been integrated with a graphical model for the calculation of quantitative data affecting the machined surface roughness. The model determines the machined surface topomorphy as a cloud of points, retrieved from the visualization system Z buffer. The current study describes the developed model for milling processes simulation in a virtual environment and the determination of the surface roughness of the processed surfaces. Also, the methodology for the verification of the quantitative data acquired by the system is presented. Results were verified with data determined in cutting experiments and by another numerical model that was integrated to the system.

INTRODUCTION

Contemporary production processes design methods employ simulation tools, like Computer Aided Manufacturing (CAM) systems and tools for determining critical quantitative data for the production processes. Most CAM systems have trivial graphics capabilities, visualizing the work-piece and a simplified geometrical model of the cutter but most importantly they have significant restrictions, such as the lack of production process parameters (depth of cut, feed, cutter wear, etc.) verification and quantitative data determination. These parameters affect the quality and the feasibility of the production process. Quantitative data, like the cutting forces and the surface roughness (Ko et al., 2003) are critical in the production process design (Zaman et al., 2006). Production

DOI: 10.4018/978-1-61520-631-5.ch005

processes quantitative data determination tools are based on analytical, numerical or experimental algorithms. These tools are posses' limited visualization capabilities.

The proposed research aims at the development of a virtual environment capable of providing complete simulation and analysis of the machining operations, thus extending CAM systems' capabilities. The system integrates CAM system functionalities with machining processes quantitative data determination models and can be used as a machining processes verification tool. A virtual environment for machining and other machine shop processes simulation was developed within a Virtual Reality platform, in order to provide higher level visualization, walk/fly through and interaction capabilities. Information about the simulated machining operations is provided in real time. In the virtual environment at the beginning a three axes milling machine is simulated. Workpiece geometry produced during the machining process is predicted and visualized in real time. For the determination of critical machining processes quantitative data, a model was developed to assess the surface roughness of the machined surface. The model exploits OpenGL functionalities. The results determined by the model are being visualized in the virtual environment.

For the verification of the quantitative data acquired by the system a two step process was employed. First surface topomorphy is verified and then the calculated surface roughness parameters are evaluated. For the verification of the model results a numerical model, experimentally verified in the past has been integrated to the system in order to compare its results and directly evaluate their accuracy. The accuracy of the model has also been verified with results determined in cutting experiments. The results were found to be in agreement with both the numerical model and the experiments. The verification process and its results are presented in the current study.

LITERATURE REVIEW

Virtual Environments for Surface Roughness Determination

Huang and Oliver (1994) developed a system for machining processes simulation in a five axes CNC machine. The system aims at the improvement of the workpiece machined surface quality by improving the cutter path. Ko et. al. (2003) developed a Virtual Manufacturing system for the determination of optimum feedrate values in 2.5 axis machining processes that provides the ability to determine cutting forces in order to improve the machined surface quality. Qui et al. (2001) and Ong et al. (2002) presented a system developed in VRML for material removal simulation. The system provides information about the required time for the completion of the machining process and quantitative data like the cutting forces, machined surface roughness, required energy and cutter wear. Bowyer et al. (1996) developed a simulation system for several types of machining operations that could be employed for design, modeling and implementation of production plans in the virtual environment, aiming at errors detection in the executed operations.

Generalized Models for Milling Process Simulation

Antoniadis et al. (2003) presented a model for surface roughness determination. In this model the workpiece is being modeled with vertical linear segments. As the cutter moves along the machining process trajectory, linear segments decrease their height to the lowest intersection position with the cutter edges. At the end of the simulation, linear segments vertices define the final machined surface. The model was experimentally verified and the calculated roughness levels were found to be in agreement with the experimental ones. This model has also been integrated in the proposed environment for the verification of the proposed graphical model. Engin et al. (2001) proposed a generalized mathematical model for predicting cutting forces, vibrations, dimensional surface finish and stability lobes in milling. The model is based in the mathematical modeling of the cutter with helical flutes defined in a parametric volume. Liu et al. (2005) developed a model for the determination of peripheral milling dynamic parameters. The geometry and kinematics of the cutter are considered for the determination of the machined surface, from which surface roughness is being calculated.

Models for Surface Roughness Determination in Milling Processes

Several analytical methods have been presented for surface roughness parameters determination in milling processes (Lou et al., 1999; Alauddin et al., 1995; Wang, & Chang, 2003; Benardos, & Vosniakos, 2002; Tseng et al., 2005; Baek et al., 2001). These methods are considering the cutting speed, the feed, the depth of cut and vibrations as parameters and employ mathematical equations, such as the multiple regression equation (Lou et al., 1999) for the determination of the surface roughness parameters. Tseng et al. (2005) state that in conventional metal removal processes an exact prediction of surface roughness is difficult to achieve, due to the stochastic nature of the machining processes and they propose the use of a data mining technique for predicting acceptable machined parts, rather than focusing on the calculation of precise surface roughness values.

The Use of OpenGL for the Determination of Machining Processes Quantitative Data

Kim et al. (2000) presented a model for cutting forces determination in ball-end milling of sculptured surfaces. For cutting forces calculation, chip thickness has to be determined from the contact area between the cutter and the workpiece. The contact area is determined from the Z-map of the surface geometry and the current cutter position. Roth et al. (2003) presented a model for the calculation of cutting forces in milling processes, which is based of an adaptive and local depth buffer. This methos allows the depth buffer to be sized to the tool as opposed to workpiece and thus improves the depth buffer size accuracy ratio drastically.

VIRTUAL ENVIRONMENT FOR MACHINING PROCESSES SIMULATION

Virtual Environment for Machining Processes Simulation Structure

For the development of the environment, the PTC Division developer toolkit and ANSI C programming language were employed. In the developed environment a machine shop is being visualized and the functional characteristics of a three axes CNC milling machine are being simulated. Virtual Research V6 Head Mounted Display, Polhemus Fastrack tracking system and 5th DT 16 data glove were integrated to the system for the immersion of the user to the virtual environment. A 3D Magellan Spacemouse is being used in order to facilitate the movement of the user in the virtual environment when the system is used in desktop mode. The integration of a 3d glasses set is expected shortly.

For the development of the system the geometrical models of the environment were produced with the use of Computer Aided Design (CAD) and dynamic geometry (polygons) tools. The machine shop building, the machines, the cutters and the environment parts where drafted with the use of Pro Engineer. Workpiece geometrical model is defined with the use of virtual environment dynamic geometry tools that provide the ability to modify the geometrical model shape in real time. The use of

Figure 1. Structure of the virtual environment for machining processes simulation

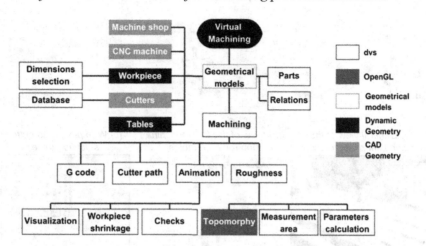

dynamic geometry is necessary, in order to visualize machining processes simulation. The material removal is visualized by modifying workpiece polygon vertices coordinates, according to cutter position in real time. Other environment objects, like 3d text and graphs were also developed with the use of appropriate virtual environment dynamic geometry tools. After the geometry was defined in the virtual environment, attributes were given to the three dimensional objects. A hierarchy between the geometrical models was build, constraints, interaction and collision attributes were defined.

A model for the determination of quantitative data related to the machined surface roughness has been developed and integrated in the virtual environment. The model determines the machined surface topomorphy and calculates the values of critical surface roughness parameters, such as the R_a, R_y, R_{ti}, R_z. The overall structure of the virtual environment for machining processes simulation is shown in *Figure 1*.

Virtual Environment for Machining Processes Simulation Functional Characteristics

The virtual environment for machining processes simulation is shown in *Figure 2a, b*. The system

interface was integrated in the virtual environment and is presented with three dimensional geometrical models. The user can fly trough, interact with all the objects and manually manipulate the CNC machine. For the execution of a machining process, the user has to select workpiece dimensions from the corresponding data table (*Figure 2c*). Workpiece is automatically installed on the CNC machine worktable. Then the user has to select cutter from the corresponding data table (*Figure 2c*). The G code program is being read from its file and the CNC machine executes the defined machining process. CNC machine axes move realistically according to the path and the feed defined in the program and spindle revolves with the predefined speed. During machining process simulation, workpiece material removal is being visualized when the cutter intersects the workpiece and data related to the process are being visualized (*Figure 2d*). Moreover, information like the G code command simulated in the CNC machine, feed, spindle speed and cutter path are visualized in a data table (*Figure 2e*). The user can fly through the environment during simulation to inspect the material removal process from different perspectives and pause, stop or restart the machining process. When the simulation is completed, quantitative data for the machining process

Figure 2. Virtual Environment for machining processes simulation

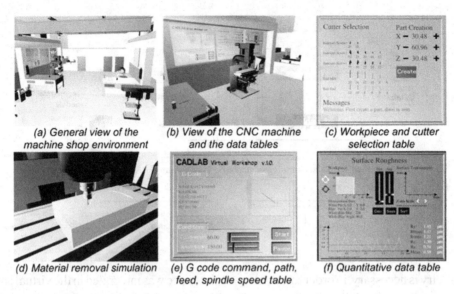

(a) General view of the machine shop environment

(b) View of the CNC machine and the data tables

(c) Workpiece and cutter selection table

(d) Material removal simulation

(e) G code command, path, feed, spindle speed table

(f) Quantitative data table

can be determined and visualized, according to user preferences (*Figure 2f*). Then user is able to select the surface roughness measurement area in the equivalent virtual environment data table and hence acquire quantitative data for surface roughness parameters and the measurement area topomorphy. This information is shown in the same data table of the virtual environment. Finally, in this data table the entire machined surface topomorphy can be visualized as a three dimensional model, that can inspected from different perspectives, due to the free movement capabilities of the user in the environment.

SURFACE ROUGHNESS THEORY

Surface roughness in machining is a parameter related to the geometrical characteristics of the abnormalities produced by the cutter in the machined surface. The size, shape and topomorphy of these abnormalities depend on (Tsai et al., 1999; Michigan Tech web site), machining parameters like, the cutting speed, feed, cutting depth, geometrical characteristics of the cutter, such as the

cutter nose radius, rake angle, side cutting edge angle and cutting edge geometry, workpiece and tool material combination and their mechanical properties, quality and type of the cutter, jigs, fixtures and lubricant used and vibrations between the cutter and the workpiece.

Surface roughness is considered to be an important parameter in machining as it affects surface quality and product functional characteristics, since good surface roughness (Machinery's Handbook 26th edition, 1995) reduces friction on the machined surface, increases product wear resistance, improves product appearance and improves mechanisms functionality.

There are several parameters for surface roughness measurement that provide different information for the measured surface. It is measured in areas of the machined surface, selected by the user and measurements refer only to the selected area. Thus, in a machined surface, a number of measurements must be performed in more than one area. Usually linear or radial measurements are taken. Linear measurements are performed in line or vertical to the feed direction for a specific distance. Radial measurements are performed around a fixed point for a specific angle. The most critical surface roughness parameters are (Thomas, 1999):

- **Mean line**: for a specific topomorphy expressed with a y(x) function, mean line intersects y(x) so that the area between y(x) and mean line is equal over and below the mean line.
- **R_a**: Mean surface roughness parameter, expressed, for a y(x) function, with the following formula: $R_a = \int\limits_0^L |y(x)|\, dx$
- **R_y**: The distance between the lowest and the highest point of the measured surface profile.
- **R_{ti}**: The measured surface profile is divided into equal parts (usually five). R_{ti} is the distance between the lowest and the highest point for each part.
- **R_z**: Is the mean value of the R_{ti}: $R_z = \dfrac{\left(R_{t1} + R_{t2} + \ldots + R_{tn}\right)}{n} = \dfrac{1}{n}\sum_{i=1}^{n} R_{ti}$

MODEL FOR SURFACE ROUGHNESS QUANTITATIVE DATA DETERMINATION IN MACHINING

Determination of the Machined Surface Topomorphy

The model for the determination of the machined surface topomorphy (Bilalis, & Petousis, 2008) was implemented in a three dimensional graphics environment developed in OpenGL *Figure 3*. In the model the cutter motion relative to the workpiece is being simulated according to cutting conditions defined in the G code file. These conditions are the tool path, the spindle speed in rpm and the feed in mm/min. During simulation the cutter sweep surface is calculated, by determining cutting edges sweep surface. From the cutting

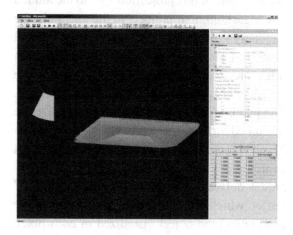

Figure 3. OpenGL machining processes simulation environment for machined surface topomorphy determination

edges sweep surface the machined surface of the process is determined.

For the determination of cutting edges sweep surface during machining simulation, the cutter is being modeled, according to the shape and number of its cutting edges. Cutting edges shape is defined from the outer edge profile of each cutting edge, which defines the overall cutter profile. Each cutting edge is being differentiated in equal elementary segments that could be considered as straight lines. The number of segments for the differentiation of the cutting edge is being chosen in the software interface. The cutter path relative to the workpiece is also being differentiated. The cutter is being successively placed in the differentiated path positions, according to the cutting conditions (spindle speed, feed). In each position the sweep surface of each elementary section is determined. The sweep surface of a cutting edge is determined by the sweep surface of all its elementary sections.

The produced sweep surface of each cutting edge is approximated by triangles. In the sweep surface there are overlapping triangles, since part of each cutting edge sweep is being overlapped by the next cutting edge sweep or the next cutter pass sweep. If the cutter sweep surface is projected from its down side, the final machined surface topomorphy is derived, since the overlapped geometry is not visible in this projection, due to the hidden line algorithm, that projects to the user only the geometry visible in each point of view. This final machined surface topomorphy is derived from this projection in the form of cloud of points. The coordinates for the cloud of points are determined. The pixels within workpiece limits visualize the machined surface. These pixels are converted into X and Y coordinates in the graphics environment coordinate system. For these pixels the Z coordinate is derived from the visualization system Z buffer, which provides the distance between the camera and the object visualized in each pixel. In surface roughness parameters determination, the difference between the lowest and the highest edge on a surface profile is considered, so this value for the Z coordinate is suitable. Calculations for surface roughness parameters are being performed in a transformed coordinate system, which is locally defined in the surface profile. The cloud of points coordinates describing the machined surface topomorphy are exported in a text file and they are used to calculate quantitative parameters for the machined surface roughness.

Calculation and Visualization of Surface Roughness Parameters

When the machine surface topomorphy is determined, it is feasible to determine surface roughness parameters. In real environments surface roughness measurements are carried out in surface regions, selected by the user. In the proposed system this procedure is being simulated in the virtual environment. A data table was developed in the virtual environment for surface roughness quantitative data visualization (*Figure 4*). On the upper left part of the table the measurement area on the workpiece machined surface is defined by the user with the use of a specially developed handler. User defines the position of each handler end. Handler ends define surface roughness measurement area

limits. The handler defines a vertical plane to the machined surface, in which topomorphy will be determined and surface roughness parameters will be calculated from this topomorphy.

For surface roughness parameters determination, cloud points on the vertical measurement plane or in a small width distance from the plane are retrieved from the file. This is necessary because the direction for measurement is randomly selected, so the number of topomorphy cloud points exactly on the measurement plane may be small and as a result surface roughness parameters calculation accuracy could be decreased.

The system calculates surface roughness parameters such as R_a, R_y, R_{ti}, R_z and surface topomorphy mean line. For the calculation of these parameters, the points retrieved from the cloud in the previous step are used. In the quantitative data table, surface topomorphy and mean line are visualized in a specially developed graph and also surface parameter values are shown. The user has the ability to create a machining process report in the form of a text file. In the machining process report file surface roughness data for the measurement region are stored and could be acquired for further use. This process can be repeated in any other region of the machined surface.

Test Case

In order to acquire results from the system, the user has to select workpiece and cutter in the virtual environment. Then, cutter path has to be produced in the form of differentiated points in a text file. This file is opened in the OpenGL machined surface topomorphy determination software tool. Machining process is simulated in the OpenGL environment and surface topomorphy is exported as a cloud of points in a text file. This file is being read in the virtual environment, to visualize surface topomorphy graph and subsequently calculate surface roughness parameter values for the measurement area the user selects.

Figure 4. Virtual environment quantitative data table

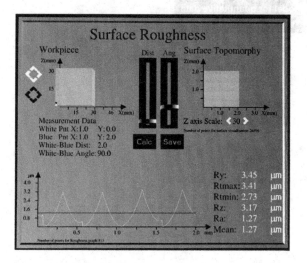

When the machining process simulation is finished in the virtual environment, workpiece appears in the quantitative data table (*Figure 4*). On top of the workpiece there is the handler for measurement area determination. The handler can alter size, position and orientation on a horizontal plane within the workpiece limits. Handler ends defining measurement area, are positioned either by direct interaction with its geometrical models or by the sliding handlers in the quantitative data table. When the measurement area is defined, by pressing "Calc" button, surface topomorphy appears in the corresponding graph. In the surface topomorphy graph mean line is shown (as a horizontal blue line). The system calculates surface roughness parameters for this topomorphy and shows their values in the quantitative data table (*Figure 4*). The user can move the handler (change its position, orientation or length) and the quantitative data for each position are calculated and shown on the table. This feature is necessary since in real surface roughness measurements usually the profiler contact element is placed in a position and measures roughness radically at a fixed radius for a specific angle (usually 180 or 360 degrees).

The system provides a feature for the creation of a machining report in the form of a text file. The system calculates and stores in this report data related to the G code file being used for simulation, the selected cutter, the selected workpiece and surface roughness parameter values for the measurement position.

By pressing the "Surf" button, the entire machined surface topomorphy defined in the cloud of points is being visualized in the virtual environment quantitative data table (*Figure 4*).

Model Verification

In this section the process for the verification of the developed surface roughness quantitative data determination model is described. The process is shown in *Figure 5* (Bilalis et al., 2009).

The results acquired by the model were verified with the experimentally verified machining simulation numerical model MSN (Milling Simulation by Needles) (Antoniadis et al., 2003) and data from experiments. The results were verified in a two steps process. First the machined surface topomorphy accuracy is validated and then the calculated parameter values are being directly compared. To accomplish that, the MSN model was integrated in the OpenGL software. This process provides direct control on model results, when conducting experiments is not possible. Moreover, a wide variety of cutting experiments was implemented to directly quantitatively and qualitatively verify the model results.

Verification with the MSN Model

The MSN model is used mainly to mathematically verify the machined surface topomorphy determined with the presented model. Moreover, surface roughness parameters values calculated with the MSN model were compared with values calculated with the presented model for identical cutting cases.

Figure 5. Quantitative data determination model verification process

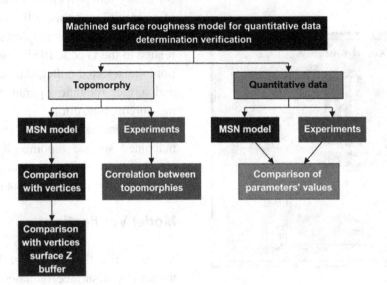

The MSN milling simulation model is being executed simultaneously with the model developed in the current study. The final machined surface is being determined with two different clouds of points, linear segments vertices and Z buffer values for the pixels within workpiece limits representing the lowest cutter sweep surface. Since both models are executed simultaneously during the machining process simulation, the two clouds of points are formed with the same cutting conditions. The machined surface determination method and the density of the workpiece discretization are different between the two models. In the MSN model the density of the workpiece discretization is determined by the number of linear segments used for the workpiece modeling. In the developed model the workpiece discretization depends on the selected zoom level during the machined surface clouds of points' formation and storage.

For the verification of the presented model, the two clouds of points are compared. The comparison aims at the determination of the Z buffer accuracy with respect to a mathematical method. Due to different workpiece discretization in the two models, Z coordinates are compared for vertices and pixels respectively having similar X and Y coordinates. For the comparison of the two clouds of points, first the discretization step in X and Y direction is determined for both clouds. From the discretization step, points with similar X and Y coordinates from both clouds are determined. For these points Z coordinate is transformed to the same coordinate system. This is necessary, since linear segment vertices Z coordinates provide the value of workpiece Z dimension at each point, while Z buffer values provide the distance between the respective pixel and the camera. Z coordinates are compared for the respective points. At each workpiece position the difference and the difference percentage are calculated. Finally, the maximum difference and difference percentage in Z direction are calculated for the two clouds of points.

The accuracy of the comparison method depends on the discretization step in the clouds of points, since, as the density of the clouds increases, the compared points are closer and the accuracy of the comparison is higher. A difference in the Z coordinate is expected since the compared points are not in the exact same position.

The second verification determines the accuracy of the cutter sweep surface. For this verification, a surface is defined by the linear segment vertices. This surface is being stored with the same method as the cutter sweep surface that is a cloud of points produced using the Z buffer. This cloud of points is compared with the cutter sweep surface cloud of points by directly comparing the Z coordinate of every pixel. Since both clouds of points in this verification are produced with the same method and at the exact same position and zoom level, the difference between them shows the level of accuracy of the machined surface determined with the current study model.

A software tool was developed, according to the described comparison methodology, for the verification of the presented model results with the MSN numerical model. The average deviation between the linear segments cloud and the cutter sweep surface cloud was 3%. The average deviation between the surface produced with the needles vertices and the cutter sweep surface cloud was 0.05%. In *Figure 6*, for the same machining operation, surface topomorphy defined by the MSN model and by the Z buffer is shown in isosurface mode with color scale, to facilitate evaluation.

The MSN model calculates the average value of surface roughness parameters (R_t, R_z) for the whole determined topomorphy in each cutting case. These values were correlated with equivalent surface roughness parameters values calculated with the presented model. The average deviation between these values was 3%.

Verification with Experimental Data

Surface roughness results acquired from the system were compared with experimental data to directly verify the developed model. A cutting case was defined. The cutting case part and its production process were designed in a CAD/CAM system. The part was manufactured with a ball-end tool with one cutting edge and different cutting conditions in CNC milling machine, using the G code file produced by the CAM system. The G code file used for the part manufacture

Figure 6. Machined surface topomorphy

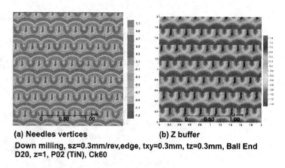

(a) Needles vertices   (b) Z buffer

Down milling, sz=0.3mm/rev,edge, txy=0.3mm, tz=0.3mm, Ball End D20, z=1, P02 (TiN), Ck60

was imported in the virtual environment for the simulation of the process, in order to ensure that the real and the virtual experiment have identical cutting parameters.

The pocket geometry of the cutting case part was constructed several times with different cutting conditions (up/down milling, change of feed, step over and depth of cut). To construct the pocket geometry, a circular trajectory was followed in all cases. The number of passes in each iteration is determined according to the step over parameter value, defined in the cutting conditions.

For the verification of the model results, machined surface topomorphy produced by the computational model was compared with the experimental topomorphy. *Figure 7* shows a typical correlation performed between the computational and the experimental results for two different cutting conditions. The left image of this figure shows the experimental topomorphy. The middle and the right image of the same figure shows the computationally produced surface topomorphy, in two different ways, in isosurface form and in 3D form. The correlation between the experimental and the computational results exhibits that the topomorphies are in good agreement, considering that there are parameters that could not be taken into account in the developed computational model.

In order to verify the quantitative data the presented model calculates, its results were compared with equivalent data determined in

Figure 7. Comparison between the experimental and the determined surface topomorphy

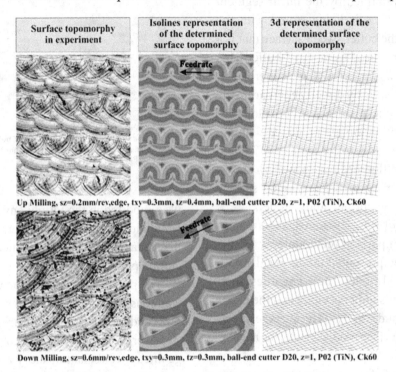

Surface topomorphy in experiment	Isolines representation of the determined surface topomorphy	3d representation of the determined surface topomorphy

Up Milling, sz=0.2mm/rev,edge, txy=0.3mm, tz=0.4mm, ball-end cutter D20, z=1, P02 (TiN), Ck60

Down Milling, sz=0.6mm/rev,edge, txy=0.3mm, tz=0.3mm, ball-end cutter D20, z=1, P02 (TiN), Ck60

the experiment. For each cutting condition in the experiment, roughness measurements were taken inside the pocket geometry of the part vertically to the feed direction, in four different areas in the trajectory. In each area measurements were taken in measurement planes with length 5mm. In *Figure 8* calculated surface roughness parameters values are compared with the equivalent values measured in the experiment for different cutting conditions. Results from the virtual environment and the experiment are in good agreement, considering that some parameters affecting surface roughness are not taken into account in the developed computational model. As it is shown in the *Figure 8*, in down milling experimental values are closer to the calculated ones. In up milling the deviation between the experimental and the calculated values is higher than in down milling. This is due to the fact that in up milling there are more vibrations than in down milling and, since vibrations are not considered in the computational model, the deviation between the experimental and the

calculated values in up milling is higher. There are more vibrations in up milling than in down milling, because in down milling cutting forces act in a direction towards the milling machine table, making the workpiece more stable than in up milling where cutting forces act in a direction opposite to the milling machine table, as they where trying to lift the workpiece from the table, making it less stable.

DISCUSSION

The presented research exploits existing computing tools, such as the PTC Division developer toolkit, ANSI C and OpenGL for the implementation of the developed machining processes simulation model. In this model different algorithms for CAM integration, cutter trajectory determination, material removal visualization, machining process simulation and machined surface roughness

Figure 8. Comparison of the calculated surface roughness parameters values with the equivalent values measured in the experiment

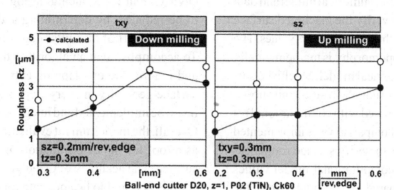

quantitative data determination were developed and integrated.

The research is focused mainly at the determination of quantitative data related to the machined surface roughness. A new model was developed for the determination of the machined surface topomorphy from the cutter sweep surface, exploiting OpenGL functionalities. The accuracy of the surface roughness results acquired by the system depends on the accuracy of the surface topomorphy determination model and the density of the cloud of points.

The accuracy of the surface topomorphy is influenced by the cutter model and trajectory discretization density, the hidden lines algorithm employed by the system and the projection type used for three dimensional graphics visualization. OpenGL built in hidden line algorithm is used. Regarding the projection type, orthographic and perspective projection is supported. Orthographic projection is used, because in perspective projection objects are deformed to create the sense of depth to the user and, since in the developed model data related to every pixel within the workpiece limits are acquired from the graphics card Z buffer, errors can arise during the storage of the machined surface cloud of points, because of the deformed visualization. The projection position and angle also affect the accuracy of the developed model, because they influence the Z buffer accuracy. The

accuracy of the Z buffer depends on projection parameters such as the horizontal and vertical distance between the camera and the surface, the field of view and the position of the near and the far clipping planes. Better Z buffer accuracy is achieved when znear plane is not close to the camera, objects are close to the znear plane and the distance between the znear and the zfar plane is small (Steve Baker, 2003). Z buffer is employed in the presented model for the determination of the machined surface triangles vertices coordinates, so it is critical to acquire the most accurate data from Z buffer, in order to determine more accurate surface roughness parameters values. Several executions of the model has shown that, when each of these parameters is in a certain range of values, the difference in the cloud points coordinates is negligible, so a set of values was selected for all machining simulations. Finally, machined surface topomorphy accuracy is influenced by the density of the cloud of points. To overcome screen pixel resolution limitations, the machined surface is zoomed on the screen in the measurement area, which usually has 5mm length as in real surface roughness measurements. The cloud of points is produced for this zoomed view, which means that for 1280X1024 screen resolution a cloud with almost 700000 points for the measurement area is produced. A cloud of points is produced in this way for each measurement area.

Regarding the verification processes followed, they employ an existing numerical model and data from experiments to verify the machined surface topomorphy and roughness parameters values. The machined surface topomorphy is mathematically verified with the numerical model. Machined surface topomorphy experimental results could not be mathematically compared with computational results, so a qualitative comparison was implemented in this case. In order to verify surface roughness parameters values, computational model values were directly compared with values from the numerical model and experiments for identical cutting conditions. Due to the stochastic nature of the machining processes (Tseng et al., 2005), average values from several measurements for both the computational model and the experiment were calculated for the comparison. According to the verification method followed, the results of the model have adequate accuracy, however some factors related to the verification process and the model need to be further discussed.

CONCLUSION

One of the aims of this research was the evaluation of the virtual environment as a machining processes simulation tool. Functionality for achieving an exact representation of reality is still missing from the developed virtual environment, but the comprehension of what is actually being carried out in the real world is improved. Because of the open architecture of the environment, it could be extended in the future in order to provide enhanced approximation of the real machine shop environment.

In the developed quantitative data determination model a new approach has been presented that exploits OpenGL functionalities. In future versions of the quantitative data determination model some issues have to be addressed in order to optimize the performance of the algorithm. It has

been identified that the information the OpenGL environment is producing during simulation has to be reduced, by determining and storing only the lower part of the cutter edges sweep surface. To accomplish that an algorithm that determines and ignores the overlapping cutter edges sweep surface geometry in every step of the simulation has to be implemented and integrated to the model. Overall, the model aims at evaluating the OpenGL as a tool for the determination of the machined surface. The accuracy of OpenGL for such applications is found to be adequate for small parts or regions of the part with dimensions within some limits. These size limits though are sufficient for surface roughness measurements.

The model is been verified with another numerical model the MSN (Antoniadis et al. 2003) and also with experimental results. Although the verification method followed does not completely confront the stochastic behavior of machining processes, it showed that the results acquired by the system are in agreement with both the employed numerical model and the experimental results, making the model suitable for integration in production design processes.

ACKNOWLEDGMENT

The project is co-funded by the European Social Fund and National Resources – EPEAEK II -IRAKLITOS

REFERENCES

Alauddin, M., Baradie, M. A., & Hashmi, M. S. J. (1995). Computer Aided analysis of a surface roughness model for end milling. Materials Processing Technology, 55, 123–127. doi:10.1016/0924-0136(95)01795-Xdoi:10.1016/0924-0136(95)01795-X

Antoniadis, A., Savakis, C., Bilalis, N., & Balouksis, A. (2003). Prediction of surface topomorphy and roughness in ball end milling. Advanced Manufacturing Technology, 21, 965–971. doi:10.1007/s00170-002-1418-8doi:10.1007/s00170-002-1418-8

Baek, D. K., Ko, T. J., & Kim, H. S. (2001). Optimization of feedrate in a face milling operation using a surface roughness model. Machine Tools and Manufacture, 41, 451–462. doi:10.1016/S0890-6955(00)00039-0doi:10.1016/S0890-6955(00)00039-0

Baker, S. (n.d.). *Learning to Love your Z-buffer*. Retrieved from http://www.sjbaker.org/steve/omniv/love_your_z_buffer.html

Benardos, P. G., & Vosniakos, G. C. (2002). Prediction of surface roughness in CNC face milling using neural networks and Taguchi's design of experiments. Robotics and Computer-integrated Manufacturing, 18(5-6), 343–354. doi:10.1016/S0736-5845(02)00005-4doi:10.1016/S0736-5845(02)00005-4

Bilalis, N., & Petousis, M., (2008). Development of a virtual environment for surface topomorphy and roughness determination in milling operations. *Transactions of the ASME, Journal of Computing and Information Science in Engineering, Special Issue Advances in Computer Aided Manufacturing, 8*(2).

Bilalis, N., Petousis, M., & Antoniadis, A. (2009). Model for surface roughness parameters determination in a virtual machine shop environment. International Journal of Advanced Manufacturing Technology, 40(11), 1137–1147. doi:10.1007/s00170-008-1441-5doi:10.1007/s00170-008-1441-5

Bowyer, A., Bayliss, G., Taylor, R., & Willis, P. (1996). A virtual factory. *International Journal of shape modeling, 2*(4), 215-226.

Engin, S., & Altintas, Y. (2001). Mechanics and dynamics of general milling cutters. Part I: helical end mills. Machine Tools and Manufacture, 41, 2195–2212. doi:10.1016/S0890-6955(01)00045-1doi:10.1016/S0890-6955(01)00045-1

Engin, S., & Altintas, Y. (2001). Mechanics and dynamics of general milling cutters. Part II: Inserted cutters. Machine Tools and Manufacture, 41, 2213–2231. doi:10.1016/S0890-6955(01)00046-3doi:10.1016/S0890-6955(01)00046-3

Huang, Y., & Oliver, J. H. (1994). NC milling error assessment and tool path correction. In *International Conference on Computer Graphics and Interactive Techniques, Proceedings of the 21st annual conference on Computer graphics and interactive techniques* (pp. 287 – 294).

Kim, G. M., Cho, P. J., & Chu, C. N. (2000). Cutting force prediction of sculptured surface ball-end milling using Z-map. Machine Tools and Manufacture, 40(2), 277–291. doi:10.1016/S0890-6955(99)00040-1doi:10.1016/S0890-6955(99)00040-1

Ko, J. H., Yun, W. S., & Cho, D. W. (2003). Off-line feed rate scheduling using virtual CNC based on an evaluation of cutting performance. CAD, 35, 383–393.

Liu, X., & Cheng, K. (2005). Modeling the machining dynamics in peripheral milling. Machine Tools and Manufacture, 45, 1301–1320. doi:10.1016/j.ijmachtools.2005.01.019doi:10.1016/j.ijmachtools.2005.01.019

Lou, M. S., Chen, J. C., & Li, C. M. (1999). Surface Roughness prediction technique for CNC End Milling. Industrial Technology, 15(1), 1–6.

(1995). Machinery's Handbook (26th ed.). New York: Industrial Press, Inc.

Michigan Tech Web Site. (n.d.). Retrieved from http://www.mfg.mtu.edu/cyberman/quality/sfinish/terminology.html

Ong, S. K., Jiang, L., & Nee, A. Y. C. (2002). An Internet Based Virtual CNC Milling System. Advanced Manufacturing Technology, 20, 20–30. doi:10.1007/s001700200119doi:10.1007/s001700200119

Qiu, Z. M., Chen, Y. P., Zhou, Z. D., Ong, S. K., & Nee, A. Y. C. (2001). Multi User NC Machining Simulation over the Web. Advanced Manufacturing Technology, 18, 1–6. doi:10.1007/PL00003949doi:10.1007/PL00003949

Roth, D., Ismail, F., & Bedi, S. (2003). Mechanistic modeling of the milling process using an adaptive depth buffer. CAD, 35(14), 1287–1303.

Thomas, T. R. (1999). Rough Surfaces (2nd ed.). New York: Imperial College Press.

Tsai, Y. H., Chen, J. C., & Lou, S. J. (1999). In-process surface recognition system based on neural networks in end milling cutting operations. International Journal of Machine Tools & Manufacture, 39(4), 583–605. doi:10.1016/S0890-6955(98)00053-4doi:10.1016/S0890-6955(98)00053-4

Tseng, T. L., Kwon, Y., & Ertekin, M. (2005). Feature based rule induction in machining operation using rough set theory for quality assurance. Robotics and Computer-integrated Manufacturing, 21, 559–567. doi:10.1016/j.rcim.2005.01.001doi:10.1016/j.rcim.2005.01.001

Wang, M. Y., & Chang, H. Y. (2003). Experimental study of surface roughness in slot end milling AL2014-T6. Machine Tools and Manufacture, 20, 1–7.

Zaman, M. T., Senthil Kumar, A., Rahman, M., & Sreeram, S. (2006). A three-dimensional analytical cutting force model for micro end milling operation. International Journal of Machine Tools & Manufacture, 46(3-4), 353–366. doi:10.1016/j.ijmachtools.2005.05.021doi:10.1016/j.ijmachtools.2005.05.021

ADDITIONAL READING

Baeka, D. K., Kob, T. J., & Kim, H. S. (2006). Chip volume prediction using a numerical control verification model. International Journal of Machine Tools & Manufacture, 46, 1326–1335. doi:10.1016/j.ijmachtools.2005.10.011doi:10.1016/j.ijmachtools.2005.10.011

Blackmore, D., Leu, M. C., & Wang, L. (1997). The sweep envelope differential equation algorithm and its application to NC machining verification. CAD, 29(9), 629–637.

Chryssolouris, G., Mavrikios, D., Fragos, D., Karabatsou, V., & Pistiolis, K. (2002). A novel virtual experimentation approach to planning and training for manufacturing processes-the virtual machine shop. International Journal of Computer Integrated Manufacturing, 15(3), 214–221. doi:10.1080/0951 1920110034978doi:10.1080/09511920110034978

Csaba, A., & Talaba, D. (2007). Design evaluation and modification of mechanical systems in virtual environments. Virtual Reality (Waltham Cross), 11, 275–285. doi:10.1007/s10055-007-0074-6doi:10.1007/s10055-007-0074-6

Ding, S., Mannan, M. A., & Poo, A. N. (2004). Oriented bounded box and octree based global interference detection in 5–axis machining of free-form surfaces. CAD, 36, 1281–1294.

Duffy, V. G., Ng, P. W., & Ramakrishnan, A. (2004). Impact of a simulated accident in virtual training on decision making performance. Industrial Ergonomics, 34, 335–348. doi:10.1016/j.ergon.2004.04.012doi:10.1016/j.ergon.2004.04.012

Fleisig, R. V., & Spence, A. D. (2005). Techniques for accelerating B-Rep based parallel machining simulation. CAD, 37, 1229–1240.

Jang, D., Kim, K., & Jung, J. (2000). Voxel-Based Virtual Multi-Axis Machining. Advanced Manufacturing Technology, 16, 709–713. doi:10.1007/s001700070022doi:10.1007/s001700070022

Jimeno, A., & Puerta, A. (2007). State of the art of the virtual reality applied to design and manufacturing processes. International Journal of Advanced Manufacturing Technology, 33, 866–874. doi:10.1007/s00170-006-0534-2doi:10.1007/s00170-006-0534-2

Li, H. Z., Liu, K., & Li, X. P. (2001). A new method for determining the undeformed chip thickness in milling. Materials Processing Technology, 113(1), 378–384. doi:10.1016/S0924-0136(01)00586-6doi:10.1016/S0924-0136(01)00586-6

Li, J. G., Zhao, H., Yao, Y. X., & Liu, C. Q. (2008). Off-line optimization on NC machining based on virtual machining. International Journal of Advanced Manufacturing Technology, 36, 908–917. doi:10.1007/s00170-006-0915-6doi:10.1007/s00170-006-0915-6

Lin, Y., & Shen, Y. L. (2004). Enhanced virtual machining for sculptured surfaces by integrating machine tool error models into NC machining simulation. Machine Tools and Manufacture, 44, 79–86. doi:10.1016/j.ijmachtools.2003.08.003doi:10.1016/j.ijmachtools.2003.08.003

Lo, C. C. (1999). Real Time generation and control of cutter path for 5 axis CNC machining. Machine Tools and Manufacture, 39, 471–478. doi:10.1016/S0890-6955(98)00040-6doi:10.1016/S0890-6955(98)00040-6

Mousavi, M., & Aziz, F. A. (2008). State of the art of haptic feedback in virtual reality in manufacturing. In *Proceedings - International Symposium on Information Technology 2008*, 3.

Peng, G., Wang, G., Liu, W., & Yu, H. (in press). A desktop virtual reality-based interactive modular fixture configuration design system. Computer Aided Design.

Peng, Q., Hall, F. R., & Lister, P. M. (2000). Application and evaluation of VR-based CAPP system. Materials processing. Technology (Elmsford, N.Y.), 107, 153–159.

Rai, J. K., & Xirouchakis, P. (2008). Finite element method based machining simulation environment for analyzing part errors induced during milling of thin-walled components. International Journal of Machine Tools & Manufacture, 48, 629–643. doi:10.1016/j.ijmachtools.2007.11.004doi:10.1016/j.ijmachtools.2007.11.004

Ratchev, S., Nikov, S., & Moualek, I. (2004). Material removal simulation of peripheral milling of thin wall low rigidity structures using FEA. Advances in Engineering Software, 35, 481–491. doi:10.1016/j.advengsoft.2004.06.011doi:10.1016/j.advengsoft.2004.06.011

Sun, S., Luo, L., Li, G., Zou, X., & Yang, J. (2008). The virtual simulation system of numerical control machining. *2008 International Workshop on Modelling, Simulation and Optimization*, 289-293.

Tian, S. J., Liu, W. H., Zhang, H., & Jia, C. Q. (2007). Research of VR-based 3D NC machining environment and key technology. Journal of System Simulation, 19(16), 3727–3730.

Tian, X., Deng, H., Fujishima, M., & Yamazaki, K. (2007). Quick 3D Modelling of Machining Environment by Means of On-machine Stereo Vision with Digital Decomposition. *Annals of the CIRP*, 56.

Wang, T. Y., Wang, G. F., Li, H. W., Lin, J. B., & Wu, Z. Y. (2002). Construction of a realistic scene in virtual turning based on a global illumination model and chip simulation. Materials Processing Technology, 129, 524–528. doi:10.1016/S0924-0136(02)00626-Xdoi:10.1016/S0924-0136(02)00626-X

Wang, W. J., Wang, T. Y., Fan, S. B., & Wang, W. Y. (2008). Research on material removal algorithm model in virtual milling process based on adaptive dynamic quadtrees algorithm. *Applied Mechanics and Materials, 10-12*, 822–827. doi:10.4028/www.scientific.net/AMM.10-12.822doi:10.4028/www.scientific.net/AMM.10-12.822

Yao, Y., Li, J., Lee, W. B., Cheung, C. F., & Yuan, Z. (2002). VMMC: A test bed for machining. *Computers in Industry, 47*, 255–268. doi:10.1016/S0166-3615(01)00153-1doi:10.1016/S0166-3615(01)00153-1

Zhang, I., Deng, J., & Chan, S. C. F. (2000). A next generation NC machining system based on an NC Feature Unit and Real Time tool path generation. *Advanced Manufacturing Technology, 16*, 889–901. doi:10.1007/s001700070007doi:10.1007/s001700070007

Chapter 6
Augmented Reality for Collaborative Assembly Design in Manufacturing Sector

Rui (Irene) Chen
The University of Sydney, Australia

Xiangyu Wang
The University of Sydney, Australia

Lei Hou
The University of Sydney, Australia

ABSTRACT

Some speculations regarding the current issues existing in current assembly work have been brought out in this chapter. The theoretical basis behind the idea that Augmented Reality systems could provide cognitive support and augmentation is established. Hence, this chapter analyses the foundations for assembly feasibility evaluation and discusses possible innovative ways to provide an efficient and robust solution for these problems of realism and efficiency in design and assembly processes. The proposed platform considers the multiple dependencies in different manufacturing sectors that allow the work to be conducted in a simultaneous way, rather than sequential order.

INTRODUCTION

For a typical machine, one may look inside and find that it consists of accessories, modules and parts which have to be combined and integrated to fulfill its function. As the last step of mechanical manufacture to satisfy the technical requirements, assembly also includes the relative works such as regulation of assembly accuracy, inspection of

DOI: 10.4018/978-1-61520-631-5.ch006

tolerance, test of integration, painting and package other than the pure combination of components. During the process, correctly guaranteeing the assembly precision of machine and components is one of the critical criteria determines the product quality. Before shaping the finished product, the traditional assembly of mechanical components is mainly on the basis of parameters deriving from assembly drawings or some business software such as CAD/CAM. Although being guaranteed a realization of strict assembly sequence and considerable assembly precision, such methods guided by assembly drawings or software also manifest their defects. Because of the lack of combination with the real environment, they can't provide a better understanding of different constrains and complicated plant environments in the real assembly circumstances while the after evaluation of assembly workload such as assembly cost, time consuming and hardship could not be easily commanded either. Moreover, concerning a large amount of components to be assembled, an obstacle to understand the assembly drawing between the designers and the assemblers has been introduced. Again, the repetitive assembly operation would also create a incorrect assembly because of the physical tiredness and the mental negligence. Accordingly, such a serious occlusion of information exchange greatly limits the development of the assembly level. To solve this problem, a concept of collaborative assembly design by using AR technology has been arisen, aiming at completing the interconnection of every character in the before-product period. This technology will allow designers, manufacturers and assemblers to collaborate in a distributed way.

This paper mainly focuses on a novel technology to evaluate mechanical assembly sequences, say, the Augmented Reality technology. Defined as the combination of the real and virtual scene, such a technology has been widely used in areas such as product maintenance (Feiner & MacIntyre & Seligmann, 1993), manufacturing (Curtis & Mizell & Gruenbaum & Janin, 1998; Sims, 1994), training (Back, 2001), battlefield (Urban, 1995; Metzger, 1993), medicine (Mellor, 1995; Uenohara & Kanade, 1995), and so on (Pope, 1994). Comparing with Virtual Reality (VR) which aims at totally mimicking the real world into the synthetic virtual perception according to the help of computer and separates the real and virtual environment, AR maintains a sense of presence in the real world and balances the perception of real and virtual world. With the help of a see-through head-mounted device, a data glove and

a tracking system, the virtual components can be placed in the real one which can be seen from the head-mounted device. Wearing eyeglasses which are also called the HMD, an operator manipulates the virtual components directly and superimposes them on the real ones with the whole process can be seen from the HMD. Besides, during the operation process of integrating the virtual objects, the operator will detect the real interferences coming from the real objects and the ambient environment that would delay the assembly schedule or need to be further modified. What is more, because of the feedback of other "non-situated" elements like recorded voice, animation, replayed video, short tips, arrows, it could simultaneously guide the operators through the whole assembly operation, release their tension and even notify an error assembly (Raghavan & Molineros & Sharma, 1999). This way, the reality being perceived is augmented. In AR, two noticeable key techniques have to be mentioned. They are the generation of assembly sequence and the superimposition of virtual objects.

The planner, a key component in the system for creating the assembly sequence and reducing the impractical or impossible subsequences while manipulating the real and virtual prototype components in an assembly environment, allows an operator to cooperate with using the assembly graph which is also called the liaison graph (Molineros, 2002). The generation and the decrease of assembly sequence are coming from the mutual behavior between the operator and the planner. With the help of the assembly graph (liaise graph) which serves as the underlying control structure, the planner utilizes precedence constrains along with the liaison graph to input all the possible assembly sequences by planner, say, a state from FFFFF to TTTTT, and then generates all the possible sequences. Following that, a mutual intercommunication between the planner and the operator is used to reduce the impractical and impossible assembly sequences. When generating the assembly sequence, the planner initiatively provides information to the augmentation system on what to display using the liaison graph which detects the interference, the inappropriate sequences like the unmatchable inserts, connections and fixing, thus largely reducing the impractical and impossible assembly sequences. In the opposite way, according to visual sensing and augmentation, the operator provides the information perceived to the planner about what parts are being manipulated or what state has been reached in the assembly representation, simultaneously a liaison has been established when graphics and augmentation cues are correctly positioned and updated. The planner could delete the finished assembly notes in the liaison graph and reduce some assembly sequences. Again, the operator provides the information to the planner on the basis of how difficult the completed assembly sequence is and then this information is used to cumulatively compute the cost of the sequence under evaluation and to eliminate other sequences (Wilson, 1995). Another technique used for augmentation is the marker capture technique where the three algorithms were used, the thresholding algorithm, the region growing algorithm and Minimum Spanning Trees (MST) algorithm (Raghavan & Molineros & Sharma, 1999; Bolt, 1980). Considering computer vision techniques offer the potential to provide rich feedback, but suffer from problems like computational complexity, calibration, occlusion caused by lighting conditions, noise, etc. Accordingly, the assembly uses markers to simplify the computer vision algorithms and makes real-time implementation feasible.

BACKGROUND

Some assembly systems based on augmented reality have been produced by the researchers. The two most important AR systems were introduced by Molineros (2002) and by Azuma (1993), they developed AR system called the AREAS and AUDIT, in which they outlined in detail the components of their systems, the principle of each operational usages such as HMD (see-through eyeglass), Camera, planner, tracker, as well as image mixing. ESKUA which is based on tangible user interfaces and carried out by Zhang, Y, Finger, S and Behrens S, is another operational platform to interact with CAD software and replace the old CAD/CAM platform concerning the limitation of environment. The camera tracking technique rested with setting a series of markers was deeply investigated by Neumann, Cho (1996) and Liverani, Amati, Caligiana (2004) to supplement the object-tracking blank that the traditional computer graphics can't realize. To test the efficiency of the AR system, especially in the assembly in manufacturing industry, researchers have carried out a great deal of work in the last few years with the help of algorithms of automatically generating the assembly sequence (Wiedenmaier & Oehme & Schmidt & Luczak, 2001; Shin & Dunston, 2008). Despite the hardships and barriers in constraints management, especially in large batch assembly, great interest in other industries is still exhibited (Pellom & Kadri, 2003). More in general, there are some defects that should be noted. At first, when assembling in the real situation where only a few accessories should be assembled, it is better to obey the instructions in assembly drawings since their simplicity, time saving and low cost. Whereas the assembly drawings become very complicated or even can't be understood by the workers with obvious ease as soon as the machine includes a large amount of accessories. Under such circumstances, reading an assembly drawing for a long time could easily create a visual and physical tiredness which lowers the assembly efficiency in the issue. Accordingly, assembly using AR technique should be employed. But in the current AR system, we still can't utilize the computer to automate the sequence of assembly in view of the conditionality of colossal algorithm and computer Graphics (Tuceryan & Greer & Whitaker & Breen & Crampton & Rose & Ahlers, 1995). Moreover, during the assembly, the mutual accuracy of position precision (straightness, parallelism and coaxiality), the mutual kinematic accuracy (driving precision and rotary accuracy) and the machining accuracy (matching quality and contact quality) must be guaranteed and if not, then rejects would be made in case the assembly accuracy can't be guaranteed.

ISSUES

Problem 1

To guarantee the possibility of high assembly accuracy, the proper assembly approaches should be employed. This way, it is significant to have the expert assemblers experienced in programming assembly path and solving assembly problem. To ensure accuracy in a multi-components assembly where includes lots of composed loops, an experienced expert assembler should design the ideal sequence of assembly by choosing the appropriate assembly approach among exchange, selection, modification and regulation approaches. Actually it often takes months or even years for a novice assembler to develop expert knowledge for assembling processes that have high complexity.

Problem 2

When assembling in the real situation where only a few accessories wait to be assembled, it is better to follow the instructions in assembly drawings due to their simplicity, time saving and low cost. Whereas the assembly drawings become very complicated or even can't be understood with obvious ease when the machine to be assembled includes a large amount of components. Under such circumstance, reading an assembly drawing for a long time could easily create a visual and physical tiredness which lowers the assembly efficiency in the issue. Accordingly, assembly using AR technique should be employed. But in the current AR system, we still can't utilize the

computer to automate the assembly sequence in view of the limitation of computer graphics and colossal algorithm. Moreover, during the assembly, the mutual position accuracy (straightness, parallelism and coaxiality), the mutual kinematic accuracy (driving precision and rotary accuracy) and the machining accuracy (matching quality and contact quality) must be guaranteed and in case the assembly accuracy can't be guaranteed, then rejects would be made.

SOLUTIONS AND RECOMMENDATIONS

The Virtual Reality concept has been implemented in various business and industrial sectors. It offers a novel approach to human-machine interactions where information is displayed in the field of vision of human operators. This helps to visualize innovative ideas and user-activated visual programming processes. This concept also turns enterprises into a modern digital factory, particularly for the manufacturing sectors where users are often geographically distributed in different locations and collaboration is of paramount importance. Efficient sharing of product data is a crucial factor for the next generation of manufacturing.

In addition good collaboration is a key value for society. Working together in real time either together in one room or remotely is important for a flexible and fast planning process. There are a small number of existing technologies and systems which provide collaborative frameworks (Chryssolouris, et al., 2007; Constantinescu, et al., 2006) not only is collaboration between people important, but also collaboration between available systems is of significance. Important features such as common data exchange formats and a common look and feel for the given user interfaces must be considered in order to offer an easy-to-use technology that hides underlying technological diversity and complexity from users.

Figure 1. Sequence planning in AR assembly system (Adapted from (Pang, et al., 2006)).

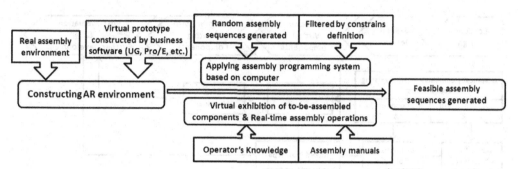

Concerning hardware ergonomics within the virtual technologies domain, a variety of devices are available which differ significantly in properties such as functionality, dimensions, weight and costs. Depending on the task and the needs of the user, the necessary hardware components have to be chosen accordingly. An example system for collaborative planning which is integrated in the Digital Factory for Human-Oriented Production System (DiFac) framework such as the IPA Collaborative Planning Table (Constantinescu & et al, 2006). It enables the collaboration of multiple involved persons, the so called "planners", for achieving the layout planning tasks. The assemblers, designers and engineers can operate with virtual objects and communicate easily and in a direct way. To collaborate with other remote users, a Multiuser Server can be employed. Files, text chat or interaction events for moving objects can be shared.

For the base components it is important to ensure the quality and robustness in order to have reliable devices for the interaction tasks. Therefore, it is envisaged that Augmented Reality (AR) systems are the most suitable for application assembly and design in manufacturing because AR ensures an efficient design, manufacture, and collaboration, as well as robust manufacturing techniques. In addition, the seamless interaction between the real and virtual world is of great importance for an easy-to-use and intuitive user interface. Again, tracking accuracy and precise registration of digital

data are key issues. This chapter discusses the possibility to build an interaction platform which integrates different input and output devices like a Holobench System, DataGlove and Tracking System. Given such an interaction platform, the user is provided with a user-friendly interface for performing different tasks throughout the Digital Factory, such as designing a workflow, through direct manipulation by virtual human metaphors.

One of most difficult tasks for engineers is the assembly sequence planning for complex products (Bolt, 1980). Many automatic systems have been used to automate the sequences of the planning process, however, the problem is that it is very hard to formalize the assembly planners' knowledge. Automatic sequence planning systems are able to generate a set of feasible sequences based on identified constraints. Unfortunately, certain constrains are difficult to identify if a good and realistic feel of the assembly process is not in place. An Augmented Reality interface mixing the real and virtual prototypes provides a better perceptive environment for engineers to experience the realistic feeling of assembly operation and identify the assembly constraints. The AR assembly environment can be integrated with an automatic assembly planning system. As an example, the methodology developed by Pang et al. (2006) for assembly sequence optimization is shown in (Figure 1).

Different engineers and designers can view and verify feasible sequences in AR environments to

Figure 2. A single interactive paradigm for an assembly task

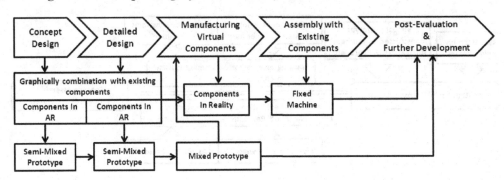

identify new constraints and decide whether there is a need to change the optimization criteria (e.g., minimal cost, minimal number of orientations, etc.). Next, engineers can go back to the Automatic Assembly Planning System to re-plan the sequences no matter where they are located, so it is especially useful during a collaborative work.

(Figure 2) describes the sequence for using the AR paradigm, starting from the concept design phase, followed by the detailed design phase, further design refinements and finally leading to building and assembly.

Concept Design Phase: Business process re-engineering is increasingly becoming the focal point of attention in today's efforts to overcome problems and deficits in the automotive and aerospace industries (e.g., integration in international markets, product complexity, increasing number of product variants, reduction in product development time and cost). Deploying Augmented Reality systems often involves several interactive paradigms for assembly tasks (See Figure 2) in which engineers and designers can experiment naturally with the prototype. The figure shows a paradigm about how a single assembly can be done with the support of Augmented Reality systems. For example, the assembly process below illustrates how a designer would refer to an AR model (e.g. a design for an aircraft) to demonstrate the practicality of several designs and choose the most suitable option corresponding to existing components. An iterative process is applied in

which increasing levels of detail and accuracy accumulates over the product design cycle. Initially, in the early concept design phases the AR model will be simplistic and lacking in detail (a rough draft of the desired end product). Gradually more and more component information is added and produces a more detailed design.

Detailed Design Phase: Engineers can analyse the AR model and provide feedback. Here the AR model gives designers the freedom to quickly and easily make changes to the specifications of their model.

Modifying a real world prototype, such as an aircraft, following the traditional methodology of creating real world prototypes for each design introduces significant inefficiencies in the design and prototyping process. It can be prohibitively expensive due to costs of materials, man hours spent in and assembly of prototypes, and other costs associated with the increased timeframe required due to a slower design and prototyping process (e.g. loss of market share due to lack of competitive advantage).

Manufacturing Virtual Components Phase: After the previous two phases the design is now starting to become relatively mature. Engineers will consult with the manufacturers of the various components (ie. component suppliers) and determine if further modifications to the AR model are required. Consultation between designers, engineers and with the component suppliers will take place in a more rapid timeframe. This promotes a more efficient form of collaboration between the interested parties.

The design cycle will move in a repetitive process of design, consultation, further design improvements, and so on. The design cycle is iterative and continually builds and improves on previous design efforts using feedback provided by engineers, component suppliers, and any other interested parties. There will be a negotiation between parties whose fields of expertise are within diverse disciplines, the AR design paradigm will facilitate better communication between these parties.

Assembly with Existing Components Phase: The various parts are purchased from component suppliers and assembled by assemblers (e.g. engineers or factory workers) in order to produce the real world product based on the AR model. The product is ready to be used without need for the production of a real world prototype.

During this phase it is expected that the engineers or designers might wish to provide further feedback in order to improve the AR model so that the assemblers could follow the AR model easily rather than the schematics diagram and make the corresponding change to the real components. The virtual phototype (AR model) will help the assemblers to produce the real world product in a more efficient way, and will provide a visual representation that is more intuitive for them to follow.

Post-Evaluation & Further Development Phase: After production of the prototype further testing and analysis will be carried out. This may result in further modification to the AR model. Due to the flexibility of the AR paradigm modifications to the AR model can be made more quickly.

Fewer changes to the design will be required at this stage, and it will be quicker to finish the assembly tasks due to improved collaboration and feedback in earlier phases.

Practically all automotive companies separate different parts to various manufacturing factors. For example, if the object consists of four plants

to be produced, then each manufacturing sector is in charge of one plant, but the important part is that the each component is required to be matched before any other steps to take further. The figure demonstrates a complicated process which using Augmented Reality concepts into a network with various departments for the components. Each sector has specialised workers in the particular domain knowledge with certain training. In the beginning the designer and engineer produce the concepts design, then with the aids of Augmented Reality systems, the virtual assembly could be formed. Meanwhile, the assemblers could see how the components should be assembled to match with some existing real components.

As an example, the assemblers of an automotive chassis in plant 2 are building the chassis based on the phototype. This plant is dependent on the production of parts from other manufacturing sectors, such as the supplier for the engine block. The manufacturer of the chassis can start to build with confidence without having to wait to receive a shipment of engine blocks from plant 1.

There are multiple dependencies between these plants, but with the network flow, each plant can monitor the other's plants' progress so there is no need to wait until the previous plant to complete their assembly task, the work can be conducted simultaneously. In addition, the efficiency could be accumulated across the assembly line between all the manufacturing plants involving in the production.

BENEFITS

Reducing Mental Workload and Cognitive Load

There is a cognitive load present in the assembly process. In the assembly task, more and more assemblers get trained with different methods. Augmented Reality systems provide a more efficient way to train the assemblers, the cognitive

Figure 3. A platform for collaborative work in assembly design simultaneously

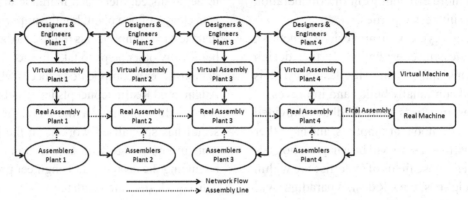

workload will be reduced as they no longer need to exert cognitive effort when trying to visualise the component based on a traditional schematic. The AR phototype will help the assemblers by providing a more natural and intuitive phototype, requiring less effort to interpret, and helping to guide them in the assembly process.

Cognitive load theory addresses how to use elementary tools for training assembly workers. For example, users prefer a graphical user interface (GUI) that uses illuminated picture based icons in order to remember where specific programs and functionality are located in the user interface. Compare this to text based icons which are less intuitive and will increase the cognitive load. Providing visual cues decreases cognitive load even if a user knows where items are located. AR provides a superior visual stimulus to the end user. Picture based icons can be used instead of plain text icons as this provides a simpler more intuitive user interface with less cognitive load.

In performing complex manufacturing work such as assembly tasks, the assembler has to reach a certain level of performance while not exceeding the mental capacity he is willing to spend. A well-designed human-machine-interface like Augmented Reality might be helpful to the worker to achieve these goals. Some studies have reported that the AR environment was less mentally demanding (Tang, et al., 2003). A well-proven method of designing such systems is to

arouse the workers, thus providing the visual cue is significant to the assembly task. The arousal level can be thought of as how much capacity you have available to work with. One finding with respect to arousal is the Yerkes-Dodson law (1908) which predicts an inverted U-shaped function between arousal and performance (See Figure 4). There is a certain relationship between the arousal level and the quality of performance. If the task is too simple or too complex, the level of arousal will go too low and too high. Only the optimal level of arousal, which is lower for more difficult or intellectually (cognitive) tasks, and higher for tasks requiring endurance and persistence, can improve the quality of performance. A visual stimulus is one of the significant senses for arousal and motivation of workers. In assembly tasks, workers often need to form the image of assembly sequences ac-

Figure 4. The Yerkes-Dodson law

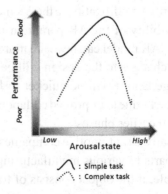

cording to the drawings, this causes some mental workload for the workers. Although some cases may only have few steps to go through, but more often the cases are much complicated. Therefore, the Augmented Reality could allow the workers to visualize the parts rather than manipulating the objects in their mind. It has been proven that if the workers do not have to mentally transform objects and keep a model of the relationship of the assembly objects to its location in working memory, they would then experience less mental workload (Tang, et al., 2003). When the assembler is being trained to read the assembly drawings, there is a large quantity of information being presented in the drawings, it could easily overload the assembler's peak arousal level (producing stress) and this results in a situation where does not want to arouse them anymore. With the assistance of Augmented Reality systems, assemblers will not be fatigued easily since the visual aids could break down the complexity and maintain the arousal at an even level.

Reduced Design Time and Errors

Physical phototyping is traditionally the main method for assembly design. With physical phototypes, engineers, designers and assemblers can easily obtain direct feedback from their senses (visual, tactile, and force, etc) in order to decide if the parts have been designed properly. During the assembly operations, it is easier to identify any unexpected drawbacks to improve the design, but that usually is very time consuming and incurs a very high cost in past years, additionally, once being made, it is difficult, time consuming and expensive to modify the initial prototype. Hence, Augmented Reality can be potentially considered as a rapid prototyping and low cost system since the technology could generate the 3D graphical models which are used to manipulate and design products using existing (or novel) parts. Furthermore, usually the assembly designer tried to avoid the errors as much as possible. However, the design

process is becoming increasingly flexible if the design process can be adopted with Augmented Reality systems since the design is changeable with changeable prototype, the 3D image will change according the manipulation from the designers so it is more efficient.

Furthermore, there seem to be two different understandings of what exactly virtual prototyping is: the "computer graphics" and the "manufacturing" point of view (Sims, 1994). During the verification between different disciplines such as designers, engineers, manufacturers and component suppliers, it is not avoidable to have some errors, some might be independent errors and some might be dependent ones. Previous study for assembly tasks have been proven that the participants who used the AR systems can produce far less dependent errors (Tang, et al., 2003). Since the visualizations provided by AR systems could help augment the assemblers' cognition and also be a more useful instructional tool compared to the paper drawings. In the past, proper design of instructional visualizations can reduce the time taken and errors made in performing a task (Molineros, 2002). To understand how to design effective visualizations, it is significant that Augmented Reality can give instant feedback, so the assembler could immediately decide if the next step should proceed before the errors to be produced.

FUTURE RESEARCH DIRECTIONS

In our future industrial case it can be aimed to enhance assembly work for sequence planning. In augmenting assembly work, the assembly worker is guided by virtual objects and visual assembly instructions.

As virtual reality has become more widespread, the demand for system developing has increased dramatically. Establishment of an AR assembly environment is an extremely complex and needs to consider many interdisciplinary issues from different domain knowledge such as design, engineering, AR technologies, assembly and manufacturing. Although there are some works which have been done in the AR assembly domain, the research in collaborative assembly design is still at the infant stage. Therefore, there are essential needs to investigate the realm of assembly process from the various disciplines in order to increase the work efficiency.

One key value for a comprehensive assembly evaluation is the physical interaction between real and virtual objects in an AR assembly environment, however there are still lots of limitations in this domain (Aliaga, 1994; Breen, et al., 19956; Vallino, 1998). For example, physical interaction between real and virtual objects in Augmented Reality should include collision detection and reaction which is significant for a comprehensive, realistic and feasible assembly and design process. If these problems cannot be solved, the AR assembly system would be hard to use in any complicated evaluation. On the other hand, at the current state of existing AR technology, the most realistic feedback can only be obtained from the direction of real object affecting the virtual components, but not vise-versa. Hence, the studies of the other way from a virtual object to the real object should be carried out as well and it has significant meaning for the future AR application in the collaboration.

CONCLUSION

This chapter discusses the current issues of assembly work and explain the reason that why the AR system could be the option to solve these problems with the potential for benefits. The proposed mixed prototyping concept from AR environment combines the advantage from the real prototype and virtual prototype which increases the efficiency and flexibility compared to the traditional method in the assembly work. In this way, it not only reduces the cost for the manufacturing industries, but also reduces the time and increase the accuracy during assembly

process. The optimized solution also offers the opportunity for different manufacturing sectors to work in a same time. This innovative idea breaks down the sequential work process for collaboration in assembly and offers a platform which supports the features of overlaying and registering information on the workspace in a spatially meaningful way in AR. Moreover, it improves the human performance and relieves some of the workers' mental workload. The AR systems offer a real time collaboration and interaction between various enterprise units allowing a fast information exchange and letting the natural separation from designers and manufacturers to be overcome.

REFERENCES

Aliaga, D. G. (1994). Virtual and real object collisions in a merged environment. In *Virtual Reality Software Technology* [Singapore: World Scientific Publishing Co.]. *Proceedings of VRST, 94*, 287–298.

Azuma, R. (1993). Tracking requirements for augmented reality. [Special issue on computer augmented environments]. *Communications of the ACM, 36*(7), 50–52. doi:10.1145/159544.159581

Bolt, R. (1980). Put-That-There: Voice and gesture at the graphics interface. *Computer Graphics, 14*(3), 262–270. doi:10.1145/965105.807503

Breen, D. E., Rose, E., & Whitaker, R. T. (1995). *Interactive Occlusion and Collision of Real and Virtual Objects in Augmented Reality*. (Technical report ECRC-95-02).

Chryssolouris, G., Pappas, M., Karabatsou, V., Mavrikios, D., & Alexopoulos, K. (2007, April). A Shared VE for Collaborative Product Development in Manufacturing Enterprises. In Li, W. D., Ong, S. K., Nee, A. Y. C., & McMahon, C. (Eds.), *Collaborative Product Design and Manufacturing Methodologies and Applications*. London: Springer-Verlag. doi:10.1007/978-1-84628-802-9_3

Constantinescu, C., Runde, C., Volkmann, J., Lalas, C., Sacco, M., Liu, D., Pavlopoulos, C., & Pappas, M. (2006). *DiFac D1 – Definition of a VR-based collaborative digital manufacturing environment.* DiFac Project (FP6-2005-IST-5-035079), v. 6.4.

Curtis, D., Mizell, D., Gruenbaum, P., & Janin, A. (1998). Several devils in the detail: Making an AR application work in the airplane factory. In *Proceedings of the International Workshop on Augmented Reality '98.*

Feiner, S., MacIntyre, B., & Seligmann, D. (1993). Knowledge-based augmented reality. [Special issue on computer augmented environments]. *Communications of the ACM, 37*(6), 53–62. doi:10.1145/159544.159587

Liverani, A., Amati, G., & Caligiana, G. (2004). A CAD-Augmented Reality Integrated Environment for Assembly Sequence Check and Interactive Validation. *Concurrent Engineering, 12*(1), 67–77. doi:10.1177/1063293X04042469

Mellor, J. P. (1995). *Enhanced reality visualization in a surgical environment. (Tech. Rep).* MIT Artificial Intelligence Laboratory.

Metzger, P. J. (1993). *Adding reality to the virtual.* Paper presented at Virtual Reality Annual Symposium, WA, USA.

Molineros, J. M. (2002). *Computer Vision and Augmented Reality for Guiding Assembly.* PA: Department of Computer Science and Engineering in Pennsylvania State University, State College.

Neumann, U., & Cho, Y. (1996). A self-tracking augmented reality system. In Proceedings of Virtual Reality Software and Technology (VRAIS96) (pp. 109–115). Hong Kong.

Pang, Y., Nee, A. Y. C., Ong, M., Yuan, S. K., & Youcef-Toumi, K. (2006). *Assembly Automation.* Bradford, UK: Emerald Group Publishing Limited.

Pellom, B., & Kadri, H. (2003). Recent Improvements in the CU SONIC ASR System for Noisy Speech: The SPINE Task. In *Proceedings of IEEE International Conference on Acoustics, Speech, and Signal Processing (ICASSP)*, Hong Kong.

Pope, A. R. (1994). *Model-based object recognition: a survey on recent research (Tech. Rep).* California: University Berkeley.

Raghavan, V., Molineros, J., & Sharma, R. (1999). Interactive Evaluation of Assembly Sequences Using Augmented Reality. *IEEE Transactions on Robotics and Automation, 15*, 435–449. doi:10.1109/70.768177

Sharma, R., & Molineros, J. (1997). *Computer vision-based augmented reality for guiding manual assembly.* Paper presented at the Virtual Reality Annual International Symposium, Atlanta, GA, USA.

Shin, D. H., & Dunston, P. S. (2008). *Evaluation of Augmented Reality in steel column inspection.* West Lafayette, IN: School of Civil Engineering, Purdue University.

Sims, D. (1994). New realities in aircraft design and manufacture. *IEEE Computer Graphics and Applications, 14*(2), 91. doi:10.1109/38.267487

Tang, A., Owen, C., Biocca, F., & Mou, W. (2003). Comparative Effectiveness of Augmented Reality in Object Assembly. In *Proc. CHI* (pp. 73-80).

Tuceryan, M., Greer, D. S., Whitaker, R. T., Breen, D. E., Crampton, C., Rose, E., & Ahlers, K. H. (1995). *Calibration requirements and procedures for a monitor-based augmented reality system.* IEEE Trans. Visual. Computer. Graph.

Uenohara, M., & Kanade, T. (1995). *Vision-based object registration for real-time image overlay* (pp. 14–22). Computer Vision, Virtual Reality and Robotics in Medicine.

Urban, E. C. (1995). The information warrior. *IEEE Spectrum, 32*(11), 66–70.

Vallino, J. R. (1998). *Interactive Augmented Reality*. University of Rochester.

Wiedenmaier, S., Oehme, O., Schmidt, L., & Luczak, H. (2001). Augmented reality for assembly process: An experimental evaluation. In *Proceedings of the IEEE and ACM International Symposium on Augmented Reality* (pp. 185–186). Los Alamitos, CA: IEEE Computer Society.

Wilson, R. H. (1995). Minimizing user queries in interactive assembly planning. *Robotics and Automation. IEEE Transactions on, 11*, 308–312.

Yerkes, R. M., & Dodson, J. D. (1908). The Relationship of Strength of Stimulus to Rapidity of Habit Formation. *The Journal of Comparative Neurology and Psychology, 18*, 459–482. doi:10.1002/cne.920180503

KEY TERMS AND DEFINITIONS

Augmented Reality: A field of computer research which deals with the combination of real-world and computer-generated data such as the computer generated scene overlaid on the real world.

Virtual Reality: A technology which allows the users to interact with a computer-simulated environment, whether that environment is a simulation of the real world or an imaginary world.

Section 3
Virtual Reality Concepts in Service Sector

Chapter 7

Virtual Reality and Neuroimaging Technologies:
Synergistic Approaches in Neuromarketing

Harrison R. Burris
DeVry University, USA

Shahid A. Sheikh
Chancellor University, USA

ABSTRACT

Marketers have long been fascinated by the possibility of understanding how consumers think and what factors stimulate favorable reactions to marketing stimuli. Marketers are now beginning to utilize neuromarketing techniques to map patterns of brain activities to ascertain how consumers evaluate products, objects, or marketing messages. Neuromarketing is relatively a new field of marketing that utilizes computer-simulated environments, such as Virtual Reality (VR) or Immersive Virtual Reality (IVR) technologies combined with neuroimaging technologies, such as Functional Magnetic Resonance Imaging (fMRI), Quantitative Electroencephalography (QEEG), Magnetoencephalography (MEG), and other means of studying human neurological responses. Marketers need this information to help gain favorable reactions to their marketing stimuli and to predict which product designs and marketing messages will appeal most and be on consumer's minds when the prospects are ready to buy.

INTRODUCTION

Marketers spend billions of dollars each year on relatively crude methods such as focus groups, questionnaires, and measurements of eye movements in the attempt to understand how the human brain makes decisions and what motivates consumers to spend. However, with advances in the fields of virtual reality and neurosciences,

marketers can now predict with relative accuracy which design or marketing message will appeal most to consumers by mapping out which parts of the brain are active when consumers look at certain products or marketing messages. These relatively new field is aptly termed as 'neuromarketing', which has stimulated significant innovations in marketing in general and in marketing research in particular. Neuromarketers combine virtual reality technologies with neuroscience, brain scanning, or neuroimaging technologies to help predict which

DOI: 10.4018/978-1-61520-631-5.ch007

marketing stimuli or marketing messages will appeal most to consumers by mapping out which parts of the brain are active when respondents look at certain stimuli or marketing messages. However, critics of this approach are concerned with the ethical and philosophical issues related to marketers' ability to probe mechanisms behind people's decision-making processes coupled with the dilemmas these advances in brain science present and who should be allowed to peek into consumers' brains.

This chapter reviews neuromarketing technologies such as computer-simulated environments combined with neuroimaging technologies utilized in neuromarketing. This chapter gives an overview and focuses on the advances in the fields of virtual reality and neuroimaging and the ability to use brain responses to ascertain how consumers evaluate marketing stimuli.

NEUROMARKETING

Marketers in the past relied on traditional market research methods such as surveys and focus groups, indirect and often inaccurate methods such as observing how consumers behave in stores, or tracking how purchases rise or fall in response to promotional campaigns or changes in pricing. However, these methods are often fraught with bias and imprecision and fail to predict consumers' thoughts and feelings. Although brain-scanning devices have been available for decades, new scanning technologies and computer processing algorithms can pinpoint more precisely which brain regions are active as people respond to products, makes, and brand choices, or are exposed to marketing stimuli such as advertisements. Neuromarketing, according to Sutherland (2007) is relatively a new field of marketing that utilizes neurosciences, computer-simulated environments, medical technologies, and other scientific means of studying human consumers' neurological, sensorimotor, cognitive, and affective responses

to marketing stimuli. Lesley Stahl, a 60 Minutes correspondent recently reported on neuroscience research into how we think and what we are thinking is advancing at a stunning rate, making it possible for the first time in human history to peer directly into the brain to read out the physical make-up of our thoughts, some would say to read our minds (Columbia Broadcasting System (CBS), 2009). Some of the medical technologies used in neuromarketing include functional magnetic resonance imaging (fMRI), magnetoencephalogram (MEG), and quantitative electroencephalogram (qEEG). Of the three, according to Kenning et al. (2007) and Kenning, Plassmann, & Ahlert (2007), fMRI, to try to figure out what we want to buy and how to sell it to us, has captured the greatest interest among market researchers and enjoyed the widest publicity.

Marketers need this information to help gain favorable reactions to their marketing stimuli and to predict which product designs and marketing messages will appeal most and be on consumer's minds when the prospects are ready to buy. With breakthroughs in neuroscience, neuromarketers can hope to see what goes on inside consumers' minds when they shop by hooking people up to functional magnetic resonance imaging (fMRI) machines to map how their neurons respond to products and pitches (Carr, 2008). The relatively new approach that combines neurosciences with marketing techniques is aptly termed neuromarketing. Gemma Calvert, co-founder of a London company called Neurosense told Leslie Stahl, a CBS's 60 Minute correspondence, that companies such as Unilever, Intel, McDonald's, Proctor & Gamble, MTV, or Viacom are already using neuromarketing techniques to predict what consumers want to buy and how to sell their desired products to them (Columbia Broadcasting System (CBS), 2009).

Some of the roots of neuromarketing go back to neuroscientist Damasio's (2005) assertion that human beings use the emotional part of the brain when making decisions, not just the rational part, which is a departure from René Descartes's Cartesian idea of the human mind as separate from bodily processes. Damasio draws on neurochemistry to support his claim that emotions play a central role in human decision-making. This claim is based on human emotions, decision-making, memory, and communication, from a neurological perspective. Damasio uses brain imaging techniques (e.g. advanced magnetic resonance scanning), and cognitive, psychophysiological, and psychophysical techniques in conjunction with virtual reality techniques in his research.

With the help of brain-scanning or neuroimaging technologies combined with Immersive Virtual Reality (IVR) technologies, such as a pair of specially adapted Sony virtual-reality goggles, a neuromarketer can predict which marketing stimuli will appeal most to consumers by mapping out which parts of the brain are active when the respondents look at certain products or marketing messages.

Another example is research conducted by Brown University professor John Donoghue, in which he used multielectrode recording arrays and fMRI techniques of brain-scanning or neuroimaging technologies in capturing brain signals (as cited in Ortiz, 2007). Donoghue and his research team then used digital signal processors (DSPs) and algorithms to translate these brain signals into a format that a computer can understand and process. Using scientific methods and advanced technologies, researchers are coming to understand how human beings process feelings that affect our decision-making processes such as purchasing decisions.

The goal for using this technology in neuromarketing is to decode which purchasing choices go into buying (Wilchalls, 2004) a particular product and to understand better how consumers make emotional connections with brands. The result can be the ability to pinpoint the preference areas of the brain. Using this data, marketers can help design better products and a more effective marketing campaign. However, because of the restrictions of the MRI scanning process, and the time required for a response to be registered in the brain and transferred to an fMRI image, other neural scanning technologies are also being investigated for their contributions to neural marketing. Several of these neural scanning technologies have the potential to use lightweight wearable sensors that would enable marketing studies in environments such as the CAVE (CAVE Automatic Virtual Environment, 2009). Other neural scanning technologies involved in research are magneto-encephalography (MEG), and quantitative electroencephalography (qEEG). Neuromarketers are beginning to combine neural scanning technologies with virtual reality technologies to get better results.

VIRTUAL REALITY

One of the computer technologies being incorporated into neuromarketing, Virtual Reality (VR), initially coined by Jaron Lanier in 1989 (as cited in Heim, 1993), is an artificial environment, created using multiple technologies, in which individuals immerse themselves and feel that this the artificial reality really does exist. Other related computer technologies include Artificial Reality (Krueger, 1991), Cyberspace (Gibson, 1984), and, more recently, Virtual Worlds (Beier, 1990). Virtual Reality, also known as the Virtual Environments (VE) has drawn much attention in the last few years and extensive media coverage caused interest to grow rapidly. However, few people really know what VR is, or what its basic principles and unresolved problems are.

According to Youngblut, Johnson, Nash, Wienclaw, and Will (1996), the idea of VR began well before the advent of the computer; however, VR, in the sense we have come to know, occurred during the past 40 years. VR pioneers such as Ivan Sutherland, Michael Noll, and Myron Krueger all had their parts to play in the creation of modern-day VR. Popular culture and science fiction both have also had profound effects on the social implications of VR.

According to Isdale (1993), originally the term VR referred to Immersive Virtual Reality (IVR) in which the user, using an electronic device such as the head-mounted display (HMD), becomes fully immersed in an artificial, three-dimensional world that is completely generated by a computer. IVR combined with brain-scanning or neuroimaging technologies can stretch a marketer's understanding of what triggers a certain response by looking deep inside consumers' brains to reveal eventually the secrets of designing and selling a more universally appealing product.

Harris, Duffy, Smith, and Stephanidis (2003) suggest that there are numerous types of VR systems, but most can be classified into one of the following three categories: Desktop VR, Video Mapping VR, and Immersive VR. In Desktop VR, a computer user views a virtual environment through one or more computer screens and can then interact with that environment, but is not immersed in it. An example of Desktop VR would be Second Life, with which a user becomes part of a VR world. Video Mapping VR uses cameras to project an image of the user into the computer program, thus creating a 2-D computer character. Blue screens used by TV weathermen that allow them to stand in front of full-sized animated weather maps and satellite images typify this technique. Although fully immersed in the environment, it is difficult to interact with the user's surroundings. Immersive VR uses a HMD to project video directly in front of the user's eyes, plays audio directly into the user's ears, and can track the movements of the user's head. A dataglove (or datasuit) is used to track movements of the user's body and duplicate them in the virtual environment (Rheingold, 1991). When the user cannot distinguish between what is real and what is not, then immersive VR has succeeded.

Beyond the immersive environment of the VR glasses and headphones is the environment of the CAVE (ADLAB, 2006) or the Immersive Cocoon (Cocciardi, 2008). In these systems, the user is inside a room or sphere, the surface of which is a seamless display system. With 3-D glasses and hand feedback (gloves or 3-D mice), the user can navigate inside a 3-D environment.

Military training and gaming industries have largely driven the rapid advances in the VR technologies and have concentrated on sight and sound, which are also major elements in marketing stimuli. In addition to sight and sound, smell and taste are also important to marketing stimuli. Virtual Reality allows users to see, hear, and will sometime soon allow the user to touch and smell objects and environments that exist only inside computers. Although not as well developed or commercialized as sight and sound, VR technology for smell and taste exists. The Smell-O-Vision system, a technique created by Hans Laube, released 30 odors during the projection of a film so that the viewer could smell what was happening in the movie *Scent of Mystery* (Smith & Kiger, 2007), and NAU is reportedly working on an immersive headset the will reproduce smells (Franklin, 2009).

The appeal of VR to a company marketing organization is its tremendous time and cost savings. No longer does an organization need to wait for an art department to make posters and no longer does it have to wait for the model makers to make handcrafted prototypes of products and store displays. With the click of a mouse, a new ad campaign or product appears, as if by magic, in a display before a prospective customer.

Potential customers can be shown advertising or products using desktop computer screens, LCD wall screen projectors, 3-D goggles, or immersive VR such as the CAVE (Cave Automatic Virtual Environment. 2009) or the Cocoon (Cocciardi, 2008).

In one recent use of VR technologies in studying buyer habits and reactions, Procter & Gamble, the U.S. multinational, used a CAVE-like environment to study the behavior of English shoppers in VR recreations of their local shops (ADLAB, 2006). Since CAVE-like environments utilize an

Figure 1.

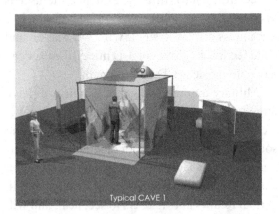

Typical CAVE 1

Figure 2.

Typical CAVE 2

Artificial Reality (AR) system, which does not require wiring human beings to use an interface, and computerized sensors perceive human actions in terms of the human body's relationship to the simulated world (Heim, 1998), the shoppers could be studied as they moved around the virtual shops. The marketers then got reactions to what the customer seesaw; they could ask questions pertaining to products, services, and other marketing stimuli; or they could watch responses such as clenching of fists, jaws, narrowing of eyes or pupils, crossing of arms, or leaning forward.

Just as computers have been making VR possible and increasing the speed of marketing studies, they have also been advancing medical imaging, both in terms of the kinds of images that can be collected and the accuracy and speed with which the computer can process the raw data into a usable image.

NEUROIMAGING

One of these imaging technologies, Magnetic Resonance Imaging (MRI), has revolutionized the way doctors visualize conditions ranging from tumors to ruptured tendons and is considered safe and noninvasive, but requires expensive machines and facilities. To help pay for MRI facilities, researchers have been looking for other applications

that could help share the cost, and marketing is one such application.

Magnetic Resonance Imaging was first used to scan a full human body in 1977 (Clare, 1997). By the early 1990s, continued improvement in the technology and research into applications of MRI scanning resulted in the realization that blood flow to the brain could be imaged. Neuroscientists adapted standard MRI scanners to produce three-dimensional images of brain activity at any particular moment. It has been known since 1890 that mental processes cause an increased flow of blood to the active area of the brain (Roy & Sherrington, 1890). MRI scans showed the part of the brain that was active (or functional), and the new technique was called fMRI for Functional MRI (Belliveau et al., 1991). The first applications of fMRI were in precise diagnoses of stroke and other brain disorders such as schizophrenia (Weinberger et al., 1996). Continued development of improved MRI equipment and processing software led to much more precise location of the active areas in a brain scan, measured precise locations of small changes in blood flow identifying what the subject was thinking at the instant an MRI image was taken, and began to correlate active brain locations with particular thoughts. MRI or fMRI do not scan brains for the words or images, but correlate the active brain area with likes or dislikes in response to marketing stimulus such as a picture.

In one example of such brain scanning or neuroimaging technologies, according to Peck (2008), neuroscientist Paul Sajda of Columbia University, uses an EEG cap taped into the brain's vision system to tell which images grabbed an individual's attention even if they are moving too fast to notice consciously.

VIRTUAL REALITY AND NEUROIMAGING IN NEUROMARKETING

Neuromarketing represents the latest extension in the use of a series of technological means to capture involuntary human responses to marketing stimuli. Brain imaging, a widely used technique in neuromarketing permitted by the latest technologies, is simply the latest in a long line of marketing research efforts used to understand better consumer reactions to marketing stimuli and messages. However, this understanding is markedly different from that obtained with traditional survey or focus group efforts in which the respondent knowingly interacts. The marketing information collected by neuromarketing might be more accurate than information collected in conventional marketing studies. According to Rowan (2004), multinationals such as Unilever and Ford are paying scientists to scan volunteers' brains. In addition, Hollywood studios are testing brain responses to film trailers, and food manufacturers are using neuro-imaging to fine-tune multi-million-dollar product launches. Several auto manufacturers such as Jaguar, Mercedes-Benz use these techniques to design and crash test their automobiles.

According to Berns, a psychiatrist at Emory University (as cited in Park, 2007), marketers can use brain imaging to gain insight into the mechanisms behind people's decisions in a way that is often difficult to get at simply by asking a person or watching his or her behavior. The high costs have somewhat limited the use of Virtual Reality and neuroimaging technologies such as fMRI and CAVE in neuromarketing. However, once market barriers of tight research budgets, complexity of the instruments, and high costs of brain-scanning or neuroimaging technologies are resolved, the neuromarketing industry is expected to develop further. With technology developers exploring many new applications, especially those involving neuroimaging, it is inevitable that brain-scanning or neuroimaging technologies would evolve into a highly sophisticated neuromarketing tools. Some of the improvements made to the technology have further enhanced the modality and many applications have adopted these systems.

According to Addison (2005), Zaltman of Harvard, toward the end of the 1990s, reported the first use of fMRI as a marketing tool. The idea of seeing what people think using fMRI was first called neuromarketing by Ale Smidts of the BrightHouse Institute for Thought Sciences, working out of the neuroscience wing of Emory University Hospital in Atlanta, Georgia (Lewis & Brigder 2005). Carr (2008) and Rowan (2004) describe neuromarketing as an approach with which marketers combine neuroscience and marketing techniques to predict how consumers will react to stimuli in the marketplace, from prices to packages to advertisements. In the words of *Forbes* magazine, the researchers at Emory's School of Medicine and Hospital are experimenting on human subjects in order to find the buy button inside the skull (Wells, 2003). The *New York Times* called the neuroscience wing at Emory University the epicenter of the neuromarketing world (Thompson, 2003).

The potential payoff of neuromarketing is that combining the ability of VR to produce products and environments with the ability of fMRI or other brain-scanning technologies to read subconscious reactions greatly enhances the accuracy and reliability of marketing studies. These neuroimaging technologies, combined with VR in which the user is fully immersed in an artificial, computer generated three-dimensional world, can stretch marketers' understanding of what triggers a certain response by looking deep inside consumers' brains to reveal the secrets of designing and selling a more universally appealing product.

According to Sutherland (2007), since it is the unconscious mind that drives how consumers respond to marketing stimuli, consumers do not really know why they buy what they buy, which is why traditional market research falls short. Sutherland reports that according to neuroscientists, there are three main parts to the brain: the human brain or cortex, the mammalian or the middle brain, and the reptilian or old brain. Of the three, the human brain, the most evolved part of the brain, is responsible for logic, learning, language, conscious thoughts, and our personalities. According to Chaudhuri (2006), the reptilian brain drives consumers' buying decisions, which neuromarketers strive to measure to predict how consumers will react to stimuli in the marketplace, from prices to packaging to advertisements. With breakthroughs in brain sciences, neuromarketers can hope to see what goes on inside consumers' minds when they shop by hooking people up to functional magnetic resonance imaging (fMRI) machines to map how their neurons respond to products and pitches (Carr, 2008). To change the content presented and to measure the response within fMRI environment, stereo goggles and headphones (Resonance Technology Inc., 2009) and stereo displays designed specifically to (Cambridge Research Systems, 2009) operate within the intense magnetic field of an MRI was all that was necessary.

The understanding gained from neuromarketing methods is also different from that obtained with observational studies in which behavior is examined, but without the ability to trace the internal roots that prompted the action. Neuromarketers believe that well-designed neuromarketing studies can provide involuntary responses, free of the biases introduced by other marketing study collection methods. Therefore, the assumption is that neuromarketing using brain images could possibly tell the marketers, which brand images, trigger the strongest subconscious responses, and which commercials or logos touch us most deeply. If these assumptions were proved correct, marketers would not have any further need for unscientific focus groups.

Marketing studies performed using neuromarketing are just the beginning. Recently, Knutson a Stanford scientist, conducted a test to measure anticipatory emotions, which are the intuitive and emotional regions of the brain that prime the decision-making process even before the cognitive areas of the brain are brought in to assess options, such as the value of a product and its price, which triggers an anticipation of pleasure or pain (Park, 2007). To test his theory, Knutson presented his subjects, while they were in the fMRI machine, with pictures of products, each followed by a price with the option of purchasing each item on display. As subjects viewed products they preferred, Knutson saw activity in the nucleus accumbens, a region of the brain involved in anticipating pleasant outcomes. If, on the other hand, the subjects thought the price of these items was too high, there was increased activity in the insula—an area involved in anticipating pain. "The idea is that if you can look into people's brains right before they make certain decisions, you can get a handle on these two feelings and do a better job of predicting what they are about to do"(Knutson, Rick, Wimmer, Prelec, and Loewenstein (2007) suggest anticipatory emotions not only bias but also drive decision making.

Knutson et al., in their article titled "Neural Predictors of Purchases," described how they used brain imaging to monitor the mental activity of shoppers as they evaluated products and prices on computer screens. By using event-related fMRI, the authors investigated how people weigh consumer preference and price factors to make purchasing decisions. The authors posit that by watching how different neural circuits light up or go dark during the buying process, they could predict whether a person would end up purchasing a product or passing it up. According to the authors, consistent with neuroimaging evidence suggesting that distinct circuits anticipate gain and loss, product preference activated the nucleus accumbens (NAcc), while excessive prices activated the insula and deactivated the mesial prefrontal cortex (MPFC) prior to the purchase decision. Activity from each of these regions independently predicted subsequent purchases beyond self-report variables. These findings suggest that activation of distinct neural circuits related to anticipatory affect precedes and supports consumers' purchasing decisions.

Virtual reality, in its present forms, can greatly enhance marketing, and in particular marketing studies. The advent of future VR that can reproduce the feel and smell of products will only further improve the usefulness of VR for marketing. If the potential of neuromarketing hinted at by the studies performed to date can be realized, it is difficult to imagine marketers having any need of other marketing study tools. VR and neural imaging will have completely changed how marketing studies are performed and the accuracy of the resulting predictions.

ILLUSTRATIVE CASES FF SUCCESSFUL USE FF NEUROIMAGING, VIRTUAL REALITY, AND NEUROMARKETING

McConnon (2007), in his article titled "If I Only Had A Brain Scan" published in *BusinessWeek,* reports that an advertising agency recently sponsored an experiment to fine-tune an ad campaign for the maker of Jack Daniels. The experiment, conducted at McLean Hospital and managed by Harvard University, scanned the brains of half-a-dozen young whiskey drinkers to gauge the emotional power of various images, including college kids drinking cocktails on spring break,

twentysomethings with flasks around a campfire, and older guys at a swanky bar.

According to Carter (2009), the carmaker Honda is one of the businesses using neuroscience to learn how and why consumers decide what to buy. Carter adds that Honda researchers use a smart garment called LifeShirt designed by US tech company VivoMetrics to monitor the emotions of buyers visiting car dealerships. Honda found the results so persuasive, Carter adds that it is remodeling showrooms and retraining staff to tailor pitches according to a potential buyer's state of mind. Carter cites yet another example of British broadcaster GMTV that uses the neuromarketing procedures to gauge receptiveness to adverts at different times of the day.

According to Lindstrom and Underhill (2008), Microsoft plans to use EEGs to record the electrical activity in people's brains to see what emotions they experience as they interact with their computers. Using brain-scanning technology, Unilever discovered not only why consumers enjoyed their best-selling Eskimo ice cream bars, but also that eating ice cream creates even greater visceral pleasure than either chocolate or yogurt.

FUTURE RESEARCH DIRECTIONS

According to Lee et al (2009), market researchers have an unparalleled opportunity to adopt cognitive neuroscientific techniques, including virtual reality and neuroimaging to redefine the new field of neuromarketing. The prohibitive factors slowing down the desired advances are the bulk, size, and cost of neuroimaging and virtual reality instruments and machines. However, neuroimaging instruments and machines manufactures such as Siemens, Sony, GE, and Philips are seeking smaller, less invasive, portable, or even mobile sensors for fMRI, EEG and other brain scanning functions. To map precise correlation of brain activity to locations within the brain, instrument makers are diligently working to increase the speed and resolution of scans. The speed improvements would enable the neuromarketers to complete a scan while the brain is still active with the response to a stimulus. The low-cost neuroimaging instruments and machines will make the equipment available to marketing researchers without the necessity to defray costs with medical scanning.

In virtual reality, manufacturers are seeking the ability for higher fidelity images, more seamless displays, and more senses simulated. In the combined area of VR and Neuromarketing research is being conducted on development of VR Neuromarketing suites, such as CAVE and COCOON and on what marketing protocols to use and what questions to answer using VR Neuromarketing.

Lindstrom and Underhill (2008) in their book *Buyology: Truth and Lies About Why We Buy* explain that companies will continue to turn to neuromarketing to better understand how consumers feel about their products. Authors predict that traditional market research will gradually take smaller role, and neuromarketing will become the primary tool companies use to predict the success or failure of their products.

CONCLUSION

The aim of this working chapter was to explore the use of numerous neuroimaging modalities in the emerging field of neuromarketing. In doing so, we presented a brief overview of the Use of Virtual Reality and Neuroimaging Technologies in the emerging field of Neuromarketing. It is our opinion that attempts, although limited to show correlations between brain activity signals and buying behaviors have proven successful. The research to increase the speed and resolution of neuroimaging instruments and machines is progressing that will allow commercialization of neuromarketing field allowing it to become an important marketing skill within a very few years.

REFERENCES

Addison, T. (2005, May). More science: more sense or nonsense? *Ad-Map, 461,* 24.

ADLAB. (2006, November 7). *P&G Creates Virtual Reality Research Room*. Retrieved from http://adverlab.blogspot.com/2006/11/pg-creates-virtual-reality-research.html

Beier, K. P. (1990). *Virtual Reality: A Short Introduction*. Retrieved from http://www-vrl.umich.edu/intro/

Belliveau, J. W., Kennedy, D. N., McKinstry, R. C., Buchbinder, B. R., Weisskoff, R. M., & Cohen, M. S. (1991). Functional mapping of the human visual cortex by magnetic resonance imaging. *Science, 254*(5032), 716–719. doi:10.1126/science.1948051

Cambridge Research Systems. (2009). *MRI–Live*. Retrieved from http://www.crsltd.com/catalog/mri-live/index.html

Carr, N. (2008, April 3). Neuromarketing could make mind reading the ad-man's ultimate tool. *The Guardian*. Retrieved from http://www.guardian.co.uk/theguardian

Carter, M. (2009, June 24). *Neuromarketing is a go*. Retrieved April 4, 2009, from http://www.wired.co.uk/wired-magazine/archive/2009/06/features/neuromarketing-is-a-go.aspx

CAVE Automatic Virtual Environment. (2009). In *Encyclopedia Britannica*. Retrieved March 19, 2009, from http://www.britannica.com/EBchecked/topic/1196650/Cave-Automatic-Virtual-Environment

CBS Interactive Inc. (2009). *Incredible Research Lets Scientists Get A Glimpse At Your Thoughts*. Retrieved April 20, 2009, from http://cnettv.cnet.com/60-minutes-mind-reading/9742-1_53-50004855.html

Chaudhuri, A. (2006). *Emotions and Reason in Consumer Behavior*. Burlington, MA: Butterworth-Heinemann.

Clare, S. (1997). *Functional MRI: Methods and Applications*. Nottingham, UK: University of Nottingham.

Cocciardi, T. (2008, September 22). *Immersive VR Cocoon Coming In 2009*. Retrieved from http://g4tv.com/thefeed/blog/post/689456/html

Damasio, A. (2005). *Descartes' Error: Emotion, Reason, and the Human Brain*. New York: Penguin.

Evans, J. R., & Abarbanel, A. (1999). *Introduction to Quantitative EEG and Neurofeedback*. London: Academic Press.

Gibson, W. K. (1984). *Neuromancer*. New York: Ace Books.

Harris, D., Duffy, V., Smith, M., & Stephanidis, C. (Eds.). (2003). *Human-Centered Computing: Cognitive, Social, and Ergonomic Aspects* (*Vol. 3*). Boca Raton, FL: CRC Press.

Heim, M. (1993). *The Metaphysics of Virtual Reality*. New York: Oxford University Press.

Heim, M. (1998). *Virtual Realism*. New York: Oxford University Press.

Hoffman, D. L. (1995). *Marketing in Hypermedia Computer-Mediated Environments: Conceptual Foundations*. Working Paper, Owen Graduate School of Management at Vanderbilt University. Retrieved from http://www2000.ogsm.vanderbilt.edu

Isdale, J. (1993). *What Is Virtual Reality? A Homebrew Introduction and Information Resource List Version 2.1*. Retrieved from ftp://ftp.hitl.washington.edu/pub/scivw/papers/whatisvr.txt

Kenning, P., Plassmann, H., & Ahlert, D. (2007). Applications of functional magnetic resonance imaging for market research. *Qualitative Market Research: An International Journal, 10*(2), 135–152. doi:10.1108/13522750710740817

Knutson, B., Rick, S., Wimmer, E., Prelec, D., & Loewenstein, G. (2007). Neural Predictors of Purchases. *Neuron, 53*(1), 147–156. doi:10.1016/j.neuron.2006.11.010

Krueger, W. M. (1991). *Artificial Reality II*. Reading, MA: Addison-Wesley Publishing Company, Inc.

Lee, N., Senior, C., Butler, M., & Fuchs, R. (2009). The Feasibility of Neuroimaging Methods in Marketing Research. *Nature Precedings*. Retrieved from http://hdl.handle.net/10101/npre.2009.2836.1

Lewis, D., & Brigder, D. (2005, July). Market Researchers Make Increasing Use of Brain Imaging. *Advances in Clinical Neuroscience and Rehabilitation, 5*(3), 35.

Lindstrom, M., & Underhill, P. (2008). *Buyology: Truth and Lies About Why We Buy*. New York: Broadway Business.

Mazuryk, T., & Gervautz, M. (1996). *Virtual Reality History, Applications, Technology, and Future*. Retrieved from http://www.cg.tuwien.ac.at/research/publications/1996/mazuryk-1996-VRH/TR-186-2-96-06Paper.pdf

McConnon, A. (2007, January 22). If I Only Had A Brain Scan. *BusinessWeek*. Retrieved from http://www.businessweek.com/magazine/content/07_04/c4018008.htm

Ortiz, S. Jr. (2007 January). Brain-Computer Interfaces: Where Human and Machine Meet. *Technology News*, 17-21.

Park, A. (2007, January 19). Marketing To Your Mind. *Time*. Retrieved from http://www.time.com/time/magazine

Peck, M. E. (2008). A Brainy Approach to Image Sorting: DARPA project reads the brain waves of image analysts to speed up intelligence triage [Electronic]. *IEEE Spectrum Online*. Retrieved on March 1, 2009, from http://spectrum.ieee.org/apr08/6121

Renvisé, P., & Morin, C. (2007). Neuromarketing: Understanding the Buy Button in Your Customer's Brain. Nashville, TN: SalesBrain, LLC

Resonance Technology Inc. (2008). *VisuaStim-Digital*. Retrieved from http://www.mrivideo.com/product/fmri/vsd.htm

Rheingold, H. (1991). *Virtual Reality. The Revolutionary Technology of Computer-Generated Artificial Worlds and How It Promises to Transform Society*. New York: Touchstone.

Rowan, D. (2004). *Neuromarketing: The search for the brain's 'buy' button*. http://www.david-rowan.com/2004_02_01_archive.html

Roy, C. S., & Sherrington, C. S. (1890). On the Regulation of the Blood-supply of the Brain. *The Journal of Physiology*, *11*(1-2), 85–158.

Sato, S. (1990). *Magnetoencephalography (Advances in Neurology)*. New York: Raven Press.

Smith, M., & Kiger, P. J. (2007). *OOPS: 20 Life Lessons From the Fiascoes That Shaped America*. New York: HarperCollins Publishers.

Sutherland, M. (2007). *Neuromarketing: What's it all about?* Presented at Australian Neuromarketing Symposium at Swinburne University (Melbourne), February 2007.

Thompson, C. (2003, October 28), There's a Sucker Born in Every Medial Prefrontal Cortex. *New York Times*.

Weinberger, D. R., Mattay, V., Callicott, J., Kotrla, K., & Santha, A., Gelderen, Peter van, Duyn, J., Moonen, C., & Frank, J. (1996, December). MRI Applications in Schizophrenia Research. *NeuroImage*, *4*(3), S118–S126. doi:10.1006/nimg.1996.0062

Wells, M. (2003, September 1). In Search of the 'Buy Button. Forbes.

Wilchalls, C. (2004, May 22). Pushing the Buy Button. *Newsweek*.

Youngblut, C., Johnson, R. E., Nash, S. H., Wienclaw, R. A., & Will, C. A. (1996). *Review of Virtual Environment Interface Technology, IDA Paper P-3186*. Retrieved from http://www.hitl.washington.edu/scivw/IDA/

Chapter 8
Agent–Based Virtual Environments for Marketing:
Processes in Commercial Sector

Rui Wang
The University of Sydney, Australia

Xiangyu Wang
The University of Sydney, Australia

ABSTRACT

This chapter investigates the use of SecondLife as a virtual environment to help the commercial sector in marketing process. It presents the use of Immersive Virtual Reality concept to design a distributed marketing system for commercial sector based on the Benford's Mixed Reality boundaries theory and Motivated Learning Agents model. System framework has been proposed in this chapter and boundaries as well as agents factors in this framework have been discussed.

INTRODUCTION

Virtual Environments (VEs) are currently being used in an increasingly wide range of areas such as simulations (Snowdon, Churchill, & Munro, 2001), games (Torres, 2008), business (Lanier & Biocca, 1992) and decision making (Lurie & Mason, 2007). One of the most popular commercialized shared virtual environment systems is SecondLife (Linden Lab, 2003). SecondLife is an Internet-based virtual world video game, which was launched on June 2003, developed by Linden Research, Inc. Although SecondLife is sometimes referred to as a game, this descrip-

DOI: 10.4018/978-1-61520-631-5.ch008

tion does not fit the standard definition. It does not have points, scores, winners or losers, levels, and end-strategy, or most of other characteristics of games. However, there are a variety of systems, which have been created within the Second Life environment. John Gage, vice president and chief researcher at Sun Microsystems, has proposed the concept that make it possible for people to build virtual products and sell them inside SecondLife (Lee, 2007). Many users have already begun to build clothes, houses and entire islands that other users can buy with Linden dollars, which can be converted from U.S. dollars. (Figure 1) shows a shopping scenario in SecondLife.

During this virtual shopping process, sellers and consumers could see each other's avatars'

Figure 1. Shopping scenario in SecondLife

location and body gestures, from which they know where and what other people are doing. Users could design their own avatars to make them unique and recognizable to others. They are also able to make their avatars have some, such as waving arms or doing a little dance, which could help express users' feeling. Second Life provides a shared virtual environment for distributed users to collaborate with certain tasks or doing business, during which users are able to communicate with each other either by text messages or verbally chatting. Currently products sold in SecondLife are generally virtual objects that are designed and created in the virtual environment; however, it is possible to connect the virtual shopping system with web based e-commerce system and further facilitate consumers' online shopping process through interfaces between SecondLife platform and web based programming languages such as php (Linden Lab, 2003). In that way, the virtual and physical worlds could be connected and products would be sold in both virtual and physical worlds.

This chapter investigates the potentials of SecondLife as a virtual environment to help the commercial sector in marketing process. The following is a working scenario: SydneyToys is a local company that produces and supplies toys to most supermarkets (retail stores) in Sydney. To make sure that each retail store has enough goods, and those products are well presented, SydneyToys

has to send a number of agents to each retail store and check the status, which unavoidably costs lots of labor, time and money.

Furthermore, due to different understanding, different agents might have different criterion when they check the situation of products in retail stores. In order to solve these problems, the work presented in this chapter develops an agent-based virtual marketing network in SecondLife environment. This virtual world connects the real world suppliers and retail stores together based on Benford's Mixed Reality boundaries theory (Benford, Greenhalgh, Reynard, Brown, & Koleva, 1998).

This virtual world adopts motivated learning agent model. The purpose of adopting the agent model is to enable the system with intelligence so that it could monitor the status in each retail store and analyze their requirements in a real time manner.

BACKGROUND

Mixed Reality Boundaries Theory

Benford et al. (Benford, et al., 1998) introduced the concept of classifying shared-space technologies by the dimensions of transportation, artificiality and spatiality. (Figure 2) offers a detailed classification of shared spaces according to the dimensions of transportation and artificiality with specific technologies.

The illustration of the broad classification of shared spaces according to transportation and artificiality highlights the close relationships between the various approaches and in turn raise the issue of how they might be integrated. Therefore it was suggested that a more systematic approach to joining physical and synthetic, and connecting local and remote spaces (Benford, et al., 1998).

As a promising approach to tackle this issue, Benford et al. (Benford, et al., 1998) broadened the definition of Mixed-Reality as "the joining together of whole environments" rather than "the

Figure 2. Detailed classification of shared spaces according to the dimensions of transportation and artificiality (Adapted from Benford, et al., 1998)

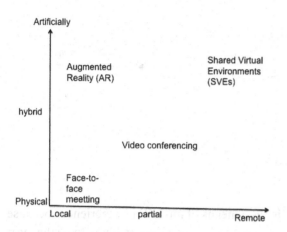

Figure 3. Creating a simple mixed-reality boundary (Adapted from Benford, et al., 1998)

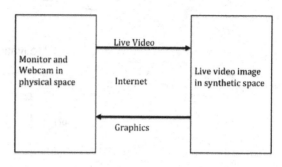

merging of real and virtual worlds" (Milgram, 1994). Based on this definition, they introduced the concept of Mixed-Reality boundaries. They developed an approach of creating transparent boundaries between physical and synthetic spaces to support new forms of awareness and communication between the inhabitants of many distributed spaces (Benford, et al., 1998).

(Figure 3) shows how a physical space might be linked to a synthetic space through the creation of a simple boundary based on Benford's theory. This is based on a combination of projecting graphics into the physical space and texturing video into the virtual space. In other words, the changing geometry of the synthetic space and the avatars within it would be transmitted across the network, rendered and then projected into the physical space. At the same time, a live video image of the physical space would be transmitted across the network and then displayed in a synthetic space through a process of dynamically texture mapping the incoming frames so that it appeared as an integrated part of the virtual environment. Consequently, the inhabitants of the physical space would see the synthetic space as an extension of their physical environment and vice versa. Given an additional audio link between the two

spaces, the inhabitants of each would be able to communicate directly with each other (Benford, et al., 1998).

Boundaries could be created between two physical spaces, two synthetic spaces, or between physical space and synthetic space. By creating those different types of boundaries, especially the physical-synthetic boundaries and synthetic-synthetic boundaries, their approach is able to join many different spaces into a much larger super-space by using multiple boundaries (Benford, et al., 1998).

Based on this theory, online stores, suppliers and customers in the three-dimensional (3D) virtual environment (SecondLife) and those in the real world could be seamlessly connected together to build up an immersive mixed world. It is supposed that in this mixed world, the marketing process could be better implemented with less cost of labour, time and money.

Motivated Learning Agents

Adopting agents in the business models is not a new topic. In Rohit and Sampath's (Rohit & Sampath, 2001) paper, several types of agents in the collaborative B2C business model and related services have been discussed, such as Interface Agent, Product Service Agent and Customer Retention Agent. It is believed that the intelligent agent based software components solves a host of problems related with the customer retention and

Figure 4. Motivated learning agent model (Adapted from Maher, et al., 2007)

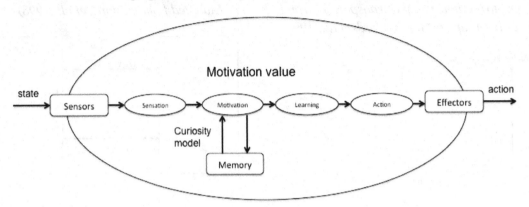

customer sales services as well as extending the horizon of the business to meet the demands in the market and as well to collaborate effectively with the peer business groups (Rohit & Sampath, 2001).

However, as the growth and rapid changing of current marketing situation, the traditional reflex agent models may not fit the needs. Agents with higher level of intelligence are in demand. Maher, Merrick, and Saunders (2007) have developed a computational model for curious environments with Motivated Learning Agents as shown in (Figure 4). Other than previous reflex Agent models, their computational model has added Motivated Agent and Learning Agent. The motivation process takes information from both the sensed environment and its own memory to trigger learning, planning, action or other Agent processes. It creates goals and stimulates action towards those goals. Agents are motivated to create goals to understand and repeat interesting events that occur in their environment. The role of motivation process in this model is to provide signals to direct the learning process. Firstly, events and observed states are received from sensation process. Then those different inputs are categorized into various types of information. Next, characteristic motivation functions are used to compute motivation values. Those values are then combined and transferred as signals and are passed to the Learning process. Learning Process is a key component of curios-

ity as a means of modelling experiences because recent experiences are more likely to be the most relevant at the current time and similar experiences from any time in the past are likely to be relevant to predict what actions to be taken at the present. Learning Process will encapsulate new knowledge as behaviours once an agent can repeat an interesting event at will (Maher, et al., 2007). In the proposed framework, there are both simple reflect agents model on the retail store side, and motivated learning agents module on the supplier side. By adopting the motivated learning agents model, the proposed system could be more self-organized and efficient.

THE PROPOSED SYSTEM

Benford's Mixed Reality boundaries theory is applied to the system proposed in this chapter as a guide to design the framework. The theory has provided a proper approach to seamlessly connect physical and synthetic environments in the system. (Figure 5) depicts the framework of the system:

Because Second Life environment has interface with other software and tools such as php and MySQL, it is possible to connect the virtual suppliers and retail stores with the selling systems in the real world. Back to the scenario in the introduction section: when a customer is intent to

Figure 5. System framework

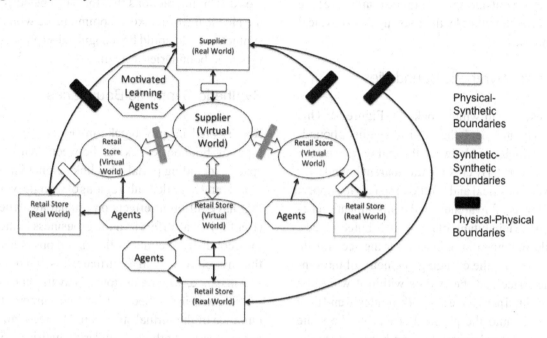

buy a toy, he/she could go to the retail store that located nearby in the physical world; alternatively, he/she could sit in front of computer in the physical world, and browse products in the virtual world. After having decided which product to buy, he/she could place the order in the virtual store, and then will get the virtual product in the virtual world, as well as the real product in the physical world later on (which will be delivered to the customer from the retail store as soon as the store receives the order in virtual world). Similarly, when a toy is sold by one retail store in the real world, it is virtually 'sold' in the virtual world retail store as well so that the retail stores and the supplier could be aware of the stock status with the supports of agents modules, which will be discussed in following sections.

Analysis of Boundaries

There are three types of boundaries between different spaces: boundaries between physical and physical environments, boundaries between physi-

cal and synthetic environments, and boundaries between two synthetic environments.

Physical-Physical Boundaries

Represented in black blocks in (Figure 5). This type of boundaries is the physical-physical boundaries, which exist in the real world, such as walls, doors, or roads that connect two physical spaces. In this scenario, the physical-physical boundaries could be the obstacles in the real world that between the supplier and retail stores. For instance, when a customer wants to buy a toy in the retail store, he/she should enter the door of the store, and the door could be recognized as a physical-physical boundary that between one physical place (the retail store) and another physical place (the outside space); moreover, when the customer leaves his/her house for the retail store, the door of his/her house could be recognized as a physical-physical boundary that exists between one physical space (the house) and another physical space (the outside space). Therefore, the three spaces (the customer's house, the outside space, and the retail store) are connected together by the two physical-physical boundaries.

Physical-Synthetic Boundaries

Represented in white blocks in (Figure 5). This type of boundaries is the physical-synthetic boundaries, which exist between the real world and the virtual world. By creating transparent boundaries between physical and synthetic spaces to support new forms of awareness and communication between the inhabitants of many distributed spaces. While implementing e-business in the SecondLife environment, the changing geometry of the synthetic space and the avatars within it would be transmitted across the network, rendered and then projected into the physical space. At the same time, the users' operations and behaviors in the physical space would be transmitted across the network and then displayed in a synthetic space through a process of dynamically animations so that it appeared as an integrated part of the virtual environment. Consequently, the inhabitants of the physical space would see the synthetic space as an extension of their physical environment and vice versa. Given an additional audio link between the two spaces, the inhabitants of each would be able to communicate directly with one another. For instance, when a customer is intent to browse and buy products within the virtual environment, he/she will be represented as a virtual avatar in SecondLife therefore he/she could enter virtual buildings, view virtual products and communicate with other virtual avatars, which represent other people in real world. The interactions that the customer in the physical world takes to communicate with the virtual world could be recognized as physical-synthetic boundaries. On the other side, the retail stores and the supplier build up virtual stores and virtual products in the SecondLife environment, and there will be a number of virtual avatars in the virtual world, which represent the sales person in the physical

world. The interactions that the sales persons in the physical world take to communicate with the synthetic world could be recognized as physical-synthetic boundaries as well.

Synthetic-Synthetic Boundaries

Represented in grey blocks in (Figure 5). This type of boundaries exists between synthetic spaces, including portals that link distinct virtual worlds and bounded sub-regions of a single world that have different effects on mutual awareness (Benford, et al., 1998). In the e-business context in SecondLife, it could be the virtual obstacles in the environment such as virtual walls and doors. For instance, when a customer's avatar enters a virtual store in the SecondLife environment, the entrance of the virtual store could be recognized as a synthetic-synthetic boundary, which links one synthetic space (the virtual building that represents the store) and another synthetic space (the outside space of the virtual store). Furthermore, the avatars could transport themselves from one space to another space in the SecondLife environment; for instance, a customer could be transported from his/her "house" to the virtual store directly. The transportation could be recognized as a synthetic-synthetic boundary as it connects two synthetic spaces, the customer's virtual house and the virtual store together.

By creating those different types of boundaries, especially the physical-synthetic boundaries and synthetic-synthetic boundaries, this approach is able to join many different spaces into a much larger super-space by using multiple boundaries. Those boundaries could exist between physical and synthetic spaces, physical and physical spaces, or synthetic and synthetic spaces. In the scenario in this chapter, by creating those three types of mixed-reality boundaries, the customers, and the retail stores and supplier in the real world, as well as those in the virtual world could be seamlessly connected.

Figure 6. Simple reflex model (Adapted from Russell, et al., 2003)

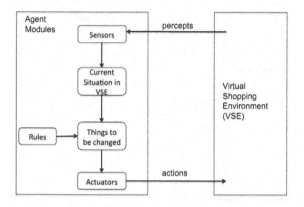

AGENTS MODULES

The agents module could exist in both real world and virtual world and they are monitoring and learning different types of evens. In real world, the agents module could be combined with the selling system and therefore monitors the marketing situation in each retail store; agent in each retail store side could tell the supplier whether a specific retail store has enough stock, and whether their products are selling in reasonable prices in that store. On the retail stores side, the simple reflex agents model is adopted, as shown in (Figure 6) (Russell, Norvig, & Canny, 2003):

In the virtual world, the agents could recognize each customer by their SecondLife user names, and record the customers' shopping preferences. In the real world, it is usually difficult to track and record customers' profile due to a number of reasons: it is difficult to identify customers; customers do not wish to participant; customers do shopping in different locations and so on.

However, in the virtual environments, the agents module could solve some of the problems. Because each user in the SecondLife environments has a unique user id, it is easy to recognize and track the users' behaviors. Some of those behaviors, such as shopping preferences, could be automatically recorded. The reflex agents module on the retail stores side is a basic agent that is rule-based. It sensors interesting events from the environment and generates reasonable effects. It could also contain search agent that automatically get useful information from Internet or database when needed. For instance, it could search for the stock status in the nearest retail store when product in the current store is sold out, and make the order automatically.

Motivated Agents Module is adopted on the supplier side, which is shown in (Figure 7) (Russell, et al., 2003). Those monitored data could be stored in the database and meanwhile sent to the supplier. The motivated agent module on the supplier side receives data from retail stores and them analyze the data. The learning process is triggered by motivated agent and encapsulates new knowledge as behavior when monitored events have been repeated. The database gets the knowledge from learning and this information could then in turn affects the motivation process; accordingly, the learning process is not only affected by current motivation, but may also by previous experiences stored in database. Database on all the retail stores sides are synchronized in real-time through network. Therefore, the agents module on supplier side gets information from each retail store. After the activation process, information is sent to effectors in all retail stores (Russell, et al., 2003).

The products are not only on sale in the real world stores; with the help of the system, they could also be sold in the virtual world. Since there are more than 2 million people playing in SecondLife and a lot of business is being processed here, it is likely that when visitors see the products in the virtual world retail store, they would like to place orders and get the goods in both the virtual and real worlds. Therefore, the real and virtual worlds are seamlessly connected.

Figure 7. Motivated learning agents model (Adapted from Russell, et al., 2003)

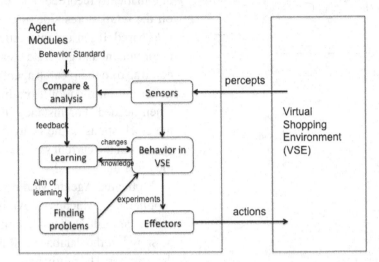

SUMMARY AND FUTURE WORK

This chapter presents the use of immersive virtual reality concept to design a distributed marketing system for commercial sector based on the Mixed Reality boundaries theory and Motivated Learning Agents model. Prototyping of the system will be developed in the future work. The system could seamlessly connect multiple physical and virtual environments together and afford benefits to the marketing process. The system framework demonstrates the potentials and possibility that it could advance the current practice of distributed marketing process.

REFERENCES

Benford, S., Greenhalgh, C., Reynard, G., Brown, C., & Koleva, B. (1998). Understanding and constructing shared spaces with mixed-reality boundaries. *ACM Transactions on Computer-Human Interaction, 5*(3), 185–223. doi:10.1145/292834.292836

Lanier, J. A., & Biocca, F. (1992). An Insider's View of the Future of Virtual Reality. *The Journal of Communication, 42*(4), 150–172. doi:10.1111/j.1460-2466.1992.tb00816.x

Lee, E. (2007). Listening in on Sun and Second Life at iMeme. *The Tech Chronicles*. Retrieved November 5, 2009, from http://www.sfgate.com/cgi-bin/blogs/techchron/detail?blogid=19&entry_id=18513

Linden Lab (Producer). (2003). *Second Life*. Podcast retrieved from http://secondlife.com/

Lurie, N. H., & Mason, C. H. (2007). Visual representation: Implications for decision making [Review]. *Journal of Marketing, 71*(1), 160–177. doi:10.1509/jmkg.71.1.160

Maher, M. L., Merrick, K., & Saunders, R. (2007, November 7). *From Passive to Proactive Design Elements: Incorporating Curious Agents into Intelligent Rooms*. Paper presented at the Computer-Aided Architectural Design Futures (CAAD Futures).

Milgram, P., Takemura, H., Utsumi, A., & Kishino, F. (1994). *Augmented Reality: A class of displays on the reality-virtuality continuum*.

Rohit, R. V., & Sampath, D. (2001). Agents Based Collaborative Framework for B2C Business Model and Related Services. In Innovative Internet Computing Systems (LNCS 2060, pp. 126-133). Berlin: Springer.

Russell, S. J., Norvig, P., & Canny, J. F. (2003). Artificial Intelligence: A Modern Approach (2nd Illustrated Ed.). Englewood Cliffs, NJ: Prentice Hall.

Snowdon, D., Churchill, E. F., & Munro, A. J. (2001). Collaborative Virtual Environments: Digital Spaces and Places for CSCW: An Introduction. In E. F. Churchill, D. N. Snowdon & A. J. Munro (Ed.), Collaborative Virtual Environments: Digital Places and Spaces for Interaction (2nd Illustrated Ed., pp. 3-17). London: Springer-Verlag.

Torres, D. (2008). On virtual environments and agents in next-generation computer games. [Review]. *The Knowledge Engineering Review, 23*(4), 389–397. doi:10.1017/S0269888908000040

Chapter 9
Implementing Virtual Reality in the Healthcare Sector

Sofia Bayona
Universidad Rey Juan Carlos, Spain

José Miguel Espadero
Universidad Rey Juan Carlos, Spain

José Manuel Fernández-Arroyo
Hospital Severo Ochoa, Spain

Luis Pastor
Universidad Rey Juan Carlos, Spain

Ángel Rodríguez
Universidad Politécnica de Madrid, Spain

ABSTRACT

This chapter will concentrate on the advantages that VR can offer to the Healthcare Sector. After a brief introduction, the second section will present an analysis of the areas where VR techniques can be successfully applied. Next section will describe some existing VR applications in healthcare. The development of a VR surgery simulator, with all the aspects that make this process challenging, will be presented on the following section. An analysis of the difficulties specific to healthcare environments while dealing with the design and development of VR applications will be covered in the next section. The last section will be devoted to conclusions and future perspectives of VR in the Healthcare Sector.

INTRODUCTION

The last decades have seen a remarkable growth of the Healthcare Sector in most societies, fuelled by advances in Medicine and an increased availability of resources. As a result, many societies present nowadays longer life expectancies and aging populations, which are more aware of health issues, in terms of demanding advanced treatments for health problems that would remain untreated just some decades ago. This places stronger demands on professionals, which have ever-increasing needs for continuous education on aspects such as learning new techniques, acquiring

DOI: 10.4018/978-1-61520-631-5.ch009

new dexterities, understanding data provided by new, complex instruments, etc.

Virtual Reality (VR) has an important role to play in this scenario. VR systems can be used for learning, training, planning and assessing techniques and interventions. The can also be helpful by facilitating the analysis and understanding of complex data. And they can even help motivate, distract and provide extra support for patients with specific some times overwhelming injuries, pain or sicknesses, such as severe burns (Hoffman, 2004).

Even though VR has a lot to offer to these domains, the Healthcare Sector is peculiar, presenting specific features that depend on its very nature. This chapter analyses the problem of designing and implementing VR applications in this sector, departing from an example of an area that has achieved a remarkable success: surgery simulation. The conclusions reached during the development of these systems can be used to cast some light on the problems associated to the development of a new VR application for the Healthcare Sector.

Regarding the case of surgical simulation, a lot of surgical procedures have a long learning curve, since they are complex to perform and require specialized training in order to obtain proficiency. Therefore, there is a strong need for learning and training the surgical skills.

During their instruction, surgeons, after a period of theoretical education, must acquire practical proficiency before being allowed to perform surgical procedures. This practical training-by-opportunity period usually consists of the observation of a number of operations performed in real patients and the gradual incorporation to auxiliary tasks, executed under strict expert supervision. This traditional training entails several disadvantages. First, the presence of beginners increases the risks involved in these procedures. Second, patients are frequently not pleased with being examined by non-experts. Third, those practical sessions constitute a bottleneck in the learning process, given the restrictions in the number of

trainees admitted to each operation. Other alternatives, such as using animals or plastic models, present problems too. For example, experimenting with animals involve legal and ethical restrictions. Additionally, they are of limited use given the anatomical differences and the expenses associated to animal maintenance. Plastic models can be quite realistic. Nevertheless, they are expensive to build, and once an incision has been made during a training session, it cannot be removed (unless the model provides extra exchangeable pieces, with its associated cost). This limits the lifespan of a plastic model before it turns into a non-realistic environment. Another limitation is that plastic models have in general a reduced number of different cases or configurations and they do not allow performing a patient specific training. Specialized courses involving cadavers are often expensive, restricted by the availability of cadavers and necessarily short. They do not suffice to achieve competency.

Simulation using Virtual Reality techniques offers a strong potential and makes it possible to conceive new solutions. Nevertheless, when designing Virtual Reality simulators, a lot of different aspects need to be considered: the interface that the surgeon will use; how to provide faithful and realistic feedback; the learning method to be applied; the process of practitioners' evaluation and, last but not least, cost. These issues support the fact that surgical simulators involve and should take into account different research lines and multiple disciplines:

- **Medicine and surgery:** it is essential to know which are the surgeons' problems and needs depending on each specialty. Surgical skills and techniques must be studied to understand how they are acquired so that learning and training deficiencies can be avoided.
- **Psychology:** task analysis is necessary to define a coherent and reliable learning program, which contains useful and effective

training exercises. In order to be able to assess the validity of a surgical simulator, metrics for response analysis and specific learning procedures have to be designed.

- **Computer Science and Engineering:** solutions that make the most of Virtual Reality potential and resources will be applied for the enhancement of algorithms so that the simulator can interact and run in real time and with enough realism.

This interdisciplinary approach makes the task of implementing Virtual Reality systems in the Healthcare Sector a difficult challenge. This chapter covers the most relevant issues and problems that must be faced when designing VR medical applications. Highlighting the key points and suggesting solutions, this chapter intends to serve as a useful reference for decision making.

WHAT CAN VR OFFER TO THE HEALTHCARE SECTOR?

Whenever an operator has to be trained to perform tasks involving risk for human beings or critical economic costs, simulators are the best choice. Very common examples can be found in industry, transportation and military environments, with flight simulators being probably the most widely publicized case. Medicine is another relevant area for simulators, with important risks that must be minimized. Medical staff must receive a very special training to perform correctly their tasks.

As mentioned above, the case of surgical simulation will be used to illustrate the issues discussed in this chapter. Within this context, the better healthcare professionals are trained, the safer healthcare procedures will be (Bayona, 2006). Surgical simulators offer new possibilities for surgeon learning, training and assessment. Virtual Reality has taken a protagonist role in healthcare, since it can provide solutions and new alternatives to help surgeons and to improve patient safety.

Nowadays, there exist a lot of surgical applications and they are becoming more powerful, useful and realistic as technology progresses.

During their instruction and residency, surgeons usually learn the basic techniques with simple training equipment, but the rest of the training is made through books and videos describing surgical procedures and techniques, specialized courses, or in the operating room, watching and participating in real operations.

Books, videos and multimedia material are particularly important and help a lot when learning anatomy, but they are not enough to acquire the necessary theoretical knowledge and practical skills necessary to safely perform surgery.

Another option of traditional apprenticeship is to attend to specialized courses. These courses often have a high cost and they are normally conducted away from the usual work centers of surgeons, implying additional travel allowances and accommodation costs. The centers where these courses are taught require specialized facilities, since they often use animals or cadavers.

In addition to the ethical dilemmas posed by the use of animals and the obvious anatomical differences, their use is becoming more and more restricted. On the other hand the cost and difficulties in obtaining cadavers is making this option increasingly more impracticable (Kauffmann, 2000).

While training in the operating room is essential and invaluable, it does not provide the optimal environment to test or practice new techniques and procedures because of the risk to the patient, the environmental stress and the limited time (since it is often not possible to increase the time of intervention). This training method also limits the dissemination of knowledge, as only a very limited number of people can be trained by an expert surgeon, and the time spent as a resident doctor is limited as well: there are restrictions on the number of hours and the number of days that a resident can work per week (Liu, Tendick, Cleary & Kaufmann, 2003).

It is expected that during this time, the future surgeon will have the opportunity to acquire the necessary knowledge and skills to become competent. However, there is no guarantee that this is the case, because the degree of proficiency achieved will depend on many factors, from prior knowledge to the pathologies of the patients he/she has had the opportunity to observe. Also, the teaching skills and patience of his/her mentor will have a strong impact on his future skills. Not all residents will have the same opportunities, so it could be said that it is an opportunist learning, being in many cases insufficient.

Virtual environments present an alternative to alleviate these deficiencies of training. In a 3D interactive simulation, surgeons using an interface can handle, cut or suture dynamic and geometrically correct models of simulated organs and tissues. As the interaction is done with a virtual anatomy, there is no risk to the patient and therefore there is less stress. Unlike learning anatomy from a book, Virtual Reality is interactive and offers navigable three-dimensional models.

Virtual Reality also provides some unique advantages: it allows the repetition of exercises and the training of skills as many times as needed until they can be completely mastered. Another benefit is that, since it is possible to generate arbitrary virtual anatomies and pathologies, surgeons can be trained to deal with atypical pathologies that might not be frequently found throughout his career, but for which they must be prepared as well. One outstanding possibility of Virtual Reality is the reconstruction of 3D models based on the real data of specific patients. This offers the opportunity of setting up simulations in which the surgeon will be able to plan and execute the procedure with a virtual model that corresponds to a particular patient that has to be operated. In a near future, it is predictable that training and accreditation in surgery will tend to standardization thanks to simulators.

Most simulators are available for surgical applications in minimally invasive surgery (MIS).

This is not a coincidence. First, there is a need for better learning and training methods for the complex techniques involved in MIS. Furthermore, the restrictions imposed by MIS make the design an implementation of Virtual Reality simulators more affordable with the current technology than it is for simulation of open surgery.

The following questions are very important to be remembered when designing a Virtual Reality simulator: What can be simulated? Is it worthy to design and implement a Virtual Reality healthcare simulator for his task? Do current traditional simulators cover the needed training? Which would be the achievable degree of realism with the current Virtual Reality technology? What would be the costs?

A Virtual Reality training system may be able to provide a non-degradable realistic environment, in which novices may learn and try as much as desired. Using such a system also reduces the trainee's stress, since the training session is no more a one opportunity procedure. Pathologies and training cases can be designed following didactic criteria. Even more, Virtual Reality allows training on real patient specific data. Assessment studies should guarantee that the skills acquired through virtual simulation are transferable to the operating room.

The following section is devoted to analyze the specific problems in this sector that could take advantage of VR techniques and applications. The analysis will depart from the healthcare problems modern societies have in the face of aging, more health-aware societies, looking for areas where VR developments can offer efficient solutions.

EXAMPLES OF VR-HEALTHCARE APPLICATIONS

Virtual Reality has been applied to many healthcare areas ranging from the visualization of medical databases to surgical procedures. If we check the two leading clinical databases – MEDLINE and

PSYCINFO – using the "Virtual Reality" keyword we can find 2601 papers listed in MEDLINE and 1865 in PSYCINFO (accessed 03 April, 2009). Another sign of the relevance of VR applied to healthcare is the great success of the annual international conference Medicine Meets Virtual Reality (MMVR, 2009).

VR applications in healthcare include:

- Remote surgery, telepresence, augmented reality surgery.
- 3D human anatomy models for education, visualization diagnosis and planning
- Architectural design for health-care facilities
- Preventive medicine and patient education
- Haptic aided rehabilitation
- Visualization of massive medical databases
- Treatment planning
- Medical therapy
- Pain control
- Psychotherapy through Virtual Reality
- Virtual patients
- Surgery simulation: for pre-operative planning, computer-aided surgical interventions, intraoperative navigation and image guided surgery, post-operative planning, education, training, rehearsal, and assessment of surgical competences.

This section presents some existing VR systems for the Healthcare Sector, together with some papers and reviews related to different application areas, such as psychotherapy, virtual patients and surgical simulators. Two interesting surveys of the application of VR techniques to healthcare are (Moline, 1997; Riva, 2002).

A complete review on VR applied to psychotherapy can be found at (Riva, 2005). Also, it is interesting to mention the Virtual Reality Medical Center (VRMC, 2009), a well-known center in which VR is currently being applied to treat anxiety and panic disorders, including specific phobias such as fear of flying, fear of driving,

fear of heights, fear of public speaking, fear of thunderstorms, claustrophobia, agoraphobia, arachnophobia, social phobia, panic disorder, and posttraumatic stress disorder due to motor vehicle accidents. In this center Virtual Reality exposure therapy (3-dimensional computer simulation) is used in combination with physiological monitoring. General stress management and relaxation skills are taught for stress-related disorders with significant success.

A remarkable effort to provide a virtual patient is SimMan®, which is a portable and advanced patient simulator for team training, with realistic anatomy and clinical functionality (SimMan®, 2009). Other interesting projects related to virtual patients are (Dickerson, 2005; Takacs, 2008). Also, Liu et al. (2003) present a through survey of surgical simulator systems, describing the components of a simulator and identifying key research questions. Leskovsky et al. (2006) offer an online repository to keep track of surgical simulators and follow the state-of-the-art in this field.

Although there are several simulators for open surgery procedures, such as (Al-khalifah, 2006), most surgical simulators address Minimal Invasive Surgery (MIS) procedures, due to the particularities of this type of interventions, e.g. Haptica Promis (2009). In general, surgical virtual simulators are often associated with specific interventions. Some examples are UroMentor (2009) associated with cytoscopy, Simbionix (GI Mentor, 2009) and AccuTouch (Immersion, 2009) associated with colonoscopy and bronchoscopy, Procedicus MIST and Procedicus VIST (Mentice, 2009) associated with intravascular procedures, or the numerous simulators, SimSurgery (2009), LapSim (2009), LapMentor (2009) or Procedicus MIST and Procedicus VIST (Mentice, 2009) associated with laparoscopy. Regarding arthroscopy simulators, most work has been devoted to knee training (Muller & Bockholt, 1998; Mabrey, Gillogly & Kasser, 2002), although two commercial simulators were developed including shoulder ar-

Figure 1. Example of surgical simulator insightArthroVR(Courtesy of GMV (©2009, GMV, Used with permission))

throscopy exercises: Procedicus VA from Mentice and *insightArthroVR®* (GMV, 2009; (See Figure 1).

A complete review on minimally invasive surgery simulators can be found in (Basdogan, 2007).

A CASE STUDY: DESIGN AND IMPLEMENTATION OF A SURGICAL SIMULATOR

Once this general panorama of VR in healthcare is presented, a particularly relevant segment will be described in more detail: surgical simulators, an area where a remarkable degree of success has been achieved. This success has been stimulated by the difficulties associated to the learning process in minimally invasive surgery and by the advantages these surgical procedures present, a fortunate coincidence that can cast some light on how to conceive successful VR applications.

The following paragraphs describe the main problems and issues that must be taken into account when designing and implementing surgical simulators. In particular, the following aspects will be addressed:

- Development of the virtual scene, surgical instruments and anatomical models.
- Scene-instrumental interaction.
- Collision detection methods
- Deformable objects simulation methods
- Sensorial stimuli synthesis

Development of the Virtual Scene, Surgical Instruments, and Anatomical Models

This section describes different alternatives for building the virtual scene, including the modeling of anatomical case-studies (both healthy and unhealthy) and the acquisition of real patient data. Also, this section covers modeling the surgical instruments.

Surgical simulators can be based on three different kinds of virtual scenes, depending of the desired system complexity and the final purpose of the simulator:

- Virtual scenes that do not try to represent the real anatomy, but a synthetic scene which will facilitate carrying out several exercises designed to train particular abilities useful for surgery, as indirect vision (the ability of working while looking at the image of a monitor) or relying on the feedback provided by touch. Those exercises must be specially designed and validated by experts on medical pedagogy to ensure that they are useful and well chosen for the instruction objectives.
- Scenes that try to represent common pathologies of human anatomy (or animal anatomy, if the simulator is oriented to veterinary). The most common use of those scenes is to create exercises where the trainee must diagnose and repair the pathology using the adequate surgical pro-

cedure. As there are a very large number of pathologies, each one is different in each patient, and sometimes a patient presents more than one pathology, it is necessary to choose just a reduced set of representative scenes that will be implemented in the simulator.

- Scenes that represent pathologies from real patients, using data acquired from medical imaging devices (such as NMR). These scenes may be used to prepare some extremely complex surgery (as the division of Siamese twins), to evaluate the risks for a new surgical procedure, to plan an intervention, to make sure that a particular surgical procedure is feasible for a specific patient, etc.

In the case of virtual scenes based in human anatomy, it is necessary to create a model to represent and simulate each organ that can be found on the virtual scenario. It is necessary to simulate not only the pathological areas that need to be analyzed and repaired, but also any organ, tissue and anatomical structure near of the area of surgery. The large number of models and the strong interaction between them produce usually a very complex scenario.

Also, it is especially difficult to acquire the physical parameters that characterize the mechanical or functional behavior of each organ, due to problems intrinsic to the measurement process, the anisotropic behavior of most tissues, etc. The "rigor mortis" produce strong differences in the rigidity values that can be measured on cadaveric organs and the rigidity of live tissues; it can be stated that the only organs with characterizations easy to acquire are bones and skin. Due to those difficulties, it is frequent to work with simplified scenes that make use of fewer elements and which do not simulate every element that may appear in a real surgery, as internal fat or capillaries near

the working area, as long as the didactic purpose of the simulator is kept.

In addition to the anatomy, it is necessary to develop also models for surgical instruments, including simple to highly complex tools, which may be covered by industry patents. For example, an arthroscopy camera uses complex optics which may be oriented by the surgeon to view in different directions. There are a large number of tools that can perform the same surgical procedure, so it is necessary to choose which surgical instruments will actually be simulated.

With respect to the way models are represented, current simulation applications which need to be executed in real-time use 3D meshes, with surface patches defined using triangular (sometimes quadrilateral) faces. This is due to the fact that the current graphics hardware is optimized for processing this kind of models, achieving excellent ratios price-performance from the point of view of their graphical output.

Scene-Instrumental Interaction

In healthcare-oriented applications, scenes are usually complex, containing both deformable and rigid objects. Accordingly, appropriate collision detection, force calculation and deformation algorithms must be developed.

The simulation of a surgery procedure in a realistic way needs the simulation of every interaction between the medical instrumental and the anatomical structures in the surgery area. As a result of this simulation, the system has to provide the current position of every instrument and organ in the scene, the new shape of every deformable model, the forces that must be sent to the haptic devices (if used) for providing touch feedback, and the sounds that must be produced.

Since the interaction between the instrumental and the anatomy is so important for providing a realistic feedback, the design and implementation of the algorithms that model this interaction is the most complex task in the development phase of any simulator. It is necessary to keep in mind some facts during the design phase:

• The simulation stage takes place within a complex scene, where objects usually have irregular geometries and intercross each another in a reduced space. In consequence, a large number of interactions between objects can happen at any time. It is therefore necessary to choose an efficient method for detecting contacts between objects and for computing the consequences of these contacts, in order to guarantee adequate response times during the simulation

• The use of thin structures, as tendons or surgical threads requires implementing collision detection algorithms which ensure temporal coherence, which guarantees detecting collisions that take place in the time between two collision tests.

• As each deformable structure can be interacting with several other structures or simulated tools (they could even present self-collisions), it is hard to use deformation methods based on pre-computed solutions. To speed-up the contact and collision detection stage it is necessary to use techniques based in hierarchical structures, such as sphere-trees, OOBB-trees or spatial hashing. Using such structures on deformable objects requires recalculating them after each deformation.

• Given the fact that different output devices demand different refresh rates, it is usually necessary to design the software architecture using independent threads, each one running at the pertinent frequency. For example, graphics devices need refresh rates between 20 and 60 Hz typically, while haptic devices use refresh rates near 1000 Hz.

The architecture of a basic simulator may be implemented using just three threads:

1. **Graphics Thread:** It creates the graphical output from the current state of each surgical tool and anatomy model in the scene. It should run at rates between 20 Hz and 60 Hz and have assigned low priority, so that it does not interrupt the physic thread.

2. **Physics Thread:** It is in charge of reading the input of the haptic devices in order to compute the position of the surgical tools, carrying out the collision detection stage and detecting interactions between models. It should also compute the new shape of the deformable models and it should also recalculate the data structures in order to accelerate the next collision detection stage. The Physics Thread should run at rates between 80 Hz. and 150 Hz in order to ensure the stability of the integration method used for computing the system response.

3. **Haptic Thread:** It should compute the output that haptic devices have to provide, at a rate above 500 Hz. (most haptic devices require to be refreshed at 1000 Hz). As this task runs at such a high frequency, it should have the highest priority and be heavily optimized, because it can use an important percentage of the total CPU time.

Depending on the specific features of the simulator, it may be even convenient to add additional threads in order to reduce the size of Physics Thread.

Collision Detection Methods

Collision detection (García-Alonso, 1994) is one of most important tasks for interactive simulators which pretend to show a realistic response. The main purpose of this task is to search whether there are contacts between any pair of objects in the scene; knowing these contacts allows computing interactions among objects (such as structures or tissues on the scene and surgical instruments), and producing repulsion forces that avoid one object to penetrate inside other. If any of the colliding object models is deformable, it is also necessary to compute the deformation suffered by this object.

Deformable objects may present heavy changes in shape before they return to their original shape (Gibson, 1997; Meier, 2005; Nealen, 2006). In consequence, it is hard to apply to them techniques which use any kind of precomputed structure such as bounding volumes. Instead, it is easier to use techniques such as spatial partitions (Teschner & Kimmerle, 2005), which make no assumptions about movement or deformation of shapes.

A specific problem present in deformable objects is autocollisions, or the collision of two parts from the same object. This is due to a deformation process which makes a part of an object to try to penetrate another part of itself. If a simulator deals with a heavily deformable organ (such as an intestine, for example) it is necessary to implement an extra test to detect and prevent this kind of collisions.

Testing any two objects for collisions requires, in principle, testing every primitive from the first object against every primitive from the second object. This process is very expensive from the computational point of view if it is solved by a brute force method as described before, so it is very important to use some technique to speed-up it. There are many scientific publications (Bergen, 2004; Ericsson, 2004; Jiménez, 2001; Lin, 1998; Lin, 2004; Teschner & Kimmerle, 2005) about how to speed-up the collision tests. Typical methods include bounding volumes, stochastic methods, distance field based techniques, visibility based techniques or spatial subdivision methods. The use of a spatial partition drastically reduces the number of primitive pairs to check, as it only checks primitive pairs allocated in the same cell of the partition (Hastings, 2005; Teschner & Heidelberger, 2003).

Deformable Objects Simulation Methods

There are a number of mathematical methods that can be used for simulating the deformations produced in non-rigid bodies such as human organs and soft tissues during simulations (Meier, 2003). The detailed description of these methods is out of the scope of this work. The most widely used are:

- Mesh-less methods: They simulate the deformable object as if it were composed of a set of particles. The position of these particles may evolve under the influence of internal forces from the model, which guaranties the internal cohesion and right distribution of particles, and external forces, generated by interactions with colliding bodies and surgery tools. The displacement of each particle is then propagated to the associated part of the model using an extrapolation schema. Some of those techniques, as SPH, are very common in fluid simulations, but they can be also used to simulate soft tissues if high cohesion forces are used (Steinmann, Otaduy & Gross, 2006).
- Mesh-based methods: They represent the model geometry as a mesh of vertex, which can be located on the surface of the model or all over its volume. Whenever a collision with any external models is detected, these methods compute the force applied to the contact area vertex, using some methods to propagate the force within the mesh while preserving its topology. The most popular techniques are based on mass-spring models (Bourguignon, 2000; Provot, 1995) and finite element methods (Bro-Nielsen, 2002). This last approach is very precise if the volume of the element is small, but reducing the volume element increases the time required to solve the system equation, making it difficult to use

it for real-time simulators (Debunne, 2000; Etzmuss, 2003; Müller, 2002; Müller, 2004; Shijven, 2003).

Sensorial Stimuli Synthesis

The main senses used during surgery learning processes are the vision and touch senses. This section focuses therefore on computing the appropriate outputs for creating graphical and haptic feedback in response to human interactions.

Visual stimuli: Most off-the shelf graphics hardware can represent 3D objects with a level of realism which is good enough to make the surgery scenario displayed on the screen easily understandable. If additional realism is needed, stereo displays can be used to add depth information, but it is usually not necessary (for example, in minimally invasive surgery only a 2D monitor is available, and a stereo display might even be inappropriate). The main problem regarding visual feedback is simulating physical processes in order to create a correct animation for real-time graphics. The behavior of fluids, free bodies floating on fluids, fat deposits, reflection and refraction of intense lights, etc., are well studied and may be simulated, but it is hard to achieve a good result while ensuring real-time response to human iterations.

Haptic stimuli: Haptic devices are needed in order to return touch and/or force feedback. Historically, there have been many haptic devices which have been specially designed for medical simulation purposes. Also, different general-purpose devices have been used for the same purpose. The following ones can be cited:

*   Laparoscopic Impulse Engine (LIE), from Immersion[1] (2009)
*   Phantom, from Sensable (2009)
*   Omega, from Force Dimension (2009)

Audible stimuli: The relevance of sound is frequently undervalued when designing simula-

tors, but its importance is sometimes critical for increasing the feeling of immersion within the virtual scene. Sounds may be directly related with simulation (as the sound from a drill to indicate its on/off state) or just come from any other sound sources usually found in the operating room during a surgery (e.g. a patient heart rate monitor). Generic hardware shipped with any modern computer may be used to synthesize or reproduce sound; for this last option, it is often difficult to register sound with an appropriate level of quality. High performance sound systems can be used for generating directional sound, but this is not usually required.

Other stimuli: Sometimes it may be useful to incorporate external stimuli to improve the feeling of immersion into the virtual scene. The use of correct ambient illumination, surgical gloves and dress, or hiding wires not present on a real surgery process may suppose an extra motivation factor that will increase the effectiveness of the learning process.

Learning Protocols Didactic Sequences

As it has been mentioned before, learning surgery through virtual simulation can contribute to improve patient safety by training surgeons so that they can perform procedures in a shorter time, enhancing economy of movements and reducing patient damage (Poss, 2000). In order to benefit from all these advantages, learning protocols and didactic sequences for learning surgical techniques must be devised. For that purpose, the exercises to be included in the simulator have to be conceived by a multidisciplinary design team, composed by surgeons, psycho-pedagogues and engineers. Surgeons should describe surgical competences and apprentices' needs. Also, surgeons, together with psycho-pedagogues, have to analyze tasks and competences in order to fix learning protocols. Last, engineers should introduce technical constraints, suggesting alternative implementations of each of the simulator features.

The first step in all this process has to be establishing learning requirements and defining the educational goals to be covered by the simulator. In order to do this, expert surgeons will define the desirable competencies to be acquired: procedure knowledge, anatomy knowledge, dexterity, decision making, stress control, etc. Then, expert surgeons and psycho-pedagogues will plan a didactic sequence of training exercises in order to provide an individualized formation. These ideas will be discussed with the engineers, who, knowing the technological constraints will study the achievable degree of realism and fidelity.

Within the planning of the didactic sequence, several aspects should be taken into account:

- Task analysis
- Avoidance of bad habits
- Definition of difficulty levels.
- Development of a library of pathologies and cases.

Task analysis is a strategy based on the curriculum of competences. It consists on decomposing the task to be learned into the different elements that form it (subtasks). It is mainly based on two theories:

- Theory of identical elements: this theory supports that complex tasks involve operations, principles and rules present in simpler tasks, which can be previously learned.
- The theory of cumulative learning affirms that simple tasks are components of more complex tasks.

There are many different alternatives to perform a task analysis (Bloom, 1956; Bloom, Masia & Krathwohl, 1964; Fleishman, 1984; Gagne & Medsker, 1995; Patrick, 1992). Two predominant options are hierarchical decomposition and the technique of critical incidents. In hierarchical decomposition, the procedure is divided into steps, tasks and subtasks, so that the movements to be performed can be analyzed (Cao, 2007). The aim of the technique of critical incidents is to identify which key events within a process can lead to success or failure. Thus, researchers should attempt to characterize events and behaviors that may lead to mistakes.

Learning errors and bad habits acquisition should be avoided above all and already anticipated at this stage. For example, an initial stage of the didactic sequence is instrumental ergonomics. The apprentice should be instructed to grasp and use the different instrumental utilized during the medical intervention. One way of doing this could be to show some images or models of the different instrumental. In some of those images, the instrumental is properly grasped whereas in others it is incorrectly held. Then, the apprentice should select the correct positions. With this simple exercise, some errors and bad habits could be prevented. Another fundamental principle is that simpler tasks must be mastered before learning higher level skills. The various levels will be overcome according to competence criteria (Aggarwal, 2006; Cao, 1999).

In a well-designed methodology, the training program must train first the tasks on a one by one basis, and then include exercises that combine them. For example, in the case of arthroscopic surgery, a simulator should allow the training of the competence of handling the arthroscope. In order to decompose this complex skill, an apprentice must first dominate the different types of arthroscope turns: the turn of the camera and the turn of the optics (or the light source) before being able to navigate inside the joint. An exercise could be designed, consisting in handling a virtual arthroscope and observing the results of turning the arthroscope and the light source not inside a joint (as it happens in real interventions), but in a familiar and intuitive scenario that will make the learning of this skill easier. In this example, the apprentice would introduce the arthroscope into a virtual operating theater whose interior would be displayed on the screen, using a fixed portal and practice the already mentioned turns. This way, he/she could focus the operating room lamp simply by turning 180° the arthroscope (i.e. looking towards the ceiling of the operating theater), increase the visual field by moving back the arthroscope or decrease the vision area by approaching it to an object. Once the apprentice masters the arthroscope's turns and is able to navigate the virtual operating room, he/she will proceed to handle the arthroscope within the virtual anatomical model of the joint.

The exercises should be designed so that they present a progressive difficulty degree. It is possible to exploit the options offered by Virtual Reality systems for showing helping elements, different viewpoints and different anatomical models. An additional feature that is sometimes helpful is the possibility of adding or eliminating anatomical layers, providing a very didactic system for a three-dimensional understanding of the anatomy.

Formative and Summative Feedback

It is essential to provide trainees with a detailed feedback about their performance (Hubal, 2000; Seymur, 2002); for example, Higgins et al. (1997) state that it is absurd to build a training simulator that does not provide useful feedback on the performance of the learner (Higgins, 1997). When residents are practicing a new procedure, it is essential for them to be aware that an error has occurred whenever it happened, so that they can adjust their performance in future attempts. Even if errors do not prevent finishing a specific task, it is important to give feedback to the apprentices regarding all of their mistakes, especially if these errors may cause harm to a patient in a short or long term.

There are two types of feedback related to apprentices' performance (Box, 2003; Van Sickle, Gallagher & Smith, 2007):

- The instantaneous feedback, based on interactive indicators, which warns immediately whenever there has been an incidence on the performance of the trainee, such as an error or a collision. This kind of feedback is part of formative assessment, i.e., it is associated with the usefulness of evaluation as a tool for improving the process of teaching and learning.

- Feedback at the end of the exercise, such as the number of goals achieved, the total errors or the time to complete the task. This is a type of summative assessment that intends to evaluate the acquired knowledge and skills and that can assign grades.

Virtual Reality simulation, as a new technology for teaching, is able to generate realistic environments (with 3D virtual anatomy based on real data), which will not deteriorate with use. Moreover, VR training allows customized instruction, tailored to individual needs and abilities; this is what is named formative itinerary (Bayona, 2007). Also, virtual simulation allows the repetition of exercises until they are performed correctly, both in terms of how they are carried out and how long it took the apprentice to perform them; a useful point is that the simulator can easily store and retrieve the learning history of each apprentice. Additionally, it can incorporate experts' knowledge through the creation of a complete set of training cases and also for conducting a formal evaluation of the exercise.

Exercises within the simulator can be repeated as many times as desired and with various configurations. The system will provide the apprentice with elements of self-learning and self-evaluation.

Once developed, Virtual Reality surgical simulators must be validated before being recognized as a training tool for the learning and assessment of surgical skills.

Assessment of Surgical Simulators

Simulators are supposed to be useful for learning and assessing skills, but this is an issue that must be rigorously demonstrated. Once they will be thoroughly validated, Virtual Reality simulators will take an essential and unavoidable role in the education of new surgeons.

Most current surgical simulators have not been thoroughly validated (Sutherland, 2006). Nevertheless, it is essential to validate a simulator before using it to assess the competence of an apprentice, since the competence level of a surgeon will determine to a great extent the success of the operation. Logbooks assess experience, but not expertise (Paisley, Baldwin, & Paterson-Brown, 2001). In medicine, surgeons deal with human lives, so safety is a key issue. Consequently, there should be a tool to control and measure the competency level. Are simulators capable of measuring this competency level? How can we assure that training with a specific simulator will improve performance in the operating theatre? Assessment studies try to offer an answer to these questions (Sutherland, 2006). Simulators have the advantage that they can register metrics automatically, but there is still not a uniform approach for measuring surgical performance (Gallagher, 2001; Kneebone, 2003).

After a surgical simulator has been designed and implemented, it is essential to validate it before it can be used for planning, training or assessing. This section proposes a scientifically sound, structured methodology to validate simulators. This content is mainly based on (Bayona, 2009). It is probable that in a not so distant future, the effectiveness of surgical procedures will be evaluated through simulation. However, for that, simulators effectiveness and validity should be shown beforehand.

To carry out the validation process, it is essential to follow a rigorous methodology, focused on testing the different types of validity. The concept of validity refers to the property to be true, correct and in accordance with reality. Consequently, the validity is composed of a set of principles as described by Moorthy et al. (2003):

- **Face validity:** is the extent to which the examination resembles real life situations, i.e., the degree to which a measure appears to be valid to the observed subject. It is important because it influences the degree of cooperation of the person being observed. According to Moorthy, in the virtual simulation domain, it could suggest how the simulator reflects the real environment.

- **Content validity:** is the extent to which the issue that is being measured is evaluated by the assessment tool. It tries to ensure that the test is an adequate and representative sample of the content it aims to assess. Experts should conduct a detailed examination of the contents to determine whether they are appropriate and specific to a particular situation. It could happen, for example, that while trying to measure technical skills, simultaneously and involuntarily the test is also measuring knowledge. Establishing content validity is subjective and based on the judgments of experts.

- **Construct validity:** tries to ensure the existence of a psychological construct which underlies and gives meaning and significance to the test scores. A common example is the ability of an assessment tool to differentiate between experts and novices performing a task (Schijven & Jakimowicz, 2003). Another focus for this study is whether the surgical skills improve with practice in the simulator (Feldman, Sherman & Fried, 2004).

- **Concurrent Validity:** is the extent to which the results of the assessment tool correlate with the gold standard for that domain. It is based on comparing the test scores with other parallel indicators or external criteria. In order to determine concurrent validity, two different measure situations are needed: one is the predictor (X) and the other is the criterion (Y). The same subjects are measured and two observations are obtained as a result: one with X and the other with Y. Normally, concurrent validity is within the last steps in the validation process, as it evaluates the effectiveness of the simulator. The most ambitious goal of a surgical simulator would be to demonstrate that the taught skills are transferable to a real procedure at the operating room.
- **Predictive validity:** is the ability of the examination to predict future performance. Predictive validity tries to ensure the degree or effectiveness of the test to predict a variable of interest. A Virtual Reality surgical simulator will have predictive validity if the score that it provides is a good indicator to predict the level of performance that the surgeon will have in the operating room.

As a previous step before defining the objectives, it is useful to raise some questions to orientate the assessment process and to help assigning priorities. Based on these questions, goals will be defined and divided into primary objectives and secondary objectives. Then, a relationship between these objectives and the different types of validity will be settled. Afterwards, hypotheses based on the stated objectives will be formulated. It must be taken into account that a hypothesis must synthesize the query that the researcher wants to answer. Feasibility and scientific relevance should be prioritized.

Once the hypotheses are established, researchers can proceed to the design of the validation study, which must consider the ethical and legal regulations in force.

Ethical aspects are covered in the Declaration of Helsinki (WMO, 1996) and the Belmont Report (BR, 1976). They are based on three basic principles of respect, beneficence and justice. Specifically they materialize in:

- The informed consent and the specific data to be collected (together with the specification of the correspondent data protection issues) will be detailed when designing the experiments.
- Favorable Risk-Benefit Ratio. The relevant risks, benefits and uncertainties related to the experiment must be clearly exposed.
- Fairness in the selection, distribution and monitoring of subjects.
- Should the experiment require the handling of hazardous substances, safe facilities and trained personnel should be available.

Legal aspects of research with humans also must be taken into account. It is important to know the current legislation to design a study conforming to the existing regulations with respect of management and confidentiality of personal data.

The experiment should focus on a determined population. Inclusion and exclusion criteria must be specified. Each study ought to justify the minimal sample size.

The type of the study should be specified (Bayona, 2009):

- Depending on its purpose (descriptive or analytical)
- Depending on the temporal direction (transverse or longitudinal studies)
- Depending on the start time of the study (prospective or retrospective)
- Depending on the allocation factor study. They can be divided into:

o Observational studies (cohort or case-control)
o Experimental studies (defining the presence or absence of a control group and the method of allocating subjects to groups)

In the case of experimental studies, the operational definition of variables will be detailed. Dependent and independent variables will be specified. Avoidance of extraneous variables should be taken into account and researchers should consider whether it is necessary to perform a habituation procedure. The variables and the procedure to register them will be specified: e.g. time of completing the task, achieved goals, manual precision, economy of movement, etc.

Actuation and observation protocols for the experiment will be established. If possible, the study must be blind. In addition to this, researchers should decide the plan for the statistical analysis of data.

Before conducting large experiments, it is advisable to undertake a pilot study involving fewer resources and with a smaller sample size, to identify potential problems or concerns regarding both the intervention and the observation protocols. The data obtained in this study will serve to make corrections in the protocol and will be used as a guide or outline of what might be found in the more comprehensive study.

Following this methodology, results will be obtained and researchers will be able to draw conclusions regarding the initial hypotheses raised.

Once a simulator will be thoroughly validated, we will use it as a tool for learning or assessing the apprentices' surgical competences. An impact on patient safety may be expected from having an objective standard evaluation tool, which could be systematically used to assess surgeons' competencies before progressing to the operating room.

Major difficulties in implementing VR systems in the Healthcare Sector

The Healthcare Sector is different from many others where VR based solutions are being developed and exploited. This section is devoted to the analysis of these differences; understanding them is essential for avoiding many pitfalls that can hamper the success of an otherwise well designed, useful VR system.

There are several factors that contribute making the Healthcare Sector different from the point of view of engineering design. The first and most significant is the relevance of its activities to the life and health of people. This is evident, but engineers should keep it in mind while trying to understand points of view and decisions made by professionals of Health. Before a system can be validated and used thoroughly it has to be proven first that the system can not harm a patient in any way. Afterwards, it has to be proven too that it is useful for the purpose it was conceived for.

Healthcare professionals are surrounded by companies and salespeople who try to convince them to use a specific solution for a range of problems. Sometimes, a seemingly valid product has shown negative or even dangerous long term side effects which did not show up at system testing. Related to this, there is another factor affecting Healthcare professionals' decisions: mass media. Any news involving the Healthcare Sector attracts a remarkable amount of public attention. In particular, negative news can be exploited as an excellent way to increase business. Finally, politics are also important, since issues regarding public health can make political parties to win or loose elections.

A logical consequence of all these factors is that Healthcare professionals end up being cautious before adopting a new solution, and acceptance of radically new approaches tends to be slower than desired by the engineers who design them. Also, established solutions and procedures are often preferred until the advantages of the new approaches are fully shown. This does not mean at all that the Healthcare Sector is against technological advance; it is probably one of the sectors where technology has made a stronger impact. It just means that new solutions need a longer time before they reach widespread acceptance.

The second issue that has hindered the development of VR systems for the Healthcare Sector is complexity, and associated to it, cost. Most of the simplification assumptions that have been taken for other fields (simplified models, simple dynamic behaviour, rigid rather than deformable entities, etc.) can not be used in many applications in this sector because they would produce extremely unrealistic outcomes. In consequence, medical VR systems require dealing with difficult problems, which –as usual in VR– need to be solved in real time. This results in longer development times and more expensive hardware and software, which can make a VR system uneconomical.

Nevertheless, there is no doubt that the future for VR in the Healthcare system is bright. Little by little, VR systems are being designed and developed, entering the market and conquering a good reputation that makes many Health professionals see VR based solutions nowadays as useful and effective. The incorporation of VR training systems to Hospitals and Universities for the education of residents will extend the use of these systems, and above all, it will change the mentality of professionals, even in the short term. Once it is shown that the VR approach is useful (at least for some situations), more and more problems will be selected as candidates for VR techniques. For that, it is important that multidisciplinary teams composed of Health Sector professionals and engineers are set up in order to detect open problems and to design effective solutions: a lack of knowledge about real needs or procedures will result in a loss of opportunities or just plain failures.

Once a well-conceived and designed VR system is developed, a new stage starts: convincing the users of the potential benefits it provides; in general, young professionals tend to be faster in adopting new technologies. In some cases, there is peculiar situation, originated by the fact that decisions about buying a new system are usually taken by senior professionals. Very often, VR systems provide feedback to rate how well professionals do the exercises, and usually this rating is based just on dexterity, hand-eye coordination and physical ability, rather than on experience, ability to correct problems, ability to make the correct decisions, etc. In consequence, senior, expert professionals tend to get lower ratings than young, inexpert professionals. This fact might produce an unconscious rejection of the whole system, precisely by the kind of people who have to decide whether the whole system is worthwhile. It is important therefore to ensure that VR systems produce practitioner assessments which take into consideration a wide range of aspects, and not just physical dexterity.

Taking into consideration all these factors, a number of issues can be taken into account while developing VR systems for the Healthcare Sector:

First, it is important to concentrate efforts in developments that do solve specific problems or provide solutions for relevant needs. For ensuring this, it is essential to ensure support and feedback from Healthcare professionals during all the stages of development, since they are the people who have a global vision of the problems existing within their field. This is just an additional statement in favour of multidisciplinary development teams, a frequent need in the VR field.

Second, the functional specifications of VR systems in the Healthcare Sector are extremely important. It is essential to avoid just as much producing irrelevant designs which do not really solve any problem as it is to avoid generating overly complex designs which will be difficult to develop and maintain and which will be very costly, in terms of both software and hardware. It is very important to balance complexity and usefulness; always, a simple solution which produces the desired effect is the best option, particularly if that simplicity avoids later on the presence of skilled operators to make the system run.

Third, VR systems for the Healthcare Sector pose a considerable challenge from the technical point of view. It is necessary still to improve many aspects: more realistic treatment of deformable tissues, organs and entities, better sensory feedback, more appropriate haptic devices, etc. Also, it is necessary to develop real time versions of complex processes such as cutting, grasping, sawing, etc.

Last, the development of VR systems for the Healthcare Sector goes far beyond the actual engineering problem. It is also important to pay attention to other aspects such as how the system will be used, what information it will return about practitioners' performance, what kind of training exercises will be set up, etc.

CONCLUSION

Finally, this section presents the most relevant conclusions achieved from the experience gathered while designing VR systems for the Healthcare Sector. These conclusions cover different issues, regarding technical and non-technical matters.

The first issue to be pointed out has been already discussed throughout this chapter: the development of VR systems for the Healthcare Sector requires setting up multidisciplinary teams. Even though this is true in general for most VR applications, the need of collaboration among professionals from different fields is even stronger in the Healthcare Sector, because of the strong contrasts with respect to other areas. From our point of view, health professionals, psychologists and engineers have to work together, because the development of such VR systems involve many tasks that have to be performed by professionals with very specific backgrounds. As usual, setting up a team with people from areas so diverse presents specific challenges and difficulties. The smoothness with which the team collaborates is a good indicator of how the different points of view are incorporated into the system.

From a technical point of view, it is necessary that Healthcare VR systems improve their performance, both in terms of realism and capabilities. This requires designing advanced hardware, better adapted to the task to be performed, as well as developing more accurate and efficient software. In surgery simulation, for example, surgeons are often presented with poor graphic and haptic responses, quite far from what would be desirable in order to achieve a realistic simulation of the operating room. Sometimes it is even more difficult to perform certain tasks in simulators providing haptic feedback through commercial devices than it is in the real case, because commercial devices adapted to such specific problems can not exactly reproduce the degrees of freedom, restrictions and responses provided by surgical tools. This problem can be solved by designing specific interaction devices. Nevertheless, adopting this solution means that the cost of the final product will be noticeable increased, a quite undesirable option for a product and a technique that have to open a new market.

As stated in previous sections, the Healthcare Sector demands dealing with problems, situations and cases that require pushing simulation algorithms beyond the current state of the art. An additional example in this line is acquiring real data from specific patients: one of the main technical challenges for the following years will be the introduction of patient specific data into simulators, mixing the virtual world with real data extracted from any of the common acquisition techniques available in Medicine (PET, MRI, etc.).

From the training and learning point of view, the lack of standards for learning assessment with simulators prevents the certification of the education received by apprentices, an important issue that should be addressed before simulators can reach a widespread acceptance and use (nowadays it is possible to find reputed professionals that are reluctant to use VR systems for education, clinging to more traditional learning methods with the argument that they are certificated). The experience achieved during the last years by apprentices and instructors has proved nevertheless that VR systems offer an excellent alternative to traditional methods, not suffering from scarcity on resources (operating rooms, instrumental, cadaveric specimens, etc.). As time goes by and the professionals educated using VR systems start reaching responsibility positions, the acceptance and diffusion of VR systems will grow.

A definite advantage of the new VR tools is the combination of cost reduction, experimental learning reproducibility and ease of storage and management of case learning history. For example, from the point of view of surgery simulation, the new methods allow the introduction of specific expert knowledge, by allowing the definition and personalization of new sets of training cases. Additionally, it is expected that defining new evaluation protocols adapted to surgical simulators will allow a more objective and formal evaluation of the future surgeons.

To conclude, even though VR systems are growing fast both in capabilities and in acceptance, it has to be kept in mind that VR systems are conceived nowadays as complementary teaching tools, not as complete substitutes of traditional teaching methods. It is hard to say whether VR systems will be the only option in the near future or not, but the present situation allows to ensure that their importance in the Healthcare Sector will grow steadily during the following decades.

ACKNOWLEDGMENT

This work has been partially funded by the Spanish Ministry of Education and Science (grant TIN2007-67188). S.B. thanks the FP7 Marie Curie Actions for the Intra European Fellowship (grant PIEF-GA-2009-236642).

REFERENCES

Aggarwal, R., Grantcharov, T., Moorthy, K., Hance, J., & Darzi, A. (2006). A competency-based virtual reality training curriculum for the acquisition of laparoscopic psychomotor skill. *American Journal of Surgery*, *191*(1), 128–133. doi:10.1016/j.amjsurg.2005.10.014

Al-khalifah, A., McCrindle, R., & Alexandrov, V. (2006). Immersive Open Surgery Simulation. In *International Conference on Computational Science ICCS 2006, Part I*, (LNCS 3991, pp. 868 – 871).

Basdogan, C., Sedef, M., Harders, M., & Wesarg, S. (2007). Vr-based simulators for training in minimally invasive surgery. *IEEE Computer Graphics and Applications*, *27*(2), 54–66. doi:10.1109/MCG.2007.51

Bayona, S. (2007). *Metodologías de aprendizaje y evaluación para simuladores quirúrgicos de realidad virtual. Aplicación en simuladores artroscópicos*. Unpublished doctoral dissertation, Universidad Rey Juan Carlos, Escuela de Informática. Móstoles, Madrid, Spain.

Bayona, S., Fernández, J. M., Bayona, P., & Pastor, L. (2009). A new assessment methodology for virtual reality surgical simulators. *Computer Animation and Virtual Worlds*, *20*(1), 39–52. doi:10.1002/cav.268

Bayona, S., García, M., Mendoza, C., & Fernández-Arroyo, J. (2006). Shoulder arthroscopy training system with force feedback. In *Proceedings of medical information visualization - biomedical visualization* (pp. 71–76). Los Alamitos, CA: IEEE Computer Society.

Bergen, G. (2004). *Collision Detection in Interactive 3D Environments*. San Francisco: Morgan Kauffman Publishers.

Bloom, B. S., & Krathwohl, D. R. (1956). *Taxonomy of Educational Objectives, Handbook 1: Cognitive Domain*. Reading, MA: Addison Wesley Publishing Company.

Bourguignon, D., & Cani, M. P. (2000). Controlling Anisotropy in Mass-Spring Systems. In *Proceedings of Eurographics Workshop on Computer Animation and Simulation (EGCAS)* (pp. 113-123). Berlin: Springer-Verlag.

Box, I. (2003). Assessing the assessment: an empirical study of an information systems development subject. In *ACE '03: Proceedings of the fifth Australasian conference on Computing education* (pp. 149-158). Darlinghurst, Australia: Australian Computer Society, Inc.

BR. (1979). *The Belmont Report - U.S. Health & Human Services*. Retrieved April 6, 2009, from www.hhs.gov/ohrp/humansubjects/guidance/belmont.htm

Bro-Nielsen, M., & Cotin, S. (2002). Real-time Volumetric Deformable Models for Surgery Simulation using Finite Elements and Condensation. In. *Proceedings of Eurographics, 15*(3), 57–66.

Cao, C. G. L. (2007). Guiding navigation in colonoscopy. *Surgical Endoscopy, 21*(3), 480–484. doi:10.1007/s00464-006-9000-3

Cao, C. G. L., MacKenzie, C. L., Ibbotson, J. A., Turner, L. J., Blair, N. P., & Nagy, A. G. (1999). Hierarchical decomposition of laparoscopic procedures. *Studies in Health Technology and Informatics, 62*, 83–89.

De Floriani, L., Kobbelt, L., & Puppo, E. (2005). A Survey on Data Structures for Level-Of-Detail Models. In Dodgson, N. A., Floater, M. S., & Sabin, M. A. (Eds.), *Advances in Multiresolution for Geometric Modelling* (pp. 49–74). Berlin: Springer Verlag. doi:10.1007/3-540-26808-1_3

Debunne, G., Cani, M. P., Desbrun, M., & Barr, A. (2000). Adaptive Simulation of Soft Bodies in Real-Time. In *Proceedings of the Computer Animation* (pp. 15-20). Washington, DC: IEEE Computer Society.

Dickerson, R., Johnsen, K., Raij, A., Lok, B., Stevens, A., Bernard, T., & Lind, S. (2005). Assessment of Synthesized Versus Recorded Speech. In *Proceedings of Medicine Meets Virtual Reality 14: Accelerating Change in Healthcare: Next Medical Toolkit, 119* (pp. 114–119). Virtual Patients.

Ericson, C. (2004). *Real-Time Collision Detection*. San Francisco: Morgan Kauffman Publishers.

Etzmuss, O., Keckeisen, M., & Strasser, W. (2003). A Fast Finite Element Solution for Cloth Modelling. In *Proceedings of 11th Pacific Conference on Computer Graphics and Applications (PG'03)* (pp. 244-251).

Feldman, L. S., Sherman, V., & Fried, G. M. (2004). Using simulators to assess laparoscopic competence: ready for widespread use? *Surgery, 135*(1), 28–42. doi:10.1016/S0039-6060(03)00155-7

Fleishman, E. A. (1984). *Taxonomies of Human Performance: The Description of Human Tasks*. New York: Academic Press Inc.

Force Dimension. (2009). *Omega and Delta haptic devices*. Retrieved April 6, 2009, from http://www.forcedimension.com/products

Gagne, R. M., & Medsker, K. L. (1995). *The Conditions of Learning: Training Applications*. London: Wadsworth Publishing.

Gallagher, A. G., Richie, K., McClure, N., & McGuigan, J. (2001). Objective psychomotor skills assessment of experienced, junior, and novice laparoscopists with virtual reality. *World Journal of Surgery, 25*(11), 1478–1483. doi:10.1007/s00268-001-0133-1

García, M., Mendoza, C., Pastor, L., & Rodríguez, A. (2006). Optimized linear FEM for modeling deformable objects. *Computer Animation and Virtual Worlds, 17*(3-4), 393–402. doi:10.1002/cav.142

García-Alonso, A., Serrano, N., & Flaquer, J. (1994). Solving the collision detection problem. *IEEE Computer Graphics and Applications, 14*(3), 36–43. doi:10.1109/38.279041

Gibson, S. F. F., & Mirtich, B. (1997). *A survey of deformable modelling in computer graphics* (Technical Report No. 97-19). MERL- A Mitshbishi Electric Research Laboratory.

GMV. (2009). *insightArthroVR*. Retrieved April 6, 2009, from http://www.insightmist.com/description/description.htm

Haptica. (2009). *ProMIS*. Retrieved April 6, 2009, from http://www.haptica.com

Hastings, E. J., Mesit, J., & Guha, R. K. (2005) Optimization of Large-Scale, Real-Time Simulations by Spatial Hashing. *Proc. of SCSC, 37*(4), 9-17.

Higgins, G. A., Merrill, G. L., Hettinger, L. J., Kaufmann, C. R., Champion, H. R., & Satava, R. M. (1997). New simulation technologies for surgical training and certification: Current status and future projections. *Presence (Cambridge, Mass.), 6*(2), 160–172.

Hoffman, H. G., Patterson, D. R., Magula, J., Carrougher, G. J., Zeltzer, K., Dagadakis, S., & Sharar, S. R. (2004). Water-friendly virtual reality pain control during wound care. *Journal of Clinical Psychology, 60*(2), 189–195. doi:10.1002/jclp.10244

Hubal, R. C., Kizakevich, P. N., Guinn, C. I., Merino, K. D., & West, S. L. (2000). The Virtual Standardized Patient. Simulated Patient-Practitioner Dialog for Patient Interview Training. *Studies in Health Technology and Informatics, 70*, 133–138.

Immersion. (2009). *AccuTouch Endoscopy Simulator*. Retrieved April 6, 2009, from http://www.immersion.com/medical/products/endoscopy/

Jiménez, P., Thomas, F., & Torras, C. (2001). 3D collision detection: a survey. *Computer Graphics, 25*(2), 269–285. doi:10.1016/S0097-8493(00)00130-8

Kaufmann, C., Zakaluzny, S., & Liu, A. (2000). First Steps in Eliminating the Need for Animals and Cadavers in Advanced Trauma Life Support. In *MICCAI '00: Proceedings of the Third International Conference on Medical Image Computing and Computer-Assisted Intervention* (pp. 618-623). London: Springer-Verlag.

Kneebone, R. (2003). Simulation in surgical training: educational issues and practical implications. *Medical Education, 37*(3), 267–277. doi:10.1046/j.1365-2923.2003.01440.x

Krathwohl, D. R., Bloom, B. S., & Masia, B. B. (1964). *Taxonomy of Educational Objectives, The Classification of Educational Goals: Handbook II, Affective Domain*. New York: David McKay.

LapMentor. (2009). Retrieved April 6, 2009, from http://www.med.umich.edu/UMCSC/equipment/lapmentor.html

LapSim. (2009). Retrieved April 6, 2009, from http://www.med.umich.edu/UMCSC/equipment/lapsim.html

Leskovsky, P., Harders, M., & Szekely, G. (2006). A web-based repository of surgical simulator projects. *Studies in Health Technology and Informatics, 119*, 311–315.

Lin, M. C., & Gottschalk, S. (1998). Collision detection between geometric models: A survey. In *Proceedings of IMA Conference on Mathematics of Surfaces, 1*, 602–608.

Lin, M. C., & Manocha, D. (2004). Collision and proximity queries. In Goodman, J. E., & O'Rourke, J. (Eds.), *Handbook of Discrete and Computational Geometry* (2nd ed.). New York: Chapman and Hall/CRC Press.

Liu, A., Tendick, F., Cleary, K., & Kaufmann, C. (2003). A survey of surgical simulation: applications, technology, and education. *Presence: Teleoper. Virtual Environ.*, *12*(6), 599–614. doi:10.1162/105474603322955905

Mabrey, J. D., Gillogly, S. D., & Kasser, J. R. (2002). Virtual reality simulation of arthroscopy of the knee. *Arthroscopy*, *18*(6). doi:10.1053/jars.2002.33790

Meier, U., López, O., Monserrat, C., Juan, M. C., & Alcañiz, M. (2005). Real-time deformable models for surgery simulation: a survey. *Computer Methods and Programs in Biomedicine*, *77*, 183–197. doi:10.1016/j.cmpb.2004.11.002

Mentice. (2009). *Procedicus MIST and Procedicus VIST.* Retrieved April 6, 2009, from http://www.mentice.com/

Mentor, G. I. (2009). *Simbionix.* Retrieved April 6, 2009, from http://www.simbionix.com/

MMVR. *Medicine Meets Virtual Reality.* (2009) Retrieved April 6, 2009, from http://www.next-med.com/

Moline, J. (1997). Virtual reality for health care: a survey. *Studies in Health Technology and Informatics*, *44*, 3–34.

Moorthy, K., Munz, Y., Sarker, S. K., & Darzi, A. (2003). Objective assessment of technical skills in surgery. *British Medical Journal*, *327*(7422), 1032–1037. doi:10.1136/bmj.327.7422.1032

Müller, M., Dorsey, J., McMillan, L., Jagnow, R., & Cutler, B. (2002). Stable Real-Time Deformations. In *Proceedings of ACM SIGGRAPH Symposium on Computer Animation (SCA)* (pp. 49-54).

Müller, M., & Gross, M. (2004) Interactive Virtual Materials. In Proceedings of Graphics Interface (GI) (pp. 239-246).

Muller, W., & Bockholt, U. (1998). The virtual reality arthroscopy training simulator. In. *Proceedings of Medicine Meets Virtual Reality*, *6*, 13–19.

Nealen, A., Müller, M., Keiser, R., Boxerman, E., & Carlson, M. (2006). Physically based deformable models in computer graphics. *Computer Graphics Forum*, *25*(4), 809–836. doi:10.1111/j.1467-8659.2006.01000.x

Paisley, A. M., Baldwin, P. J., & Paterson-Brown, S. (2001). Validity of surgical simulation for the assessment of operative skill. *Journal of Surgery (British)*, *88*(11), 1525–1532. doi:10.1046/j.0007-1323.2001.01880.x

Patrick, J. (1992). *Training: Research and Practice.* New York: Academic Press.

Poss, R., Mabrey, J. D., Gillogly, S. D., Kasser, J. R., Sweeney, H. J., & Zarins, B. (2000). Development of a virtual reality arthroscopic knee simulator. *Journal of Bone and Joint Surgery (Am)*, *82*(10), 1495–1499.

Provot, X. (1995). Deformation constraints in a mass-spring model to describe rigid cloth behavior. In *Proceedings of Graphics Interface* (pp. 147–154). Canadian Human-Computer Communications Society.

Riva, G. (2002). Virtual Reality for Health Care: The Status of Research. *Cyberpsychology & Behavior*, *5*(3), 219–225. doi:10.1089/109493102760147213

Riva, G. (2005). Virtual Reality in Psychotherapy [Review]. *Cyberpsychology & Behavior*, *8*(3), 220–240. doi:10.1089/cpb.2005.8.220

Schijven, M., & Jakimowicz, J. (2003). Construct validity: experts and novices performing on the Xitact LS500 laparoscopy simulator. *Surgical Endoscopy*, *17*(5), 803–810. doi:10.1007/s00464-002-9151-9

Sensable. (2009) *Phantom Omni devices*. Retrieved April 6, 2009, from http://www.sensable.com/products-haptic-devices.htm

Seymour, N. E., Gallagher, A. G., & Roman, S. A., OBrien, M. K., Bansal, V. K., Andersen, D. K., & Satava, R. M. (2002). Virtual reality training improves operating room performance: results of a randomized, double-blinded study. *Annals of Surgery*, *236*(4), 458–463. doi:10.1097/00000658-200210000-00008

SimMan. (2009). Retrieved April 6, 2009, from http://www.laerdal.com/document.asp?docid=1022609

SimSurgery. (2009). Retrieved April 6, 2009, from http://www.simsurgery.no/

Steinemann, D., Otaduy, M. A., & Gross, M. (2006). Fast arbitrary splitting of deforming objects. In *SCA '06: Proceedings of the 2006 ACM SIGGRAPH/Eurographics symposium on Computer animation* (pp. 63-72). Aire-la-Ville, Switzerland: Eurographics Association.

Sutherland, L., Middleton, P., Anthony, A., Hamdorf, J., Cregan, P., & Scott, D. (2006). Surgical simulation: a systematic review. *Annals of Surgery*, *243*(3), 291–300. doi:10.1097/01.sla.0000200839.93965.26

Takacs, B., Hanak, D., & Voshburg, K. G. (2008) A Virtual Reality Patient and Environments for Image Guided Diagnosis. In Proceedings of Medical Imaging and Augmented Reality: MIAR 2008 (LNCS 5128, pp. 279–288).

Teschner, M., Heidelberger, B., Müller, M., Pomeranets, D., & Gross, M. (2003). Optimized spatial hashing for collision detection of deformable objects. In *Proceedings of Vision, Modeling* (pp. 47–54). Visualization.

Teschner, M., Kimmerle, S., Heidelgerger, B., Zachmann, G., Raghupathi, L., & Fuhrmann, A. (2005). Collision detection in deformable objects. *Computer Graphics Forum*, 61–81. doi:10.1111/j.1467-8659.2005.00829.x

UroMentor. (2009). Retrieved April 6, 2009, from http://www.med.umich.edu/UMCSC/equipment/uromentor.html

Van Sickle, K. R., Gallagher, A. G., & Smith, C. D. (2007). The effect of escalating feedback on the acquisition of psychomotor skills for laparoscopy. *Surgical Endoscopy*, *21*(2), 220–224. doi:10.1007/s00464-005-0847-5

VRMC. *Virtual Reality Medical Center*. (2009) Retrieved April 6, 2009, from http://www.vrphobia.com/

WMO: World Medical Organization. (1996). Declaration of Helsinki. *British Medical Journal*, *313*(7070), 1448–1449.

ADDITIONAL READING

Al-khalifah, A., & Roberts, D. (2004). Survey of modeling approaches for medical simulators. In *Proc. 5th Intl conf. disability, virtual reality & assoc. tech.*, Oxford, UK (pp. 321-329).

Allard, J., Cotin, S., Faure, F., Bensoussan, P., Poyer, F., & Duriez, C. (2007). SOFA an open source framework for medical simulation. In *Medicine meets virtual reality* (pp. 13–19). MMVR.

Bartrolí, A. V. i, König, A., & Gröller, M. E. (2000). Cylindrical approximation of tubular organs for virtual endoscopy. In Proceedings of computer graphics and imaging (pp. 283-289). New York: IASTED/ACTA Press.

Bayona, S., Fernández, J., Martín, I., & Bayona, P. (2008). Assessment study of *insightArthroVR®* arthroscopy virtual training simulator: face, content, and construct validities. *Journal of Robotic Surgery, 2*(3), 151–158. doi:10.1007/s11701-008-0101-y

Bimber, O., & Raskar, R. (2005). *Spatial augmented reality: Merging real and virtual worlds.* New York: A. K. Peters, Ltd.

Bro-Nielsen, M., & Cotin, S. (2002). Real-time volumetric deformable models for surgery simulation using finite elements and condensation. *Proceedings of Eurographics, 15*(3), 57–66.

Broeren, J., Rydmark, M., & Sunnerhagen, K. S. (2004). Virtual reality and haptics as a training device for movement rehabilitation after stroke: A single-case study. *Archives of Physical Medicine and Rehabilitation, 85*(8), 1247–1250. doi:10.1016/j.apmr.2003.09.020

Bruyns, C., Senger, S., Menon, A., Montgomery, K., Wildermuth, S., & Boyle, R. (2002). A survey of interactive mesh-cutting techniques and a new method for implementing generalized interactive mesh cutting using virtual tools. *Journal of Visualization and Computer Animation, 13*(1), 21–42. doi:10.1002/vis.275

Burdea, G. C., & Coiffet, P. (2003). Virtual reality technology, second edition with CD-ROM. New York: Wiley-IEEE Press.

Burgert, O., Gessat, M., Jacobs, S., Falk, V., & Lemke, H. (2008). Steps towards open standards for medical virtual reality systems. *Studies in Health Technology and Informatics, 132*, 62–77.

Burgert, O., Neumuth, T., Audette, M., Pössneck, A., Mayoral, R., & Dietz, A. (2007). Requirement specification for surgical simulation systems with surgical workflows. In *Medicine meets virtual reality* (Vol. 15, pp. 58–63). Amsterdam: IOS Press.

Chen, P., Barner, K. E., & Steiner, K. V. (2006). A displacement driven real-time deformable model for haptic surgery. In *HAPTICS '06: Proceedings of the symposium on haptic interfaces for virtual environment and teleoperator systems (HAPTICS'06)* (pp. 499-505). Washington, DC: IEEE Computer Society.

Dunkin, B., Adrales, G., Apelgre, K., & Mellinger, J. (2007). Surgical simulation: a current review. *Surgical Endoscopy, 21*(3), 357–366. doi:10.1007/s00464-006-9072-0

Flynn, D., van Schaik, P., Blackman, T., Femcott, C., Hobbs, B., & Calderon, C. (2003). Developing a virtual reality-based methodology for people with dementia: A feasibility study. *Cyberpsychology & Behavior, 6*(6), 591–611. doi:10.1089/109493103322725379

Fried, G. (2006). Lessons from the surgical experience with simulators: incorporation into training and utilization in determining competency. *Gastrointestinal Endoscopy Clinics of North America, 16*(3), 425–434. doi:10.1016/j.giec.2006.03.009

Green, P., Hill, J., Jensen, J., & Shah, A. (1995). Telepresence surgery. *IEEE Engineering in Medicine and Biology Magazine, 14*(3), 324–329. doi:10.1109/51.391769

Kneebone, R. (2003). Simulation in surgical training: educational issues and practical implications. *Medical Education, 37*(3), 267–277. doi:10.1046/j.1365-2923.2003.01440.x

Ku, J., Cho, W., Kim, J. J., Peled, A., Wiederhold, B. K., & Wiederhold, M. D. (2003). A virtual environment for investigating schizophrenic patients' characteristics: Assessment of cognitive and navigation ability. *Cyberpsychology & Behavior, 6*(4), 397–404. doi:10.1089/109493103322278781

Kühnapfel, U. G., Çakmak, H. K., & Maaß, H. (2000). Endoscopic surgery training using virtual reality and deformable tissue simulation. *Computers & Graphics*, *24*(5), 671–682. doi:10.1016/S0097-8493(00)00070-4

Lacey, G., Ryan, D., Cassidy, D., & Young, D. (2007). Mixed-reality simulation of minimally invasive surgeries. *IEEE MultiMedia*, *14*(4), 76–87. doi:10.1109/MMUL.2007.79

Lamata, P., Gómez, E. J., Sánchez-Margallo, F. M., López Monserrat, C., & García, V. (2007). SINERGIA laparoscopic virtual reality simulator: Didactic design and technical development. *Comput. Methods Prog. Bio-med.*, *85*(3), 273–283.

Lemke, H. U., Vannier, M. W., Inamura, K., Farman, A. G., & Doi, K. (Eds.). (2001). *Proceedings of Computer Assisted Radiology and Surgery (CARS'2001)*. Berlin: Elsevier.

Lin, M. C., & Otaduy, M. A. (Eds.). (2008). *Haptic rendering: Foundations, algorithms and applications*. Natick, MA: A. K. Peters, Ltd.

Massie, T. H., & Salisbury, K. (1994). The phantom haptic interface: A device for probing virtual objects. In *Procceedings of the ASME winter annual meeting, Symposium on haptic interfaces for virtual environment and teleoperator systems*, Chicago, IL (pp. 295-302).

McLaughlin, M. L., Sukhatme, G., & Hespanha, J. (Eds.). (2002). *Touch in virtual environments. Haptics and the design of interactive systems*. Englewood Cliffs, NJ: Prentice Hall.

Meier, U., López, O., Monserrat, C., Juan, M. C., & Alcañiz, M. (2005). Real-time deformable models for surgery simulation: a survey. *Computer Methods and Programs in Biomedicine*, *77*(3), 183–197. doi:10.1016/j.cmpb.2004.11.002

Mendoza, C. A. (2003). *Soft tissue interactive simulations for medical applications including 3D cutting and force feedback*. Unpublished doctoral dissertation, INRIA Rhone-Alpes, Institut National Polytechnique de Grenoble, France.

Mor, A. B., & Kanade, T. (2000). Modifying soft tissue models: Progressive cutting with minimal new element creation. In *MICCAI'00: Proceedings of the third international conference on medical image computing and computer-assisted intervention* (pp. 598-607). London: Springer-Verlag.

Nash, E. B., Edwards, G. W., & Thompson, J. A., & Bar_eld, W. (2000). A review of presence and performance in virtual environments. *International Journal of Human-Computer Interaction*, *12*(1), 1–41. doi:10.1207/S15327590IJHC1201_1

Nienhuys, H., & van der Stappen, A. (2001, October). A surgery simulation supporting cuts and finite element deformation. In W. Niessen & M. Viergever (Eds.), Proc. Of the 4th international conference on medical image computing and computer assisted intervention (Vol. 2208, pp. 153–160). Utrecht, The Netherlands: MICCAI.

Novák, Z., Krupa, P., & Chrastina, J. (2001). 3D Spinal canal reconstruction: virtual reality and postsurgical reality. In Lemke, H. U., Vannier, M. W., Inamura, K., Farman, A. G., & Doi, K. (Eds.), *CARS* (*Vol. 1230*, pp. 57–61). Elsevier.

Nunes, F. L. S., & Costa, R. M. E. M. (2008). The virtual reality challenges in the health care area: a panoramic view. In *SAC '08: Proceedings of the 2008 ACM symposium on applied computing* (pp. 1312-1316). New York: ACM.

Paloc, C., Kitney, R., Bello, F., & Darzi, A. (2001). Virtual reality surgical training and assessment system. In Lemke, H. U., Vannier, M. W., Inamura, K., Farman, A. G., & Doi, K. (Eds.), *CARS* (*Vol. 1230*, pp. 210–217). Amsterdam: Elsevier.

Peters, T., & Cleary, K. (Eds.). (2008). *Image-guided interventions: Technology and applications*. Berlin: Springer. doi:10.1007/978-0-387-73858-1

Pflesser, B., Petersik, A., Tiede, U., Höehne, K. H., & Leuwer, R. (2002). Volume cutting for virtual petrous bone surgery. *Computer Aided Surgery*, *7*(2), 74–83. doi:10.3109/10929080209146018

Rizzo, A. A., Buckwalter, J. G., & Neumann, U. (1997, December). Virtual reality and cognitive rehabilitation: A brief review of the future. *The Journal of Head Trauma Rehabilitation*, *12*(6), 1–15. doi:10.1097/00001199-199712000-00002

Salisbury, K., Conti, F., & Barbagli, F. (2004). Haptic rendering: Introductory concepts. *IEEE Computer Graphics and Applications*, *24*(2), 24–32. doi:10.1109/MCG.2004.1274058

Sherman, W. R., & Craig, A. B. (2003). *Understanding virtual reality. interface, application, and design*. San Francisco: Morgan Kaufmann Publishers.

Srinivasan, M. A., & Basdogan, C. (1997). Haptics in virtual environments: taxonomy, research status, and challenges. *Computers & Graphics*, *21*(4), 393–404. doi:10.1016/S0097-8493(97)00030-7

Sutcliffe, A. G., & Kaur, K. D. (2000, November). Evaluating the usability of virtual reality user interfaces. *Behaviour & Information Technology*, *19*(6), 415–426. doi:10.1080/014492900750052679

Thurfjell, L., McLaughlin, J., Mattson, J., & Lammertse, P. (2002). Haptic interaction with virtual objects: the technology and some applications. *The Industrial Robot*, *29*(3), 210–215. doi:10.1108/01439910210425487

Traub, J., Sielhorst, T., Heining, S.-M., & Navab, N. (2008). Advanced display and visualization concepts for image guided surgery. *J. Display Technology*, *4*(4), 483–490. doi:10.1109/JDT.2008.2006510

Vafai, N. M., Payandeh, S., & Dill, J. (2006). Toward haptic rendering for a virtual dissection. In *ICMI '06: Proceedings of the 8th international conference on multimodal interfaces* (pp. 310-317). New York: ACM Press.

Vince, J. (2004). *Introduction to virtual reality*. Berlin: Springer Verlag.

Voß, G., Hahn, J., Müller, W., & Lindemann, R. (1999). Virtual cutting of anatomical structures. In Westwood, J. D. (Ed.), *Medicine meets virtual reality 1999 (MMVR'99)* (pp. 381–383). Amsterdam: IOS Press.

Wang, P., Becker, A. A., Jones, I. A., Glover, A. T., Benford, S. D., & Greenhalgh, C. M. (2007). Virtual reality simulation of surgery with haptic feedback based on the boundary element method. *Computers & Structures*, *85*(7-8), 331–339. doi:10.1016/j.compstruc.2006.11.021

ENDNOTE

[1]   NOTE: Immersion Corporation does not commercialize Laparoscopic Impulse Engine devices anymore, since the creation of its own subdivision to develop medical simulators. Instead, they sell several complete medical simulators as *insightArthroVR®* for arthroscopy, LapVR® for laparoscopy and CathLabVR® for endovascular procedures.

Section 4
Virtual Modeling in Virtual Communities and Static Images

Chapter 10
Social Impact and Challenges of Virtual Reality Communities

Rafael Capilla
Universidad Rey Juan Carlos, Spain

ABSTRACT

The phenomenon of virtual reality has crossed geographical and social barriers since virtual reality applications started to be used massively by non-expert users. The development of high-cost and complex virtual reality applications for concrete domains and highly skilled users have widened its scope to the general public, which exploits the Internet to create, share, and configure virtual communities of users and avatars that transcend organizational, political, cultural and social barriers. This chapter analyses the social impact of different software platforms and environments that can be used to create virtual communities, and also how these platforms provide different collaborative capabilities among their members. The author also analyzes how virtual reality technology impacts in the creation and use of virtual communities, as well as outlining the benefits and drawbacks in a globalized context.

INTRODUCTION

The era of Internet has brought the globalization of the activities that ease the ways in which users and organizations share information and communicate each other. The enormous growth and popularity of social networks that enable the creation of virtual communities of users that share common interests is becoming a social phenomenon which transcends cultural, political and geographical barriers worldwide. Several social networks with similar and different aims (e.g.: Facebook, Tuenti, aSW, LinkedIn, MyYearbook) have achieved a great success as they count with thousands of users all around the world. Social networks form a structure made of nodes (i.e.: individuals or organizations) that are tied by one or more interdependencies such as: ideas, financial, cultural, social status, friendship and so on. Members of a social network can join or leave freely the networks to which they belong, while in other cases an invitation is required and

DOI: 10.4018/978-1-61520-631-5.ch010

approved to keep under control the virtual community. Today, social network analysis (Wasserman & Faust, 1994; Breiger, 2004; Freeman, 2004; Freeman, 2006) has emerged as a key technique of study in sociology and information science which uses collaboration graphs to illustrate the relationships between humans.

Generally speaking, users of social networks often interact using a Web portal which contains a variety of third-party applications available for the members of a given virtual community. In addition, virtual reality (VR) technology enhances communication in virtual communities by adding new on-line communication and display capabilities for virtual users. Virtual reality software for virtual communities like Second Life, provides on-line sharing and communication facilities where the virtual users (i.e.: avatars) interact in a virtual world to express their ideas, friendliness, or conflicts with other avatars. Moreover, advanced communication facilities provided by distributed Web applications constitute one of the existing challenges that are leveraging the popularity of virtual reality technology in an affordable manner. In this chapter we will analyze the characteristics and the social impact of social networks in the today's society as well as the use virtual reality technology in modern virtual communities.

BACKGROUND VIRTUAL REALITY TECHNOLOGY FOR VIRTUAL COMMUNITIES

Since Ivan E. Sutherland pioneered the computer graphics research, and implemented the first head-mounted-display (HMD) using wire-frame graphics (Sutherland, 1968), was not until 1989 when several VR developers, like Jaron Lanier used extensively the term of virtual reality to refer to computer technology that allows users to experience a three-dimensional environment which simulates the real world. Compared to traditional desktop applications, virtual reality is a complex and expensive software technology that uses special hardware devices to simulate the real world in which users are immersed in a virtual environment and they can interact with other avatars and virtual objects. Developing VR applications is not easy and flexible software architectures are needed (Capilla et al., 2008). Today, the complexity and specialization of current virtual reality applications (e.g.: military, health, simulators) has led to other type of VR applications that can be easily used by the general public, making virtual reality a massive and affordable technology for many. Presently, three kinds of applications can be used to create virtual reality communities, but this classification is continuously growing:

1. **Massively multiplayer online games (MMOG):** Are computer games that enable hundreds or thousands of players, all of the interacting in a game which is connected using Internet protocols. A wide list of different types of games is available, such as: action games (e.g.: Startport), sports (e.g.: Hattrick), building games (e.g.: Blockland), exploration (e.g.: Uru live), flight simulation (e.g.: IVAO, VATSIM), real-time strategy games (e.g.: DarkSpace), or social games (e.g.: Club Penguin, EGO, Nicktropolis, Second Life). Other subcategories can be defined under MMOG. Some of the MMOG games are free play while others required a paid subscription. In other cases, free play games include advertising or micro-transactions between players (e.g.: Ashen empires, Audition online, Bang howdy, etc). These micro-transactions encompass purchase of items or resources for the winning of the game, payment using a virtual and non real currency, bonuses, or expansion packs among others. Many of these games are commercial releases while others are still beta versions.

2. **Metaplace:** Is a software platform which brings virtual reality technology to the

Web as a way to democratize the development of virtual worlds. Metaplace uses the MMO markup language (often known as the Second Life on the Web). Metaplace's users can build 3D online worlds for PC or even mobile devices without any special skills or knowledge about VR programming languages. Hence, Metaplace offers virtual worlds opened up to all. Broadly speaking, Metaplace's users can generate online contents and the platform provides facilities for amateurs to publish their own virtual worlds. Because the official client uses Flash technology, user can deliver 2D or 2.5D virtual spaces rather than real 3D objects, but companies like Metaplace Inc. (formerly *Areae*) are promoting to support 3D functionality. With Metaplace, users can create virtual worlds as any content in the Web as they can use a markup language, style sheets, or scripting languages combined with Flash technology.

3. **Second Life:** Second life (SL) from Linden Lab is an online virtual reality community that makes an extensively use of VR technology (3D objects, avatars) to allow user interaction represented by an avatar (i.e.: a Resident in SL terminology). SL offers an effective platform for synchronous communications (Edwards, 2006) which is used by several organizations like IBM. Second Life exploits Internet to communicate the client installed in a PC with SL servers. A second life virtual user can communicate and interact with other avatars in many different virtual worlds, and they can form temporal groups or smaller communities of users sharing common interests (e.g.: a political party). Second life has achieved a strong social impact that widens and empowers other traditional communication ways like walls or email. Moreover, second life residents can change their appearance as they would like to be in "a second life" different from the

Figure 1. A Second Life resident interacting in a virtual world(© 2009, R.Capilla)

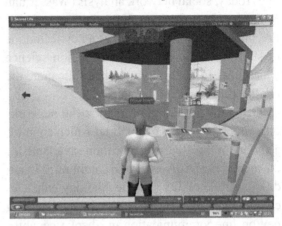

real one (even the gender). They can also be engaged in many activities, just as people do in the real life. Interaction can be done using chat or instant messaging once users have met in the virtual scene. Second life encompasses also different subcultures and events (i.e.: games, contests, nightlife). SL offers the Linden scripting language (LSL) for programming and interacting with the 3D objects and primitives for building SL virtual worlds, as well as a built-in 3D modeler that allows Residents to create complex objects from a set of basic building blocks or primitives. For business goals, SL offers users Linden dollars (L\$) that allow users to buy, sell, or rent trade lands, goods, or services. (Figure 1) displays a Second Life's avatar interacting in a virtual world.

CHARACTERISTICS AND LIFECYCLE OF VIRTUAL COMMUNITIES

Users join virtual communities for a certain time, which depends of the user's goals and expectations or the type of the virtual community. In the case of MMOG, users interact with of the community members until the game ends. In those cases where users belong to a virtual community for a long time, a membership life cycle (Kim, 2000) for online communities states that members of virtual communities begin their life in a community as visitors or lurkers (i.e.: a person who reads discussions on a message board, or chat room or any other interactive system, but rarely if ever posts or participates). Members start their activity in the community as novice and after contributing for a sustained period of time they become more expert or regulars. In a further step of the lifecycle they can become or act as leaders, and finally once they have contributed to the community for some time they become elders and in some cases leave the community. This life cycle can be applied to many virtual communities in different areas of expertise. The characteristics of communities in practice and its lifecycle has been also studied by Wenger (2007), as members with similar interests are seeking peer-to-peer connections both in the real life or in the virtual community to which they belong. A similar life cycle has been proposed by Lave and Wenger (1991), where users become part of a virtual community. The authors propose the following five types of trajectories

1. **Peripheral (i.e. Lurker):** An outside and unstructured participation.
2. **Inbound (i.e. Novice):** Newcomers are invested in the community and are expected towards full participation.
3. **Insider (i.e. Regular):** Full committed community participant.
4. **Boundary (i.e. Leader):** Leader sustains membership participation and brokers interactions with other members.
5. **Outbound (i.e. Elder):** Members leave the community due to new relationships, new positions, or new expectations.

Example: Facebook

According to the previous life cycle, we outline an example of a trajectory of a Facebook user.

Peripheral (Lurker): Observing the community and viewing content and types of users, groups of interests, and third-party applications. Does not add to the community any data or discussion.

Inbound (Novice): Just beginning to join and starts to provide some personal information. Occasionally can post some a comment, start some discussion using the wall, or seek for friends occasionally.

Insider (Regular): He/she adds to the community discussion and content as well as interacts regularly with other users, provide comments and answers to ongoing discussions, post new information and add new applications to enhance collaborative profile's features.

Boundary (Leader): The user is recognized as a senior participant in one or several areas or group of interest and he/she creates new groups in order to attract new or existing members. Other community members may ask for the opinion of the leader as he/she acts as an active contributor and trusted member.

Outbound (Elder): The member leaves the community for a variety of reasons, such as lack of time or interest, friends that left the community, got a new job, appearance of new communities (new competitors) which may offer better interaction capabilities, etc.

Virtual communities often share a set of common characteristics. According to Wenger (2007), *"in a nutshell, communities of practice are groups of people who share a concern or a passion for something they do and learn how to do it better as they interact regularly"*. The author mentions three elements that are crucial in distinguishing a community of practice from other groups and communities:

1. **The domain:** A community of practice has an identity defined by a shared domain of interest. Membership therefore implies a commitment to the domain, and a shared competence that distinguishes members from other people.
2. **The community:** Members engage in joint activities and discussions, help others, and share information, as a way to build relationships that enable them to learn from each other.
3. **The practice:** Members of a community develop a shared repertoire of resources: experiences, stories, tools, and ways of addressing problems. This effort takes time and sustained interaction.

Other characteristics may refer to the structure or formality of the organization, as some of them are more fluid than others while in some cases they have very strict rules for the permanence of the members. For instance, the policy of aSW says that you should not contact any member you don't know or you haven't contact before. Otherwise and depending the number of declines or ignores from members you have contacted, you will increase the risk to lost your right to connect.

Virtual communities promote a new form of democratic space to share and debate new and existing ideas, which are often organized in hundreds of groups of interests where users can join and or leave freely. Users interact with others preserving their privacy as they avoid a physical interaction, and they don't need to employ time to move to a specific physical location to discuss with other members because they are not tied to a specific location. Hence, the effectiveness of Internet constitutes certainly a key advantage to create more and more virtual communities in the cyberspace. Virtual communities constitute in practice an effective way of informal knowledge sharing available for their members, in addition to weblogs and wikis, to create volatile and non-

volatile lightweight knowledge, support collaboration between people, and support knowledge organization (Lee et al, 2003).

In addition, collaborative virtual environment is one the major characteristics of these platforms that memberships exploit to get in touch with other members from the same or a different community. Such collaborative capabilities (e.g.: CSCW – Computer Support Cooperative Learning) are discussed, for instance, in Second Life (De Lucia et al., 2008), as a groupware feature demanded by virtual community users. The authors investigate how SL can enable teams to work together and they propose the so-called SLMeeting software to enhance communication facilities of traditional meeting rooms by supporting the management of collaborative activities (e.g.: booking list, meeting chat room, voting participant palette, timekeeping clock, etc.). SL residents interact with SLMeeting objects on behalf of the SLScript programming language.

In general, virtual community members use, seek, and build communities for several activities, like: (i) socialization (entertainment, meetings, and discussion), work together (business, overcome geographical barriers), (ii) have topical conversations (issues), (iii) buy and sell (marketplace), and so on. All these activities impact in the relationships among the members of the communication and in the social aspects.

SOCIAL IMPACT OF VIRTUAL COMMUNITIES

Virtual communities have achieved in the recent years an enormous popularity and a great impact in the today's society. Lesser and Storck (2001) mention that the social capital ("*those tangible substances that count for most in the daily lives of people*", Hanifan, 1920) implicit in communities of practice leads to behavioural change, which produces an increment of knowledge that influence positively. Kim (2000) points out the difference between traditional structured online communities (message boards, traditional chat rooms), and more individual-centric social tools (blogs, instant messaging), and suggests the latter are gaining in popularity. He also discusses the term "desocialization" to refer to a less frequent interaction between humans in traditional settings, in contrast to the increasing in virtual socialization of the today's societies.

At present, the social implications of virtual communities are enormous as they count with thousands or millions affiliate members which are organized in sub-communities according to cultural, political, or economical interests among others. Hence, the potential of community leaders to convoke people with a common goal on behalf of the advantage of Internet, and independently of the temporality of the mission, is a determinant factor that may destabilize the, for instance, current political status.

Popularity and Growth of Virtual Communities

Social networking sites are going globally, and the continuous growth of virtual communities has lead to a social phenomenon with important implications in the real world (e.g.: hundreds of people with a common interest that have been formally convoked to an event, replacing in some cases SMS or email). Wellman (2000) highlights the growth of such communities and sees in them the potential to develop significant relationships chosen by their members which enable to build specialized relationships. Statistics show that the number of memberships or affiliates of major virtual communities grows daily. For instance, Second Life statistics report by Feb 2009 1.402.491 users logged in during last 60 days and 12.2 million registered users. MySpace and Facebook are the biggest social networks as they count with more than 175 and 110 million active members respectively (more than 70% of Facebook users

are outside the United States), but some of these user profiles belong to restaurants, organizations, associations and other private business. Other statistics from Facebook reflect how often users updated pages, become fans of pages every day, or how many contents are uploaded or created per month. The Spanish social network Tuenti.com reports 12.077.000 visitors by the end of Nov 2008. We have to differentiate between registered users and only visitors, but we can use both data to reflect the trend of growth, popularity, or interest of a particular community or social network. According to different sources, there is some important discrepancy about the real number of registered users in Tuenti and recent news reported that it counts with 4.3 million registered users. The growth of Tuenti in 2008 with respect to the previous year was estimated in 770% (El periódico de Aragón newspaper, March 2009). Tools like Google Trends can be used to compare the trend of visitors of most popular social networks.

Smaller and more private communities like aSW (a small world) counts with nearly 423000 members. LinkedIn has around 36 million members and is currently adding 25 new members every minute of every day. The statistics mentioned before show that the increasing number memberships (Social networks count with nearly 300 million users worldwide - ABC newspaper, Feb 22nd 2009 -) belonging to one or several social and virtual networks has a strong social impact. A recent study in Spain (March 2009), reports that the 50.8% of Spanish Internet users are registered in some of the existing social networks like Facebook or Tuenti, 23.4% of these users belong to more than one social network and 71.7% of them use these tools for personal relationships.

(Figure 2) displays the approximate number of registered users of top social networks. Continuously, updated news report the war of numbers between top social networks, as these data vary every day and should be revisited frequently. We couldn't find reliable data of registered users for Tuenti.

Figure 2. Worldwide distribution of memberships of top virtual communities (March, 2009)(© 2009, R.Capilla)

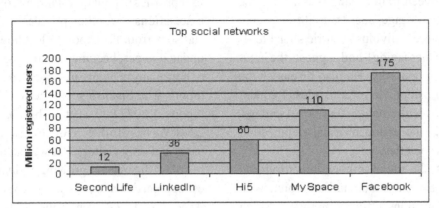

Social Implications

The analysis of social factors is important for virtual communities in the way we need to understand the behaviour of their members. As predicted by Negroponte (1995), *"we will socialise in digital neighbourhoods'"*, and the Internet is indeed a powerful mechanism that promotes communication among individuals. As mentioned in (Crow and Allan, 1994), traditional communities are disappearing as people become less generally socially because of racial, religious, or political problems. Hence, virtual communities are leading the transformation of sociability and they have a strong influence in their members as well as in the today's society. Several implications can be derived from the use of these portals where thousands users belonging to several countries with different or similar political ideas and cultural factors interact. As geographical barriers are broken with the massive introduction of the use of virtual communities, users from different countries can interact much faster than using for instance, traditional email systems, and news or comments are posted instantly to one or several memberships in order to receive a quick response.

According to the survey reported in (Lin, 2008), quality of information, member satisfaction, trust, and social usefulness are additional key factors in implementing successful virtual communities. The study reported in Lin (2008) examines trust and social usefulness as highly pertinent features for virtual communities. From a social perspective, belonging to a virtual community promotes social relationships (Hampton and Wellman, 2001). Social factors like trustworthiness and reciprocity between members are important factors for the survival of the community. In order to highlight the importance of social factors in the today's virtual communities we analyze different social characteristics as an indication to estimate the degree of impact of virtual communities in the daily's life of citizens and how the use of virtual networks may affect to the relationships of citizens.

Time spent on virtual communities and social networks soaring: The time spent by members of virtual communities constitutes an important factor because it can distract people during their daily work in the office. As reported by (The Marketplace, 2009), Second Life residents logged nearly 400 million hours in 2008, growing 61% over 2007. In the fourth quarter of 2008 residents spent 112 million hours and peak concurrent users of 76,000 grew approximately 30% over 2007. LinkedIn reported in Feb 2009 that 5.2 million users have five or less connections. Also, the 28.6% of Spanish Internet users access social networks daily and a 41% access at

Figure 3. Average age of members of major virtual communities (March, 2009)(© 2009, R.Capilla)

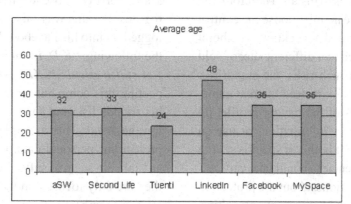

least one time per week (ABC newspaper, March 2009). This trend reflects that the time and the activity spent by users on top virtual communities is increasing every, as community memberships perceive the need to be permanently connected and updated about news or comments posted by other members.

Age of users: The age of members of virtual communities are important to know the profile and preferences of users. Tuenti is more oriented to young people while others like LinkedIn focus on the professional experience and skills; hence age of memberships should be greater. As reported in (ABC newspaper, Feb 22nd 2009), the average age of Tuenti is 23-24 years old and in Spain, and 7 out of 10 users have less than 35 years old. Other demographic data reveal in the period May 2006-2007 (Comscore, http://www.comscore.com) that the major growth of Facebook users occurred among 24-35 years old, while most of these users are older than 35. Second life stats reported in 2007 that 33 years old was the average age of SL users, and the 27.5% of active users have among 18-25. (Figure 3) reports the distribution of the average age of some social networks. The average age of aSW members is 32, while 95% o the audience is above 25.

In general, the age of virtual community memberships may vary depending of the purpose of the social network or smaller sub-community. Gener-

ally speaking teenagers and younger people are expected to spend more time playing multimedia online games rather than medium-age and older users. Thus, different market opportunities can be exploited according to the age of the users. (Figure 3) displays the distribution of the average age of members from some major social networks.

Legal issues, privacy, and risks for social network memberships: According to the Spanish data protection act (LOPD), users less than 14 years old need permission from their parents to belong to any social network as this kind of Web portals are not free of risks for young people. As an example, the minimum age to register an account on MySpace is 14, and profiles with ages set from 14 to 15 years are automatically private, while users whose ages are set at 16 or over have the option to set their profile to public viewing. There are a lot of threats from unknown users that require the protection of younger users from murderers or criminals. The LOPD law warns users that the risks for security are very important. Privacy of personal information (e.g.: address, photo, contact information) is one of the important issues that require special treatment by social networks. A frequent practice happens when social networks sell the personal data of their members. For instance, a Facebook user who gives access to a third party application should authorize first to allow his/her personal information to the owner of the application he/she wants to install. Therefore, the social network and the member loose the control of its own information and never know whether it will be used, published in a different site, or sold it to others. To avoid such risks, the authorities advice users to use a nick instead the real name, use thumbnail images of the picture profile, do not publish real contact information, or use an email address that don't bother if spam is sent to it. Data protection agencies should take care, according to local regulations, about the protection of personal data of social network memberships. To avoid risks, the IBM has launched the utility so-called *privacy-aware maketplace* (PaMP) as a Facebook application based on Ruby on the Rails technology that empowers users to control all aspects of their data to be set and propagated. The PaMP applications uses two different scales to compare the privacy level of users to a recommended score. Hence, different Web and open social networks can exploit the advantages of PaMP applications and users can adjust their privacy settings according to their preferences.

Other recent case referred to privacy was reported by the EFE press agency (London, Feb 2009), K. S., a British teenager was sacked for calling job boring on Facebook. She made the comment about a Marketing & Logistics company in Essex, (U.K.) as she was not happy in her job. The girl didn't mention the name of the company when she posted comments about her job but she invited other stuff members to read them. B. B., a representative from the TUC trade union said "*employees need to protect their privacy online and employers should be less sensitive to criticism*", and also "*just because snooping on personal conversations is possible these days, it doesn't make it healthy*". In this case, the lack of regulation about private comments between members of the same network or simply friends may lead to unpredictable consequences like the one described before. Another similar situation (Feb 2009) happened with K. D., a skiving Aussie who fingered on Facebook and emailed his manager

asking for 1 day absence in his work for medical reasons, but this was false. Afterwards, the guy logged on into his Facebook's profile and posted the following: "*K.D. is not going to work, fuck it I'm still trashed.SICKIE WOO!*". The problem posting this comment was that his boss was in his friends list, and saw the message discovering the fraud. This example shows the need to protect our personal data. Other networks such as LinkedIn seem to suffer less these problems as they are only focused on the professional career of their members.

Social networks sometimes commit abuses about the personal information stored, and users often ignore privacy policies as they are longs texts complex to understand and difficult to read. Abuses in massive marketing posts is another typical situation often committed, as for instance 100.000 small advertisers and the 66% of big USA companies use Facebook for sending offers. To protect users, some social networks like Tuenti are not indexed by search engines in order to avoid spam to their members. At present, Facebook is revisiting its own declaration of rights and responsibilities, and allow registered users be an active part as they could review and vote new procedures to define a new declaration of rights and responsibilities that will guide the behaviour of their memberships. Therefore, it is expected to count with a new way to control future legal issues, and members will have the opportunity to perform such review. Moreover, Facebook plans to support assemblies every 30 days once after the announcement of the declaration of new principles.

Another important fact was the recent murder in Spain of Marta, a young girl 17 years old (Feb 2009) which provoked a quick reaction of the friends of the victim in the Tuenti social network, and many of them attempted to collaborate with the police and also reproach the murderers because the assassin was an old boyfriend of the victim. "Tuenti seeks Marta", was the popular call launched on Tuenti in order to attract people to help police in the search of the body. A special event was created in Tuenti for helping with the investigation and 500.000 users were notified through this event. Thus, social networks can be quite useful to call up memberships and help the society in such cases.

Political influence: Winning an election in a country or region, organizing a protest against political ideas and politicians, or convoke people to strike, are clear examples of the influence of social networks and virtual communities that are quickly replacing SMS mobile phone technology for the same goal in a cheaper and faster way, but also because much more people can be convoked using social networks with less effort and cost. For instance, in the Spanish municipal elections held in 2007, political party offices of the conservatory and socialist parties were burnt in Second Life. In the same election period, the leader of the Spanish communist party gave a speech in Second Life using an avatar with similar appearance to the real person, such as (Figure 4) shows. Another example happened in Second Life relates a recent poll where Second Life residents preferred Obama to McCain by over 2 to 1.

Just taking a quick look to virtual communities like Facebook, we can find many sub-communities related to political ideas or concrete facts, where community members can express their opinion or agree and disagree about recent political decisions that affect to their current life or next future. Virtual political communities are growing faster as they promote new forms of discussion on the Internet. The popularization of virtual communities has a strong impact on the democratization of Internet, as it allows memberships to effectively support political communication. Also, political leaders engage or attract thousands of members as supporters or simply fans which leverage their popularity during, for instance, campaigns. Again, virtual networks replace more traditional communication systems like SMS messaging system, used apparently by members of the Spanish socialist party in 2004 to influence the result of the national elections when Islamic terrorists put bombs in

Figure 4. Avatar of the Spanish communist party leader in Second Life(© 2007, ElMundo newspaper)

Spanish regional trains killing two hundred people. Now, virtual spaces offer enhanced capabilities to convoke people to events as well as enable on-line and instant discussion about a topic and using for instance the wall facility to post instant messages. In not so opened or democratic countries, an emerging civil society using Internet reduces political barriers and debates political reform on behalf of social networks. For instance, Facebook is growing on 250.000 members in China per day in a fierce competition with Myspace.

THE MARKETPLACE

In addition to social factors, trading between memberships is a reality. Social networks connect people at low cost which can be beneficial for entrepreneurs and small business looking to expand their contact base. The economical analysis of social interactions (Manski, 2000) constitutes an additional motivation for membership interaction in addition to other social factors. For instance, bars and restaurants are very active in advertising daily to customers subscribe to an entertainment community in order to be informed about upcoming events by means of banners or text announcements. Since businesses operate globally, social networks facilitate users to keep in touch with contacts around the world. Any event posted in a given community (e.g.: aSW)

Figure 5. Second Life positive monthly Linden dollar flow trend (March 2009)(© 2009, R.Capilla)

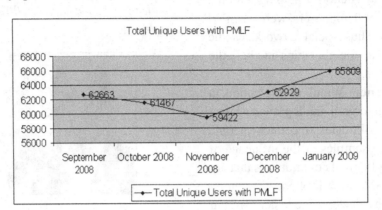

is received by the members of that community via email, which are notified also about who is attending or not to a particular event.

Business in social network happens when people purchase or sell goods or services, which can be done using a virtual currency offered by the software platform supporting the virtual community or in other cases real money is used in off-line business transactions. As reported in (The Marketplace, 2009), nearly USD$35 million is traded between Second Life residents each month, and SL economy has grown to become one of the world's largest user-generated virtual economies. Second Life uses Linden dollars (L$) as virtual currency for trading between SL residents, and in 2008 more than USD $100 million worth of L$ were bought and sold. Second Life offers

members a land use fee which is monthly charge in addition to membership fees (i.e., US$9.95/month Premium Membership). For instance, an entire region with 65,536 m2 will cost US$195 monthly VAT excluded. A detailed price list is applicable depending of the country, membership category, or land purchase. SL residents exchange volume increased 33% or land owned by Residents increased 82% over 2007. (Figure 5) displays a short history of the evolution of positive monthly Linden dollar flow (PMLF) of SL users (March 3rd 2009).

(Figure 6) displays the evolution of Second Life in-world business profits distribution in USD dollars for Jan 2009. As we can see in the figure, greater incomes are up to $ 100 USD. The range

Figure 6. Second Life in world business profits distribution in Jan 2009(© 2009, R.Capilla)

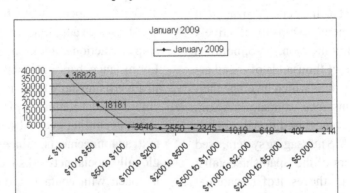

Figure 7. Second Life month customer spending distribution in Jan 2009(© 2009, R.Capilla)

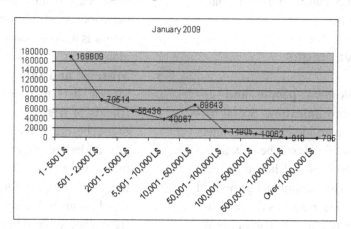

between $ 200 USD and $ 1000 USD is also significant but above this amount it decreases faster.

(Figure 7) displays the monthly customer spending distribution in Jan 2009 for a total of 442.143 customers. As we can see, most SL customers trade Linden dollars (L$) up to 50.000 L$.

In aSW, trading between members is realized posting the goods in a buy and sell section. Cars, watches, cameras, jewels, fashion, holiday houses, many of them luxury goods, are offered only to aSW memberships which have to establish contact using email or chat facilities before the business take place. For instance, in March 2009, aSW counts with nearly 23.140 buy/sell advertisements posted. No virtual payment or additional business transaction facilities is offered in this exclusive community, which bases their personal relationships on previous contacts between trusted members and where social status is a sign of elite distinction. In other cases, free services can be offered or posted to strengthen relationships, like parties or social events.

Another example of social networking being used for business purposes is LinkedIn which claims to have more than 20 million registered users from 150 different industries and uses the Web portal as a business meeting point to answer technical questions, find business partners, seek for a job, or simply be in touch with other profes-

sionals. Hence, a professional network is used for business marketplace and replaces in some cases the traditional face-to-face meeting. Other forms of business are provided by dating sites, where community members are looking for a couple, short-term or sporadic relationship. Payment is done in most cases using a credit card or bank transfer. Differently from professional networks like LinkedIn, including personal information is usually discouraged for safety reasons, and also, a fee is usually required to access the members' profile. Popular sites like Match.com or Meetic are decreasing the number of affiliates in favor of social networks like Facebook.

As we can see from the previous data, trading and business using virtual or real currency using social network portals has a high impact in the today's economy, as memberships can establish real businesses according to their interests.

BENEFITS AND DRAWBACKS OF VIRTUAL COMMUNITIES

There are several pros and cons we can extract from our analysis of social networks and virtual communities. In some cases, an advantage can be a disadvantage at the same time, so community members should be very careful during the daily interaction with others.

Benefits and Advantages

- **Find know/unknown people and enhance social communication**: Social networking allows us to identify and connect with friends. Old friends can be now found in social communities and hence to reestablish contact. The continuous growth of virtual communities increases the possibility to know new people but also unknown persons.
- **New business/job/travel opportunities:** Communities like LinkedIn offer and excellent way to be in touch with other professionals while others like aSW offer good business opportunities.
- **Trust and help:** Sometimes people travel alone across the world for business reasons and knowing friends who can help in a different country or simple provide useful information which increases trust. Trustfulness results key for the success of the interaction between members and the social portal should control a bad use of the community members.

Drawbacks and Disadvantages

- **Unprotected personal data**: There is a high risk when we allow access tot third-party applications in our social network as they can capture all our personal information and make a bad or abusive use of it (e.g.: sell our contact information or use it for massive emailing). Also, criminals can find in social communities an inexhaustible source of personal information.
- **Ineffective work:** Much time spent by users interacting in a social network during the daily working schedule may lead to decrease the productivity at work under a

more relaxed ambient. In addition to social networks, the traditional messenger application is a clear example of wasted time in many cases.

- **Mistrust and safety:** Sometimes we add to our list unknown people or simply friends of friends who have never known or met before. We should keep our community under control and be aware that there many invitations from unknown people that might be risky for our privacy and personal security. We should deny invitations from people we don't know, but unfortunately, in many cases the curiosity to establish contact with unknown people is higher that the potential risks.

DISCUSSION

In this chapter we have stressed the importance of modern social networks and virtual communities and its influence in the today's society. Our study shows that several technologies (i.e.: MMOG, virtual reality, Web technology) can be used and combined to create a virtual community of interest, where users engage one or several communities. More connections imply in most cases more possibilities to know other people and to benefit from new contacts. As a result, the social network or virtual community grows as well as its popularity. Most of the existing communities share a set of common characteristics but they differ in others, mostly depending on the specific goal, mission, age, or activity of the participants.

Also, social and economical factors have been discussed. Business and new job opportunities constitute another strong motivation to join a community. There are many more areas that can be analyzed to know how much a particular community can impact in our life. In our analysis we have focused on major virtual communities, some of them make extensive use of virtual reality as an affordable technology for many. With respect to the social implications, we have discussed the trust, social usefulness, influence of the time spent by users, the age of the participants, legal issues, and privacy among others. As all major communities are soaring faster, these and other implications in the today's societies are changing the way by which, we as human or individuals, we establish relationships with peers or groups of interest. In this sense, social networks promote the appearance of community leaders in the virtual space that could also become leaders in the real life.

Joining a virtual community can sometimes be risky, and this should be carefully balanced, especially for young members that require more protection. Virtual communities offer lots of advantages which in some case can turn in disadvantages or risks, so we have to measure the use in time and form of the communities to which we belong and don't try to replace real life relationships with exclusively virtual ones. Finally, virtual communities based on virtual reality technology provide a three dimensional perspective of our avatars interacting with others in a virtual environment, but in some cases this is perceived more a game rather an effective way of relationship with others.

FUTURE RESEARCH DIRECTIONS

New challenges arise from the use of virtual reality technology for virtual communities and social networking. In addition to laptop applications where users exploit the benefits and services offered by virtual portals, the massive use of handheld devices (Weng, 2007) like: PDA, IPhone, or Blackberry, provide new ways of remote access to virtual communities on behalf of the software installed in handheld devices. Hence, users can be in touch as they are moving worldwide. In addition, MMOG could be played in gaming consoles or PDA (e.g.: SOL – Shadow of Legend), but virtual reality applications require much more processing and memory capacity to run VR mobile applica-

tions. As MySpace and Facebook are turning into mobile, mobile social networking can offer new capabilities like geosocial search (already offered by aSW but in the Web portal) to, for instance, locate users using wireless technology. As an example, *mobikade* is a free mobile social networking service aiming to bring Japanese mobile social networking services sites to Europe, and it differs from other social networking by the fact that it is an exclusively mobile based and accessible only through the mobile phone.

Also, social networks for professionals like LinkedIn can be improved using federated services to locate experts in the net. Job seekers can use this kind of technology or specialized web portals to offer additional services those current social networks don't provide or simply are not interested on them. Federated social networks or federated identity management are also research fields to explore. The XMPP protocol can help in this research area. Moreover, transferring user's identity (OpenID) from one network to another constitutes a hot research topic to analyze data portability and single digital identity across the Internet.

Related to VR technology, where users are immersed in a virtual world using a computer, *telepresence* refers to a user interacting in a real environment. Telepresence (Minski, 1980; Sheridan, 1994) comprises a set of technologies which allow a person to feel as if they were present at a location other than the true location. Telepresence systems provide the required stimuli that the user perceives no differences from actual presence. Telepresence can be used in a variety of applications like: remote meetings, teleconferencing, remote surgery, or education among others. Also, Bracken and Lombard (2004) suggested that people interact with computers socially. Some commercial telepresence systems are already available from Digital Video Enterprises, Polycom, HP, IBM (Debuts Sametime 3D) or Cisco Systems (WebEx, 2009). Compared to other traditional teleconferencing systems, telepresence

Figure 8. Cisco telepresence system for teleconferencing and remote meetings(© 2009, Cisco Telepresence Solution)

brings users to have a face-to-face meeting without travelling long distances, which brings enormous time and cost reduction. As an example, (Figure 8) provides an image from Cisco Telepresence System 3000 used for a virtual meeting, where part of the attendees are virtual participants.

CONCLUSION

This chapter analyzed the most visible impact of modern virtual communities with special focus in virtual reality technology. The topics covered in this chapter tried to provide some guidance for memberships of these communities and for newcomers. We have also highlighted the benefits and the risks of an extensive use of virtual communities, but also that new opportunities can be derived from a rational use of social networks. As a concluding remark we can say that the popularity of Web social portals and also the use of virtual reality technology still need to advance to produce better influence in our societies, but never try to replace the interaction that happens in the real world.

REFERENCES

A Small World. (2009). Retrieved from http://www.asmallworld.net

Bracken, C., & Lombard, M. (2004). Social presence and children: Praise, intrinsic motivation, and learning with computers. *The Journal of Communication, 54*, 22–37. doi:10.1111/j.1460-2466.2004.tb02611.x

Breiger, R. L. (2004). The Analysis of Social Networks. In Hardy, M., & Bryman, A. (Eds.), *Handbook of Data Analysis* (pp. 505–526). London: Sage Publications.

Capilla, R., Martinez, M., Nava, F., & Muñoz, C. (2008). Architecting Virtual Reality Systems. In *Designing Software Intensive Systems: Methods and Principles*. Hershey, PA: IGI Global.

Cisco Telepresence Solution. (n.d.). Retrieved from http://www.cisco.com/en/US/prod/collateral/ps7060/ps8329/ps8330/ps7073/prod_brochure0900aecd8054c9c0.pdf

Cisco Webex. (2009). Retrieved from http://www.webex.com

Crow, G., & Allan, G. (1994). *Community Life. An introduction to local social relations*. Hemel Hempstead, UK: Harvester Wheatsheaf.

De Lucia, A., Francese, R., Passero, I., & Tortora, G. (2008). *SLMeeting: supporting collaborative work in Second Life* (pp. 301–304). AVI.

Edwards, C. (2006). *Another World*. IEEE Engineering & Technology.

Facebook. (2009). Retrieved from http://www.facebook.com

Freeman, L. (2004). *The Development of Social Network Analysis: A Study in the Sociology of Science*. Vancouver, Canada: Empirical Press.

Freeman, L. (2006). *The Development of Social Network Analysis*. Vancouver, Canada: Empirical Press.

Hampton, K., & Wellman, W. (2001). Long distance community in network society: contact and support beyond Netville. *The American Behavioral Scientist, 45*(3), 476–495. doi:10.1177/00027640121957303

Hanifan, L. J. (1920). *The Community Center.* Boston: Silver Burdett.

Kim, A. J. (2000). *Community Building on the Web: Secret Strategies for Successful Online Communities.* Berkeley, CA: Peachpit Press.

Kim, A. J. (2004). Emergent Purpose. *Musings of a Social Architect.* Retrieved from http://socialarchitect.typepad.com/musings/2004/01/emergent_purpos.html

Lave, J., & Wenger, E. (1991). *Situated Learning. Legitimate peripheral participation.* Cambridge, UK: University of Cambridge.

Lee, F. S., Vogel, D., & Limayen, M. (2003). Virtual Community Informatics: a review and research agenda. *Journal of Information Technology Theory and Applications, 5*(1), 47–61.

Lesser, E. L., & Storck, J. (2001). Communities of practice and organizational performance. *IBM Systems Journal, 40*(4). doi:10.1147/sj.404.0831

Lin, H.-F. (2008). Determinants of successful virtual communities: Contributions from system characteristics and social factors. *Information & Management, 45*(8), 522–527. doi:10.1016/j.im.2008.08.002

LinkedIn. (2009). Retrieved from http://www.linkedin.com

Manski, C. F. (2000). Economic Analysis of Social Interactions. *The Journal of Economic Perspectives, 14*, 115–136. doi:10.1257/jep.14.3.115

Minski, M. (1980). Telepresence. *OMNI magazine,* 45-51.

Negroponte, N. (1995). *Being Digital.* London: Hodder and Stoughton.

Second Life. (2009). Retrieved from http://secondlife.com

Sheridan, T. B. (1994). Further musings on the psychophysics of presence. *Presence (Cambridge, Mass.), 5*, 241–246.

Sutherland, I. E. (1968). A head-mounted three-dimensional display. In *Proceeding of the Fall Joint Computer Conference. AFIPS Conference Proceedings* (Vol. 33, pp. 757- 764). Arlington, VA: AFIPS.

The Marketplace. (2009). Retrieved from http://secondlife.com/whatis/marketplace.php

Wasserman, S., & Faust, K. (1994). *Social Network Analysis: Methods and Applications.* Cambridge, UK: Cambridge University Press.

Wellman, B. (2000). Physical Place and Cyber-Place: The rise of Networked Individualism. *International Journal of Urban and Regional Research, 25*(2), 227–252. doi:10.1111/1468-2427.00309

Weng, M. (2007). *A Multimedia Social-Networking Community for Mobile Devices Interactive Telecommunications Program.* Tisch School of the Arts/ New York University.

Wenger, E. (2007). *Communities of practice. A brief introduction.* Retrieved from http://www.ewenger.com/theory

ADDITIONAL READING

Adler, P., & Kwon, S. (2002). Social capital: Prospects for a new concept. *Academy of Management Review, 2781*, 17–40. doi:10.2307/4134367

Bartle, R. A. (2004). *Designing virtual worlds.* Indianapolis, IN: New Riders.

Biocca, F., & Levy, M. R. (1995). *Communication in the Age of Virtual Reality.* Mahwah, NJ: Lawrence Erlbaum Associates.

Borgatti, S., & Cross, R. (2003). A relational view of information seeking and learning in social networks. *Management Science, 49*, 432–445. doi:10.1287/mnsc.49.4.432.14428

Burdea, G., & Coffet, P. (2003). *Virtual Reality Technology* (2nd ed.). New York: Wiley-IEEE Press.

Chi, E. H. (2008). The Social Web: Research and Opportunities. *IEEE Computer, 41*(9), 88–91.

Cloud computing. (2009). In *Wikipedia, the Free Encyclopaedia*. http://en.wikipedia.org/wiki/Cloud_computing

Crowston, K., & Howinson, J. (2005). The Social Structure of Free and Open Source Software Development. *First Monday, 10*(2).

Crowston, K., & Sieber, S. (2007). Virtuality and Virtualization. In *Proceedings of the International Federation of Information Processing Working Groups 8.2 on Information Systems and Organizations and 9.5 on Virtuality and Society*, Portland, Oregon, USA.

Evans, B. M., & Chi, E. H. (2008). Towards a model of understanding social search. In *ACM Conference on Computer Supported Cooperative Work (CSCW 2008)*, San Diego, CA, USA (pp. 485-494).

Evans, D. A., Feldman, S., Chi, E. D., Milic-Frayling, N., & Perisic, I. (2008). The social (open) workspace. In *Proceedings of the 17th ACM Conference on Information and Knowledge Management (CIKM 2008)*, Napa Valley, California, USA. *eXtensible Messaging and Presence Protocol.* (2009). Retrieved from http://es.wikipedia.org/wiki/XMPP

Federated Services. (2009). Retrieved from http://www.federatedservices.com/

Grau, O. (2003). *Virtual Art: From Illusion to Immersion*. Cambridge, MA: MIT Press.

Heer, J., & Boyd, D. (2005). Vizster: Visualizing Online Social Networks. In *IEEE Symposium on Information Visualization (InfoVis 2005)*, Minneapolis, MN.

Matsuo, Y., Mori, J., Hamasaki, J., Nishimura, T., Takeda, H., Hasida, K., & Ishizuka, M. (2007). POLYPHONET: An advanced social network extraction system from the Web. *Journal of Web Semantics, 5*(4), 262–278. doi:10.1016/j.websem.2007.09.002

Mennecke, B. E. (2008), Second Life and other Virtual Worlds: A Roadmap for Research. *Communications of the AIS, 20*(20).

Mika, P. (2004). Bootstrapping the FOAF-web: An Experiment in Social Network Mining. In *1st Workshop on Friend of a Friend, Social Networking and the Semantic Web*, Galway, Ireland.

Mutton, P. (2004). Inferring and Visualizing Social Networks on Internet Relay Chat. In Proceedings of Information Visualization (IV 2004), London, UK (pp. 35-43).

Open, I. *D.* (2009). Retrieved from http://openid.net/

Preece, J., & Maloney-Krichmar, D. (2003). Online Communities. In Jacko, J., & Sears, A. (Eds.), *Handbook of Human Computer Interaction* (pp. 596–620). Mahwah, NJ: Lawrence Erlbaum Associates Inc. Publishers.

Rheingold, H. (2001). In Press, M. I. T., Ed.). Cambridge, MA: The Virtual Community.

Scott, J. P. (2000). *Social Network Analysis* (2nd ed.). Thousand Oaks, CA: Sage Publications.

WebEx. (2009). Retrieved from http://www.webex.com/

Yingzi, J. Matsuo, Y., & Ishizuka, M. (2007). Extracting Social Networks Among Various Entities on the Web. 4th European Semantic Web Conference, ESWC 2007. Springer-Verlag LNCS 4519, 251-266.

Chapter 11
Application of Topographical Capture Techniques for Modelling Virtual Reality:
From the Static Object to the Human Figure

Mercedes Farjas Abadía
Universidad Politécnica de Madrid, Spain

Manuel Sillero Quintana
Universidad Politécnica de Madrid, Spain

Pedro Ángel Merino Calvo
Universidad Politécnica de Madrid, Spain

ABSTRACT

Since the dawn of time man has attempted to represent the human figure with techniques ranging from simple drawings to techniques that manage to reflect the movement of body segments. In parallel, cartographic techniques have developed very advanced capture and 3D representation systems, but even though they have been applied in recent years to other sciences, they have not been applied yet to virtual reality. The appearance of the laser acquisition systems has enabled us to acquire data without discrimination on points and to get quick 3D models. This situation allows us to work directly on the concept of surface and to analyze it from the uniqueness of the detail, compared to traditional systems which capture points for, later, imaging surfaces from them. Under this prism, a research group was formed by graduates in Physical Activity and Sport and in Cartography, in order to bring together both sciences and to improve techniques of capture and representation of the human body. The road is not completely gone, but some results have been obtained and are presented in this work.

DOI: 10.4018/978-1-61520-631-5.ch011

INTRODUCTION

Nowadays, the term *"Virtual Reality"* is associated to multiple disciplines, both in research and practical applications, but its ultimate goal in all of them is very similar: to produce an illusion of reality, which can be subject to a practical, technical or conceptual application. Since the 50's, when they were started to nowadays, the capture, processing and representation systems have been varied, evolving in a parallel way to the computers, essential for the mathematical calculations.

Direct applications of virtual reality range from medicine to engineering, from computer games to advertising. In all those fields, simulations provide an effective and efficient support to its technical or practical goals.

If we consider the processing hardware and software, we see that has changed dramatically. In some cases, it is difficult to distinguish between real and fictitious when you see some pieces of work of virtual reality. In a deeper analysis, we can conclude that the problems are in the collection of data, since in many cases much of the work is done through techniques of image designing and processing.

In this report, we propose a new technique to capture the information that is going to by virtualized, basing it in real-world data collection using a 3D scanner. This technique provides us with a virtual model of reality with metric data, which we can say that is a perfect representation of reality. The study develops model tests in laboratory and real environments, trials with static human models, leaving the door open to the modelling of the human figure as a moving object.

Before going further in the work, we would like that you turn the light back with us, so that when you read, you will understand the steps taken since the beginning of the topography until the representation of the human figure by topographic as a result of biomechanical studies.

At present we are working on virtual reality techniques, but it has not always been our goal, as traditionally the development of the topography has focused on modelling and representation of terrain in all its aspects. A few years ago, a group of people considered that topographic techniques and virtual reality had progressed in two parallel but not crossed ways, or, in other words, advancing without looking each other.

Throughout time, topographic and cartographic engineering technologies have been working on the acquisition of data using different equipment and topographic, photogrammetric and geodetic methods in order to represent 2D and 3D objects, buildings, statues and archaeological sites, focusing the research on obtaining and modelling those elements with sufficient metric precision.

It is said that any investigation begins when we are faced with a question or uncertainty that makes us question the situation and initiate a search. And we have the following question: Can our techniques for capturing and modelling to contribute something to the virtual reality and biomechanics?

We believe that one of the fundamentals of virtual reality is three-dimensional interactive computer simulation, so that the user is introduced in an artificial environment that is perceived as real, allowing you to interact in a virtual world that has the ability to maintain a two-way correspondence with the real world. The more closely approximates the information captured to the reality, the better the interrelationships between the virtual and the real. If we apply these concepts to biomechanics, as a multidisciplinary study of the measurements of the human body in movement, we can be at the gates to get almost perfect representations of the reality with virtual models.

In short, we have to understand both the functional and the physical variability in subject's movement, and how these components interact and how they could be improved. The study of the dialectical relationship structure-function, is a basic tool with a strong genetic dependence for the identification of future athletes.

Under this view, in recent decades, and in parallel with the evolution of virtual reality, sports science has tried to analyze and explain the different aspects of the human figure and its movement through various sports disciplines, in order to propose procedures for evaluating and improving the actions of the athletes by virtual models. Thus we can observe as the conventional training methods in elite athletes have been complemented by technologic advances for analyzing and quantifying the parameters involved in the performance. At present it is impossible to reach the maximum goals in sports without the help of high technology.

From this viewpoint, we considered a quantum leap in the object of study. If we were able to represent all types of surfaces:

Why not introduce real coordinates and the variable time in these virtual representations?

If we could represent, controlling the accuracy in the final model and choosing the proper technique for that purpose, a surface at a time *"A"* and *"B"* at a later time (e.g. on a glacier to analyze the displacement of moraines, or on a Cathedral deterioration over time), the new variable could also be monitored and would be defined by Δt.

Once we entered into concept of metric representation of *"dynamic surfaces"*, it was an adventure to go beyond the measured object. It was an experience to observe the surroundings and people close to zero velocity, not considering the scenarios as empty, in an isolated way, but with his players and considering the human movement slowed until a *"moment"* becomes a *"taking"* in the data acquisition process.

The results that we obtained, along with the emergence of new equipment and technologies in topography, let us accept the hypothesis of the project, and our ability to look forward again and again, investing hours and hours (the time variable again) in the design and implementation of the first tests.

After having the idea, accepting the challenge and setting the scientific context and the human team, the viability was assured thanks to Leica Geosystems and the company 3D ICOM, which always provided us with their last generation equipments.

We show you now a glimpse of these new technologies in the field of virtualization and its application to sports; technologies that should have assessed by the reader.

VIRTUAL REALITY DEVICES TO CAPTURE INFORMATION

In a model of virtual reality we have to fulfil some minimum requirements of simulation or representative capacity, user-model interaction and sensory perception of the user. Even as the last is the most important, it directly depends on the quality of the simulation we obtain as a result of the input images we use, because depending on their proximity to reality we can convince the users of the accuracy of the parallel reality that we offer them.

Currently, systems for image capture require huge processing times and in some cases somewhat tedious, so the incorporation of topographic techniques (3D scanner) will allow us to capture the real shape quick and eliminating most of the post-processing tasks. This situation coupled with the precision of the shots and the availability of space-time metrics, will enable the virtual reality model, once completed, to interact with the user in an image very close to reality, where three-dimensional movements can be controlled by the metric component that is provided, a way of solving some of the problems existing today.

This relationship between the use of coordinates of space and time, allows us to overcome the barriers of space and time, and it could allow us to set up an environment where information provided by the model and the perception that the user receives are interlaced in a direct and two-way; that is an unknown situation with a huge potential in the development of virtual reality interfaces.

The application of these results allows us to move between the topology of three-dimensional virtual reality or immersive and the non immersive Internet-based, being the last one the more accepted by users, and where the method can produce more tangible benefits. We can sustain this assertion, since in applications where the user is a component of the virtual world, the nearest is the image recognition, the better the acceptance of the system, but if we apply the system to maintain the heritage of a nation or, in archaeology, as a method to aid in the exploration and subsequent modelling, the benefits increase exponentially, allowing us not only to identify the precise site and its environment, but also knowing their temporal variations, or enable people located in different places to make a virtual visit, simultaneously, as if actually they were in that place, even being in the other side of the earth.

If we consider the user interface based in video-mapping, where the person or environment is filmed in advance and incorporated into the computer by graphics simulations, the result is, without any doubt, closer to reality but still not perfect. The use of 3D scanning systems will allow us that the person, image, or environment to introduce into the model is a clone of the reality, a young teacher who comes to surprise the viewer, allowing the illusion is created with realism such that people can doubt where is the line between the real and the virtual world.

Today, we are coming into a world where reality is pure coincidence, and the virtual environment with be as normal as the real one, like a cyberspace where space-time relations are not just virtual, but will be part of our lives and we will assume it. In this situation, the better defined are the models, the better will be the acceptance by the users. For example, the success of the clothing shops will depend on the availability of an implemented system for virtually testing how fit us some clothing.

In these terms, the virtual world is made up of geometric shapes produced by a computerized

Figure 1. Human face capture by scanner (2008) Equipment Konica Minolta VI-9i

graphic system; this geometry is interlaced forming meshes, which in turn represent objects, and the objects virtual scenarios. If we increase the geometric quality of the original polygons (best shots and more accuracy), we can offer more quality in the virtual model. But at present this quality improvement requires us to have more processing capacity and consequently increases the cost. The incorporation of capture systems based on topographic techniques, allows us to not only improving the quality of the images, but also improving and reducing the subsequent processing times to the minimum, as we shall see later on specific developments.

At present, the scanner system operating perfectly in static 3D objects, but there is a problem that affects the time delay of the system, so that the shots with dynamic objects appeared to move; so that, the capacity to respond to this issue is today insurmountable, but moving at the pace that this technology does, this problem will be an anecdote in a few years. We face a similar situation to the beginnings of photography when they were required seconds for taking a good pictures, and the modern digital cameras are able to take hundred of high definition pictures per second. It is only a matter of time, to improve the technique to obtain the results described in this paper, so that, we can consider it as a beginning or a window open for further studies to a fully development of the system. (See Figure 1)

TOPOGRAPHIC AND CARTOGRAPHIC TECHNIQUES AS AN ALTERNATIVE

In parallel with advances in virtual reality, the mapping techniques have evolved to very fast allowing us access to information almost in real time, but its use has been limited to the representation of the earth's surface and in some cases, very recent ones, to the cataloguing of the artistic heritage.

The increasing use of the advances that occurred in media and technology in recent years has led to the introduction of graphics systems as indispensable tools in teaching and learning processes. The use of the computer as an audiovisual tool at work, and its computational power, allows the design of models and processes with a high potential for development, expression and operability.

The graphical representation has always been an essential complement for any type of biomechanical analysis, as the kinematic and kinetic variables obtained from it allow statistical studies and simulations (digital models) of the movement of the human body.

At present the results depends on method of capture, where the variables space and time play a decisive role in obtaining good results, which are operational in a short space of time.

In a review of the state of the art, as regards the representation of human figures, static or dynamic, we can see that the modern systems apply techniques based on photographic or opto-electronic systems. Both systems record the spatial position of a number of spatial markers associated with the body surface, whose movement supposedly reflects the movement of body segments. Thus, it is difficult take decisions regarding the relationship of markers with the anatomical characteristics of the structure that lies below.

In the course of science, topographic and cartographic techniques have traditionally been linked to the study and representation of the terrain, in any of its states or situations, resulting in

Figure 2. Capture of the Cibeles fountain by Laser equipment UPM-Leica (2003) CYRAX 2500 Leica- Geosystem

digital images, in two or three dimensions, which were implemented for having maps as a result. But these monothematic techniques have been gradually changing its design to become more generalist and multidisciplinary and, presently, they have became an essential support for different studies or scientific projects. They are remarkable the advances that have occurred in the study and cataloguing of architectural works or in supporting the analysis of deformation of materials.

Let's see two different examples:

a. Gathering data through a continuous digital picture sensor system. (See Figure 2)
b. Data collection by laser system without prism.

Currently, the technological development allows the acquisition of information with laser systems without prism, which allow us the data acquisition without discrimination on points (without markers), and therefore they need not be placed in advance any element facilitate the calculation process later. As a direct consequence, we have that the collection of data can be executed faster and most importantly minimizing the subsequent process of calculation.

Under these systems, the representation is done on all of the selected area, obtaining a two-dimensional and/or three-dimensional continuous image of the represented figure, in which the density of points will be accord to the desired precision. Allowing us to work on the *"concept"* surface directly, analyzing it from the uniqueness of detail, compared to traditional systems which record points to imagine surfaces from them.

In 2004 a group of people, including the authors of this work, they posed the following question:

Do topographers' capture systems and their analysis methodology can be used to generate virtual reality models, and in particular, the representation of the human body and its biomechanical analysis?

To find answers, we began research in this field. We started to work on the doctoral thesis of Pedro Calvo Merino untitled *"Three-dimensional modelling of the human figure through mapping techniques and their application the moving object"*, which is currently in edition process, and some final works to obtain the Engineering degree in Topography. We have used some of their results as part of the contents of this work.

We tried to define a methodology to be able to capture and generate virtual representation of the static human figure, and establish some parameters in order to apply directly the 3D laser scanner on the sport disciplines in which biomechanics have a relevant role.

To do so, we have settled the following targets:

1. Analysis of the current methodologies and their capture parameters applied to static objects and their virtual representations.
2. Analysis of the mechanisms and parameters that can influence the acquisition of the human figure, in order to apply them to sports.
3. Development of methodology of capture based on a laser system without prism.
4. Representation of the three-dimensional human figure on a digital format, in real time and using real coordinates, allowing its metric analysis.

Based on the above targets, they have been defined the following specific objectives:

1. Image capture and formation of a 3D model.
2. Analysis of its application to the moving object.

Since obtaining the first results, we note that the use of this technology allowed us to work with both the object and the human figure in real time, compared to other systems that require a large computer processing time. At the same time, it was confirmed that its main advantage would be the high degree of similarity to the real model, with a minimum post-processing time, and subsequently allowing modelling the human figure very close to real time.

Compared to traditional capture systems through photogrammetric or optoelectronic systems, the methodology of the 3D laser systems is reduced in the number of stages.

We believe we are on the way to obtain inertial parameters suitable for biomechanical modelling of the human body, involving on it the use of anatomical points and segments under an interconnected on a local or real reference system, where there is an interrelationship of those anatomical points on the surface of the human body with the space.

This paper will try to define and open a door to a new system for capturing and representing the human figure, as a primary step for the study of human motion in real time. It also try to describe our findings on trying to develop, validate and apply a work methodology with direct applications in sports where the biomechanics and virtual representation has an important role.

DESCRIPTION OF CAPTURE SYSTEM

New technologies may allow describing, analyzing, evaluating and modelling statically and cinematically the environment and the human figure and its movement (cinematic analysis), and then resolve and optimize the biomechanical analysis, through representations of the model with details and temporal patterns which were unthinkable some years ago.

The capture system using 3D scanner consists of devices that analyze a real object, inanimate or animated, to produce a near-real representation of it, as a points cloud with geometry and metric. This allows us to model not only a rapid modelling process, but also, thanks to the availability of metrics, modifying the position of the model without changing its real geometry.

3D scanners are classified according to the measurement system: contact and non-contact with the object. Focusing on the non-contact type, are classified into two categories: active (emit some kind of radiation) and passive (do not emit any kind of radiation). In this paper we will focus on the non-contact scanners with active pulsed laser beam, which are the best suited to the capture of data for virtual reality applications. At the moment, they are widely used in many applications: topographic representations of the land, industry, maintenance of cultural heritage, or film and video games edition.

If we focus on the models currently on the market, there are different systems but they all have common characteristics in their basic technology (pulsed laser beam, no markers are required to objects to capture the environmental conditions of work, etc.), which we will try to show in the following paragraphs.

In the pulsed laser beam equipments, it is measured flight time (going and back) for each point on the object's surface. These devices have a timer with a resolution of 1 picoseconds, allowing us to produce beam of diameter smaller than 6 mm at a distance of 50 m from the object. Taking a step forward, they have been linked to the technique of laser beam of modulated amplitude, in which the system scans continuously an object through a variable beam, by using rotating mirrors. With one of these systems the team was able to capture the energy reflected from the object, by comparing the shape of the reflected wave with modulation released and, later, calculating the distance of the object and consequently their spatial coordinates. As a result, all points were captured from the beginning on three-dimensional coordinates into a local reference system, allowing its analysis and conversion to various formats. This is one of the added values of the 3D laser scanners compared to traditional capture systems (Barber, Mills, & Bryan, 2004).

When we make a comparison of traditional methods based on photogrammetry and optoelectronics compared to laser scanning systems, we obtain the following advantages of the latter over the former (Demir et al., 2004):

- Recording of direct points of the object in 3D. Capture in real time.
- Provides a lot of points from the surface, allowing a more realistic and complete analysis of the object.
- It is an excellent technique for the description and representation of irregular surfaces.
- The final results are available in a very short period of time.

When $"c"$ is the speed of the pulsed light and $"t"$ is flight time (going and back), we have simply that space travel is $(t \cdot c) / 2$. As speed of the laser beam is a constant, the calculation of the distance will depend only on the flight time, which is currently around 3 picoseconds. Considering samples of 1mm in the surface, the estimated time for scanning an object sized 50 x 180 cm (body) located 50 meters away, with a rate of 200,000 points per second, is approximately 5 seconds.

The distance of a point and its direction (polar coordinates) is calculated by changing the direction of the pulse using a rotating mirror method. The rotating mirror device is commonly used because they are much lighter than prism and it can be rotated much faster and with superior accuracy.

To capture technique uses the continuous beam of laser amplitude modulation, where the scanner scans an object through the beam of a continuous variable, using rotating mirrors. With this system the team is able to capture the energy reflected from the object, comparing the shape of the reflected wave with modulation issued and calculate the distance of the object and consequently their spatial coordinates. As a result, all points are captured from the beginning three-dimensional coordinates on a local reference system, allowing its analysis, or export to various formats, this is one of the added value of the 3D laser scanners compared to traditional systems of capture.

There are different capture systems based on laser systems in the market, the most important are the ScanStation 2 and the HDS6100 of Leica-Geosystem (Leica Geosystems, 2005), the Trimble GX 3D Scanner, and the VI-9i or VI910 of Konica Minolta.

All of them are based on a system of continuous laser beam, allowing high speed scanning from 100,000 points / sec to 500,000 points / second, while providing a complete horizontal visual field (±360°) and ±135° in vertical. They provide high accuracy (± 0.05 mm in the VI-92), even at great distances, thanks to the great intensity and the beam generated by each pulse of short wavelength, which combined with the optical compensation schemes and the dynamic expansion of the laser scanning, allows very accurate captures of surfaces with different levels of reflection.

Capture methods are often based on laser optical triangulation, providing a points cloud that automatically generate a polygonal mesh with all the information connected, thereby geometric ambiguities are eliminated and the final result is improved, allowing to apply 24bit textures – real color and consequently obtaining the continuity of the elements represented virtually.

The most relevant characteristics of the equipment are:

- Laser scan for high precision and speed capture using the pulse laser system, with double mirror optics and servo-mechanisms.
- Luminosity: Operating with bright light and complete darkness.
- Allows a scan of 20.000 m³ to 50 meters and 160.000 m³ to 100 meters.
- The range varies from one computer to another, for example the ScanStation 2 has a range of 300 m with 90% reflectivity.
- Capture precision < 4 mm to 50 meters and resolution < 1 mm at distances between 5 and 50 meters and angles of ± 60 micro-radians.
- Density vertical scanning 1,000 points/column and horizontal scanning 1000 points/raw.
- Measurement precision P2P between ±0.05 mm and ±4 mm.
- Capture time less than 5 minutes, depending on the volume: if we consider 1 column/sec for 1000 points/column, 2 columns/sec for 200 points/column but, considering little volumes, values are 0.3 seconds for 80,000 points and 2.5 seconds for 300,000 points.
- Visual field complete (±360°) in horizontal and ±135° in vertical, both under solar light and complete darkness.
- Direct interface and on real-time connection with the computer.
- Colour video camera integrated with a resolution of 680 x 480 pixel.

How Do They Work?

- Focus the scanner onto the area of interest.
- The video camera integrated in the team, made a first quick capture, which is sent to a computer connected to it.
- Implementation of a rapid scan capture in order to get a 3D preview to provide us in-

formation about the depth of the capture (blind or dark areas).

- The operator selects the desired area, accuracy, resolution and other required parameters.
- Starts the capture of the object. To do this within the system, two mirrors perform a quick and systematic scan by laser pulses on the selected area, using the technique of *"flying time"* to take the measurement of each pulse of the laser. The system does not require the use of reflectors (markers).
- For each laser pulse, they are calculated distances and tiny integrated optical decoders perform angular measurements, obtaining primary polar coordinates, which are transformed into Cartesian coordinates (X, Y, Z).
- The resulting positions are displayed graphically on the computer screen in real time (as soon as they are calculated).

CAPTURE AND PROCESSING SOFTWARE

As an example, we briefly describe the Cyclone software of Leica Geosystems. Most of them have a similar nature.

Cyclone software is a modular PC software to operate the scanner Cyrax. It processes 3D point clouds in an efficient and manages projects from 3D laser scanner. Makes a thorough record of each detail, allowing a quickly and safely integration of different scans, taking only certain points in common.

The system has a wide range of tools for working with images and models in three dimensions. Its most important features are:

- Total control of the scanner and process from the PC through the communication of the scanner and the PC by a standard Ethernet connection.

- Fast capture of the digital video image in 4-bit true colour with 630 x 480 pixels resolution.
- Adjust parameters in detail: accuracy, density of points, etc.
- Fast conversion of the point cloud in a triangular mesh surface.
- Generation of digital models using mesh.
- Generation of surfaces and maps of intensity.
- Calculation of volumes on the mesh.
- 3D modelling from point clouds, by intelligent algorithms.
- Record multiple scans. With overlapping functions, geometric adjustment, adjustment of spatial coordinates, and so on.
- Instantaneous calculation of distances between two points and from the scanner at any point of the object.
- Allows displacement, flight, zoom and free-rotation of the 3D models.
- Texturing of the point cloud.
- Viewing selected items with parameterized intensity.
- Filters to enter data and information based on distance and intensity ranges.
- Geo-referencing and processing of the points in space.
- Record multiple scanning processes.
- Measures on the model (ΛX, ΛY, ΛZ), using P2P techniques.
- Export formats: VRML, DXF, DGN, text (X, Y, Z, color), PTS, Warefront OBJ, etc.

  It is required a PC with the following characteristics:
- Windows 2000 (SP2 or higher), Windows XP (Professional or Home Edition, SP2).
- Monitor: minimum resolution of 800 x 600 pixel.
- Pentium 4 2 GHz or higher.
- 512 MB RAM (1 GB recommended).
- SVGA - OpenGL Graphic Card.
- 10/100 Ethernet Network Card.
- Disk: minimum 10 Gb.

Figure 3. Survey of virtual representation at 1 / 500 of the archaeological area of Mleiha in the Emirate of Sharjah with GPS receivers

Figure 4. Digital model of the Torreón Guzmanes (Avila), produced by a laser three-dimensional 3D Trimble GS200

THE CAPTURE OF THE STATIC OBJECT RESULTS OBTAINED IN FIELD WORKS

As mentioned above, the first applications of laser systems were only topographical and, recently, for cataloguing of heritage. On them, three-dimensional models were obtained which allowed carrying out studies, analyzing proposals and making decisions on geographic areas or archaeological sites. In the following figures we present some of the results. (See Figure 3) and (Figure 4)

The progress occurred in data acquisition systems with 3D scanning techniques during the last years it has been both in the collection of data in continuous mode and in bypassing the selection of points in the field and avoiding the subjectivity remaining in the results. Data capture is automatically done in the field and, later, in the cabinet, it is made the selection of information.

This technique is being used, quite successfully, in some models as *"Tyrannosaurus Rex"* by the Carregie Museum of Natural History (Pittsburgh, PA) or the *"Statue of Liberty"* in New York by The College of Architecture at Texas Tech University in cooperation with the Historic American

Buildings Survery and the National Park Service, as representative examples.

On the other hand, the use of these systems has proliferated in the so-called *"Reverse engineering"* consisting of duplication of pieces or components without the aid of drawings and/or documentation, by creating 3D virtual models from an existing object for obtaining a copy as accurate as possible.

In terms of the metrics, the modelling process is concluded with the generation of the mesh of triangles that represent the surface of the object by a finite set of surface elements (triangles). But from the standpoint of representation, the results can be improved by applying textures to the surface that resemble those of the constituent material of the object, simulating different lighting effects and getting shaded representations of the object from different viewpoints, including stereoscopic images and animations.

Our experience with the station Leica TC 305 (direct measure without prism) had allowed us to work with beams of discrete points, interconnected by minimum squared adjustments. The equipment Geosystem Leica Cyrax 2500 made it possible to continue this line of study using continuous sequence of points, applying 3D laser technology to archaeological pieces and other heritage items. (See Figure 5) and (Figure 6)

The methodology consisted of placing the scanner on a tripod and connected to a laptop. The scanner was oriented to the selected area to scan and it began the acquisition of data. The equipment needed only fifteen minutes to complete the acquisition providing in real-time the point cloud and triangle mesh.

The precision was ±4 mm in distances and ±60 microradians in angles. The ability to data capture reached 1,000 points per second, achieving a precision in the beam of 1.2 mm. The cloud of points was managed by the specific software that has modules for calculation and modelling in two and three dimensions. As the fourth coordinate, it was recorded the light intensity.

In the project *"La Lonja de Valencia (Spain)"* (See Figure 5) and (Figure 6), they were carried out additional data captures with the laser equipment in remote areas, in order to represent the vaults of the main courtyard. It is surprising how easily is the process of providing textures to the model using the software provided with the laser scaning equipment. This task can be performed in situ, having the final image just after finishing the data capture of the point cloud.

Within this general framework for data acquisition, we search for new models of cartographic representation and experiment with new technologies, always maintaining the metric relations between the data, and creating models or prototypes. In this way, through the digital models, we extended to three dimensions the baseline scenario, without losing the possibility of obtaining traditional cartographic models.

HUMAN REPRESENTATION ACHIEVEMENTS IN THE FIELD WORKS

Since ancient times, men have tried to show their immediate reality and the environment around

Figure 5. (A) Modelling La Lonja de Valencia (B) The Central vault of La Lonja de Valencia

5 (A)

5 (B)

Figure 6. Three-dimensional model of the facade of the church of Santa Teresa (Ávila) by the 3D laser scanner Trimble GS200

them, either as art or as for technical proposes, focusing on the representation of the human figure in motion and trying to exaggerate its traits. Until today, the representation of the human figure and its dynamics has been a hotspot for artists, thinkers and scientists, using variety of materials and technical supports for that.

As a reality or necessity, it become a science study: kinanthropometry, which seeks to measure and represent the human figure, moving or static, with the greatest realism possible, to apply their findings to the various sports or in addition to advances in medicine (Carter, 1982).

The word Kinanthropometry derives from the Greek *"Kinein"* which means movement, movement, *"Anthropos"* which means human, and finally *"Metrein"*, which means measurements. Carter (1982), defined it as *"the study of size, proportion, maturation, body composition and form, to describe the physical characteristics, assess and represent the growth, nutrition and the effects of training"*. We can consider it as an interface between the quantitative morphology and physiology, or structure and function to help interpret the dynamics of growth, exercise, nutrition and the influence of the physical human movement.

In the Esparza's work (1993), we find references explaining who the body shape and performance are intimately related and the typology of the athlete plays a decisive role in sports performance. This means that the ability to perform work or exercise will be closely related to the amount and proportion of different tissues and body segments that make up the human body and to the economy in the management of the movements.

This science was born as an interdisciplinary scientific field (anthropologists, doctors, nutritionists, physiologists, biomechanical, physical education teachers, among others), to unify criteria and methods in the assessment study of man in motion. It aims to analyze the correlation of morphological and physiological responses, considered as a bridge between the relationship structure-function.

Advances in techniques of virtual representation has evolved dramatically, but always associated with photogrammetric, optoelectronic or video systems, to get sensations very close to reality, but having insufficient density of points and especially metrics, they have been unrealistic simulations until now.

In parallel with these developments, topographic and cartographic techniques have been progressing in their capture systems, making the presentation of information almost in real time, but its implementation has been traditionally limited to the representation of the earth's surface and, in some cases, very recently, to the documentation of the artistic heritage, but always away from the systems for virtual representation in applications which are in the field of topography or cartography.

Today, the graphic representation of the environment and humans, as part of it, is a necessary complement to a number of activities: documentation of heritage, traffic accidents, reconstruction of criminal scenarios, civil engineering, animations and films, etc. The kinematic and kinetic variables obtained allow statistical studies and simulations using virtual models (digital models) to describe the behaviour of human beings and their environment. However, the techniques used are limited by the method of capture, in which the variables space and time play a decisive role in obtaining operating and accurate results in a short space of time.

By linking topographic techniques, biomechanics, and virtual modelling applications for the capture and representation of human body and its movement, we can obtain results both on the functional variability and on the physical variability of subject in motion, and understand how these components interact and how they could be improved. The study of the dialectical relationship between structure and function is a basic tool with a strong genetic dependence for the identification of future athletes.

We can consider that one of the basics of biomechanics is the multidisciplinary study of the measurements of the human body, its movement and derivations thereof. Under this multi-character, great advances have been developed through the interest and perseverance of many researchers and their contributions, to incorporate new methods and refine the measurement instruments.

In recent decades, and in parallel with the evolution of other disciplines that work with graphical representation or use graphic systems as a support, they have tried to analyze and explain several aspects of the human figure and its movement in the environment that surround it, being a clear example of this many sporting disciplines, in which it is necessary to establish procedures for evaluating and improving the athletes performance. Thus, we see how conventional training in elite athletes has been complemented by advances in technology to analyze and quantify the parameters involved in the performance. Nowadays, it is impossible to reach the international level in any sport without the assistance of high technology.

TECHNIQUES USED TODAY IN BIOMECHANICS

The use of photography has been for over a century the most relevant technique applied to biomechanical analysis of human movement. Photogrammetry is *"a set of techniques to obtain information regarding the size, position and orientation of a physical object and its environment, through film, measurement and mathematical calculations on these measurement"*, where the spatial coordinates of the points of interest (anatomical points) are calculated from the planar coordinates of images from at least two cameras (Woltring, 1995).

In these techniques, data acquisition requires the matching of points to represent by the operator (passive or active markers in terms of brightness), and the individual capture of each one of them. After selecting and measuring each point and with a laborious calculation of the data, it could be reconstructed the element under study (in example a double somersault). This technique of modelling followed a line of work that went *"from the point to the surface"* and with a huge

human intervention in the intermediate stages (Soto, 1995).

In these measurement protocols, entries were limited to taking the spatial position of a small number of points (markers), all attached to the body surface, and whose motion approximates the motion of the segments that form the union of these points (Vera, 1989; Zatsiorski & Donskoi, 1988). This capture method represents a partial aspect of reality, because it transform the information obtained from sensors (limited in number and position) from an recorded image and their further processing, digitalization and modelling, into a numerical representation that can be processed by a computer, forcing all to a high consumption of resources and time.

Subsequently, they began to be used for optoelectronic systems, based on the use of TV cameras capable of detecting the position of passive or active markers in terms of brightness, in real time. These systems have been employed in the field of biomechanics of human movement under laboratory conditions. In the 90s, even today, There are used systems as ELITE (Elaboratore di Immagini Televisive, Center of Bioengineering of Milan, 1983), VICON VX (VInes CONverter for Biomechanics, University of Strathclycle, 1989), PREMIUM (Precision Motion Analysis System), or Expert HirRes Vision 3D (High Resolution 3D Motion Analysis System). They are classified according to the sensors they use: PSD (Position Sensitive Devices), CCD (Charge Coupled Devices, online or in area), among others.

All this systems are multi-camera equipments. The coordinates of the markers are computed in almost real time, which partly reduces the further process of data. But we still have a geometric picture of the human figure, formed by a limited number of points, so the result is very biased and poorly defined.

These systems, and other similar with little variations, always rely on the use of active or passive markers, being the passive the ones with a best performance (better space-time resolution and non-simulated identification of markers), but it is always necessary to use interpolation procedures to estimate the position of the markers in the same instant of time, resulting in a distortion of the final results. All this leads us to have some systematic errors caused by distortion of the image, scale errors, accidental errors (incorrect placement of the markers, errors in scanning, error in the mathematical processing, etc.), which cause problems in the reconstruction of coordinates in space-time and, as result, in the representation of the human figure and its movement.

At present the use of Automatic Motion Capture 3D, such as VICON, determines the position of reflective markers attached to the body of the subject. These are taken up by a set of 6 infrared cameras that record the movement with frequencies between 60 and 1000 Hz. This capture must be done indoors, under controlled and calibrated conditions, as it is necessary to have geometric reference system. This condition affects the athlete's actions, because they do not perform on their natural work conditions and environment.

The main purpose of the system is to collect the movements of an athlete to apply them to a later animation work, resulting in a film of a few seconds of the performed movement. We must consider that each second of animation requires approximately one hour of post-processing work by computer systems and specialized software, as Mocap and Motion Builder, and after that tedious process, you get a 3D animation of the athlete which is feasible for biomechanical analysis because it include a set of mechanical variables.

This system is widely used in the film industry (Titanic, Star Wars, The Mask, Harry Potter, etc.).

Within the work done in Spain at present, apart from the above, you can highlight the following:

- The Institute of Biomechanics of Valencia (IBV), where the system *"Kinescan/IBV"*, similar to VICON, can perform a complete analysis of movements in 3D based on digital video technology with reflective markers. This system has a post-process of the captured images by manual digitizing, and as a result, the application provides information about the three-dimensional movement of people in space: velocity, acceleration, mechanical impulses, moments angular or energy.

- The Faculty of Physical Activity and Sport at the University of Granada, particularly the Biomechanics Research Group. It has to be highlighted their work on three-dimensional photogrammetry, performance evaluation and quantitative analysis of sport.

- The group of Biomechanics and Ergonomics of the Center for Innovation in the Industrial Enterprise (CINEI), Department of Technology of the Universitat Jaume I of Castellon. To measure the movement they use high speed B/W digital video cameras (Speedcam +500), which allow an analysis of 2D motion. Complementing, they have digital cameras (used for postural measures) and specific gloves to measure the position of the hands (18 sensors Cyberglove).

In conclusion, we note that the common denominator of all these systems is that the methodology for obtaining representative points of the human figure:

- They use capture system based on video or digital photography.
- It is necessary to use markers attached on the human body, which limits the number of metric points to be captured.
- The data collection is done *"in door"* and under predefined conditions.
- They have a very laborious post-treatment process.
- In some cases, between the data collection and the delivery of the results, there is a

long time and the conditions of the athlete may have changed.

A NEW PROPOSAL BY THE USE OF SYSTEMS BASED ON LASER CAPTURE

Some years ago, our working group was looking for new capture and modelling systems. We tried to link capture and mapping cartographic techniques and the systems used in virtual reality techniques, which did not allow metric relationships between the reality and the final model. In this way, we extended to three dimensions the stage. Without losing the reference to the traditional mapping models, we conduct tests that would allow us to develop a simple working procedure, valid for obtaining rapid and real representation of reality with above all, dimensional metrics.

As a subject of study, we focused on the human body because, as we have seen in previous examples, the static object was being handled at that time with very positive results.

The road was not easy because the laser systems without prism were not very common as there were only three companies that sold them and they were very expensive, so that, the number of equipment in Spain was reduced and its availability for our tests was very limited. But it was a fact that its use would allow us to test data capture without discrimination of markers, and to capture the whole human figure, not only a limited number of points. If we add the rapidly in the point capture, completely and unlimited, and the small post-processing required to achieve a three-dimensional digital image with real coordinates (on a grid and capable of performing actual measurements on the same), the methodology allowed us working with special data on real-time, where the space-time relationship, it was defined at the time that the capture was made.

Our first objective was to obtain inertial parameters suitable for modelling of the human body, involving on it the use of anatomical points and segments interconnected under a local or real reference system where there were an interrelationship between them and the rest of points of the human body under study. In order to do that, the following practical experiences were carried out:

- We studied, at the technical level, the work that had been carried on the heritage, focusing on statues and irregular patterns. In this review, we obtained the first information to plan further experiences, focusing on the representation of the human figure.

- Initially, in order to get an idea of the goodness of the system and initial capture parameters, we planned the capture of a static non-human element; we used a wood model commonly used by painters. The results were very exciting because we will have in a short period of a three-dimensional model of high quality.

- In the context of the final work of the degree *"A comparative study of details from a survey of classical precision and a lift with 3D laser system: The Warrior of Xian"* (School of Topography, Geodesy and Cartography), it was carried out a pilot study with a static human figure, showing as result a mesh of points equidistant, which encouraged us to continue our investigations in this direction.

- Then, we planned the first study of the male human figure, using a model (Figure 7). They were made several shots under different static positions of the body in order to obtain as much information as possible from the results. The results provided us with a cloud of point at intervals of 5 mm, so we got a continuous graphical representation of the human figure.

- We proceeded to repeat the previous test, but this time with a female human figure. See (Figure 8) (A), (B) and (C)

Figure 7. (A) Picture of the laboratory test Figure Madrid -2005 (B) The digital model obtained Madrid -2005

7 (A)

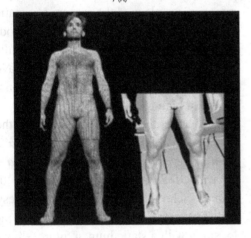

7 (B)

Figure 8. (A) Picture of the test with a female model Madrid -2005 (B) Digital pictures obtained by rotation of the model Madrid -2005 (C) Detail of the obtained digital female model Madrid -2005

8 (A)

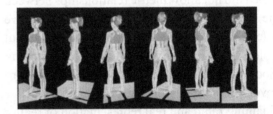

8 (B)

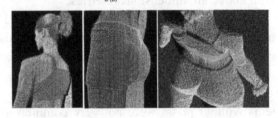

8 (C)

In both cases the results were very acceptable and provided us with a very rich experience for future experiments.

In a second test, the high-speed capture protocols of the equipments (1 to 3 seconds) were used to provide some results on the environment and movement occurring in it.

The results were more striking than those obtained previously, because in seconds we had available on the computer screen a raw 3D image of the surroundings without any post processing. However, it appeared the problem of shadows and blind spots produced by the system itself.

• After analyzing the results obtained for whole-body models, we proceeded to perform a test of a body part in more detail. This was based on the study of human arm. Implemented within the framework of a final work of the degree at School of Topography, Geodesy and Cartography (Ibáñez & Jiménez, 2006): *"An approach to anthropology in sport by mapping techniques based on laser-scanning systems: Survey a 3D human arm."* The results were acceptable, showing metrics precisions around 6.3 mm between the mesh points. An unexpected result was the colour textures offered by the model after texturing, once analyzed the colour textures seemed to correspond with muscle relaxation and contraction, opening this results another line of possible future research.

- After carrying out successfully the last experiences, we were ready to perform the first study of the movement, which had not been previously performed in the world. The results were not the most optimal, but they served to correct the capture parameters and to design the following experiences.

- Based on the analysis of previous results, we proceeded to design and conduct a test in laboratory conditions. We design a ramp with a known slope for rolling down a ball which was moving with a controlled speed. With this test we had two targets: (See Figure 9)
  ○ Study of the movement of the ball rolling down, considering it as a 3D object.
  ○ Study of the velocity and acceleration of the ball in all its way at intervals of 1 mm.

- With the above results, it was designed an experiment in real environment conditions: a race in the running track. We studied the evolution of the velocities and accelerations alone a 100 meters race. As a result we can see in the picture below the acceleration or deceleration caused by steps of the athlete, which form the "v shapes" in the image. [Figure 10]

- At present we keep on working on different experiences of motion capture and its possible applications to sports, without conclusive results but very hopeful. In parallel, we are working on systems for real-time 3D representations by virtual images (holograms), in order to perform an accurate representation of the human body. In this vein, we have opened a way for research by looking at metrics in video

Figure 9. (A) Picture of the setting of the study of velocity and acceleration of a ball Madrid -2007 (B) Picture of the results of the study of velocity and acceleration of a ball Madrid -2007

9 (A)

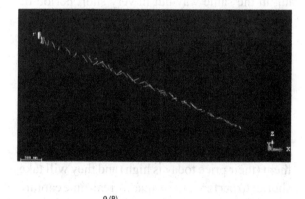

9 (B)

Figure 10. Results of the acceleration of a 100 m athleteMadrid - 2008

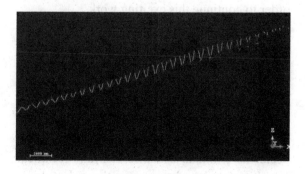

capturing systems and its real 3D representation, which combined with 3D laser captures, could allow a process of capture and analysis almost in real time.

CONCLUSION

In the last five years, the 3D laser capture systems have had a stunning technological improvement, and its tendency is to achieve a higher improvement in medium term. The situation is similar to the development of conventional photography: 100 years ago a man should pose for not less than 5 minutes in order to have a picture, and now in seconds we got a lot of high quality shots. Thus, following the example, these systems are evolving in the same way but in very short period of time, they are evolving from low resolution and high capture time to high resolution and shorter capture times in just one decade.

The members of this working group are in direct contact with the companies who sell these systems, and based on their experience, they understand that in 5 years time these equipments will be affordable to all individuals who need them (their price today is high) and they will take shorter to perform a high quality real-time capture of a moving object. However, the working principles and calculations that have been described in this work will not vary much and, therefore, we believe that the results we are getting are useful not only for the development of better equipments by companies, but also for future researchers in order to continue this exciting work.

Is worth noting the support and interest aroused by this study in institutions such as *EPOCH-European Network-European Research Network on Excellence in Processing Open Cultural Heritage*, IST-2002-507382, framed in the Sixth Framework Program of the European Union, and in other sports clubs, research institutions (traffic accidents, criminal, insurance, etc..) and Technical Faculties (engineering, aeronautics, seismology, mining, archaeology, etc.).

As we have commented, the project is currently underway. The 90% of the program has been already concluded, so we can offer partial results of the work done. Some the initial results will be released in the doctoral thesis of Pedro Calvo Merino, under the title *"Three-dimensional modelling of the human figure using mapping and its application to the moving object"*, which is in phase of completion.

REFERENCES

Adams, L. (1992). Programación gráfica. Técnicas avanzadas de modelado, acabado y animación 3D. Madrid, España: ANAYA Multimedia SA.

Allard, P., Stokes, I. A. F., & Blanchi, J. P. (1995). *Three-dimensional analysis of human movement.* Chicago: Human Kinetics.

Barber, D., Mills, J., & Bryan, P. (2004). Towards A Standard Specification For Terrestrial Laser Scaning. In *Cultural Heritage. Presented at International Society for Photogrammetry and Remote Sensing.* Antalya: Istambul.

Borg, C. E., & Margin, M. (2003). Escáneres 3D de largo alcance: ¿Avanzando hacia una herramienta híbrida o hacia una metodología híbrida? *Datum XXI*, *1*(5), 42–46.

Bracci, S., Falletti, F., & Scopigno, M. M. R. (2004). Explorando David: diagnóstico y estado de la conservación. Roma, Italia: Giunti Press.

Carter, J. E. L. (1982). *Physical structure of Olympic athletes. Part I: The Montreal Olympic Games anthropological project.* Basel, Switzerland: Krager.

Demir, N., Bayram, B., Alkış, Z., Helvaci, C., Çetin, I., & Vögtle, T. (2004). *Laser scanning for terrestial photogrammetry, alternativa system or combined with traditional system?* Presented at International Society for Photogrammetry and Remote Sensing, Istambul.

Donskoi, D., & Zatsiorski, V. M. (1988). *Biomecánica de los ejercicios físicos*. La Habana, Cuba: Pueblo y Educación.

Esparza, F. (1993). *Manual de cineantropometría*. Pamplona, España: FEMEDE.

García, P. (n. d.). *Kinantropometria o cineantropometria: Definición y alcance social [Versión electrónica]*. Universidad de Caracas. Retrieved February 8, 2005, from http://www.rendeportin.com.ve/kinan.htm

Ghosh, S. K. (1979). *Analytical photogrammetry* [Forogrametría analítica]. New York: Pergamon Press.

Gonzalez-Aguilera, D. (2001). *Consideraciones sobre el análisis de la fiabilidad en el patrimonio edificado. Fiabilidad y fotogrametría arquitectónica [Versión electrónica]*. REDCientifica. Retrieved November 8, 2004, from http://www.redcientifica.com/imprimir/doc200111070001.html

Hogarth, B. (1996). *Dynamic Anatomic*. Köln, Germany: Benedikt Taschen Verlag GmbH.

Ibáñez, S., & Jiménez, J. (2006). *Aproximación a la antropología en el deporte mediante técnicas cartográficas basadas en sistemas láser-escáner: Levantamiento 3D de un brazo humano*. Unpublished bachelor dissertation, Universidad Politécnica de Madrid (UPM).

Ikemoto, L., Gelfand, N., & Levoy, M. (2003). *A hierarchical method for aligning warped meshes [Un método jerárquico para alinear acoplamientos combados]*. Paper presented at the Fourth International Conference on 3D Imaging and Modeling (3DIM), October 6-10, 2003, Banff, Alberta, Canada.

Leica Geosystems. (2005). *Documentación Técnica y Manuales de Referencia sobre sistemas láser* [Electronic Version]. Retrieved from http://www.leica-geosystems.com/es/index.htm

Lerma, J. L. (1999). Reconocimiento de materiales y deterioros en fachadas arquitectónicas. *Datum XXI, 1*(0), 25–27.

Leva, P. (1994). *Adjustments to Zatsiorsky-Seluyanov's segment inertia parameter. Kinesiology Department*. Bloomington, IN: Indiana University.

Levoy, M., Rusinkiewicz, S., Ginzton, M., & Ginsberg, J. (2000). *The digital Michelangelo project: 3d scanning of large statues*. Department of Computer Science and Engineering, University of Washington. Retrieved October 6, 2004, from http://graphics.stanford.edu/papers/dmich-sig00/dmich-sig00.html

Moeslund, T. B., Madsen, C. B., & Granum, E. (2003). *Modelling the 3d pose of human arm and shoulder complex utilisima only two parameters*. Paper presented at the meeting International Conference of Model-based Imaging, Rendering, Image Analysis and Graphical Special Effects, Rocquencourt, Francia (pp. 11-19).

Ojeda, J. C., Martinez, R., Gonzalez, F., & Sanchez, J. A. (2002). Generación de modelos tridimensionales de curvas y túneles. *Mapping-Interactivo, Artículo 180*. Retrieved October 4, 2004, from http://www.mappinginteractivo.com/plantilla-egeo.asp?id_articulo=180

Rusinkiewicz, S., & Levoy, M. (2000). *QsPlat: A multiresolution point rendering system for large meshes*. Paper presented at the meeting SIGGRAPH 2000, Computer Graphics Proceedings (pp 343-352). Retrieved September 7, 2004, from http://graphics.stanford.edu/papers/qsplat/qsplat_paper.pdf

Salinas, F. S., & Velilla, C. (2003). Estudio métrico por fotogrametría terrestre: Documentación de pequeños monumentos [Versión electrónica]. *Mapping-Interactivo, Artículo 175*. Retrieved October 4, 2004, from http://www.mappinginteractivo.com/plantilla-egeo.asp?id_articulo=175

Shulz, T., & Ingensand, H. (2004). *Terrestrial Lasser Scanning: Investigations and Applications for High Precision Scanning*. Paper presented at the meeting FIG Working Week of Athens.

Soto, V. M. (1995). *Desarrollo de un sistema para el análisis biomecánico tridimensional del deporte y la representación gráfica realista del cuerpo humano*. Tesis Doctoral, Facultad de Ciencias de la Actividad Física y el Deporte, Universidad de Granada, España.

Vera, P. (1989). Técnicas de análisis en biomecánica deportiva: estado actual y perspectivas. Presented at Jornadas Unisport sobre tecnología del deporte, Málaga.

Vozikus, G. (2004). *Lasser Scanning: New method for recording and documentation in Archaeology*. Paper presented at the meeting FIG Working Week of Athens. Retrieved October 13, 2004, from http://www.fig.net/pub/athens/papers/wsa1/WSA1_4_Vozikis_et_al.pdf

Warn, H., Marschner, S., Levoy, M., & Hanrohon, P. (2000). A practical model for subsurface light transport. In SIGGRAPH 2000 (Computer Graphics Proceedings).

Woltring, H. J. (1995). *Smoothong and differentiation techineques applied to 3D data*. Champaign, IL: Human Kinetic.

Zatsiorski, V. M., & Donskoi, D. (1988). *Biomecánica de los ejercicios físicos*. La Habana, Cuba: Pueblo y Educación.

Chapter 12
Virtual Modelling of Prehistoric Sites and Artefacts by Automatic Point-Cloud Surveys

Mercedes Farjas
Universidad Politécnica de Madrid, Spain

Francisco J. García-Lázaro
Universidad Politécnica de Madrid, Spain

Julio Zancajo
Universidad de Salamanca, Spain

Teresa Mostaza
Universidad de Salamanca, Spain

Nieves Quesada
Universidad Politécnica de Valencia, Spain

ABSTRACT

This chapter presents laser scanner systems as a new method of automatic data acquisition for use in archaeological research. The operation of the equipment is briefly described and results are presented from its application in two Spanish archaelogical sites: Abrigo de Buendía (Cuenca), Atapuerca (Burgos). Together with these systems, point cloud measuring photogrammetric methods are revised. Photogrammetry has been widely used in heritage documentation and in no way is to be relegated by the new scanning techniques. Instead, Photogrammetry upgrades its methods by applying digital approaches so that it becomes competitive in both, operational costs and results. Nevertheless, Photogrammetry and laser scanner systems should be regarded as complementary rather than competing techniques. To illustrate photogrammetric methods their application to generate the Digital Surface Model of an epigraph is described. The authors' research group endeavours to combine teaching and research in its different fields of activity. Initial data are acquired in project-based teaching situations and international seminars or other activities. Students thus have the opportunity to become familiar with new methodologies while collecting material for analytical studies.

DOI: 10.4018/978-1-61520-631-5.ch012

INTRODUCTION

The approach used in this paper is based on Topography, a science that Norman Thomas defined as "*The art of determining the relative positions of distinctive features on portions of the Earth's surface*" (Thomas, 1958) and Buckner as "*The science and art of taking the measurements necessary to determine the relative position of points on, in or under the Earth's surface, or to locate points in a specific position*" (Buckner, 1983).

Although the concept has not changed with time, the techniques, instruments and methods used have undergone considerable changes, but the objective is still to define the position of one point in relation to another, by planimetry, altimetry or, in the case of laser scanning equipment, by three-dimensional capture.

At the beginning of 2003, Leica Geosystems put a CYRAX HDS 2500 laser scanner at our disposal. Since that time we have used the system on two lines of investigation: topographic and photogrammetric methodologies; analysing their potential and the possibility of combining both approaches.

One of these lines is in investigating how photogrammetry can simplify processes, create protocols and automate advanced instrument and software processes. The other uses the topographical approach to bring discrete three-dimensional modelling closer to metric continuity by means of higher point-densities, which in one way or another facilitate the representation of the object under study. Laser scanners also add improved features to metric quality in such a way that the full potential of this combination has still not been fully explored.

After deciding that our objective was to initiate future researchers in this method, we selected case studies which would make use of the new technology. Due to lack of space we have to leave for a further article the work dealing with metric representation by automatic photogrammetric processes, as well as describing other experiments with low-level aerial photography from remote-controlled helicopters and projects involving the modelling of palaeographic samples. About photogrammetric methods we are going to present a briefly case study description.

INTRODUCTION TO LASER SCANNERS

A 3D scanner is a data acquisition system which analyses an object or surface to acquire information on its shape, measurements and colour. This information can subsequently be used to construct three-dimensional models and extrapolate the shape of the object under study.

3D scanners operate in a way very similar to cameras. Like cameras, they have a conical field of vision and can acquire information from lighted surfaces. While a camera acquires colour information on the surfaces within its field of vision, 3D scanners capture other surface data, so that by combining geometrical features with photographs the optimum representation of the object is achieved.

An introductory text on the subject in Spanish can be found in Farjas and García-Lázaro (2008).

The type of 3D scanner normally used in three-dimensional modelling is an active non-contact scanner, which is placed at a certain distance from the object and projects a beam onto the object or its surroundings from short or long range. The type of beam used may be light, ultrasound or x-rays. Long range systems work at distances of from 3 to 300 metres and provide measurements correct to within one centimetre. Short range systems are placed at less than 3 metres and are correct to less than a millimetre. There may also be differences in the type of measuring system and the type of sweep. The different systems include the following:

Different types of measuring system:

- **Time of flight scanners:** Distance is measured from the time needed by a photodiode to emit and receive a laser beam. This type is suitable for exterior mid and long range applications and can reach almost to 1000 metres. Most time-of-flight 3D laser measurement systems are comparable to a motorised prismless total station equipped with CCD sensor and distance measurement. They carry out automatic sweeps to measure distances and encode the horizontal and vertical pulse projection angles to determine the spatial coordinates of each point. The beam aperture angle determines the spatial resolution of the exploration. Distances of up to 100 m can be measured to within 3-10 mm. These systems are used for long distance operations and also for LIDAR aerial surveys.
- **Phase difference scanners:** This type measures the distance to the object by means of the phase difference between the emitted and received signals, following the general formula of wave distanciometers. The procedure is similar to that of prismless total stations. Phase difference systems are normally used for interior and exterior mid range applications of up to 100 m and are accurate to within 1 cm.
- **Optical laser triangulation scanner:** This type calculates spatial coordinates from the direct intersection, in a method similar to stereophotogrammetry, except that it has an emitting diode (laser scanner) at one end and a receiving diode (CCD video camera) at the other, so that only one camera is necessary. 340,000-pixel spatial resolutions can be obtained with an estimated

accuracy of around 2 mm for distances of up to 2 m.

Types of sweep:

- **Camera scanner:** 60° x 60° maximum field window.
- **Panoramic scanner:** carries out sweeps around two axes (vertical and horizontal). The vertical sweep is complete, interrupted only by the base of the instrument itself. Maximum sweep vision field is 360° x 310°.
- **Hybrid scanner:** a combination of the two preceding systems, with a 360° x 60° capture zone.

At the present time, research is being carried out to develop a kinetic laser scanner sweep system in real time with a synchronised combination of GPS and inertial positioning systems.

The typical components in a laser scanner are the following:

- **Data capture system:** Based on a laser beam combined with a deviation system that permits the capture of all points in the sweep area. The data obtained consist of the three-dimensional coordinates of each point. The latest models also record reflected wave intensity.
- **Camera:** In some cases the system has a built-in camera (normally low resolution), and in others it is not included. Except in optical triangulation, the images captured from the sweep area are generally used to facilitate the subsequent identification of the points. They may also be used to give texture to models and create orthoimages.
- **Data processing computer programs:** Since the system produces a large quantity of data for processing, special programs

must be used, basically to extract and model surfaces from the raw point cloud and also to reference in a single system of coordinates the different clouds obtained from different scans.

- **Spatial positioning:** systems (optional), generally GPS, other systems may be optional.

GENERAL WORKING PROCEDURES WITH LASER SCANNERS SYSTEMS

Operations with terrestrial laser scanners are divided into three phases; data acquisition, post-processing and visualisation.

Data Acquisition

During the data capture process, attention must be given to the number of batteries available and their operating time, atmospheric and solar radiation effects, surface features and reflectance, possible difficulties in transporting the laser equipment, as well as other questions such as the possible danger involved in using of the laser and the appropriate precautions.

A preliminary study of the object is fundamental to trouble-free data acquisition, as it can help to avoid mistakes in merging the different sweeps, redundancies can be minimised and optimal use be made of scanning time and data estimates can be made for each area.

The point density attainable by the system depends on distance from the target, the resolution chosen, the precision established for the project and capture time.

To ensure complete digitilisation of the zone, care must be taken in designing the number of laser scans and their locations. The minimum number of sightings should be made to obtain the lowest number of shaded areas and gaps, with a common overlap zone between the different beams. Minimum sweep overlap threshold is usually between 10-39%.

The capture system records the coordinates in the scanner's reference system. This is different for each sighting, so that each laser data capture must be referred to a single global or local reference system for the set of sweeps. Often, targets are needed specifically designed to link, register or georeference different coordinate systems from different topographical sightings. If they are not available, most software programs are able to search for common points and merge the different sweeps semi-automatically

Data Processing

After acquisition the data is processed. Most laser scanner systems include a specific data processing and viewing program capable of processing the large quantity of points data from each scan. The traditional CAD system alone could not deal with such a large amount of information.

In general, the initial data processing is as follows:

- Registration of each point cloud with the reference system chosen for the project, generally local or global.
- Pre-editing of each scan. If this is too dense, points can be reduced to a manageable size by cleaning.
- Filtering of information to eliminate overlapping areas.
- Elimination of undesirable or erroneous points, e.g. persons or objects that get in the way during a scan.
- 3D segmentation of point clouds.
- Extraction of geometries
- Modelling of 3D entities
- Filling in zones empty of points.
- Simplification of the entities.

Most of these processes are carried out interactively. Semi-automatic and automatic algorithms are now being developed to optimise handling of laser data. However, the opacity of the algorithms used by manufacturers and the small amount of experience acquired to date in data acquisition mean that it is often necessary to perform the processes manually.

Visualisation of the Results

Visualisation can be carried out either before or after data processing. The quality of the final result largely depends on how well the data processing phase was performed.

Visualisations that can be obtained after data processing are the following:

- Pure point clouds or with assigned reflected intensity or texture levels if cameras are also used.
- Triangulated surface mesh
- Shaded surfaces
- Geometric models of simple figures or entities.
- Orthoimages, if laser data are combined with images and photogrammetry is used.
- Animations

Final results can be delivered in the form of:

- Point clouds that can be processed in CAD (dwg and dgn) environments.
- CAD 3D (dxf) file
- CAD 2D (dxf) file
- Modelling file
- ASCII file of the required points
- TIN 3D texturisation
- Animated films
- PDS and AutoPlant files for use with software in industrial plants.

Case 1. Modelling of Archaelogical Site by Long-Range Laser Scanner Abrigo De Buendía Project (Alos & Minzateanu, 2007)

The objective of this project was to construct a digital model of the terrain of the archaeological site at Castejón to obtain a map of the zone and its surroundings and also a digital reconstruction of the remains. When the data was obtained in 2005 we decided to consider 3D laser scanning as a possible alternative to photogrammetry.

Abrigo de Buendía is an archaeological site in Castejón, Spain, in the north west of the province of Cuenca, and belongs to the Autonomous Community of Castilla – La Mancha, at about 150 km from Madrid. The site was discovered in 1983 by Juan Vicent and Fernando Velasco. Carbon dating placed the site at about 15,000 BC. The first digs were carried out in July 2005 supervised by I. de la Torre and J. Vicent.

Data Acquisition

The first stage of the site modelling project involved the creation of a basic point network to give coverage to the site using GPS technology georeferenced to the Spanish geodesic system.

To preserve the geodesic points for future campaigns, they were placed on iron-reinforced concrete bases on firm ground.

Positions were chosen by the relative static method, which allows the coordinates of one receiver to be obtained from those of an another, which defines the work reference system to within 5-10 mm ±1 ppm.

The points observed with GPS were obtained in the WGS84 reference system. To transform its coordinates into the official Spanish system at that time (ED50 in UTM projection on Hayford's ellipsoid) they were transformed with REGENTE vertex data (Spanish geodesic reference frame-

Figure 1. Geodetic Network, "Los Gaviluchos" Point & Leica GPS System 500

Figure 2. Trimble GX-200 data acquisition and detail of the raw point cloud

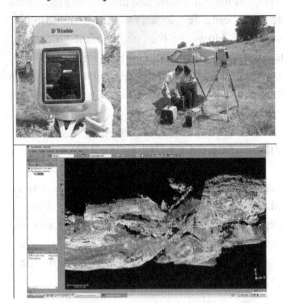

work) from the sheets adjacent to the site. (See Figure 1).

After the construction of the basic grid, the necessary scans were made to model the surroundings of the Abrigo de Buendía by the Real Time Kinematic (RTK) method.

From the basic known coordinates belonging to the basic grid, four scans of the site were performed. The terrestrial laser scanner used was the Trimble GX-200, which obtained 3D coordinates (x, y and z) from the points observed with the instrument reference system (Figure 2). Reflected beam light intensity was also recorded for each point.

The parameters defined for this task were:

- Recognition of spheres: 2-3 minutes per sphere. Spheres were positioned evenly throughout the site.
- Scan stations: i.e. every scan would be performed from a point of known coordinates.
- A filter was used for distances between 50 – 70 m.
- Direct visualisation of scanned points on the screen with the option of real time geometric analysis.

Coordinates of the points that could not be reached by the scanner were taken by a Leica TCR 705 total station (which offers the option of operating without a prism reflector).

When the field work had been completed all the data acquired was filed in a computer using PointScape software.

Data Processing

Field data were in the form of homogeneous point clouds in a reference system. Trimble RealWorks was used to merge scans and data into a single model. Sphere recognition was performed automatically and the total cloud points were obtained in the reference system of coordinates calculated for the basic grid.

Several possible alternative software systems were assessed for data processing in a search for a program that had not been produced by the system manufacturer and LandDesktop 2006 from AutoDesk was finally selected. Due to the limitations of the computer system, the block had to be divided into three parts for model editing. Points were cleaned from all three parts and the segments were then re-joined to form a single surface model.

For surface visualisation regular 15 x 7.5 cm grids were used for zones that required greater detail, as in the cliff face and in a zone containing a recent rock fall.

The complete 3D model of the prehistoric site, supplemented by the data collected by the total station, was then inserted into the general model of the surrounding area obtained by RTK and GPS. This operation was performed manually due to the rugged terrain.

Before contour mapping, different variables had to be configured, such as equidistance, contour intervals, line types and styles, colours, text styles, justification, etc. Finally, Autocad 2007 was used to generate the model both for rendering and visual styles.

One of the aims of the project was to map the area surrounding the site. For this, scales were used according to the feature density of the terrain, e.g. 1/1000, 1/200, 1/100, as well as 3D views to represent the cliff face of the site from different perspectives.

For altimetry, manually and automatically obtained contour lines were used. Vertical surfaces were modelled manually since no software could be found capable of doing this operation. The rest of the site was contoured automatically and then checked manually.

The zone of greatest interest, close to the vertical rock face where the archaeological remains had been found, was modelled in two sections on a scale of 1/100 to show greater detail in altimetry.

Conclusion

Of the advantages of using laser scanners for three-dimensional modelling, the following can be mentioned:

- A large amount of topographical information can be captured rapidly on almost any type of surface (except matt black and those with high reflectance).
- Accuracy of measurements can be ensured

to within 1 cm.
- Information can be stored directly onto a hard disk.
- Rapid access to the point clouds obtained, with verification *in situ.*
- Files can be converted to different formats.

However, there are also disadvantages:

- The equipment, program and complementary equipment are very expensive.
- Powerful computers and programs are needed to handle large point clouds, as file capacities of 200 Mb can easily be reached.
- The equipment itself is bulky and needs to be transported with care.
- A plentiful electrical power supply is necessary in the form of motor generators or batteries, neither of which is easily transported over difficult terrain.
- Experienced technicians are needed to operate control software.
- In extensive non-geometrical surfaces with a lot of noise it may be difficult to distinguish the target from surrounding features in the acquired data.

The project had a total budget of €32,600 and even though the objectives were achieved we consider that this amount would be beyond the means of most archaeological teams.

Case 2: Modelling of Archaelogical Site by Long and Short-Range Laser Scanner Galeria-Zarpazos Site in Atapuerca (Vazquez Pelaez, 2007)

This project was planned by the ERASMUS program and involved students and teachers from universities from Spain, Germany and the USA.

The principle objective was to provide exchanges for teachers and students in subjects related to the conservation of the national heritage, applying digital techniques to collect geometrical

Figure 3. Atapuerca archaeological site, Spain

information, including data acquisition by GPS receivers, topographic total stations, 3D laser scanners and remote controlled helicopters.

The specific objectives were:

- To learn to place the geometrical documentation of heritage sites in the chain of value of the national heritage.
- To learn the fundamentals of geometric registration systems.
- To acquire skills in handling the equipment.
- To assess the possibilities of applying such methods to archaeology.

From the educational point of view, the objectives were:

- To allow students to meet people from other cultures.
- To practice all the phases involved in the process: data acquisition, basic data processing, obtaining results.
- To allow them to take part in an actual archaeological project.
- To integrate information technologies into archaeological documentation systems.
- To work with specialists from other disciplines, including geography, archaeology and terrain engineering.
- To provide students with experience in operating systems that may not be available

in their own universities due to their high cost.

Activities focused on carrying out specific projects on the documentation of heritage sites, one of which is described below. The experience took place in the archaeological site of Galería-Zarpazos at Atapuerca (Burgos, Spain). A theoretical explanation was provided by an archaeologist on a visit to the site; data acquisition and the use of the equipment was planned; tasks were assigned in the use of the equipment; data were acquired; basic processing was performed; and finally the students compiled a preliminary report of the results.

The Galería-Zarpazos site is in the zone known as the *Trinchera del ferrocarril* at the Atapuerca archaeological site (Figure 3) in a low mountain range in the province of Burgos in the Community of Castilla and León. It was declared a World Heritage site in 2000 due to the exceptionally important archaeological and paleontological finds made there.

The finds are exceptional due to the abundance of fossil specimens in a good state of conservation. The stone tools found there date from the early Stone Age almost up to the Bronze Age. Remains have been found of a new species of cave-dwelling bear, *Ursus dolinensis*. The most important finds are of human remains, found in different sites, which is unusual, believed to be the oldest found in Europe. These include *Homo antecessor,* the last of the common Neanderthal species, *Homo sapiens*, and the pre-Neanderthal *Homo heidelbergensis*.

The Zarpazos gallery was among the first to be systematically excavated within the *Trinchera,* which is an underground trench which comes up to the surface in the form of a chimney. The main entrance is on the left hand side of the site and is known as the *Covacha de los Zarpazos*. The project aimed to create a three-dimensional model of this zone by 3D laser scanner.

As in the previously described project, a GPS grid was established to cover the entire zone and linked to the Spanish geodesic system. A precision polygonal was then performed inside the trench itself, where the site is located, so as to be able to radiate to the targets of the laser scanner system.

The polygonisation grid was necessary since GPS observation was impossible inside the trench with 20 m high vertical walls. The three-tripod observation method was used for this secondary grid, with a complete 360° turn at each scan. The GPS grid was observed by three GPS Leica 500 with the necessary complementary equipment.

The GPS positioning of the exterior grid was the so-called rapid - static method, which works with pseudo distances and phase. Distance increments were calculated to within a millimetre. When all the data from all the GPS observations had been imported, as well as data from the antenna situated in Burgos and the necessary data for the days when the observations were carried out, the processing parameters were configured using the Leica Geo Office v 6.0. The final coordinates of the vertices were calculated by the official Spanish system, 1950 Datum Europeo in UTM projection.

After the minimum square adjustment, the error ellipse values were obtained, as well as the standard deviations regarding the position of each base with respect to the points considered to be fixed.

When the geodesic link, the basic grid and the polygonisation grid had been observed, all the references and control points of each site were registered and registration began with the Z+F IMAGER 5006 3D scanner provided by HafenCity University, Hamburg, Germany.

The topographical references for the laser scanner consisted of marks impressed on thick laminated paper of different sizes. These were observed with the TCR 705 station.

The Z+F IMAGER 5006 scanner works by directing a laser beam at the centre of a rotating mirror, which diverts the laser in vertical rota-

tion and scans the entire surroundings. Angular encoders measure the rotation of the mirror and the horizontal rotation of the base. The measuring system is based on phase difference technology and transmits different waves at various longitudes. The distance between the scanner and the target is calculated from the phase difference between the transmitted and received waves.

The system can measure distances of between 0.5 to 80 m. The manufacturer guarantees precision within 1.5 mm at 50 m. The chief advantage of the phase difference method is the point capture speed, which can reach up to 5000,000 points per second, compared to the 4,000 points p/s of the time of flight method.

The scanner is panoramic, with a useful beam vision of 310° vertically and 360° horizontally, with maximum angular resolution of 10 gons.

Two different software programs were used to process the data.. One was the scanner's own software, *Z+F Láser Control,* used in the field work and pre-processing. The other, used for the point cloud processing, was the RealWorks program.

The zone was studied previous to the scanning operation to identify its features and restrictions and to decide on the number of stations necessary and their placement. The zone was divided in two; one consisted of the *Galeria,* having walls 17 m long and 8 m tall at the highest point; the other was to the left of this site, known as *Zarpazos,* a cavity about 5 m long, 6 m deep and with a maximum height of 7 m.

The site was given photo coverage by a camera placed very close to the scanner station. Photography was carried out at the same time as scanning, but changes in sunlight and cloud conditions meant that shots had to be repeated on several occasions. Three or four photographs were taken in each position, changing the light settings in each one. Those considered the most suitable for the project were selected.

Scans were taken from seven positions to cover the entire site, leaving considerable overlaps be-

Figure 4. Scan view and target measurement

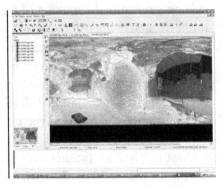

tween the segments. Two scans were taken from inside the *Zarpazos* gallery.

A point cloud defining the geometry of the target can be obtained by 3D laser scanning in real time.

Z+F Láser Control software was used for initial data processing.

The first steps were as follows:

- Import sweeps
- Clean data
- Merge sweeps
- Georeferencing
- Export sweeps

When the point clouds had been imported, they could be viewed in two-dimensional projection, as in a photograph, or in three dimensions. Readings were included of the coordinates and the reflected light intensity at each of the points.

The scanner is programmed for indiscriminate registration according to a criteria of angular distances. Erroneous points can be eliminated automatically by a series of programmed masks, which block them from being visualised on the screen if they comply with certain pre-defined spatial conditions.

After cloud importing and filtering, the instrument reference system coordinates, different for each station, are transformed into a single reference system.

To determine the transformation parameters, the coordinates of the corresponding points in both reference systems, the original and the final, must be known. However, the laser scanner does not register singular points such as corners or the geometrical centres of targets, but rather selects a series of points evenly distributed around the surface.

Target signals were used in this project and the centres of the signals were identified manually (See Figure 4). To do this correctly, it was important for the scanner to be able to register the reflected light intensity besides the points' spatial coordinates. In this way, visualising the cloud points would be similar to visualising a black-and-white photograph.

After identifying all the target signals in the different sweeps, the centre of each one was identified manually.

All topographical references were measured and the point clouds were registered. A three-dimensional Helmert transformation was used to convert the scanner reference system to the selected reference system.

Figure 5. Digital model of Galeria and solid representation of Zarpazos

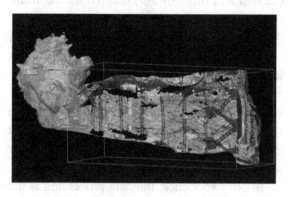

EXPORT OF SWEEPS

In this phase the sweeps are exported from the Z+F (*zfprj) program to the RealWorks (*rwp) format. This consists of obtaining an XYZ file, the only format shared by both RealWorks (*rwp) and Z+F. Besides the XYZ information, the intensity value of each pixel is incorporated. Seven text archives of over 1 Gb each were obtained for every sweep

After importing the files, the point clouds were edited. The necessary steps in this stage were the following:

- Import clouds
- Merge point clouds
- Eliminate noise
- Triangulation
- Assign textures to model

Two methods were used to eliminate noise. One method eliminated scanned areas not needed for the site model and the other gained space on the hard disk by filtering out unnecessary points. The elements removed included scaffolding, parts of the site not included in the model and the zones outside the site itself. In this way, the point cloud was reduced from a size of 38 million points to 15 million.

Finally, spatial filtering was carried out by using the distances between points to reduce the number of points and save processing time in the remaining tasks. The centimetre was chosen as the filtering unit. All points at less than one cm from another were eliminated and a homogeneous cloud was thus obtained. This reduced the cloud size by about 10 million points.

With all the unnecessary points cleaned from the point cloud, the triangular grid (TIN) was edited. This grid was composed of triangles whose 3 vertices were 3 different cloud points. No points remained inside the triangles, no two triangles overlapped and the entire point cloud was composed of a single geometry. This grid took a whole day to process. Editing the grid consisted of eliminating irregular or oversized triangles. The grid was also softened to improve its visual appearance.

Before starting the texture matching process, the best photos were selected for each zone and these were then modified as to lighting, contrast, etc. with the PhotoShop program, which was also used to eliminate noise. When all the photos had consistent colours, texture matching began. Images were exported to RealWorks. Points on the photos were matched with the coinciding points on the previously obtained grid. Textures could be matched with four points but satisfactory results were only obtained with at least seven points. An unlimited number of points could be chosen; the greater the number of points the better the results.

When a photo was assigned to the grid, the photo was cut as required to fit the grid and an overlap was left to ensure a good final result.

RESULTS OBTAINED

The final results of the data processing were a three-dimensional model, orthophotographs and videos of the *Galería-Zarpazos* site (See Figure 5). Two independent digital models were also obtained, one for the *Galería* and one for *Zarpazos*.

The next phase was to create orthophotos. 3D point clouds that contained radiometric informa-

Figure 6. Final maps with the orthomosaic of Galeria and ZarpazosConclusions of the project

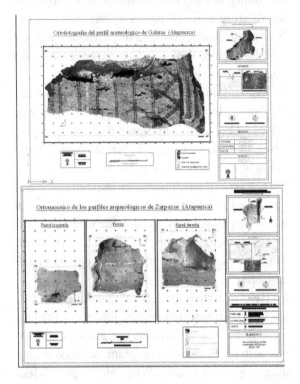

tion were used for this purpose. An orthogonal projection of the point cloud onto a previously defined vertical plane was carried out. The steps involved in this process were as follows:

*   Definition of the projection plane and its parameters: direction of the axes, situation of the plane by coordinates, plane orientation angle.
*   Selection of the zone of interest.
*   Selection of image resolution, which depended entirely on the image quality and not on that of the digital model. All the orthophotos were made to a 3 mm pixel size.

The orthophotos were then exported to a CAD document for editing in cartographic form by AutoCad (See Figure 6).

Four orthophotos were obtained: one of the *Galeria* and three of *Zarpazos* (from the front, right wall and left wall to form an orthomosaic). A1 paper size format was chosen on a scale of 1/30.

This project was executed with the latest technology in the field of data capture, processing and 3D modelling and has shown that a 3D laser scanner system permits the acquisition of a large volume of data in great detail in a short time and that the data can be visualised on a laptop computer screen in real time.

In our experience, the data processing is the most complicated part of the process since it deals with large quantities of information, which means that only computers with large data processing capacity can be used for the purpose.

The time needed for data capture is much less than that needed by the classical topographical survey. A total station needs about 30 s to measure a point, while a 3D laser scanner can measure up to 150,000 points in the same time.

We consider that the overall objectives of the project have been achieved, having obtained a complete and detailed geometry of the *Galeria - Zarpazos* archaeological site. However, we also consider that the data processing programs need to be improved on, for example, in the form of new algorithms to make easier the handling of the large volume of data and facilitate interacting with other design programs.

During the 2008 campaign at the Atapuerca archaeological site, short range laser scanner data capture was incorporated into the project. New metric information on the features were thus added to the existing 3D models. Detailed scans were also carried out to register bear paw marks found on the walls. These data are at present being processed and the results are expected to be published shortly.

Short-range scanning technology was also included in the third project we carried out on the *Guilanya* engravings, which is described below.

REVIEW OF PHOTOGRAMMETRIC METHODS

Photogrammetry has been defined as "the science or art of obtaining reliable measurements by means of photographs" (Thompson & others, 1966, p. 4), where the term "art" is to be understood in the sense of a skill developed through experience. The principle of Photogrammetry is finding the intersection in object space of at least two conjugate rays coming from perspective bundles, constructed from overlapping photographs of the object being measured. This requires some parameters to be either known or determined on the job: the camera internal orientation parameters, which allow reconstructing a perspective bundle of rays from a photograph, and the external orientation parameters, which account for camera positions and attitudes.

Like laser scanning, Photogrammetry is a non-contact, non-destructive measuring technique. So, international organizations as UNESCO and ICOMOS (International Council on Monuments and Sites) have recommended the use of Photogrammetry for heritage documentation and preserving (Carbonell, 1989:321). Despite the very high costs of traditional analogue or analytical photogrammetric equipments which included high precision optical-mechanical stereoplotters and calibrated cameras, Photogrammetry has been widely applied to these tasks.

A work participated by one of the authors of this chapter will be briefly referred to as an example. In 1977, a photogrammetric survey of Altamira Cave pictographs (Santander, Spain) was carried out. Fifty pairs of photographs were taken with a Jenoptik UMK 10/1318 camera and processed by means of two analogue plotters, namely a Wild A-10 autograph and a Galileo Santoni IV stereo-cartograph (Llanos & García-Lázaro, 1983). The final product was a collection of ¼ scale maps of the cave ceiling. 2 mm interval contours were used for relief representation and the boundaries of the figures were delineated.

After the digital revolution, costless personal computers and off-the-shelf digital cameras can be used to perform complete, highly automated photogrammetric workflows. Measuring software is still somewhat expensive but its price is much lower than that of traditional equipments, even if currency depreciation is not accounted for. 20 years ago the price of a complete photogrammetric equipment consisting of a metric camera and an analytical stereoplotter could be so high as 120000 € (nominal). Today, some 15000 € can buy an equipment with better performances in both, affordable data set size and processing time. Thus photogrammetric methods are easier and cheaper nowadays and their use in heritage tasks can be even wider than in the past.

Automatic photogrammetric measuring software is based on digital image correlation algorithms: points on one image are sampled at a specified step and a reference window is defined in a neighbourhood of each point. A search roving window is defined and moved over a second, overlapping image, to seek for the conjugate of each sampled point. Several statistics criteria exist to determine whether a pair of conjugated points has been identified. Upon identification, conjugate rays are reconstructed and their intersections found using the internal and external orientation parameters.

These methods allow point measurement at a rate similar to that of laser scanners (Fryer & others, 2006). XYZ accuracy of photogrammetric point-clouds has been said to be poorer but emerging trends like image correlation of multiple convergent photographs (Remondino, 2008) are rapidly changing this scenario: more than two conjugate rays result in increased intersection reliability and convergent images allow conjugate rays to intersect at an angle close to 90° achieving the best accuracies. With these new methods, metric quality of photogrammetric and laser scanner point cloud measurements can be regarded as similar.

A PHOTOGRAMMETRIC STUDY CASE DIGITAL SURFACE MODEL OF AN EPIGRAPH

To illustrate the potential of high resolution Photogrammetry, a very short range photogrammetric work (camera-to-object distance = 0.5 m) will be described. This work (currently in process) is included in PADCAM, a project related to archaeological and documental heritage in Madrid Region (Spain), and funded by the Regional Government.

One of this project research lines deals with the potential of new technologies in Epigraphy, which can be defined as "an auxiliary science to History that studies the inscriptions on enduring substances" (Meyer & others, 2006 p. 1605) or "the study or science of epigraphs or inscriptions, esp. of ancient inscriptions" (Epigraphy, n. d.). A variety of methods and disciplines can be ancillary to this science.

From a geometric point of view epigraphs can be thought as abrupt changes in the shape of the engraved surface. Photogrammetry derivates 3D reliable information about the shape of an object from photographs, and can thus be regarded as one of the disciplines that are called for by Epigraphy. Several papers report the use of Photogrammetry in geometric description of epigraphs. Most referred works, however, describe just two-dimensional characterizations of symbols and letters, full 3D documentation of epigraphs being regarded as further research (Jobst, 1999). Reported 3D photogrammetric surveys are concerned at most with the spatial shape of the surface where symbols are engraved, so that it can be draped onto a plane in order to measure 2D shape of symbols (Meyer & others, 2004).

In the work presented here a digital surface model of an epigraph is being generated by photogrammetric methods, accounting for the 3D shape of the grooves that configure the symbols. The epigraph is engraved on a $2' \times 2' \times 2''$ brick (*Later Bipedalis*), dated in the last years of the Roman Empire, and reused to cover one of the graves in a Visigothic necropolis found in Madrid. There are some characters and symbols engraved on the brick surface, their dimensions being in the order of 2 mm depth, 1 cm width, and several cm in length. So, a resolution of at least 0.2 mm in object space is required for an accurate geometric description of the grooves.

Object space resolution achieved by photogrammetric methods depends mainly on image resolution, photo scale and base length (i. e., the distance between the perspective centers of two adjacent images). Large image scales are more easily obtained with medium to large format image cameras, but medium format high resolution digital cameras were regarded as too expensive for the first steps of the research.

An analogue 6 cm × 6 cm format Kiev 88 camera was used, the photographs being digitized later on by means of an available Delta GeoSystems photogrammetric scanner. Resolution of digital images was 8 microns per pixel (53 megapixels per image), with a positional accuracy of image points better than ±2 microns rms.

Camera focus was set at the shortest range (0.5 m) to get both, the largest possible photographic scale and focus setting repeatability, such that the image principal distance can be considered fixed in all the photographs. A calibration of the camera at these settings (comprising principal distance, principal point position related to image corners and the first coefficient of radial symmetric distortion) was available from a previous work.

Photo scale of the brick images was 1/5, the complete photographic coverage of the brick requiring 18 partially overlapping images arranged in 3 strips. Toroidal signals fixed to strings were used for control points and the strings were held close to the brick surface avoiding any damage. XYZ coordinates of control points were determined by topographic methods with an accuracy of ±0.1 mm rms.

Digi 3D V2005.0.25 photogrammetric software (© Manuel Quirós & José A. Martínez-Torres 2000-2005) is used to adjust the pairs of adjacent

Figure 7. (A), (B) and (C) tree overlapping photographs (D) shaded relief rendering of the brick DSM generated out of them partial (E) detail of the gridded surface

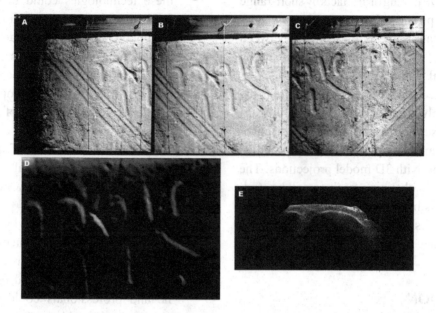

photographs and automatically generate a 3D point cloud from them by means of image correlation. Sampling step in this measurement process is 0.5 mm in object space. Point clouds are merged when completed and a regular 0.25 mm × 0.25 mm grid DSM is generated out of them.

Figure shows tree consecutive overlapping photographs (A, B, C), a shaded relief rendering of the brick DSM portion generated out of them (D), and a detail of the gridded surface (E). This last demonstrates how an extremely detailed representation of the grooves shape can be achieved. DSMs of this kind provide the researcher with a numeric high resolution replica of the object, which can further be used in a non-contact fashion to obtain accurate measures and carry out reliable analysis, not to mention the possibility of creating geometrically truly virtual realistic representations of any kind of heritage pieces.

(Figure 7) depicts tree consecutive overlapping photographs (A, B, C), a shaded relief rendering of the brick DSM portion generated out of them (D), and a detail of the gridded surface (E). This last demonstrates how an extremely detailed rep-

resentation of the grooves shape can be achieved. DSMs of this kind provide the researcher with a numeric high resolution replica of the object, which can further be used in a non-contact fashion to obtain accurate measures and carry out reliable analysis, not to mention the possibility of creating geometrically truly virtual realistic representations of any kind of heritage pieces

FUTURE RESEARCH DIRECTIONS

As can be deduced from the work carried out in this project, the objective of our 3D Modelling Laboratory to examine the capacity of 3D laser scanner systems to model archaeological artefacts and compare the results to those obtained by photogrammetry, and to optimise registration by combining and innovating in both technologies.

Another archaeological area which we have begun to investigate could be termed "The geodesic approach to imaging artefacts and obtaining two-dimensional graphic documents."

Since millimetric precision can now be achieved in 3D imaging of artefacts by short-range scanners, the problem that now makes a geodesic approach advisable is the conflict between 3D results and the 2D tracings made on site by archaeological teams.

As in the geodesic sciences, with regard to the problems involved in representing the Earth's surface on a flat surface, our objective is to discover how tracings made form artefacts can be studied in combination with 3D model projections. The method used for obtaining tracings will be studied and, if possible, a non-orthogonal 3D model projection process obtained from scanner systems will be developed.

CONCLUSION

This chapter has presented long range 3D laser scanner technology applied to archaeological sites and photogrammetric methods applied to artefacts.

The advantages of the new systems include the rapid and precise acquisition of the register, enormous potential to obtain new products after post-processing and the excellent visualisation of results in different digital formats.

Some other features are:

- Laser systems provide very accurate models and need very little time for data acquisition. Short range systems give models with particularly accurate spatial resolution.
- The amount of information stored in the system programs is difficult to handle in post-processing. This problem can be eased by using precision mechanical engineering programs such as RapidForm 2006.
- A great number of specialised programs are available to handle topographical laser scanner registers and are recommended for use in post-processing when data are acquired with a scanner of the same make as the software. The results are of good quality and the process is relatively fast.

- The present high cost involved in using these technologies could be expected to fall in the future, so that their use will in all likelihood become more widespread.
- The 3D images and colours of the virtual model confer a realistic appearance on the artefact which is very appropriate for the publication and exhibition of archaeological relics.
- The exact reconstruction of the geometry helps to preserve original artefacts and also to make the public aware of national archaeological treasures.
- It would now be possible, by means of an Internet page, to simultaneously register and publicise archaeological finds from any part of the world, and both the public and professionals could also consult experts in the subject of metrics (angles, distances, areas, volumes, etc.).
- Format compatibility and standardisation should be encouraged so that digital models can be visualised from any computer screen.
- After a 3D laser scanner data capture, geometric representations of artefacts exist on paper (orthoimages) and can be reproduced exactly.
- Surveys or microtopographical representations allow archaeological pieces to be perfectly defined and can be used for visual presentations on computer screens or on paper.
- Integrating laser scanner methodologies means that software quality inspection tools can check results by comparing captures.
- Laser scanning is a powerful technology that has many applications in different branches of science.
- Short, medium and long range terrestrial scanners can be integrated with older systems, such as GPS, Photogrammetry, Topography and Geographical Information Systems (GIS).

REFERENCES

Alós, D., & Minzateanu, R. (2007). *Proyecto e implantación de una red básica para dar cobertura al yacimiento del refugio paleolítico el abrigo de Buendía situado en Castejón (Cuenca). Obtención de cartografía y de un modelo tridimensional del refugio.* Unpublished bachelor dissertation, Universidad Politécnica de Madrid (UPM).

Buckner, R. B. (1983). Surveying measurements and their Analysis. Rancho Cordova, CA: Landmark Enterprises.

Carbonell, M. (1989). Architectural Photogrammetry. In H. M. Karara (Ed.), Non-Topographic Photogrammetry (pp. 321–347). Falls Church, VA: American Society of Photogrammetry and Remote Sensing.

Epigraphy. (n.d.). *Dictionary.com Unabridged* (v. 1.1). Retrieved March 11, 2009, from http://dictionary.reference.com/browse/epigraphy

Farjas, M., & García-Lázaro, F. J. (Eds.). (2008). Modelización Tridimensional y Sistemas Laser Escaner. Madrid, Spain: La Ergástula.

Fryer, J., Mitchell, H., & Chandler, J. (2006). The Power of Photogrammetry. *Asian Surveying and Mapping.* Retrieved March 5, 2008, from http://www.asmmag.com/news/the-power-of-photogrammetry

Jiménez-Riesco, D. (2008). *Representación Tridimensional de los Grabados de Guilanya mediante laser escaner 3D. Museo de Solsona (Lerida).* Unpublished bachelor dissertation, Universidad Politécnica de Madrid (UPM).

Jobst, M. (1999). The Photogrammetric Documentation of Epigraphs with Small Format Cameras. In *CIPA 1999 XVII International Symposium*, Recife/Olinda, Brazil. Retrieved February 10, 2009, from http://cipa.icomos.org/fileadmin/papers/olinda/99c509.pdf

Karara, H. M. (Ed.). (1989). Non -Topographic Photogrammetry. Falls Church, VA: American Society of Photogrammetry and Remote Sensing.

Llanos, A., & García-Lázaro, F. J. (1983). Photogrammetric Surveying of the Cave Pictographs of Altamira. Jenaer Rundschau, 4(83), 193–197.

Meyer, É., Grussenmeyer, P., Tidafi, T., Parisel, C., & Revez, J. (2004). Photogrammetry for the epigraphic survey in the great hypostyle hall of Karnak temple: a new approach, In *Proceedings of the XXth Congress of the International Society of Photogrammetry and Remote Sensing,* Istanbul, Turkey, 12–23 July 2004 (pp. 377–382).

Meyer, É., Grussenmeyer, P., Tidafi, T., Parisel, C., & Revez, J. (2006). A computerized solution for the epigraphic survey in Egyptian Temples. Journal of Archaeological Science, 33(11), 1605–1616. doi:10.1016/j.jas.2006.02.016doi:10.1016/j.jas.2006.02.016

Remondino, F. (2008). *Detailed image-based geometric reconstruction of heritage objects.* Retrieved September 2, 2008, from http://www.photogrammetry.ethz.ch/general/persons/fabio/remondino_sgpbf07.pdf

Thomas, N. W. (1958). Surveying. London: Edward Arnold.

Thompson, M., Eller, R., Radionski, W., & Speert, J. (1966). Manual of Photogrammetry (3rd ed., Vol. 1). Falls Church, VA: American Society of Photogrammetry and Remote Sensing.

Vázquez Pelaez, S. (2007). *Levantamiento mediante Láser Escáner 3D de la zona de Los Zarpazos en el yacimiento arqueológico de Atapuerca (Burgos).* Unpublished bachelor dissertation, Universidad Politécnica de Madrid (UPM).

Compilation of References

A Small World. (2009). Retrieved from http://www.asmallworld.net

Aamisepp, H., & Nilsson, D. (2003). *Haptic Hardware Support in 3D Game Engine.* Master of Science thesis, Department of Computer Science, Lund Institute of Technology.

Adachi, Y., Kumano, T., & Ogino, K. (1995). Intermediate Representation for Stiff Virtual Objects. In *Proc. IEEE Virtual Reality Annual Intl. Symp* (pp. 203-210).

Adams, L. (1992). Programación gráfica. Técnicas avanzadas de modelado, acabado y animación 3D. Madrid, España: ANAYA Multimedia SA.

Adamson, A., & Alexa, M. (2004). Approximating Bounded, Non-orientable Surfaces from Points. *Shape Modeling Internations.* Retrieved from http://www.computer.org/portal/web/csdl/doi/10.1109/SMI.2004.1314511

Addison, T. (2005, May). More science: more sense or nonsense? *Ad-Map, 461,* 24.

ADLAB. (2006, November 7). *P&G Creates Virtual Reality Research Room.* Retrieved from http://adverlab.blogspot.com/2006/11/pg-creates-virtual-reality-research.html

Adrians, P., & Zantige, D. (1996). *Data Mining.* London: Addison-Wesley.

Agarwal, P. K., Basch, J., Guibas, L. J., Hershberger, J., & Zhang, L. (2002). Deformable free space tiling for kinetic collision detection. *The International Journal of Robotics Research, 21*(3), 179–197.

Agarwal, P., de Berg, M., Gudemundsson, J., Hammar, M., & Haverkort, H. (2002). Box-Trees and R-Trees with Near-Optimal Query Time. *Discrete & Computational Geometry, 28,* 291–312.

Agarwal, P., Guibas, L., Nguyen, A., Russel, D., & Zhang, L. (2004). Collision Detection for Deforming Necklaces. In CGTA: Computational Geometry: Theory and applications, 28(2-3), 137-163.

Agarwal, P., Krishnan, S., Mustafa, N., & Venkatasubramanian, S. (2003). Streaming Geometric Optimization Using Graphics Hardware. In *11th European Symposium on Algorithms.*

Agarwal, R., & Brown, P. (2007). *How Innovators connect.* Mumbai, India: Himalaya Publishing House.

Aggarwal, R., Grantcharov, T., Moorthy, K., Hance, J., & Darzi, A. (2006). A competency-based virtual reality training curriculum for the acquisition of laparoscopic psychomotor skill. *American Journal of Surgery, 191*(1), 128–133. doi:10.1016/j.amjsurg.2005.10.014

Alauddin, M., Baradie, M. A., & Hashmi, M. S. J. (1995). Computer Aided analysis of a surface roughness model for end milling. Materials Processing Technology, 55, 123–127. doi:10.1016/0924-0136(95)01795-Xdoi:10.1016/0924-0136(95)01795-X

Aliaga, D. G. (1994). Virtual and real object collisions in a merged environment. In *Virtual Reality Software Technology* [Singapore: World Scientific Publishing Co.]. *Proceedings of VRST, 94,* 287–298.

Al-khalifah, A., McCrindle, R., & Alexandrov, V. (2006). Immersive Open Surgery Simulation. In *International*

Conference on Computational Science ICCS 2006, Part I, (LNCS 3991, pp. 868 – 871).

Allard, P., Stokes, I. A. F., & Blanchi, J. P. (1995). *Three-dimensional analysis of human movement*. Chicago: Human Kinetics.

Alós, D., & Minzateanu, R. (2007). *Proyecto e implantación de una red básica para dar cobertura al yacimiento del refugio paleolítico el abrigo de Buendía situado en Castejón (Cuenca). Obtención de cartografía y de un modelo tridimensional del refugio*. Unpublished bachelor dissertation, Universidad Politécnica de Madrid (UPM).

Antoniadis, A., Savakis, C., Bilalis, N., & Balouksis, A. (2003). Prediction of surface topomorphy and roughness in ball end milling. Advanced Manufacturing Technology, 21, 965–971. doi:10.1007/s00170-002-1418-8doi:10.1007/s00170-002-1418-8

Asghar, M. W., & Barner, K. E. (2001). Nonlinear Multiresolution Techniques with Applications to Scientific Visualization in a Haptic Environment. *IEEE Transactions on Visualization and Computer Graphics*, 7(1), 76–93. doi:10.1109/2945.910825

Azuma, R. (1993). Tracking requirements for augmented reality. [Special issue on computer augmented environments]. *Communications of the ACM*, 36(7), 50–52. doi:10.1145/159544.159581

Bach, J., Guibas, L., & Hershberger, J. (1997). Data Structures for Mobile Data. In *SODA: ACM-SIAM Symposium on Discrete Algorithms (A Conference on Theoretical and Experimental Analysis of Discrete Algorithms)*. Retrieved from http://citeseer.ist.psu.edu/145907.html

Baciu, G., & Wong, W. S.-K. (2002). Hardware-assisted self-collision for deformable surfaces. In *Proceedings of the ACM Symposium on Virual Reality Software and Technology (VRST)* (pp. 129-136). Retrieved from http://doi.acm.org/10.1145/585740.585762

Baciu, G., & Wong, W. S.-K. (2003). Image-Based Techniques in a Hybrid Collision Detector. *IEEE Transactions on Visualization and Computer Graphics*, 9, 254–271.

Baek, D. K., Ko, T. J., & Kim, H. S. (2001). Optimization of feedrate in a face milling operation using a surface roughness model. Machine Tools and Manufacture, 41, 451–462. doi:10.1016/S0890-6955(00)00039-0doi:10.1016/S0890-6955(00)00039-0

Baker, S. (n.d.). *Learning to Love your Z-buffer*. Retrieved from http://www.sjbaker.org/steve/omniv/love_your_z_buffer.html

Bala, K., Walter, B., & Greenberg, D. P. (2003, July). Combining edges and points for interactive high-quality rendering. In. *Proceedings of SIGGRAPH*, 22, 631–640.

Bandara, W., Gable, G., & Rosemann, M. (2005). Factors and Measures of Business Process Modeling: Model Building Through a Multiple Case Study. *European Journal of Information Systems*, 14(4), 347–360. doi:10.1057/palgrave.ejis.3000546

Barber, D., Mills, J., & Bryan, P. (2004). Towards A Standard Specification For Terrestrial Laser Scaning. In *Cultural Heritage. Presented at International Society for Photogrammetry and Remote Sensing*. Antalya: Istambul.

Barzel, R., Hughes, J., & Wood, D. N. (1996). Plausible Motion Simulation for Computer Graphics Animation. In R. Boulic & G. Hégron (Eds.), *Proceedings of the Eurographics Workshop Computer Animations and Simulation* (pp. 183-197).

Basdogan, C. (2001). Real-time Simulation of Dynamically Deformable Finite Element Models Using Modal Analysis and Spectral Lanczos Decomposition Methods. In Medicine Meets Virtual Reality (pp. 46-52).

Basdogan, C., Sedef, M., Harders, M., & Wesarg, S. (2007). Vr-based simulators for training in minimally invasive surgery. *IEEE Computer Graphics and Applications*, 27(2), 54–66. doi:10.1109/MCG.2007.51

Bayona, S. (2007). *Metodologías de aprendizaje y evaluación para simuladores quirúrgicos de realidad virtual. Aplicación en simuladores artroscópicos*. Unpublished doctoral dissertation, Universidad Rey Juan Carlos, Escuela de Informática. Móstoles, Madrid, Spain.

Bayona, S., Fernández, J. M., Bayona, P., & Pastor, L. (2009). A new assessment methodology for virtual reality surgical simulators. *Computer Animation and Virtual Worlds, 20*(1), 39–52. doi:10.1002/cav.268

Bayona, S., García, M., Mendoza, C., & Fernández-Arroyo, J. (2006). Shoulder arthroscopy training system with force feedback. In *Proceedings of medical information visualization - biomedical visualization* (pp. 71–76). Los Alamitos, CA: IEEE Computer Society.

Beier, K. P. (1990). *Virtual Reality: A Short Introduction.* Retrieved from http://www-vrl.umich.edu/intro/

Belliveau, J. W., Kennedy, D. N., McKinstry, R. C., Buchbinder, B. R., Weisskoff, R. M., & Cohen, M. S. (1991). Functional mapping of the human visual cortex by magnetic resonance imaging. *Science, 254*(5032), 716–719. doi:10.1126/science.1948051

Benardos, P. G., & Vosniakos, G. C. (2002). Prediction of surface roughness in CNC face milling using neural networks and Taguchi's design of experiments. Robotics and Computer-integrated Manufacturing, 18(5-6), 343–354. doi:10.1016/S0736-5845(02)00005-4doi:10.1016/S0736-5845(02)00005-4

Benford, S., Greenhalgh, C., Reynard, G., Brown, C., & Koleva, B. (1998). Understanding and constructing shared spaces with mixed-reality boundaries. *ACM Transactions on Computer-Human Interaction, 5*(3), 185–223. doi:10.1145/292834.292836

Bergen, G. (2004). *Collision Detection in Interactive 3D Environments.* San Francisco: Morgan Kauffman Publishers.

Bilalis, N., & Petousis, M., (2008). Development of a virtual environment for surface topomorphy and roughness determination in milling operations. *Transactions of the ASME, Journal of Computing and Information Science in Engineering, Special Issue Advances in Computer Aided Manufacturing, 8*(2).

Bilalis, N., Petousis, M., & Antoniadis, A. (2009). Model for surface roughness parameters determination in a virtual machine shop environment. International Journal of Advanced Manufacturing Technology, 40(11), 1137–1147. doi:10.1007/s00170-008-1441-5doi:10.1007/s00170-008-1441-5

Birgin, E. G., & Sobral, F. N. C. (2008). Minimizing the object dimensions in circle and sphere packing problems. *Computers & OR, 35*(7), 2357-2375. Retrieved from http://dx.doi.org/10.1016/j.cor.2006.11.002

Bloom, B. S., & Krathwohl, D. R. (1956). *Taxonomy of Educational Objectives, Handbook 1: Cognitive Domain.* Reading, MA: Addison Wesley Publishing Company.

Bobrik, R., Bobrik, R., Reichert, M., & Bauer, T. (2005). *Requirements for the visualization of system-spanning business processes.* Paper presented at the Sixteenth International Workshop on Database and Expert Systems Applications.

Bolt, R. (1980). Put-That-There: Voice and gesture at the graphics interface. *Computer Graphics, 14*(3), 262–270. doi:10.1145/965105.807503

Bonsu, S. K., & Darmody, A. (2008). Co-creating Second Life. *Journal of Macromarketing, 28*(4), 355–368. doi:10.1177/0276146708325396

Bontis, N. (2002). Managing organizational Knowledge by diagnosing Intellectual Capital. In Weicho, C., & Bontis, N. (Eds.), *The Strategic Management of Intellectual Capital and organizational knowledge.* Oxford, UK: Oxford University Press.

Borg, C. E., & Margin, M. (2003). Escáneres 3D de largo alcance: ¿Avanzando hacia una herramienta híbrida o hacia una metodología híbrida? *Datum XXI, 1*(5), 42–46.

Borrel, P., & Rappoport, A. (1994). Simple Constrained Deformation for Geometric Modeling and Interactive Design. *ACM Transactions on Graphics, 13*(2), 137–155. doi:10.1145/176579.176581

Botsch, M., & Kobbelt, L. (2005). Real-time Shape Editing Using Radial Basis Functions. [Proceedings of Eurographics]. *Computer Graphics Forum, 24*(3), 611–621. doi:10.1111/j.1467-8659.2005.00886.x

Bourguignon, D., & Cani, M. P. (2000). Controlling Anisotropy in Mass-Spring Systems. In *Proceedings of Eurographics Workshop on Computer Animation and Simulation (EGCAS)* (pp. 113-123). Berlin: Springer-Verlag.

Bowyer, A., Bayliss, G., Taylor, R., & Willis, P. (1996). A virtual factory. *International Journal of shape modeling, 2*(4), 215-226.

Box, I. (2003). Assessing the assessment: an empirical study of an information systems development subject. In *ACE '03: Proceedings of the fifth Australasian conference on Computing education* (pp. 149-158). Darlinghurst, Australia: Australian Computer Society, Inc.

Boyer, B. (2008). *MGS4 Dominates June NPD, Drives PS3 Sales*. Retrieved October 2008, from http://www.gamasutra.com/php-bin/news_index.php?story=19476

BR. (1979). *The Belmont Report - U.S. Health & Human Services*. Retrieved April 6, 2009, from www.hhs.gov/ohrp/humansubjects/guidance/belmont.htm

Bracci, S., Falletti, F., & Scopigno, M. M. R. (2004). Explorando David: diagnóstico y estado de la conservación. Roma, Italia: Giunti Press.

Bracken, C., & Lombard, M. (2004). Social presence and children: Praise, intrinsic motivation, and learning with computers. *The Journal of Communication, 54*, 22–37. doi:10.1111/j.1460-2466.2004.tb02611.x

Bradshaw, G., & O'Sullivan, C. (2004). Adaptive medial-axis approximation for sphere-tree construction. *ACM Transactions on Graphics, 23*(1), 1–26. Retrieved from http://visinfo.zib.de/ELlib/Show?EVL-2004-1.

Breen, D. E., Rose, E., & Whitaker, R. T. (1995). *Interactive Occlusion and Collision of Real and Virtual Objects in Augmented Reality*. (Technical report ECRC-95-02).

Breiger, R. L. (2004). The Analysis of Social Networks. In Hardy, M., & Bryman, A. (Eds.), *Handbook of Data Analysis* (pp. 505–526). London: Sage Publications.

Bro-Nielsen, M., & Cotin, S. (2002). Real-time Volumetric Deformable Models for Surgery Simulation using Finite Elements and Condensation. In. *Proceedings of Eurographics, 15*(3), 57–66.

Brown, R. A., Lim, A. E., Wong, Y. L., Heng, S.-M., & Wallace, D. M. (2006). Gameplay workflow: a distributed game control approach. In *2006 International Conference on Game Research and Development*, Fremantle, Australia.

Buckner, R. B. (1983). Surveying measurements and their Analysis. Rancho Cordova, CA: Landmark Enterprises.

Cambridge Research Systems. (2009). *MRI – Live*. Retrieved from http://www.crsltd.com/catalog/mri-live/index.html

Cameron, S. (1997). Enhancing GJK: Computing Minimum and Penetration Distances between Convex Polyhedra. In *Proceedings of International Conference on Robotics and Automation* (pp. 3112-3117).

Cao, C. G. L. (2007). Guiding navigation in colonoscopy. *Surgical Endoscopy, 21*(3), 480–484. doi:10.1007/s00464-006-9000-3

Cao, C. G. L., MacKenzie, C. L., Ibbotson, J. A., Turner, L. J., Blair, N. P., & Nagy, A. G. (1999). Hierarchical decomposition of laparoscopic procedures. *Studies in Health Technology and Informatics, 62*, 83–89.

Capilla, R., Martinez, M., Nava, F., & Muñoz, C. (2008). Architecting Virtual Reality Systems. In *Designing Software Intensive Systems: Methods and Principles*. Hershey, PA: IGI Global.

Carbonell, M. (1989). Architectural Photogrammetry. In H. M. Karara (Ed.), Non-Topographic Photogrammetry (pp. 321–347). Falls Church, VA: American Society of Photogrammetry and Remote Sensing.

Carr, N. (2008, April 3). Neuromarketing could make mind reading the ad-man's ultimate tool. *The Guardian*. Retrieved from http://www.guardian.co.uk/theguardian

Carter, J. E. L. (1982). *Physical structure of Olympic athletes. Part I: The Montreal Olympic Games anthropological project*. Basel, Switzerland: Krager.

Carter, M. (2009, June 24). *Neuromarketing is a go*. Retrieved April 4, 2009, from http://www.wired.co.uk/wired-magazine/archive/2009/06/features/neuromarketing-is-a-go.aspx

CaseWise. (2008). *CaseWise*. Retrieved October 2008, from http://www.casewise.com

CAVE Automatic Virtual Environment. (2009). In *Encyclopedia Britannica*. Retrieved March 19, 2009, from http://www.britannica.com/EBchecked/topic/1196650/Cave-Automatic-Virtual-Environment

CBS Interactive Inc. (2009). *Incredible Research Lets Scientists Get A Glimpse At Your Thoughts*. Retrieved April 20, 2009, from http://cnettv.cnet.com/60-minutes-mind-reading/9742-1_53-50004855.html

Chaudhuri, A. (2006). *Emotions and Reason in Consumer Behavior*. Burlington, MA: Butterworth-Heinemann.

Chen, H., & Sun, H. (2002). Real-time Haptic Sculpting in Virtual Volume Space. In *International Conference Proceedings of ACM VRST 2002* (pp. 81-88).

Chen, H., & Sun, H. (2006). Body-based Haptic Interaction Model for Touch-enabled Environments. *MIT Journal of PRESENCE: Teleoperators and Virtual Environments*, *15*(2), 186–203. doi:10.1162/pres.2006.15.2.186

Chen, H., Sun, H., & Jin, X. (2007). Interactive Soft-touch Dynamic Deformation. *Journal of Computer Animation and Virtual Worlds*, *18*, 153–163. doi:10.1002/cav.171

Chen, J.-S., & Li, T.-Y. (1998). Incremental 3 D Collision Detection with Hierarchical Data Structures. In *Proceedings of the ACM symposium on Virtual reality software and technology table of contents* (Vol. 22, pp. 139-144). Retrieved from http://portal.acm.org/citation.cfm?id=293701.293719

Chen, K. W., Heng, P. A., & Sun, H. (2000). Direct Haptic Rendering of Isosurface by Intermediate Representation. In *International Conference Proceedings of ACM VRST 2000* (pp. 188-194).

Choi, K. S., Sun, H., & Heng, P. A. (2003). Interactive Deformation of Soft Tissues with Haptic Feedback for Medical Learning. *IEEE Transactions on Information Technology in Biomedicine*, *7*(4), 358–363. doi:10.1109/TITB.2003.821311

Chorafas, D. N., & Steinhann, H. (1995). *An Introduction to Visualizaton, Virtual Reality*. Upper Saddle River, NJ: Prentice Hall.

Chryssolouris, G., Pappas, M., Karabatsou, V., Mavrikios, D., & Alexopoulos, K. (2007, April). A Shared VE for Collaborative Product Development in Manufacturing Enterprises. In Li, W. D., Ong, S. K., Nee, A. Y. C., & McMahon, C. (Eds.), *Collaborative Product Design and Manufacturing Methodologies and Applications*. London: Springer-Verlag. doi:10.1007/978-1-84628-802-9_3

Cisco Telepresence Solution. (n.d.). Retrieved from http://www.cisco.com/en/US/prod/collateral/ps7060/ps8329/ps8330/ps7073/prod_brochure0900aecd8054c9c0.pdf

Cisco Webex. (2009). Retrieved from http://www.webex.com

Clapes, M., Gonzalez-hidalgo, M., Mir-Torrres, A., & Palmer-Rodriguez, P. A. (2008). Interactive Constrained Deformations of NURBS Surfaces: N-SCODEF. In *Articulated Motion and Deformable Objects 2008* (LNCS5098, pp. 359-369). Berlin: Springer-Verlag.

Clare, S. (1997). *Functional MRI: Methods and Applications*. Nottingham, UK: University of Nottingham.

Cocciardi, T. (2008, September 22). *Immersive VR Cocoon Coming In 2009*. Retrieved from http://g4tv.com/thefeed/blog/post/689456/html

Cockburn, A., & McKenzie, B. (2004). Evaluating Spatial Memory in Two and Three Dimensions. *International Journal of Human-Computer Studies*, *61*(30), 359–373. doi:10.1016/j.ijhcs.2004.01.005

Colgate, J. E., Stanley, M. C., & Brown, J. M. (1995). Issues in the Haptic Display of Tool Use. In *Proc. Of IEEE/RSJ International Conference on Intelligent Robots and Systems* (pp. 140-145).

Constantinescu, C., Runde, C., Volkmann, J., Lalas, C., Sacco, M., Liu, D., Pavlopoulos, C., & Pappas, M. (2006). *DiFac D1 – Definition of a VR-based collaborative digital manufacturing environment*. DiFac Project (FP6-2005-IST-5-035079), v. 6.4.

Cottrell, M., Hammer, B., Hasenfuß, A., & Villmann, T. (2006). Batch and Median Neural Gas. *Neural Networks*, *19*(6-7), 762–771.

Crow, G., & Allan, G. (1994). *Community Life. An introduction to local social relations.* Hemel Hempstead, UK: Harvester Wheatsheaf.

Curtis, D., Mizell, D., Gruenbaum, P., & Janin, A. (1998). Several devils in the detail: Making an AR application work in the airplane factory. In *Proceedings of the International Workshop on Augmented Reality '98.*

Dachille, F., Qin, H., & Kaufman, A. (2001). A Novel Haptics-based Interface and Sculpting System for Physics-based Geometric Design. *Journal of Computer Aided Design, 33*(5), 403–420. doi:10.1016/S0010-4485(00)00131-7

Dachille, F., Qin, H., Kaufman, A., & El-sana, J. (1999). Haptic Sculpting of Dynamic Surfaces. In *ACM Symposium on Interactive 3D Graphics 1999* (pp. 103-110).

Damasio, A. (2005). *Descartes' Error: Emotion, Reason, and the Human Brain.* New York: Penguin.

De Floriani, L., Kobbelt, L., & Puppo, E. (2005). A Survey on Data Structures for Level-Of-Detail Models. In Dodgson, N. A., Floater, M. S., & Sabin, M. A. (Eds.), *Advances in Multiresolution for Geometric Modelling* (pp. 49–74). Berlin: Springer Verlag. doi:10.1007/3-540-26808-1_3

De Lucia, A., Francese, R., Passero, I., & Tortora, G. (2008). *SLMeeting: supporting collaborative work in Second Life* (pp. 301–304). AVI.

Debunne, G., Cani, M. P., Desbrun, M., & Barr, A. (2000). Adaptive Simulation of Soft Bodies in Real-Time. In *Proceedings of the Computer Animation* (pp. 15-20). Washington, DC: IEEE Computer Society.

Decker, G., Dijkman, R., Dumas, M., & García-Bañuelos, L. (2008). Transforming BPMN Diagrams into YAWL Nets. In *Business Process Management* (pp. 386–389). Berlin: Springer. doi:10.1007/978-3-540-85758-7_30

Demir, N., Bayram, B., Alkış, Z., Helvaci, C., Çetin, I., & Vögtle, T. (2004). *Laser scanning for terrestial photogrammetry, alternativa system or combined with traditional system?* Presented at International Society for Photogrammetry and Remote Sensing, Istambul.

Dickerson, R., Johnsen, K., Raij, A., Lok, B., Stevens, A., Bernard, T., & Lind, S. (2005). Assessment of Synthesized Versus Recorded Speech. In *Proceedings of Medicine Meets Virtual Reality 14: Accelerating Change in Healthcare: Next Medical Toolkit, 119* (pp. 114–119). Virtual Patients.

Donskoi, D., & Zatsiorski, V. M. (1988). *Biomecánica de los ejercicios físicos.* La Habana, Cuba: Pueblo y Educación.

Du, H., & Qin, H. (2000). Direct Manipulation and Interactive Sculpting of PDE Surfaces. *Journal of Comput Graph Forum (Eurographics 2000), 19*(3), 261–270.

Edery, D., & Mollick, E. (2008). *Changing the Game: How Video Games Are Transforming the Future of Business.* Upper Saddle River, NJ: FT Press.

Edwards, C. (2006). *Another World.* IEEE Engineering & Technology.

Edwards, J., & Luecke, G. (1996). Physically based Models for Use in a Force Feedback Virtual Environment. In *Japan/USA Symposium on Flexible Automation, ASME 1996* (pp. 221-228).

Ehmann, S. A., & Lin, M. C. (2001). Accurate and Fast Proximity Queries Between Polyhedra Using Convex Surface Decomposition. *Computer Graphics Forum, 20*, 500–510.

Engin, S., & Altintas, Y. (2001). Mechanics and dynamics of general milling cutters. Part I: helical end mills. Machine Tools and Manufacture, 41, 2195–2212. doi:10.1016/S0890-6955(01)00045-1doi:10.1016/S0890-6955(01)00045-1

Engin, S., & Altintas, Y. (2001). Mechanics and dynamics of general milling cutters. Part II: Inserted cutters. Machine Tools and Manufacture, 41, 2213–2231. doi:10.1016/S0890-6955(01)00046-3doi:10.1016/S0890-6955(01)00046-3

English, M. J., & Baker, W. H. Jr. (2006). *Winning the knowledge transfer race.* New Delhi: Tata McGraw Hill.

Epigraphy. (n.d.). *Dictionary.com Unabridged* (v. 1.1). Retrieved March 11, 2009, from http://dictionary.reference.com/browse/epigraphy

Ericson, C. (2004). *Real-Time Collision Detection*. San Francisco: Morgan Kaufman.

ESA. (2008). *Industry Facts.* Retrieved October 2008, from http://www.theesa.com/facts/index.asp

Esparza, F. (1993). *Manual de cineantropometría*. Pamplona, España: FEMEDE.

Estrin, J. (2009). *Closing the innovation gap*. New Delhi: Tata McGraw Hill.

Etzmuss, O., Keckeisen, M., & Strasser, W. (2003). A Fast Finite Element Solution for Cloth Modelling. In *Proceedings of 11th Pacific Conference on Computer Graphics and Applications (PG'03)* (pp. 244-251).

Evans, J. R., & Abarbanel, A. (1999). *Introduction to Quantitative EEG and Neurofeedback*. London: Academic Press.

Facebook. (2009). Retrieved from http://www.facebook.com

Farjas, M., & García-Lázaro, F. J. (Eds.). (2008). Modelización Tridimensional y Sistemas Laser Escaner. Madrid, Spain: La Ergástula.

Feiner, S., MacIntyre, B., & Seligmann, D. (1993). Knowledge-based augmented reality. [Special issue on computer augmented environments]. *Communications of the ACM, 37*(6), 53–62. doi:10.1145/159544.159587

Feldman, L. S., Sherman, V., & Fried, G. M. (2004). Using simulators to assess laparoscopic competence: ready for widespread use? *Surgery, 135*(1), 28–42. doi:10.1016/S0039-6060(03)00155-7

Fisher, S., & Lin, M. (2001). Fast Penetration Depth Estimation for Elastic Bodies Using Deformed Distance Fields. In *Proceedings of International Conference on Intelligent Robots and Systems (IROS)*. Retrieved from http://gamma.cs.unc.edu/DDF/

Fleishman, E. A. (1984). *Taxonomies of Human Performance: The Description of Human Tasks*. New York: Academic Press Inc.

Force Dimension. (2009). *Omega and Delta haptic devices.* Retrieved April 6, 2009, from http://www.forcedimension.com/products

Foskey, M., Otaduy, M. A., & Lin, M. C. (2005). ArtNova: Touch-enabled 3D Model Design. In *International Conference on Computer Graphics and Interactive Techniques* (pp.188-195).

Freeman, L. (2004). *The Development of Social Network Analysis: A Study in the Sociology of Science*. Vancouver, Canada: Empirical Press.

Fritz, J. P., & Barner, K. E. (1999). Design of a Haptic Data Visualization System for People with Visual Impairments. *IEEE Transactions on Neural Systems and Rehabilitation Engineering, 7*(3), 372–384.

Fryer, J., Mitchell, H., & Chandler, J. (2006). The Power of Photogrammetry. *Asian Surveying and Mapping*. Retrieved March 5, 2008, from http://www.asmmag.com/news/the-power-of-photogrammetry

Fuller, T., Argyle, P., & Moran, P. (2004). Meta-rules for Entrepreneurial Foresight. In Soukas, H. T., & Shepherd, J. (Eds.), *Managing the Future*. Oxford, UK: Blackwell Publishing.

Gagne, R. M., & Medsker, K. L. (1995). *The Conditions of Learning: Training Applications*. London: Wadsworth Publishing.

Gallagher, A. G., Richie, K., McClure, N., & McGuigan, J. (2001). Objective psychomotor skills assessment of experienced, junior, and novice laparoscopists with virtual reality. *World Journal of Surgery, 25*(11), 1478–1483. doi:10.1007/s00268-001-0133-1

Gallagher, A. G., Ritter, E. M., Champion, H., Higgins, G., Fried, M. P., & Moses, G. (2005). Virtual Reality Simulation for the Operating Room Proficiency-Based Training as a Paradigm Shift in Surgical Skills Training. *Annals of Surgery, 241*(2), 364–372. doi:10.1097/01.sla.0000151982.85062.80

García, M., Mendoza, C., Pastor, L., & Rodríguez, A. (2006). Optimized linear FEM for modeling deformable objects. *Computer Animation and Virtual Worlds, 17*(3-4), 393–402. doi:10.1002/cav.142

García, P. (n. d.). *Kinantropometria o cineantropometria: Definición y alcance social [Versión electrónica]*. Universidad de Caracas. Retrieved February 8, 2005, from http://www.rendeportin.com.ve/kinan.htm

García-Alonso, A., Serrano, N., & Flaquer, J. (1994). Solving the collision detection problem. *IEEE Computer Graphics and Applications*, *14*(3), 36–43. doi:10.1109/38.279041

Gärtner, B. (1999). Fast and Robust Smallest Enclosing Balls. In J. Nesetril (Eds.), *Lecture Notes in Computer Science* (Vol. 1643, pp. 325–338). Retrieved from http://link.springer.de/link/service/series/0558/bibs/1643/16430325.htm

Ghosh, S. K. (1979). *Analytical photogrammetry* [Forogrametría analítica]. New York: Pergamon Press.

Gibson, S. F. F., & Mirtich, B. (1997). *A survey of deformable modelling in computer graphics* (Technical Report No. 97-19). MERL- A Mitshbishi Electric Research Laboratory.

Gibson, W. K. (1984). *Neuromancer.* New York: Ace Books.

Gilbert, E. G., Johnson, D. W., & Keerthi, S. S. (1988). A Fast Procedure for Computing the Distance Between Complex Objects in Three-Dimensional Space. *IEEE Journal on Robotics and Automation*, *4*, 193–203.

GMV. (2009). *insightArthroVR.* Retrieved April 6, 2009, from http://www.insightmist.com/description/description.htm

Gomes de Sa, A., & Zachmann, G. (1998). Integrating Virtual Reality for Virtual Prototyping. In *Proceedings of the 1998 ASME Design Engineering Technical Conferences.* DETC98/CIE-5536.

Gomes de Sa, A., & Zachmann, G. (1999). Virtual Reality as a Tool for Verification of Assembly and Maintenance Processes. *Computers & Graphics*, *23*, 389–403.

Gonzalez-Aguilera, D. (2001). *Consideraciones sobre el análisis de la fiabilidad en el patrimonio edificado. Fiabilidad y fotogrametría arquitectónica [Versión electrónica]. REDCientífica.* Retrieved November 8, 2004, from http://www.redcientifica.com/imprimir/doc200111070001.html

Gooch, A., Gooch, B., Shirley, P. S., & Cohen, E. (1998). A Non-Photorealistic Lighting Model for Automatic Technical Illustration. In SIGGRAPH 98 (pp. 447-452).

Gottschalk, S., Lin, M., & Manocha, D. (1996). OBB-Tree: A Hierarchical Structure for Rapid Interference Detection. In H. Rushmeier (Eds.), *SIGGRAPH 96 Conference Proceedings* (pp. 171–180), New Orleans, Louisiana.

Govindaraju, N., Redon, S., Lin, M. C., & Manocha, D. (2003 July). Cullide - Interactive Collision Detection Between Complex Models in Large Environments Using Graphics Hardware. In *Proceedings of Graphics Hardware*, San Diego, California (pp. 41-50). Retrieved from http://graphics.stanford.edu/papers/photongfx/

Gress, A., & Zachmann, G. (2003). Object-Space Interference Detection on Programmable Graphics Hardware. In M. L. Lucian & M. Neamtu (Eds.), *SIAM Conf. on Geometric Design and Computing* (pp. 311–328).

Gress, A., & Zachmann, G. (2006). *GPU-ABiSort: Optimal Parallel Sorting on Stream Architectures* (Technical Report IfI-06-11). Clausthal-Zellerfeld, Germany: TU Clausthal. Retrieved from http://cg.in.tu-clausthal.de/publications.shtml

Halstead, M., Kass, M., & DeRose, T. (1993). Efficient, Fair Interpolation Using Catmull-Clark Surfaces. In *Computer Graphics* (*Proceedings of SIGGRAPH '93*) (pp. 35-44).

Hampton, K., & Wellman, W. (2001). Long distance community in network society: contact and support beyond Netville. *The American Behavioral Scientist*, *45*(3), 476–495. doi:10.1177/00027640121957303

Hanifan, L. J. (1920). *The Community Center.* Boston: Silver Burdett.

Hansen, C. D., & Johnson, C. R. (Eds.). (2005). *The Visualization Handbook.* Amsterdam: Elsevier-Butterworth Heinemann.

Haptica. (2009). *ProMIS.* Retrieved April 6, 2009, from http://www.haptica.com

Harris, D., Duffy, V., Smith, M., & Stephanidis, C. (Eds.). (2003). *Human-Centered Computing: Cognitive,*

225

Social, and Ergonomic Aspects (*Vol. 3*). Boca Raton, FL: CRC Press.

Hastings, E. J., Mesit, J., & Guha, R. K. (2005) Optimization of Large-Scale, Real-Time Simulations by Spatial Hashing. *Proc. of SCSC, 37*(4), 9-17.

Hecker, C. (1996). *Physics, the Next Frontier* (pp. 12–20). Game Developers Magazine.

Heim, M. (1993). *The Metaphysics of Virtual Reality*. New York: Oxford University Press.

Heim, M. (1998). *Virtual Realism*. New York: Oxford University Press.

Higashi, M., Aoki, N., & Kaneko, T. (2002). Application of Haptic Navigation to Modify Free-form Surfaces Through Specified Points and Curves. *Journal of Computing and Information Science in Engineering, 2*, 265–276. doi:10.1115/1.1559581

Higgins, G. A., Merrill, G. L., Hettinger, L. J., Kaufmann, C. R., Champion, H. R., & Satava, R. M. (1997). New simulation technologies for surgical training and certification: Current status and future projections. *Presence (Cambridge, Mass.), 6*(2), 160–172.

Hill, J. B., Cantara, M., Kerremans, M., & Plummer, D. C. (2009). *ID Number: G00164485 Magic Quadrant for Business Process Management Suites*.

Hoffman, D. L. (1995). *Marketing in Hypermedia Computer-Mediated Environments: Conceptual Foundations*. Working Paper, Owen Graduate School of Management at Vanderbilt University. Retrieved from http://www2000.ogsm.vanderbilt.edu

Hoffman, H. G., Patterson, D. R., Magula, J., Carrougher, G. J., Zeltzer, K., Dagadakis, S., & Sharar, S. R. (2004). Water-friendly virtual reality pain control during wound care. *Journal of Clinical Psychology, 60*(2), 189–195. doi:10.1002/jclp.10244

Hogarth, B. (1996). *Dynamic Anatomic*. Köln, Germany: Benedikt Taschen Verlag GmbH.

Huang, Y., & Oliver, J. H. (1994). NC milling error assessment and tool path correction. In *International Conference on Computer Graphics and Interactive Techniques, Proceedings of the 21st annual conference on Computer graphics and interactive techniques* (pp. 287 – 294).

Hubal, R. C., Kizakevich, P. N., Guinn, C. I., Merino, K. D., & West, S. L. (2000). The Virtual Standardized Patient. Simulated Patient-Practitioner Dialog for Patient Interview Training. *Studies in Health Technology and Informatics, 70*, 133–138.

Hubbard, P. M. (1995). Collision detection for interactive graphics applications. In IEEE Transactions on Visualization and Computer Graphics (Vol. 1, pp. 218–230).

Hubbard, P. M. (1996). Approximating Polyhedra with Spheres for Time-Critical Collision Detection. *ACM Transactions on Graphics, 15*, 179–210.

Huh, S., Metaxas, D. N., & Badler, N. I. (2001 November). Collision Resolutions in Cloth Simulation. In *IEEE Computer Animation Conference,* Seoul, Korea.

Humphries, M., Hawkins, M. W., & Dy, M. C. (1999). *Data Warehousing: Architecture and Implementation*. Englewood Cliffs, NJ: Prentice Hall. Joseph, J., & Fellenstein, C. (2004). *Grid Computing*. New Delhi: Pearson Education.

Ibáñez, S., & Jiménez, J. (2006). *Aproximación a la antropología en el deporte mediante técnicas cartográficas basadas en sistemas láser-escáner: Levantamiento 3D de un brazo humano*. Unpublished bachelor dissertation, Universidad Politécnica de Madrid (UPM).

IBM. (2008). *Innov8 Web Site*. Retrieved March 2008, from http://www-304.ibm.com/jct03001c/software/solutions/soa/innov8.html

IDS-Scheer. (2008). *ARIS*. Retrieved October 2008, from http://www.ids-scheer.com

Ikemoto, L., Gelfand, N., & Levoy, M. (2003). *A hierarchical method for aligning warped meshes [Un método jerárquico para alinear acoplamientos combados]*. Paper presented at the Fourth International Conference on 3D Imaging and Modeling (3DIM), October 6-10, 2003, Banff, Alberta, Canada.

Immersion. (2009). *AccuTouch Endoscopy Simulator*. Retrieved April 6, 2009, from http://www.immersion. com/medical/products/endoscopy/

Interactive-Software. (2008). *Interactive Software Systems*. Retrieved October 2008, from http://www. interactive-software.de/

Isdale, J. (1993). *What Is Virtual Reality? A Homebrew Introduction and Information Resource List Version 2.1*. Retrieved from ftp://ftp.hitl.washington.edu/pub/scivw/ papers/whatisvr.txt

James, D., & Pai, D. (1999). ARTDEFO: Accurate Real Time Deformable Objects. In *SIGGRAPH Conference Proceedings* (pp.65-72).

Jiménez, P., Thomas, F., & Torras, C. (2001). 3D collision detection: a survey. *Computer Graphics, 25*(2), 269–285. doi:10.1016/S0097-8493(00)00130-8

Jiménez-Riesco, D. (2008). *Representación Tridimensional de los Grabados de Guilanya mediante laser escaner 3D. Museo de Solsona (Lerida)*. Unpublished bachelor dissertation, Universidad Politécnica de Madrid (UPM).

Jobst, M. (1999). The Photogrammetric Documentation of Epigraphs with Small Format Cameras. In *CIPA 1999 XVII International Symposium*, Recife/Olinda, Brazil. Retrieved February 10, 2009, from http://cipa.icomos.org/ fileadmin/papers/olinda/99c509.pdf

Johnson, D. E., & Cohen, E. (1998). A Framework for Efficient Minimum Distance Computations. In *Proceedings of the IEEE International Conference on Robotics and Automation (ICRA-98)* (pp. 3678–3684).

Johnson, D. E., & Willemsen, P. (2003). Six Degree-of-Freedom Haptic Rendering of Complex Polygonal Model. In *HAPTICS* (pp. 229–235). Retrieved from http://csdl. computer.org/comp/proceedings/haptics/2003/1890/00 /18900229abs.htm

Jörg Becker. Martin Kugeler, & Rosemann, M. (Eds.). (2003). Process Management: A Guide for the Design of Business Processes. Berlin: Springer-Verlag.

Kapasi, U. J., Rixner, S., Dally, W. J., Khailany, B., Ahn, J. H., Mattson, P., & Owens, J. D. (2003). Programmable Stream Processors. In IEEE Computer (pp. 54–61).

Karara, H. M. (Ed.). (1989). Non -Topographic Photogrammetry. Falls Church, VA: American Society of Photogrammetry and Remote Sensing.

Kaufmann, C., Zakaluzny, S., & Liu, A. (2000). First Steps in Eliminating the Need for Animals and Cadavers in Advanced Trauma Life Support. In *MICCAI '00: Proceedings of the Third International Conference on Medical Image Computing and Computer-Assisted Intervention* (pp. 618-623). London: Springer-Verlag.

Kenning, P., Plassmann, H., & Ahlert, D. (2007). Applications of functional magnetic resonance imaging for market research. *Qualitative Market Research: An International Journal, 10*(2), 135–152. doi:10.1108/13522750710740817

Kim, A. J. (2000). *Community Building on the Web: Secret Strategies for Successful Online Communities*. Berkeley, CA: Peachpit Press.

Kim, A. J. (2004). Emergent Purpose. *Musings of a Social Architect*. Retrieved from http://socialarchitect.typepad. com/musings/2004/01/emergent_purpos.html

Kim, G. M., Cho, P. J., & Chu, C. N. (2000). Cutting force prediction of sculptured surface ball-end milling using Z-map. Machine Tools and Manufacture, 40(2), 277–291. doi:10.1016/S0890-6955(99)00040-1doi:10.1016/S0890-6955(99)00040-1

Kitamura, Y., Smith, A., Takemura, H., & Kishino, F. (1998). A Real-Time Algorithm for Accurate Collision Detection for Deformable Polyhedral Objects. *Presence (Cambridge, Mass.), 7*(1).

Klein, J., & Zachmann, G. (2003). ADB-Trees: Controlling the Error of Time-Critical Collision Detection. In 8th International Fall Workshop Vision, Modeling, and Visualization (VMV.). Munich, Germany: University München.

Klein, J., & Zachmann, G. (2003). Time-Critical Collision Detection Using an Average-Case Approach. In *Proceedings of ACM Symposium on Virtual Reality Software and Technology (VRST)* (pp. 22–31). Retrieved from http://www.gabrielzachmann.org/

Klein, J., & Zachmann, G. (2004). Nice and Fast Implicit Surfaces over Noisy Point Clouds. In *SIGGRAPH Pro-*

ceedings. Retrieved from http://www.gabrielzachmann. org/

Klein, J., & Zachmann, G. (2004). Point Cloud Collision Detection, Computer Graphics forum. In []. Retrieved from http://www.gabrielzachmann.org/]. *Proceedings of EUROGRAPHICS, 23*, 567–576.

Klein, J., & Zachmann, G. (2004). Proximity Graphs for Defining Surfaces over Point Clouds. In M. Alexa, M. Gross, H.-P. Pfister, & S. Rusinkiewicz (Eds.), *Symposium on Point-Based Graphics* (pp. 131–138). Zürich, Switzerland: ETHZ. Retrieved from http://www. gabrielzachmann.org/

Klosowski, J. T., Held, M., Mitchell, J. S. B., Sowrizal, H., & Zikan, K. (1998). Efficient Collision Detection Using Bounding Volume Hierarchies of k-DOPs. *IEEE Transactions on Visualization and Computer Graphics, 4*, 21–36.

Kneebone, R. (2003). Simulation in surgical training: educational issues and practical implications. *Medical Education, 37*(3), 267–277. doi:10.1046/j.1365-2923.2003.01440.x

Knott, D., & Pai, D. K. (2003). CInDeR: Collision and Interference Detection in Real-Time Using Graphics Hardware. In *Proceedings of Graphics Interface*, Halifax, Nova Scotia, Canada, June 11-13. Retrieved from http://www.cs.rutgers.edu/~dpai/papers/KnottPai03.pdf

Knutson, B., Rick, S., Wimmer, E., Prelec, D., & Loewenstein, G. (2007). Neural Predictors of Purchases. *Neuron, 53*(1), 147–156. doi:10.1016/j.neuron.2006.11.010

Ko, J. H., Yun, W. S., & Cho, D. W. (2003). Off-line feed rate scheduling using virtual CNC based on an evaluation of cutting performance. CAD, 35, 383–393.

Krathwohl, D. R., Bloom, B. S., & Masia, B. B. (1964). *Taxonomy of Educational Objectives, The Classification of Educational Goals: Handbook II, Affective Domain.* New York: David McKay.

Krueger, W. M. (1991). *Artificial Reality II.* Reading, MA: Addison-Wesley Publishing Company, Inc.

La Rosa, M., Dumas, M., ter Hofstede, A. H. M., Mendling, J., & Gottschalk, F. (2008). Beyond Control-Flow: Extending Business Process Configuration to Roles and Objects. In *27th Proceeding of International Conference on Conceptual Modeling*, Barcelona, Spain.

Lai, M. J. (1992). Fortran Subroutines for B-nets of Box Splines on Three- and Four-directional Meshes. *Numerical Algorithms, 2*, 33–38. doi:10.1007/BF02142204

Lander, J. (1999). *Graphic Content - collision response: bouncy, trouncy, fun* (pp. 15–19). Game Developers Magazine.

Lander, J. (2000). Graphic Content - in This Corner: the Crusher. *Game Developer Magazine*, 17-22.

Lanier, J. A., & Biocca, F. (1992). An Insider's View of the Future of Virtual Reality. *The Journal of Communication, 42*(4), 150–172. doi:10.1111/j.1460-2466.1992.tb00816.x

Lanquetin, S., Raffin, R., & Neveu, M. (2006). Generalized SCODEF Deformations on Subdivision Surfaces. In Articulated Motion and Deformable Objects (LNCS 4069, pp.132-142). Berlin: Springer-Verlag.

LapMentor. (2009). Retrieved April 6, 2009, from http://www.med.umich.edu/UMCSC/equipment/lapmentor. html

LapSim. (2009). Retrieved April 6, 2009, from http://www.med.umich.edu/UMCSC/equipment/lapsim.html

Larsen, E., Gottschalk, S., Lin, M., & Monocha, D. (1999). *Fast proximity queries with swept sphere volumes.* Technical Report TR99-018.

Larsson, T., & Akenine-Möller, T. (2001). *Collision Detection for Continuously Deforming Bodies* (pp. 325–333). Eurographics.

Lau, R., Chan, O., Luk, M., & Li, F. (2002). A Collision Detection Method for Deformable Objects. In *Proceedings of the ACM Symposium on Virtual Reality Software and Technology (VRST)* (pp. 113–120). Retrieved from http://doi.acm.org/10.1145/585740.585760

Lave, J., & Wenger, E. (1991). *Situated Learning. Legitimate peripheral participation.* Cambridge, UK: University of Cambridge.

Lee, E. (2007). Listening in on Sun and Second Life at iMeme. *The Tech Chronicles*. Retrieved November 5, 2009, from http://www.sfgate.com/cgi-bin/blogs/tech-chron/detail?blogid=19&entry_id=18513

Lee, F. S., Vogel, D., & Limayen, M. (2003). Virtual Community Informatics: a review and research agenda. *Journal of Information Technology Theory and Applications, 5*(1), 47–61.

Lee, N., Senior, C., Butler, M., & Fuchs, R. (2009). The Feasibility of Neuroimaging Methods in Marketing Research. *Nature Precedings*. Retrieved from http://hdl.handle.net/10101/npre.2009.2836.1

Leica Geosystems. (2005). *Documentación Técnica y Manuales de Referencia sobre sistemas láser* [Electronic Version]. Retrieved from http://www.leica-geosystems.com/es/index.htm

Lerma, J. L. (1999). Reconocimiento de materiales y deterioros en fachadas arquitectónicas. *Datum XXI, 1*(0), 25–27.

Leskovsky, P., Harders, M., & Szekely, G. (2006). A web-based repository of surgical simulator projects. *Studies in Health Technology and Informatics, 119*, 311–315.

Lesser, E. L., & Storck, J. (2001). Communities of practice and organizational performance. *IBM Systems Journal, 40*(4). doi:10.1147/sj.404.0831

Lessig, L. (2000). *Code and Other Laws of Cyberspace*. New York: Basic Books.

Leva, P. (1994). *Adjustments to Zatsiorsky-Seluyanov's segment inertia parameter. Kinesiology Department.* Bloomington, IN: Indiana University.

Levoy, M., Rusinkiewicz, S., Ginzton, M., & Ginsberg, J. (2000). *The digital Michelangelo project: 3d scanning of large statues.* Department of Computer Science and Engineering, University of Washington. Retrieved October 6, 2004, from http://graphics.stanford.edu/papers/dmich-sig00/dmich-sig00.html

Lewis, D., & Brigder, D. (2005, July). Market Researchers Make Increasing Use of Brain Imaging. *Advances in Clinical Neuroscience and Rehabilitation, 5*(3), 35.

Lewis, M., & Slack, N. (Eds.). (2003). *Operations Management: Critical Perspectives on Business and Management*. London: Routledge.

Lin, H.-F. (2008). Determinants of successful virtual communities: Contributions from system characteristics and social factors. *Information & Management, 45*(8), 522–527. doi:10.1016/j.im.2008.08.002

Lin, M. C., & Gottschalk, S. (1998). Collision detection between geometric models: A survey. In. *Proceedings of IMA Conference on Mathematics of Surfaces, 1*, 602–608.

Lin, M. C., & Manocha, D. (2004). Collision and proximity queries. In Goodman, J. E., & O'Rourke, J. (Eds.), *Handbook of Discrete and Computational Geometry* (2nd ed.). New York: Chapman and Hall/CRC Press.

Lin, M., Manocha, D., Cohen, J., & Gottschalk, S. (1996). Collision Detection: Algorithms and Applications. In Laumond, J.-P., & Overmars, M. (Eds.), *Proceedings of Algorithms for Robotics Motion and Manipulation* (pp. 129–142).

Linden Lab (Producer). (2003). *Second Life*. Podcast retrieved from http://secondlife.com/

Linden. (2008). *Second Life*. Retrieved October 2008, from http://www.secondlife.com

Lindstrom, M., & Underhill, P. (2008). *Buyology: Truth and Lies About Why We Buy*. New York: Broadway Business.

LinkedIn. (2009). Retrieved from http://www.linkedin.com

Liu, A., Tendick, F., Cleary, K., & Kaufmann, C. (2003). A survey of surgical simulation: applications, technology, and education. *Presence: Teleoper. Virtual Environ., 12*(6), 599–614. doi:10.1162/105474603322955905

Liu, X., & Cheng, K. (2005). Modeling the machining dynamics in peripheral milling. *Machine Tools and Manufacture, 45*, 1301–1320. doi:10.1016/j.ijmachtools.2005.01.019doi:10.1016/j.ijmachtools.2005.01.019

Liverani, A., Amati, G., & Caligiana, G. (2004). A CAD-Augmented Reality Integrated Environment for Assembly Sequence Check and Interactive Validation. *Concurrent Engineering, 12*(1), 67–77. doi:10.1177/1063293X04042469

Llanos, A., & García-Lázaro, F. J. (1983). Photogrammetric Surveying of the Cave Pictographs of Altamira. Jenaer Rundschau, 4(83), 193–197.

Lombardo, J.-C., Cani, M.-P., & Neyret, F. (1999). Real-time collision detection for virtual surgery. In *Proceedings of Computer Animation*, Geneva, Switzerland, May 26-28. Retrieved from http://www.evasion.imag.fr/Publications/1999/LCN99

Loop, C. (1987). *Smooth Subdivision Surfaces based on Triangles*. MS thesis, Department of Mathematics, University of Utah.

Lou, M. S., Chen, J. C., & Li, C. M. (1999). Surface Roughness prediction technique for CNC End Milling. Industrial Technology, 15(1), 1–6.

Lurie, N. H., & Mason, C. H. (2007). Visual representation: Implications for decision making [Review]. *Journal of Marketing, 71*(1), 160–177. doi:10.1509/jmkg.71.1.160

Mabrey, J. D., Gillogly, S. D., & Kasser, J. R. (2002). Virtual reality simulation of arthroscopy of the knee. *Arthroscopy, 18*(6). doi:10.1053/jars.2002.33790

Magnenat-Thalmann, N., Montagnol, M., Bonanni, U., & Gupta, R. (2007). Visuo-Haptic Interface for Hair. In *2007 International Conference on Cyberworlds* (pp. 3-12).

Maher, M. L., Merrick, K., & Saunders, R. (2007, November 7). *From Passive to Proactive Design Elements: Incorporating Curious Agents into Intelligent Rooms*. Paper presented at the Computer-Aided Architectural Design Futures (CAAD Futures).

Mandal, C., Qin, H., & Vemuri, B. C. (2000). A Novel FEM-based Dynamic Framework for Subdivision Surfaces. *Computer Aided Design, 32*, 479–497. doi:10.1016/S0010-4485(00)00037-3

Manski, C. F. (2000). Economic Analysis of Social Interactions. *The Journal of Economic Perspectives, 14*, 115–136. doi:10.1257/jep.14.3.115

Massie, T. H., & Salisbury, J. K. (1994). The PHANToM Haptic Interface: A Device for Probing Virtual Object. In *Proceedings of the ASME Winter Annual Meeting, Symposium on Haptic Interfaces for Virtual Environment and Teleoperator Systems*.

Mazuryk, T., & Gervautz, M. (1996). *Virtual Reality History, Applications, Technology, and Future*. Retrieved from http://www.cg.tuwien.ac.at/research/publications/1996/mazuryk-1996-VRH/TR-186-2-96-06Paper.pdf

McConnon, A. (2007, January 22). If I Only Had A Brain Scan. *BusinessWeek*. Retrieved from http://www.businessweek.com/magazine/content/07_04/c4018008.htm

McDonnell, K., Qin, H., & Wlodarczyk, R. (2001). Virtual Clay: a Real-time Sculpting System with Haptic Toolkits. In *Proc. of 2001 ACM Symp. on Interactive 3D Graphics* (pp. 179-190).

Mcneely, W. A., Puterbaugh, K. D., & Troy, J. J. (1999). Six Degrees-of-Freedom Haptic Rendering Using Voxel Sampling. In. *Proceedings of SIGGRAPH, 99*, 401–408.

Meier, U., López, O., Monserrat, C., Juan, M. C., & Alcañiz, M. (2005). Real-time deformable models for surgery simulation: a survey. *Computer Methods and Programs in Biomedicine, 77*, 183–197. doi:10.1016/j.cmpb.2004.11.002

Mellor, J. P. (1995). *Enhanced reality visualization in a surgical environment. (Tech. Rep)*. MIT Artificial Intelligence Laboratory.

Mendoza, C., & O'Sullivan, C. (2006). Interruptible collision detection for deformable objects. *Computers & Graphics, 30*, 432–438. Retrieved from http://dx.doi.org/10.1016/j.cag.2006.02.018.

Mentice. (2009). *Procedicus MIST and Procedicus VIST*. Retrieved April 6, 2009, from http://www.mentice.com/

Mentor, G. I. (2009). *Simbionix*. Retrieved April 6, 2009, from http://www.simbionix.com/

Metzger, P. J. (1993). *Adding reality to the virtual*. Paper presented at Virtual Reality Annual Symposium, WA, USA.

Meyer, É., Grussenmeyer, P., Tidafi, T., Parisel, C., & Revez, J. (2004). Photogrammetry for the epigraphic survey in the great hypostyle hall of Karnak temple: a new approach, In *Proceedings of the XXth Congress of the International Society of Photogrammetry and Remote Sensing,* Istanbul, Turkey, 12–23 July 2004 (pp. 377–382).

Meyer, É., Grussenmeyer, P., Tidafi, T., Parisel, C., & Revez, J. (2006). A computerized solution for the epigraphic survey in Egyptian Temples. Journal of Archaeological Science, 33(11), 1605–1616. doi:10.1016/j.jas.2006.02.016doi:10.1016/j.jas.2006.02.016

Mezger, J., Kimmerle, S., & Etzmuss, O. (2003). Hierarchical Techniques in Collision Detection for Cloth Animation. *Journal of WSCG.* Retrieved from http://wscg.zcu.cz/wscg2003/Papers_2003/G97.pdf

Michigan Tech Web Site. (n.d.). Retrieved from http://www.mfg.mtu.edu/cyberman/quality/sfinish/terminology.html

Milgram, P., Takemura, H., Utsumi, A., & Kishino, F. (1994). *Augmented Reality: A class of displays on the reality-virtuality continuum.*

Minski, M. (1980). Telepresence. *OMNI magazine,* 45-51.

MMVR. *Medicine Meets Virtual Reality.* (2009) Retrieved April 6, 2009, from http://www.nextmed.com/

Moeslund, T. B., Madsen, C. B., & Granum, E. (2003). *Modelling the 3d pose of human arm and shoulder complex utilisima only two parameters.* Paper presented at the meeting International Conference of Model-based Imaging, Rendering, Image Analysis and Graphical Special Effects, Rocquencourt, Francia (pp. 11-19).

Moline, J. (1997). Virtual reality for health care: a survey. *Studies in Health Technology and Informatics, 44,* 3–34.

Molineros, J. M. (2002). *Computer Vision and Augmented Reality for Guiding Assembly.* PA: Department of Computer Science and Engineering in Pennsylvania State University, State College.

Moorthy, K., Munz, Y., Sarker, S. K., & Darzi, A. (2003). Objective assessment of technical skills in surgery. *British Medical Journal, 327*(7422), 1032–1037. doi:10.1136/bmj.327.7422.1032

Morris, D. (2006). *Algorithms and Data Structures for Haptic Rendering: Curve Constraints, Distance Maps, and Data Logging.* Technical Report 2006-06.

Muehlen, M. Z., & Recker, J. (2008). How Much Language is Enough? Theoretical and Practical Use of the Business Process Modeling Notation. In *20th International Conference on Advanced Information Systems Engineering (CAiSE 2008),* Montpellier, France.

Müller, M., & Gross, M. (2004) Interactive Virtual Materials. In Proceedings of Graphics Interface (GI) (pp. 239-246).

Müller, M., Dorsey, J., McMillan, L., Jagnow, R., & Cutler, B. (2002). Stable Real-Time Deformations. In *Proceedings of ACM SIGGRAPH Symposium on Computer Animation (SCA)* (pp. 49-54).

Muller, W., & Bockholt, U. (1998). The virtual reality arthroscopy training simulator. In. *Proceedings of Medicine Meets Virtual Reality, 6,* 13–19.

Myszkowski, K., Okunev, O. G., & Kunii, T. L. (1995). Fast collision detection between complexsolids using rasterizing graphics hardware. *The Visual Computer, 11,* 497–512.

Nair, M., Assman, T. M., & Shariffadeen. (2009). Managing Innovation in the Network Economy: Lessons for Countries in the Asia Pacific Region. In S. Akhtar & P. Arinto (Eds.), *Digital Review of Asia Pacific 2009–2010 Managing Innovation in the Network Economy.* New Delhi: Sage Publications.

Narayanan, V. K., & Fashey, L. (2004). Invention and Navigation as contrasting metaphors of the pathways to the future. In Tsoukas, H., & Shepherd, J. (Eds.), *Managing the Future.* Oxford, UK: Blackwell Publishing.

Nealen, A., Müller, M., Keiser, R., Boxerman, E., & Carlson, M. (2006). Physically based deformable models in computer graphics. *Computer Graphics Forum, 25*(4), 809–836. doi:10.1111/j.1467-8659.2006.01000.x

Negroponte, N. (1995). *Being Digital*. London: Hodder and Stoughton.

Neumann, U., & Cho, Y. (1996). A self-tracking augmented reality system. In Proceedings of Virtual Reality Software and Technology (VRAIS96) (pp. 109–115). Hong Kong.

Nishita, T., & Nakamae, E. (1994). A Method for Displaying Metaballs by Using Bezier Clipping. *Computer Graphics Forum*, *13*(3), 271–280. doi:10.1111/1467-8659.1330271

O'Brien, J. F., & Hodgins, J. K. (1999). Graphical modeling and animation of brittle fracture. In *SIGGRAPH '99: Proceedings of the 26th annual conference on Computer graphics and interactive techniques*, New York, NY, USA (pp. 137–146).

Ojeda, J. C., Martinez, R., Gonzalez, F., & Sanchez, J. A. (2002). Generación de modelos tridimensionales de curvas y túneles. *Mapping-Interactivo, Artículo 180*. Retrieved October 4, 2004, from http://www.mappinginteractivo.com/plantilla-egeo.asp?id_articulo=180

OMG. (2006). *Business Process Modeling Notation Specification*. Retrieved March 29, 2008, from www.bpmn.org

Ong, C., & Gilbert, E. (1996). Growth Distances: New Measures For Object Separation And Penetration. *IEEE Transactions on Robotics and Automation*, *12*(6), 888–903.

Ong, S. K., Jiang, L., & Nee, A. Y. C. (2002). An Internet Based Virtual CNC Milling System. Advanced Manufacturing Technology, 20, 20–30. doi:10.1007/s001700200119doi:10.1007/s001700200119

OnMap. (2008). *OnMap*. Retrieved April, 2008, from http://www.onmap.fr/

Ooi, B., McDonell, K., & Sacks-Davis, R. (1987). Spatial kd-tree: An indexing mechanism for spatial databases. In IEEE COMPSAC (pp. 433–438).

Ortiz, S. Jr. (2007 January). Brain-Computer Interfaces: Where Human and Machine Meet. *Technology News*, 17-21.

Ouyang, C., La Rosa, M., ter Hofstede, A. H. M., Dumas, M., & Shortland, K. (2008). Toward Web-Scale Workflows for Film Production. *Internet Computing, IEEE, 2008*(October), 53–61. doi:10.1109/MIC.2008.115

Paisley, A. M., Baldwin, P. J., & Paterson-Brown, S. (2001). Validity of surgical simulation for the assessment of operative skill. *Journal of Surgery (British)*, *88*(11), 1525–1532. doi:10.1046/j.0007-1323.2001.01880.x

Palmer, I. J., & Grimsdale, R. L. (1995). Collision Detection for Animation using Sphere-Trees. *In Proceedings of EUROGRAPHICS* (Vol. 14, pp. 105–116).

Pang, Y., Nee, A. Y. C., Ong, M., Yuan, S. K., & Youcef-Toumi, K. (2006). *Assembly Automation*. Bradford, UK: Emerald Group Publishing Limited.

Park, A. (2007, January 19). Marketing To Your Mind. *Time*. Retrieved from http://www.time.com/time/magazine

Patrick, J. (1992). *Training: Research and Practice*. New York: Academic Press.

Peck, M. E. (2008). A Brainy Approach to Image Sorting: DARPA project reads the brain waves of image analysts to speed up intelligence triage [Electronic]. *IEEE Spectrum Online*. Retrieved on March 1, 2009, from http://spectrum.ieee.org/apr08/6121

Pellom, B., & Kadri, H. (2003). Recent Improvements in the CU SONIC ASR System for Noisy Speech: The SPINE Task. In *Proceedings of IEEE International Conference on Acoustics, Speech, and Signal Processing (ICASSP)*, Hong Kong.

Pfister, H., Zwicker, M., van Baar, J., & Gross, M. (2000). Surfels: Surface Elements as Rendering Primitives. In *Proceedings of SIGGRAPH* (pp. 335–342). Retrieved from http://visinfo.zib.de/EVlib/Show?EVL-2000-69

Ponamgi, M., Cohen, J., Lin, M., & Manocha, D. (1995). Incremental Algorithms for Collision Detection between General Solid Models. In *Proceedings of the third ACM symposium on Solid modeling and applications* (pp. 293-304). Retrieved from http://portal.acm.org/citation.cfm?id=218076.

Pope, A. R. (1994). *Model-based object recognition: a survey on recent research (Tech. Rep)*. California: University Berkeley.

Poss, R., Mabrey, J. D., Gillogly, S. D., Kasser, J. R., Sweeney, H. J., & Zarins, B. (2000). Development of a virtual reality arthroscopic knee simulator. *Journal of Bone and Joint Surgery (Am)*, *82*(10), 1495–1499.

Prahalad, C. K., & Hamel, G. (2001). The Core Competence of the Corporation. In Zack, M. H. (Ed.), *Knowledge and Strategy*. New Delhi: Butterworth Heinemann.

Provot, X. (1995). Deformation constraints in a mass-spring model to describe rigid cloth behavior. In *Proceedings of Graphics Interface* (pp. 147–154). Canadian Human-Computer Communications Society.

Puangmali, P., Althoefer, K., Seneviratne, L. D., Murphy, D., & Dasgupta, P. (2008). State-of-the-Art in Force and Tactile Sensing for Minimally Invasive Surgery. *IEEE Sensors Journal*, *8*(4), 371–381. doi:10.1109/JSEN.2008.917481

Qin, H., Mandal, C., & Vemuri, B. C. (1998). Dynamic Catmull-Clark Subdivision Surfaces. *IEEE Transactions on Visualization and Computer Graphics*, *4*(3), 215–229. doi:10.1109/2945.722296

Qin, K., Chang, Z., Wang, H., & Li, D. (2002). Physics-based Loop Surface Modeling. *Journal of Computer Science and Technology*, *17*(6), 851–858. doi:10.1007/BF02960776

Qin, K., Wang, H., Li, D., Kikinis, R., & Halle, M. (2001). Physics-based Subdivision Surface Modeling for Medical Imaging and Simulation. In *Proceedings of MIAR'2001*, Hong Kong (pp. 117-124).

Qiu, Z. M., Chen, Y. P., Zhou, Z. D., Ong, S. K., & Nee, A. Y. C. (2001). Multi User NC Machining Simulation over the Web. Advanced Manufacturing Technology, 18, 1–6. doi:10.1007/PL00003949doi:10.1007/PL00003949

Quinlan, S. (1994). Efficient distance computation between non-convex objects. In *Proceedings of International Conference on Robotics and Automation*. (pp. 3324–3329). Retrieved from http://eprints.kfupm.edu.sa/36777/1/36777.pdf

Raghavan, V., Molineros, J., & Sharma, R. (1999). Interactive Evaluation of Assembly Sequences Using Augmented Reality. *IEEE Transactions on Robotics and Automation*, *15*, 435–449. doi:10.1109/70.768177

Recker, J. (2006). *Process Modeling in the 21st Century*. Retrieved October 2008, from http://www.bptrends.com/publicationfiles/05-06-ART-ProcessModeling21stCent-Recker1.pdf

Remondino, F. (2008). *Detailed image-based geometric reconstruction of heritage objects*. Retrieved September 2, 2008, from http://www.photogrammetry.ethz.ch/general/persons/fabio/remondino_sgpbf07.pdf

Renvisé, P., & Morin, C. (2007). Neuromarketing: Understanding the Buy Button in Your Customer's Brain. Nashville, TN: SalesBrain, LLC

Resonance Technology Inc. (2008). *VisuaStimDigital*. Retrieved from http://www.mrivideo.com/product/fmri/vsd.htm

Rheingold, H. (1991). *Virtual Reality. The Revolutionary Technology of Computer-Generated Artificial Worlds and How It Promises to Transform Society*. New York: Touchstone.

Riva, G. (2002). Virtual Reality for Health Care: The Status of Research. *Cyberpsychology & Behavior*, *5*(3), 219–225. doi:10.1089/109493102760147213

Riva, G. (2005). Virtual Reality in Psychotherapy [Review]. *Cyberpsychology & Behavior*, *8*(3), 220–240. doi:10.1089/cpb.2005.8.220

Rohit, R. V., & Sampath, D. (2001). Agents Based Collaborative Framework for B2C Business Model and Related Services. In Innovative Internet Computing Systems (LNCS 2060, pp. 126-133). Berlin: Springer.

Rolfe, J. M., & Staples, K. J. (Eds.). (1988). *Flight Simulation*. Cambridge, UK: Cambridge University Press.

Roth, D., Ismail, F., & Bedi, S. (2003). Mechanistic modeling of the milling process using an adaptive depth buffer. CAD, 35(14), 1287–1303.

Rouse, R. (2000). *Designing Design Tools*. Retrieved October 2008, from http://www.gamasutra.com/features/20000323/rouse_01.htm

Rowan, D. (2004). *Neuromarketing: The search for the brain's 'buy' button*. http://www.davidrowan.com/2004_02_01_archive.html

Roy, C. S., & Sherrington, C. S. (1890). On the Regulation of the Blood-supply of the Brain. *The Journal of Physiology, 11*(1-2), 85–158.

Rozinat, A., Wynn, M. T., van der Aalst, W. M. P., ter Hofstede, A. H. M., & Fidge, C. J. (2009). *Workflow Simulation for Operational Decision Support*. Accepted for Data and Knowledge Engineering.

Rozwell, C. (2008). *Michelin Uses Virtual Environment to Teach Complex Material*. Stamford, CT: Gartner.

Rusinkiewicz, S., & Levoy, M. (2000). *QsPlat: A multi-resolution point rendering system for large meshes*. Paper presented at the meeting SIGGRAPH 2000, Computer Graphics Proceedings (pp 343-352). Retrieved September 7, 2004, from http://graphics.stanford.edu/papers/qsplat/qsplat_paper.pdf

Rusinkiewicz, S., Hall-Holt, O., & Levoy, M. (2002). Real-time 3D model acquisition. *ACM Transactions on Graphics, 21*, 438–446.

Ruspini, D. C., Kolarov, K., & Khatib, O. (1997). The Haptic Display of Complex Graphical Environments. In *SIGGRAPH 97 Conference Proceedings* (pp. 345 – 352).

Russell, N., van der Aalst, W. M. P., ter Hofstede, A. H. M., & Edmond, D. (2005). *Workflow Resource Patterns: Identification, Representation and Tool Support*. Paper presented at the CAiSE 2005.

Russell, S. J., Norvig, P., & Canny, J. F. (2003). Artificial Intelligence: A Modern Approach (2nd Illustrated Ed.). Englewood Cliffs, NJ: Prentice Hall.

Salinas, F. S., & Velilla, C. (2003). Estudio métrico por fotogrametría terrestre: Documentación de pequeños monumentos [Versión electrónica]. *Mapping-Interactivo, Artículo 175*. Retrieved October 4, 2004, from http://www.mappinginteractivo.com/plantilla-egeo.asp?id_articulo=175

Sato, S. (1990). *Magnetoencephalography (Advances in Neurology)*. New York: Raven Press.

Schijven, M., & Jakimowicz, J. (2003). Construct validity: experts and novices performing on the Xitact LS500 laparoscopy simulator. *Surgical Endoscopy, 17*(5), 803–810. doi:10.1007/s00464-002-9151-9

Schuermann, A. (2006). On packing spheres into containers (about Kepler's finite sphere packing problem). *Documenta Mathematica, 11*, 393–406. Retrieved from http://arxiv.org/abs/math/0506200.

Second Life. (2009). Retrieved from http://secondlife.com

Sensable. (2009) *Phantom Omni devices*. Retrieved April 6, 2009, from http://www.sensable.com/products-haptic-devices.htm

Seo, Y., Lee, B. C., Kim, Y., Kim, J. P., & Ryu, J. (2007). K-HapticModeler: A Haptic Modeling Scope and Basic Framework. In *IEEE International Workshop on Haptic, Audio and Visual Environments and Games HAVE 2007* (pp. 136 – 141).

Seymour, N. E., Gallagher, A. G., & Roman, S. A., OBrien, M. K., Bansal, V. K., Andersen, D. K., & Satava, R. M. (2002). Virtual reality training improves operating room performance: results of a randomized, double-blinded study. *Annals of Surgery, 236*(4), 458–463. doi:10.1097/00000658-200210000-00008

Sharma, R., & Molineros, J. (1997). *Computer vision-based augmented reality for guiding manual assembly*. Paper presented at the Virtual Reality Annual International Symposium, Atlanta, GA, USA.

Sheridan, T. B. (1994). Further musings on the psychophysics of presence. *Presence (Cambridge, Mass.), 5*, 241–246.

Shin, D. H., & Dunston, P. S. (2008). *Evaluation of Augmented Reality in steel column inspection*. West Lafayette, IN: School of Civil Engineering, Purdue University.

Shinya, M., & Forgue, M.-C. (1991). Interference detection through rasterization. *The Journal of Visualization and Computer Animation, 2,* 132–134.

Shulz, T., & Ingensand, H. (2004). *Terrestrial Lasser Scanning: Investigations and Applications for High Precision Scanning.* Paper presented at the meeting FIG Working Week of Athens.

SimMan. (2009). Retrieved April 6, 2009, from http://www.laerdal.com/document.asp?docid=1022609

Sims, D. (1994). New realities in aircraft design and manufacture. *IEEE Computer Graphics and Applications, 14*(2), 91. doi:10.1109/38.267487

SimSurgery. (2009). Retrieved April 6, 2009, from http://www.simsurgery.no/

Smith, M., & Kiger, P. J. (2007). *OOPS: 20 Life Lessons From the Fiascoes That Shaped America.* New York: HarperCollins Publishers.

Smith, R. (2006). Technology Disruption in the Simulation Industry. *The Journal of Defense Modeling and Simulation: Applications, Methodology. Technology (Elmsford, N.Y.), 3*(1).

Snowdon, D., Churchill, E. F., & Munro, A. J. (2001). Collaborative Virtual Environments: Digital Spaces and Places for CSCW: An Introduction. In E. F. Churchill, D. N. Snowdon & A. J. Munro (Ed.), Collaborative Virtual Environments: Digital Places and Spaces for Interaction (2nd Illustrated Ed., pp. 3-17). London: Springer-Verlag.

Soto, V. M. (1995). *Desarrollo de un sistema para el análisis biomecánico tridimensional del deporte y la representación gráfica realista del cuerpo humano.* Tesis Doctoral, Facultad de Ciencias de la Actividad Física y el Deporte, Universidad de Granada, España.

Stam, J. (1998a). Evaluation of Loop Subdivision Surfaces. In SIGGRAPH'98.

Stam, J. (1998b). Exact Evaluation of Catmull-Clark Subdivision Surfaces at Arbitrary Parameter Values. In *Computer Graphics* (*Proceedings of SIGGRAPH '98*) (pp. 395-404).

Steinemann, D., Otaduy, M. A., & Gross, M. (2006). Fast arbitrary splitting of deforming objects. In *SCA '06: Proceedings of the 2006 ACM SIGGRAPH/Eurographics symposium on Computer animation* (pp. 63-72). Aire-la-Ville, Switzerland: Eurographics Association.

Sutherland, I. E. (1968). A head-mounted three-dimensional display. In *Proceeding of the Fall Joint Computer Conference. AFIPS Conference Proceedings* (Vol. 33, pp. 757- 764). Arlington, VA: AFIPS.

Sutherland, L., Middleton, P., Anthony, A., Hamdorf, J., Cregan, P., & Scott, D. (2006). Surgical simulation: a systematic review. *Annals of Surgery, 243*(3), 291–300. doi:10.1097/01.sla.0000200839.93965.26

Sutherland, M. (2007). *Neuromarketing: What's it all about?* Presented at Australian Neuromarketing Symposium at Swinburne University (Melbourne), February 2007.

Tahmincioglu, E. (2008). First Stop: Second Life. *Business Week: Small Biz,* 41-45.

Takacs, B., Hanak, D., & Voshburg, K. G. (2008) A Virtual Reality Patient and Environments for Image Guided Diagnosis. In Proceedings of Medical Imaging and Augmented Reality: MIAR 2008 (LNCS 5128, pp. 279–288).

Tang, A., Owen, C., Biocca, F., & Mou, W. (2003). Comparative Effectiveness of Augmented Reality in Object Assembly. In *Proc. CHI* (pp. 73-80).

Tavanti, M., & Lind, M. (2001). *2D vs 3D, implications on spatial memory.* Paper presented at the IEEE Symposium on Information Visualization (INFOVIS 2001).

Teschner, M., Heidelberger, B., Manocha, D., Govindaraju, N., Zachmann, G., Kimmerle, S., et al. (2005). Collision Handling in Dynamic Simulation Environments. In *Eurographics Tutorial # 2* (pp. 1–4). Retrieved from http://www.gabrielzachmann.org/

Teschner, M., Heidelberger, B., Müller, M., Pomeranets, D., & Gross, M. (2003). Optimized spatial hashing for collision detection of deformable objects. In *Proceedings of Vision, Modeling* (pp. 47–54). Visualization.

Teschner, M., Kimmerle, S., Zachmann, G., Heidelberger, B., Raghupathi, L., Fuhrmann, A., et al. (2004). Collision Detection for Deformable Objects. In *Proceedings of Eurographics State-of-the-Art Report*, Grenoble, France (pp. 119–139). Retrieved from http://www.gabrielzachmann.org/

The Marketplace. (2009). Retrieved from http://secondlife.com/whatis/marketplace.php

Thomas, N. W. (1958). Surveying. London: Edward Arnold.

Thomas, T. R. (1999). Rough Surfaces (2nd ed.). New York: Imperial College Press.

Thompson, C. (2003, October 28), There's a Sucker Born in Every Medial Prefrontal Cortex. *New York Times*.

Thompson, M., Eller, R., Radionski, W., & Speert, J. (1966). Manual of Photogrammetry (3rd ed., Vol. 1). Falls Church, VA: American Society of Photogrammetry and Remote Sensing.

Torres, D. (2008). On virtual environments and agents in next-generation computer games. [Review]. *The Knowledge Engineering Review*, 23(4), 389–397. doi:10.1017/S0269888908000040

Tsai, Y. H., Chen, J. C., & Lou, S. J. (1999). In-process surface recognition system based on neural networks in end milling cutting operations. International Journal of Machine Tools & Manufacture, 39(4), 583–605. doi:10.1016/S0890-6955(98)00053-4doi:10.1016/S0890-6955(98)00053-4

Tseng, T. L., Kwon, Y., & Ertekin, M. (2005). Feature based rule induction in machining operation using rough set theory for quality assurance. Robotics and Computer-integrated Manufacturing, 21, 559–567. doi:10.1016/j.rcim.2005.01.001doi:10.1016/j.rcim.2005.01.001

Tuceryan, M., Greer, D. S., Whitaker, R. T., Breen, D. E., Crampton, C., Rose, E., & Ahlers, K. H. (1995). *Calibration requirements and procedures for a monitor-based augmented reality system*. IEEE Trans. Visual. Computer. Graph.

Tufte, E. (1983). *The Visual Display of Quantitative Information*. Cheshire, CT: Graphics Press.

Turburn, E., Aronson, J. E., & Liang, T.-P. (2005). *Decision Support Systems and Intelligent Systems*. New Delhi: Prentice Hall of India Private Ltd

Uenohara, M., & Kanade, T. (1995). *Vision-based object registration for real-time image overlay* (pp. 14–22). Computer Vision, Virtual Reality and Robotics in Medicine.

Uno, S., & Slater, M. (1997 March). The sensitivity of presence to collision response. In *Proceedings of IEEE Virtual Reality Annual International Symposium (VRAIS)*, Albuquerque, New Mexico (pp. 95).

Urban, E. C. (1995). The information warrior. *IEEE Spectrum*, 32(11), 66–70.

UroMentor. (2009). Retrieved April 6, 2009, from http://www.med.umich.edu/UMCSC/equipment/uromentor.html

Vallino, J. R. (1998). *Interactive Augmented Reality*. University of Rochester.

van den Bergen, G. (1997). Efficient Collision Detection of Complex Deformable Models using AABB Trees. *Journal of Graphics Tools*, 2(4), 1–13.

van den Bergen, G. (1999). A Fast and Robust GJK Implementation for Collision Detection of Convex Objects. *Journal of Graphics Tools: JGT*, 4(2), 7–25.

van den Bergen, G. (2001). 3D Game Objects. In *Game developers conference*. Proximity Queries and Penetration Depth Computation on.

van den Bergen, G. (2003). *Collision Detection in Interactive 3D Environments*. San Francisco: Morgan Kaufman.

van der Aalst, W. M. P., & ter Hofstede, A. H. M. (2005). YAWL: Yet Another Workflow Language. *Information Systems*, 30(4), 245–275. doi:10.1016/j.is.2004.02.002

van der Aalst, W. M. P., & van Hee, K. (2004). *Workflow Management Models, Methods, and Systems*. Boston: MIT Press.

Van Sickle, K. R., Gallagher, A. G., & Smith, C. D. (2007). The effect of escalating feedback on the acquisition of psychomotor skills for laparoscopy. *Surgical Endoscopy, 21*(2), 220–224. doi:10.1007/s00464-005-0847-5

Vázquez Pelaez, S. (2007). *Levantamiento mediante Láser Escáner 3D de la zona de Los Zarpazos en el yacimiento arqueológico de Atapuerca (Burgos)*. Unpublished bachelor dissertation, Universidad Politécnica de Madrid (UPM).

Vera, P. (1989). Técnicas de análisis en biomecánica deportiva: estado actual y perspectivas. Presented at Jornadas Unisport sobre tecnología del deporte, Málaga.

Volino, P., Davy, P., Bonanni, U., Luible, C., Magnenat-Thalmann, N., Mäkinen, M., & Meinander, H. (2007). From Measured Physical Parameters to the Haptic Feeling of Fabric. *The Visual Computer, 23*(2), 133–142. doi:10.1007/s00371-006-0034-2

Vozikus, G. (2004). *Lasser Scanning: New method for recording and documentation in Archaeology*. Paper presented at the meeting FIG Working Week of Athens. Retrieved October 13, 2004, from http://www.fig.net/pub/athens/papers/wsa1/WSA1_4_Vozikis_et_al.pdf

VRMC. *Virtual Reality Medical Center*. (2009) Retrieved April 6, 2009, from http://www.vrphobia.com/

Wächter, C., & Keller, A. (2006). Instant Ray Tracing: The Bounding Interval Hierarchy. In T. Akenine-Möller & W. Heidrich (Eds.), *Eurographics Workshop/ Symposium on Rendering* (pp. 139–149). Retrieved from http://www.eg.org/EG/DL/WS/EGWR/EGSR06/139-149.pdf

Wang, M. Y., & Chang, H. Y. (2003). Experimental study of surface roughness in slot end milling AL2014-T6. Machine Tools and Manufacture, 20, 1–7.

Warn, H., Marschner, S., Levoy, M., & Hanrohon, P. (2000). A practical model for subsurface light transport. In SIGGRAPH 2000 (Computer Graphics Proceedings).

Wasserman, S., & Faust, K. (1994). *Social Network Analysis: Methods and Applications*. Cambridge, UK: Cambridge University Press.

Weber, B., & Reichert, M. U. (2008). Refactoring Process Models in Large Process Repositories. In *20th Int'l Conf. on Advanced Information Systems Engineering*

(CAiSE'08) (pp. 124-139). Montpellier, France: Springer Verlag.

Weinberger, D. R., Mattay, V., Callicott, J., Kotrla, K., & Santha, A., Gelderen, Peter van, Duyn, J., Moonen, C., & Frank, J. (1996, December). MRI Applications in Schizophrenia Research. *NeuroImage, 4*(3), S118–S126. doi:10.1006/nimg.1996.0062

Weller, R., & Zachmann, G. (2006). Kinetic Separation Lists for Continuous Collision Detection of Deformable Objects. In *Third Workshop in Virtual Reality Interactions and Physical Simulation (Vriphys)*, Madrid, Spain, November 6-7. Retrieved from http://cg.in.tu-clausthal.de/papers/vriphys06/vriphys_kinetic_separation_list.pdf

Weller, R., & Zachmann, G. (2009 August). A Unified Approach for Physically-Based Simulations and Haptic Rendering. In *Sandbox 2009: ACM SIGGRAPH Video Game Proceedings*, New Orleans, LA, USA. Retrieved from http://cg.in.tu-clausthal.de/papers/siggraph09/IST-SiggraphGames.pdf

Weller, R., & Zachmann, G. (2009 June). Inner Sphere Trees for Proximity and Penetration Queries. In *Robotics: Science and Systems Conference (RSS)*, Seattle, WA, USA. Retrieved from http://cg.in.tu-clausthal.de/research/ist

Weller, R., & Zachmann, G. (2009). Stable 6-DOF Haptic Rendering with Inner Sphere Trees, in International Design Engineering Technical Conferences & Computers and Information. In *Engineering Conference*. (IDETC/CIE), San Diego, CA, USA. September. Retrieved from http://cg.in.tu-clausthal.de/research/ist

Wellman, B. (2000). Physical Place and Cyber-Place: The rise of Networked Individualism. *International Journal of Urban and Regional Research, 25*(2), 227–252. doi:10.1111/1468-2427.00309

Wells, M. (2003, September 1). In Search of the 'Buy Button. Forbes.

Weng, M. (2007). *A Multimedia Social-Networking Community for Mobile Devices Interactive Telecommunications Program*. Tisch School of the Arts/ New York University.

Wenger, E. (2007). *Communities of practice. A brief introduction.* Retrieved from http://www.ewenger.com/theory

Wiedenmaier, S., Oehme, O., Schmidt, L., & Luczak, H. (2001). Augmented reality for assembly process: An experimental evaluation. In *Proceedings of the IEEE and ACM International Symposium on Augmented Reality* (pp. 185–186). Los Alamitos, CA: IEEE Computer Society.

Wilchalls, C. (2004, May 22). Pushing the Buy Button. *Newsweek.*

Wilson, R. H. (1995). Minimizing user queries in interactive assembly planning. *Robotics and Automation. IEEE Transactions on, 11*, 308–312.

Witkin, A. (2001). *Constrained Dynamics.* SIGGRAPH.

WMO: World Medical Organization. (1996). Declaration of Helsinki. *British Medical Journal, 313*(7070), 1448–1449.

Wolfgang, M.-W., Reginald, J., Meehae, S., Jochen, Q., Haibin, W., & Yongmin, Z. (2002). Best modeling methods: virtual factory: highly interactive visualisation for manufacturing. In *Proceedings of the 34th conference on Winter simulation: exploring new frontiers.* San Diego, CA: Winter Simulation Conference.

Woltring, H. J. (1995). *Smoothong and differentiation techineques applied to 3D data.* Champaign, IL: Human Kinetic.

Yerkes, R. M., & Dodson, J. D. (1908). The Relationship of Strength of Stimulus to Rapidity of Habit Formation. *The Journal of Comparative Neurology and Psychology, 18*, 459–482. doi:10.1002/cne.920180503

Youngblut, C., Johnson, R. E., Nash, S. H., Wienclaw, R. A., & Will, C. A. (1996). *Review of Virtual Environment Interface Technology, IDA Paper P-3186.* Retrieved from http://www.hitl.washington.edu/scivw/IDA/

Zachmann, G. (1998 March). Rapid Collision Detection by Dynamically Aligned DOP-Trees. In *Proceedings of IEEE Virtual Reality Annual International Symposium* (VRAIS '98), Atlanta, Georgia (pp. 90–97).

Zachmann, G. (2002). Minimal Hierarchical Collision Detection. *In Proceedings of ACM Symposium on Virtual Reality Software and Technology (VRST).* Hong Kong, China, (pp. 121– 128). November 11-13. http://www.gabrielzachmann.org/

Zachmann, G., & Weller, R. (2006). Kinetic Bounding Volume Hierarchies for Deformable Objects. In *ACM Int'l Conf. on Virtual Reality Continuum and Its Applications (VRCIA).* Hong Kong, China, June 14-17. Retrieved from http://www.gabrielzachmann.org/

Zaman, M. T., Senthil Kumar, A., Rahman, M., & Sreeram, S. (2006). A three-dimensional analytical cutting force model for micro end milling operation. International Journal of Machine Tools & Manufacture, 46(3-4), 353–366. doi:10.1016/j.ijmachtools.2005.05.021doi:10.1016/j.ijmachtools.2005.05.021

Zatsiorski, V. M., & Donskoi, D. (1988). *Biomecánica de los ejercicios físicos.* La Habana, Cuba: Pueblo y Educación.

Zhang, L., Kim, Y. J., Varadhan, G., & Manocha, D. (2007). Generalized penetration depth computation. *Computer Aided Design, 39*, 625–638. Retrieved from http://dx.doi.org/10.1016/j.cad.2007.05.012.

Zhao, H., & Cao, J. (2007). A business process simulation environment based on workflow and multi-agent. In Industrial Engineering and Engineering Management (pp. 1777-1781).

Zilles, C. B., & Salisbury, J. K. (1995). A Constraint-based God-Object Method for Haptic Display. In *Proceedings of the 1995 IEEE/RSJ International Conference on Intelligent Robots and Systems* (pp. 146-151).

Zwicker, M., Pfister, H., van Baar, J., & Gross, M. (2002). EWA Splatting. *IEEE Transactions on Visualization and Computer Graphics, 8*, 223–238. Retrieved from http://csdl.computer.org/comp/trans/tg/2002/03/v0223abs.htm.

About the Contributors

N. Raghavendra Rao is a Professor at VIT University Chennai, India. Dr.Rao has a Masters degree in Commerce from Osmania University and a PhD in Finance from the University of Poona. He has also three post graduate diplomas in the areas of Financial Management, Portfolio Management and Tax Laws from the University of Madras. He has a rare distinction of having experience in the combined areas of Information Technology and Business applications. His rich experience in Industry is matched with a parallel academic experience in Management & IT in Business Schools. He has over two decades of experience in the development of application software related to manufacturing, service oriented organizations, financial institutions and business enterprises. He contributes chapters for books. He presents papers related to Information technology and Knowledge Management at National and International conferences. He contributes articles on Information Technology to main stream news papers and journals. His area of research interest is Mobile Computing, Space Technology and Knowledge Management.

***

Sofia Bayona received her degree on Computer Science and Engineering from the Universidad Rey Juan Carlos in 2002. In 2003, she researched at INRIA Rhone-Alpes, France. She obtained her PhD in Computer Science from Universidad Rey Juan Carlos in Madrid in 2007. From October 2003 until September 2009, she held a position of full-time Assistant Professor at the University Rey Juan Carlos, in Madrid. Currently, she is a FP7 Marie Curie Intra European Fellow working at the Imperial College London (grant PIEF-GA-2009-236642). She is the publicity co-chair of Madrid ACM SIGGRAPH Professional Chapter. Her research interests are virtual reality, simulation and presence.

Nikolaos Bilalis is Professor of Computer Aided Manufacturing, Department of Production and Management Engineering, Technical University of Crete, Director of CAD Laboratory. He is a Dipl.-Eng. Mechanical-Electrical from National Technical University of Athens, M.Sc. Aston University of Birmingham, UK, Ph.D. Loughborough University of Technology, UK. Its Research Interests are on Technologies for Product and Process Development and Integration, CAD/CAM/CAE/CAPP, Rapid Prototyping and Rapid Tooling, Reverse Engineering, Virtual Environments for Product development, Product Modeling and Design for Disassembly, Product Innovation and Manufacturing Excellence. He worked in the Greek Aerospace Industry and he serves now as a consultant to Industry. He has an extensive participation in numerous European and National research and development projects and he has acted as evaluators in various committees for research and development, innovation, patents and investments in high technology. He has published more than 100 papers in scientific journals and International Conferences.

Ross Brown is a Senior Lecturer with the Faculty of Science and Technology, Queensland University of Technology, Brisbane, where he is the Software Technologies Coordinator for the Bachelor of Games and Interactive Entertainment . He is also a member of the Business Process Management (BPM) Research Cluster, an internationally leading research group in the BPM domain. His main research interests are in the application of games technology to other application domains. In particular, his latest research covers the development of virtual environment technology for educational applications, representation of business processes, urban planning and mining. He has been using the Open Source Virtual World Open Simulator to enable people to visualise information and processes to obtain insight into complex scenarios for all stakeholders at both naive and expert levels. Ross's work within the Education and New Media research project in the Smart Services CRC is focussed on the provision of easy to use software tools for educators to create lesson plans within collaborative virtual environments. The research will utilise a combination of virtual world and business process workflow technology that will guide educators in the process of creating quality interactive lessons.

Harrison R. Burris is the Professor of Business Information Systems, DeVry University.

Rafael Capilla is a an assistant professor of software engineering at the Universidad Rey Juan Carlos of Madrid (Spain), and he holds a PhD in Computer Science from the same university. He worked as a senior analyst for 2 years in a telecommunications company and more than eight years as Unix system administrator. He has participated in several Spanish and European research projects and he is co-author of more than 30 international referred conference papers, one book about web programming, 4 book chapters and 3 international journals. His research interest focuses on software architecture, particularly in architectural design decisions, product-line engineering and variability management, Internet technologies, and applications for mobile devices.

Hui Chen received the B.S. and M.S. degrees in computer science from Shandong University, P.R. China, and received the Ph.D. degree in computer science from the Chinese University of Hong Kong, Hong Kong. Dr. Chen has published more than twenty technical papers refereed, including MIT Journal of PRESENCE: Teleoperators and Virtual Environments, Journal of Virtual Reality: Research, Development and Applications, Computer Animation and Virtual Worlds, and international conferences. She is currently an assistant professor in the Center for Human-Computer Interaction, Shenzhen Institute of Advanced Integration Technology, Chinese Academy of Sciences/The Chinese University of Hong Kong, Shenzhen Institute of Advanced Technology, Chinese Academy of Sciences, Shenzhen, China. Her research interests include haptics simulations, virtual reality, computer-assisted surgery, and interactive computer graphics.

Rui (Irene) Chen is currently a PHD candidate in the department of Design lab at the University of Sydney. She has been actively involved in the following funded projects: " US National Science Foundation (NSF): "Skill Development and Transfer from Virtual Training Systems", University of Sydney Faculty of Architecture Research-enhanced Learning and Teaching Scholarship Grant: "Immersive Augmented Reality Experiential Learning Space for Urban Design" and Chartered Institute of Building (CIOB) Australasia Research Development Grant: "Smart Construction Site: increasing awareness of construction assets". Her main research area is using the Tangible Augmented Reality systems to enhance the learning education in design activities. Her research interests cross from Augmented Reality,

Augmented Virtuality, Mixed Reality and Virtual Reality Applications; Educational Psychology and Computer-Supported Cooperative Work. She has also been published at several refereed international conferences, as well as in journals and has authored book chapters through her research.

Jose M. Espadero received his degree in Computer Science and Engineering from the Universidad Politécnica de Madrid in 1998. His PhD is centred on 3D modelling and Virtual Reality. He belongs to the Technical Staff in the University Rey Juan Carlos (Madrid, Spain) as the responsible of the Virtual Reality Laboratory. He has published works in the fields of computer graphics and virtual reality.

Mercedes Farjas graduated at the Universidad Politécnica de Madrid (UPM) in 1982 as an engineering surveyor. After a few years with Universidad Politécnica de Las Palmas de Gran Canarias she returned to Madrid as Surveyor to the City Council. In 1989 she took a post as assistant professor at UPM, and during these years she completed first BSc and the PhD in Educational Science and then BSc in Geodesy and Cartographical Engineering. In 1996 she was made professor in Cartography and Surveying at UPM, where she was instrumental in setting up the research group Cartography applied in Archaeology and Heritage. She is leading the research topic New Technologies in Cultural Heritage, in the UPM Laboratory *Cultural Heritage Management and New Technologies.*

Jose M. Fernandez-Arroyo received his M.D degree from the U. Complutense de Madrid in 1989. He is specialist in Traumatology and Orthopaedics since 1988 and works in a public Hospital in Madrid. He works in arthroscopy and teaches arthroscopic techniques. His research interests include the development of arthroscopic simulators with virtual reality systems. He has published works in the fields of traumatology and virtual reality simulators.

Francisco J. García Lázaro: PH Doctor, (Universidad Nacional de Educación a Distancia. Faculty of Geography, 2006). Joined the Universidad Politécnica de Madrid (UPM) Staff in 1991; hitherto working in the Departament of Surveying and Cartographic Engineering of UPM. His areas of research are GIS & Spatial Analysis and Photogrammetric Applications, having been involved in two projects related to those areas. Author or co-author of 10 presented papers to international symposia.

Lei Hou is a Phd Student in design computing in USYD with his backgroud mechanical engineering. The aim of his Ph.D. research project is to experimentally investigate the effects of the synchronous merging of virtual entities into real environments on assembly design of the industrial product development as the research purpose. The focus is on the issues of assembly interference detection assembly workload evaluation, perceptual and cognitive performance in product assembly design by using AR.

Pedro Merino, graduated at the Universidad Politécnica de Madrid (UPM) in 1983 as an engineering surveyor and got his BSc in Geodesy and Cartographical in 1998. He completed several masters, and participated in nacional and internacional simposia as a Computing Expert. Since 1984 he is working as an expert on Surveying, Mapping and Computing to the National Geographic Institute, and the National Affairs Administration.

Teresa Mostaza graduated at the Universidad Politécnica de Madrid (UPM) in 1992 as an engineering surveyor. BSc in Geodesy and Cartographical Engineering in 2005 and Dr Engineer in Geodesy and Cartography in 2007. She collaborates as 3D laser scanner technical assessor in companies of the sector and in Seminars and workshops.

Luis Pastor received the BSEE degree from the Universidad Politécnica de Madrid in 1981, the MSEE degree from Drexel University in 1983, and the PhD degree from the Universidad Politécnica de Madrid in 1985. Currently he is Professor in the University Rey Juan Carlos (Madrid, Spain). His research interests include image processing and synthesis, virtual reality, 3D modelling and parallel computing.

Markos Petousis is a Dr. Mechanical Engineer. He is a Dipl.-Eng. Mechanical Engineering from the Mechanical and Aeronautics Engineering Department of the University of Patras, Greece, MSc in production systems from the Department of Production and Management Engineering of the Technical University of Crete and Ph.D. from the same Department. His Phd is in the area of virtual reality and machining processes simulation. His Research Interests are on Technologies for Products Development, CAD/CAM/CAE/CAPP, Rapid Prototyping and Rapid Tooling, Reverse Engineering and Virtual Environments for Product development. He worked for several successfully completed European and National research and development projects over the past 15 years. Currently he is working at the Technological Educational Institute of TEI, where he teaches CAD/CAM and machining processes.

Nieves Quesada graduated at the Universidad Politécnica de Madrid (UPM) in 1992 as an engineering surveyor and in 2009 as Engineer in Geodesy and Cartography. She has experience in GPS technologies, cartography and surveying. Joined the Universidad Politécnica de Valencia (UPV) Staff in 1996.

Rune Rasmussen is an Associate Lecturer in the Faculty of Science and Technology at the Queensland University of Technology in Brisbane. Rune is a unit coordinator in the area software technologies for the Bachelor of Games and Interactive Entertainment within the Information Technology cluster. He is also a member of the Business Process Management (BPM) Research group, which is an internationally leading research group in the BPM domain. His main research interests are Artificial Intelligence and Human-Computer interfacing in the application domain of serious games. His research interests extend from research he did for his PhD thesis in solving and creating artificial players for board games, where his algorithm for solving a board game called Hex (a problem known to be NP-Hard) is still the state-of-the-art approach. His latest research activities involve the development of virtual environment technologies for educational applications. Rune's work within the Education and New Media research group in the Smart Services CRC is focused on delivering reusable software tools for educators to create lesson plans within collaborative virtual environments.

Angel Rodriguez received his degree in Computer Science and Engineering and the PhD degree from the Universidad Politécnica de Madrid in 1991 and 1999 respectively. His PhD was centered on the tasks of modeling and recognizing 3D objects in parallel architectures. He is an Associate Professor at the Photonics Technology Department, Universidad Politecnica de Madrid (UPM), Spain and has published works in the fields of parallel computer systems, computer vision and computer graphics. He is an IEEE and an ACM member.

Shahid A. Sheikh is the Provost and Chief Academic Officer at Chancellor University, and Jack Welch Institute of Management. He received his doctorate from Pepperdine University in Organizational Change.

Manuel Sillero Quintana has a degree in both in Physical Activity and Sport Sciences and in Optometry. He is intern proffesor at the Physical Activity and Sports Science Faculty of the Technical University of Madrid where he is responsible of the Physical Activity and Sport Analysis Laboratory of the Faculty and leads research projects on intangible heritage and sport science, focused mainly on sports vision.

Hanqiu Sun received M.S. in electrical engineering from University of British Columbia, and Ph.D. in computer science from University of Alberta, Canada. Dr. Sun has published more than hundred technical papers refereed, including MIT Journal of PRESENCE: Teleoperators and Virtual Environments, IEEE Transactions on Visualization and Computer Graphics, Journal of Virtual Reality: Research, Development and Applications, Computational Geometry: Theory and Applications, IEEE Transactions on Information Technology in BioMedicine, IEEE Journal of Computer Graphics and Applications, refereed book chapters and international conferences. She is currently an associate professor at the Dept. of CS&E of The Chinese University of Hong Kong. Her research interests include virtual reality, interactive graphics/animation, hypermedia, computer-assisted surgery, mobile image/video processing and navigation, realistic haptics simulations. Contact her at hanqiu@cse.cuhk.edu.hk

Rui Wang is a Master by Philosophy student in Design Lab, Faculty of Architecture, Design and Planning, the University of Sydney. Her research interests are consumers' involvement and trust issues in Mixed-Reality supported electronic commerce systems and environments under the supervision of Dr. Xiangyu Wang.

Xiangyu Wang is Lecturer in Design Computing at the Faculty of Architecture, Design & Planning, at the University of Sydney. He obtained his Ph.D. degree in Civil Engineering at Purdue University in 2005. Dr. Wang's work is featured with highly interdisciplinary research across Design, Computer Engineering, Construction, and Human Factors. His specific research interests include virtual environments for design, human-computer interactions, computer-supported cooperative work, and construction automation and robotics. He is now supervising five Ph.D. students and has published over 140 refereed articles into a wide range of highly recognized international journals and conferences (ASCE, IEEE, ACM, etc.). He was also awarded a US National Science Foundation grant to investigate skill development through virtual technologies.

Gabriel Zachmann is professor for computer graphics at Clausthal University, Germany. He is also the head of the Computer Graphics Group in the Computer Science Department. Prior to that, he was assistant professor in the computer graphics group at Bonn University, Germany, and head of the research group for novel interaction methods in virtual prototyping. In 2000, Dr. Zachmann received his PhD in computer science from Darmstadt University. From 1994 until 2001, he was with the Virtual Reality group at the Fraunhofer Institute for Computer Graphics in Darmstadt, where he carried out many industrial projects in the area of virtual prototyping. He was one of the pioneers in Europe who helped develop first Virtual Reality applications for the automotive manufacturing domain. Dr. Zachmann's research interests include geometric algorithms for computer graphics, in particular collision detection and related topics, virtual prototyping, computer vision based hand tracking, immersive visualization, virtual cities, and others.

José Julio Zancajo Jimeno, titular professor in the Escuela Politécnica Superior de Ávila (Universidad de Salamanca), graduated at the Universidad Politécnica de Madrid (UPM) in 1992 as an engineering surveyor and Dr Engineer in Geodesy and Cartography.

Index

Symbols

3D business process visualisations 75
3D entertainment environments 69
3D environments 69, 74, 121
3D graphical models 113
3D images 196, 216
3D laser scanners 186, 187, 188, 189, 191, 208
3D laser scanning 205, 210
3D laser systems 186
3D modelling 212, 215
3D models 181, 186, 189, 207, 212, 216
3D objects 147, 166, 182, 184
3D online worlds 166
3D representations 197
3D representation systems 181
3D scanners 182, 183, 187, 201, 202, 209
3D scanning systems 184
3D simulations 73
3D virtual anatomy 149
3D visualisation 69, 73, 74, 84
3D worlds 83, 84

A

agents module 132, 135
agoraphobia 142
anchor nodes 25, 26, 31
artificial reality 120, 122, 127, 228
augmented reality (AR) 105, 106, 107, 108, 109, 110, 111, 112, 113, 114, 115, 116, 221, 223, 229, 231, 233, 234, 235, 236, 238
augmented reality (AR) model 110, 111
augmented reality (AR) systems 105, 107, 108, 110, 111, 113, 114

augmented reality (AR) technique 107, 108

B

batch neural gas clustering algorithm (BNG) 52
biomechanical analysis 185, 186, 193, 194
biomechanics 181, 182, 186, 192, 193
bounding volume (BV) 37, 39, 40, 41, 42, 43, 44, 45, 46, 47, 48, 49, 50, 51, 52, 61, 66, 67
bounding volume hierarchy (BVH) 37, 38, 40, 46, 47, 48, 49, 50, 52, 53, 54, 55
bounding volume test tree (BVTT) 48, 49
brain-scanning technology 125
business enterprises 1, 3, 6, 9, 11, 12
business intelligence 6
business models 1, 8, 12
business process lifecycle 84
business process management (BPM) 68, 70, 71, 72, 73, 74, 75, 80, 84, 85
business process modelling 68, 69, 70, 71, 81, 84
business process modelling notation (BPMN) 71, 72, 75, 85, 223
business process models 68, 70, 71, 80, 84
business software 105
buyology 126, 127
Buyology 126

C

capture systems 184, 186, 187, 188, 192, 198
central processing unit (CPU) 37, 40, 53, 58, 69
claustrophobia 142
cloud of points 88, 94, 95, 96, 97, 99

cognitive load 105, 111, 112

cognitive load theory 112

cognitive neuroscientific techniques 125

collision detection 36, 37, 38, 39, 40, 41, 42, 43, 44, 45, 46, 47, 48, 50, 53, 58, 59, 61, 62, 63, 64, 65, 218, 226, 230, 231

Columbia Broadcasting System (CBS) 119, 126

community members 166, 167, 168, 173, 175, 176

computer aided design (CAD) 90, 97, 101, 102, 228, 233

computer aided manufacturing (CAM) 88, 89, 97, 98

computer aided manufacturing (CAM) systems 88, 89

computer support cooperative learning (CSCW) 168, 180

customer retention agent 131

cyberspace 120, 168, 184

Cybertouch glove 61

D

DataGlove 109

data mining 2, 5, 12, 218

data warehouses 2, 4, 5

deformable objects 14, 15, 16, 17, 22, 26, 31

degree of freedom (DOF) 59, 60, 66, 237

Descartes, René 120

desktop publishing 73

Digital Factory for Human-Oriented Production System (DiFac) 109, 115, 222

digital signal processors (DSP) 120

Digital Surface Model 201

dynamic objects 14, 31, 184

E

e-business 134

e-commerce 130

embedded knowledge 6

F

Facebook 164, 167, 169, 171, 172, 173, 175, 177, 178

flight simulation 165

functional magnetic resonance imaging (fMRI) 118, 119, 120, 122, 123, 124, 125

G

game environments 73

games industry, the 73

games studios 73

games technology 69, 74

geographical information systems (GIS) 216

geometry-based methods 16, 22

global economy 1

globalization 4, 8, 9

global positioning system (GPS) 203, 204, 205, 206, 207, 208, 209, 216

graphical model 88, 90

graphical user interface (GUI) 112

graphics processing unit (GPU) 37, 40, 41, 61, 63, 69, 225

grid computing 2, 4, 8, 12, 226

H

haptic-constraint modeling 26, 29

haptic-constraint tools 15, 26, 29

haptic information 14

haptic interaction 14, 16, 18, 21, 24, 26, 30

haptic interface point (HIP) 16, 18, 27, 28, 29

haptic rendering 36, 37, 55, 56, 58

haptics 14, 15, 16, 17, 21, 22, 23, 26, 31, 32, 34, 35, 223

haptic sensations 14

head-mounted display (HMD) 106, 107, 121, 165

heads up display (HUD) 78

healthcare 138, 139, 140, 141, 142, 143, 144, 152, 153, 154, 155, 156, 223

healthcare sector 81, 138, 139, 140, 142, 152, 153, 154, 155

hidden line algorithm 94, 99

high definition pictures 184

Holobench system 109

holograms 197

I

immersive virtual reality (IVR) 118, 120, 121, 129